THE OPEN CHAMPIONSHIP

THE HERALD BOOK OF

THE OPEN

CHAMPIONSHIP

**DOUGLAS LOWE
& ALEX BROWNLIE**

First published 2000
by Black and White Publishing Ltd, Edinburgh
ISBN 1 902927 07 9
Copyright © Scottish Media Newspapers Limited
Introduction © Douglas Lowe and Alex Brownlie

British Library Cataloguing in Publication Data:
A catalogue record for this book is available
from the British Library.

Printed by Bookprint

CONTENTS

ACKNOWLEDGEMENTS

Special thanks to Elinor Clark, curator of the British Golf
Museum at St Andrews, particularly for the precise dates of each
Open without which the microfilm search for *Herald* reports
would have been a nightmare. Further help was gratefully
received from Hamish Frew, archivist at Prestwick Golf Club,
David Joy of St Andrews, and staff at the Herald, Mitchell
(Glasgow) and University of St Andrews libraries.

INTRODUCTION

The *Glasgow Herald* (now *The Herald*) was first published on January 27, 1783, and is the oldest existing English-language newspaper in the world with a continuous history. The first edition carried the official dispatch announcing the Versailles Treaty that gave the United States of America their official independence. It would be less than 150 years before an American citizen took the Open Championship trophy on its first of many trips across the Atlantic.

The *Herald* was 77 years old when the first Open was staged and of the 128 Opens contained in this book, the *Herald* carried immediate reports on 123, a creditable record. The sad omissions are 1865, 1866, 1867, 1868 and 1870, all relating to the Challenge Belt. One is tempted to suggest that the sports editor of the time should be retrospectively sacked. In mitigation, it would have needed clairvoyant qualities to foresee the huge development of what was then a small tournament.

There was no competition in 1871 and henceforth reports of the contest for the Challenge Cup, now the famous silver claret jug, are uninterrupted with the exception of the play-off report of the 1911 Open. It was published, but the copy recorded on microfilm is so badly damaged as to be unreadable. Brief reports of the missing bits gleaned from other sources have been included and, as this is an official *Herald* publication, the record might now be regarded as complete. Better late than never.

The Open was staged over a single day up to 1891. Thereafter, the reports included in this book are of the final day's play, each with brief introductions containing the early action and other relevant details. Most reports were written against severe deadlines for the next day's edition with the exception of the phase of Saturday finishes. These reports were published on Monday and were, of necessity, written in a more considered style.

There is also a pedantic inconsistency in that some "day after" reports were written under a dateline so that action is described as having happened "today" and others without a dateline when events occurred "yesterday". For practical reasons as much as anything else these have been left as they were published originally. For clarification, the dates given at the start of the Herald reports are those of the Open and not the date of publication.

The early reports are, by modern standards, highly unsatisfactory. There is little description of the important action and in a few instances priority is given to club affairs. By the 1890s the other extreme had been reached. These reports have been exuberantly cut back while making every effort to preserve the writing style of the day. We consider it less than a literary crime to spare readers mind-numbingly boring blow-by-blow accounts of rounds by some players who were barely even in contention. It would also be safe to deduce that Old Tom Morris and his contemporaries were never subjected to the now customary ordeal of a formal press conference.

These reservations about the early years apart, the *Herald* reports collectively represent extremely fine writing, especially given the pressure under which they were written. This reflects profound interest in the game both by the *Herald* and its readers who have consistently demanded golf coverage of the highest standard. Moreover, it is a unique collection as, to the best of our knowledge, it is the first time such a compilation has been undertaken.

For almost a hundred years, the *Herald's* reporters were anonymous. The first by-lined *Herald* golf correspondent was Cyril Horne in 1958, though his style is detectable for many years before. In 1964 came the inimitable Raymond Jacobs, whose reports ran until 1995. John Huggan wrote the following two while 1998 marked the arrival of the current golf correspondent, Ian Broadley.

A great deal of care has been taken to check and double-check accuracy. However, with such a welter of facts and figures it will be a surprise if, unwittingly, a few have not slipped through the net. Should that be the case, and it will be a delight if it isn't, we wish to be corrected and will duly take stroke and distance and play three off the tee if and when this book is updated.

DL & AB

CHAPTER ONE

PRESTWICK
THE EARLY YEARS 1860-1870

THE CHALLENGE BELT

Eight men shared one dream. The scale may have changed a hundredfold and more since the beginning one cold October morning at Prestwick but the dream has remained the same, passed down from generation to generation – to be champion golfer of the world, no more, no less. The legacy of this relentless pursuit of the glittering prize is a litany of tales of triumph and tragedy, of dazzling brilliance and human frailty.

The pioneers of 1860 are the spiritual ancestors of every golfer who would dare to try.

They were dressed in flat caps, woollen jackets, plus fours and sturdy brogues and accompanied by ragamuffin caddies carrying hickory clubs under their arms and a plentiful supply of gutties in their pockets. The courses, by modern standards, were rough and ready, the greens simply cut a little shorter, but they were the same for everyone. They would play the ball as it lay. There was no set rule for the size of hole and the idea of a special teeing area was still in the future.

The speed of play by modern standards was exceptional. Until 1892 the Open was completed in a day with some players not starting before noon. Granted, the courses were shorter then than now – Prestwick's 12 holes measured 3799 yards, the equivalent of 5698 yards for 18 holes – but even so the 36 holes must have taken less than six hours even though many holes were played blind.

Of the 12-hole Prestwick course on which the first 12 Opens were played, Horace Hutchinson, a prominent amateur and later essayist, commented: "They lay in deep dells among these sandhills, and you lofted over the intervening mountain of sand; and there was all the fascinating excitement, as you climbed to the top of it, of seeing how near to the hole your ball might have happened to roll."

The cream of the world's golfers, predominantly Scots, were treated with a patronising attitude by well-to-do club members, who organised the competition and put up prizes but would not allow them into the clubhouse. Techniques were vastly different, but the game was essentially the same, to hole out in the fewest number of strokes. The passion engendered by this futile pursuit is what has made the game great. It always mattered and never more so than in the Open Championship.

In 1860 there were fewer than 30 golf clubs in Scotland and only three elsewhere – Blackheath, North Manchester and Calcutta. Having consulted them all about a tournament to establish the champion golfer with little positive response, Prestwick Golf Club took the decision to run it independently.

They commissioned the prize, a red leather belt, the silver buckle engraved with the Arms of Prestwick Burgh and golfing scenes, at a cost of £25. They then announced to all clubs that any professional could enter on the condition that "the players shall be known and respectable cadies [sic]". The competition would be over 36 holes, three rounds of the then 12-hole course. This attracted an entry of eight players, seven from Scottish clubs and one from Blackheath. The contestants gathered outside the nearby Red Lion Hotel where the rules were read out to them before each signed acceptance.

The rules were:
1. The party winning the Belt shall always leave the Belt with the Treasurer of the Club until he produces a guarantee to the satisfaction of the above Committee that the Belt shall be safely kept and laid on the table at the next Meeting to compete for it until it becomes the property of the winner by being won three years in succession and that under a penalty of £25 sterling.
2. That each party of competitors shall have a marker appointed by this Club.
3. The game shall be played according to the rules of the Prestwick Golf Club.

The eight then moved down to the course to commence play at noon. First off were Tom Morris (Prestwick) and Robert Andrew (Perth). The Open Championship was under way.

1 8 6 0

17 OCTOBER

Great Golf Match on Prestwick Links for a Challenge Belt – The members of the Prestwick Golf Club lately resolved to give a Challenge Belt, to be played for by professional golfers, and they invited the various golf clubs in England and Scotland to name and send the best players on their links, not exceeding three from any one club, to compete for it.

The game was viewed with great interest by professionals, both in England and Scotland, and during the last week a good number of them have been practising for the match on the Prestwick Links.

The game was to be 36 holes, or three rounds of the links. The player who succeeded in holing his ball in the fewest number of strokes to be the winner; and the winner of the belt for three successive years to keep it.

The match came off yesterday when there was a good turn out of the lovers of this fine game to see the play of the crack professionals who had entered themselves for the prize.

They were as follows: William Park, of Musselburgh; Tom Morris, of Prestwick; Andrew (the Rook), of Perth; Steele, of Bruntsfield; Smith, of do; Brown, of Blackheath; Strath, of St Andrews; and Charles Hunter, of the St Nicholas Club, Prestwick.

The day was rather unfavourable for good play, the wind being high and frequently blowing in fitful gusts. The competitors started in four pairs, each pair accompanied by a marker, appointed by the Prestwick Club.

The following gentlemen acted as markers: Mr Gillon, of Wallhouse; Captain James, Captain Pratt, and Major Fairlie.

The principal contest lay between Park and Morris. In the first round Park scored 55, and Morris 58, leaving 3 in favour of Park; in the next round they scored 59 each; in the third round Park made 60, Tom 59, leaving the Musselburgh player the winner by two holes [sic]. Andrew (the Rook) was next. The play, despite the high wind, was considered to be very good.

The belt is a very handsome one, being made of red morocco, mounted with plates of silver, containing representations of players, clubs, &c.

1860, 1863, 1866, 1875
WILLIE PARK SR

Willie Park, like most professionals of his time, earned his living by making clubs and balls and keeping the greens at his native Musselburgh. A farmer's son, he learned to play golf with only one club, hooked at the end like a shinty stick, which he used equally for driving and putting.

He was 27 when he won the inaugural Open but his reputation was well established by then. He had a standing advertisement in a newspaper offering "to play anyone in the world for £100". It was a vast sum of money in those days, and there were few takers. He was also reputed to have challenged members to a game under a handicap system. He would play standing on one leg, using one hand – and rarely lost. For a bet, he also played nine holes teeing the ball each time on the face of a watch without damaging it.

In serious play, Park's swing was described by a contemporary as "most graceful and easy with a pause at the end of it, but if any part of his game is to be particularised it is his putting".

Of those who did take up the £100 challenge, Tom Morris Sr won once out of four attempts and, in 1867, as a foretaste of the next era of domination, Park was beaten by a 16-year-old prodigy, Tom Morris Jr.

Park and his great rival Old Tom Morris were rarely successful as partners. Park's succinct comment was: "I aye liket best to play against Old Tom."

Park, who lived to be 70, won his first Open four years before the birth of his son, Willie Park Jr, who would make an even greater impact on the game than his father.

1 8 6 1

Scoring on the first Open was considered high, and some amateurs felt they could compete favourably. So, 1861 represented the first true Open, contested as it was by 10 professionals and eight amateurs, none of whom as it happened competed favourably at all and their scores were excluded from the Glasgow Herald's *report. Markers accompanied the professionals but the amateurs were considered above this and went out without official observers.*

26 SEPTEMBER

Prestwick Golf Club – There was a large concourse of people on the Prestwick Links yesterday, to witness the annual competition for the Challenge Belt, given by the club. Five pairs of professionals, and an equal number of gentlemen players, started for three rounds of the course. The interest of the contest was centred on the professionals who made a fine display of science and skill. We are glad to say that Tom Morris, the professional keeper of the Prestwick Links, carried off the Belt in 163 strokes; W Park, Musselburgh (who won it last year), 2d, in 167; W Dow, Musselburgh, 3d, in 171; and D Park, Musselburgh, 4th, in 172. Several matches took place today; but in the afternoon the weather became wet and disagreeable, sending all but the keenest golfers off the Links.

From other sources it is gathered that Park paid the penalty for an over-ambitious shot in the third round. After two rounds of 54, Park headed Morris by two, but in steadily worsening weather the defending champion attempted to carry the Alps guarding the second hole with his second shot with disastrous results. It took him three strokes to extricate himself from the sandhills. Morris gradually edged in front and at the second last hole, Short, Morris, with a fine tee shot and a good putt, made 2 while Park could manage just a 3. At the final hole Morris found water but elected to play the ball as it lay and made a good shot, eventually holing out in 5 for a 53, a course record. The leading amateur, 21 shots behind the winner, was Colonel J O Fairlie, a former captain of the Royal and Ancient. It was appropriate he should take the amateur prize not only because it was he who had pursued the idea of establishing the Challenge Belt but also because he had brought Tom Morris from St Andrews to Prestwick.

Tom Morris named his third son after the Colonel, and young Morris, who became known as Jof, was an Open contender several times without winning.

1861, 1862, 1864, 1867
TOM MORRIS SR

Old Tom, as he became known, was born in North Street, St Andrews, in 1821. Had it not been for his outstanding golfing ability he would probably have been a carpenter. He was 40 when he won his first Open. His fourth win in 1867 at the age of 46 years and 99 days remains the record for the oldest winner. He also holds the record for the winning margin of 13 shots in 1862.

He read the Bible and swam in the sea every day and his secret of longevity, he maintained, was to sleep with the window open.

Morris, the son of a handloom weaver, is said to have started playing the Old Course at the age of six. By his own account he could not remember a time when he did not play golf, starting out with a left hand below right grip which he later switched to the more conventional right below left. His swing was described as "slow and laboured but using clubs with supple shafts with plenty of life".

In pre-Open days he partnered Allan Robertson, who is widely regarded as golf's first professional, in big-money challenge matches and usually won. In 1851, after a squabble with Robertson, who resisted the introduction of gutta-percha balls to replace the more labour-intensive featheries, he went to Prestwick as Keeper of the Greens. As a greenkeeper he had two dicta – "mair saun (more sand)" and "nae Sunday play – the course needs a rest even if the gowfers don't".

A formidable player, he did however have a weakness on the greens. His reputation was such that the local postman was in no doubt about the identity of the recipient of a letter addressed: "The Misser of Short Putts, Prestwick."

The Royal and Ancient Club brought him back to St Andrews in 1864 when the multiple Open champion was "solemnly handed the implements of his trade – a barrow, a spade and a shovel".

He played in almost every Open from 1860 to 1896 – 12 years before his death – and his final appearance was at the age of 75 by which time he was regarded as golf's patriarch.

Latterly he became a pioneer of golf course architecture and he had a hand in laying out, among others, Lahinch, Westward Ho!, Muirfield and Royal County Down, although his methods nowadays are regarded as simplistic. His fee was £1 a day plus travelling expenses. Old Tom was the first to be appointed honorary professional when he retired in 1904 at the age of 83 and the eighteenth green of the Old Course is named the Tom Morris Green in his memory.

1862

The entry was well down for the third "Open", partly because the prospect of competing against Park and Morris was a daunting one. Morris's eventual 13-stroke victory is a record intact in year 2000. Another reason why there was a poor entry in 1862 was the small amount of prize-money that was paid only to the second and third placed players. The winner received nothing. Still, four professionals and four amateurs entered the fray. If the Open had already assumed national importance, this was not evident in the Herald's *report which gave priority to club affairs.*

11 SEPTEMBER

Prestwick Golf Club – The autumn meeting of this club was held at Prestwick on Wednesday and Thursday. There was a good turnout of members. The Right Hon. the Earl of Eglinton and Winton was elected president of the club. On Wednesday, after the usual business had been transacted, several "pairs" started for the Eglinton Gold Medal, which, after some fine play was won by Colonel J O Fairlie, of Coodham.

The match for the Challenge Belt excited great interest. The first year it was gained by Park, of Musselburgh, while last year it was carried off by Tom Morris, of Prestwick. These two fine players met this year on equal terms, and the interest was great to see who would for the second time carry off the palm of victory.

Tom made a fine start and finished his first round in 52 strokes; his second round he made in 55, and his third in 56 strokes, making a total of 163. Park was not so successful, his first round taking 58 strokes, completing the three rounds in 176, or 13 more than Tom Morris. Should Tom win the belt next season it will become his own property.

A young player, of the name of Dow, gave good promise of becoming a fine golfer, for it was thought at one time he would come in second

The weather was splendid during both days, and a great many spectators were present on both occasions. A good deal of playing took place among the members, and the Links were never in better condition for the prosecution of this noble and invigorating game.

1863

The fund was raised to a total of £10, nothing still to the winner but £5 for second, £3 for third and a donation of £2 from the Edinburgh Burgess Club going to the fourth. The entry rose to 15, including five amateurs. The prize fund was to rise to £15 in 1864 and to £20 the following year, on both occasions the winners receiving the most money.

The reference below to Park winning by "two holes" instead of two strokes, as was similarly reported in 1860, might be regarded as a slip. Most golf at this time was matchplay but the Open was and always has been strokeplay.

18 SEPTEMBER

Golfing at Prestwick – The annual meeting of the Prestwick Golf Club took place on Thursday, when Andrew Gillon, Esq, of Wallhouse, was unanimously elected captain of the club for the ensuing year, in room of the Earl of Eglinton and Winton. The competition for the gold medal was gained by Robert Clark, Esq., Edinburgh, who completed the two rounds in 120 strokes. On Friday, seven pairs started for the Challenge Belt. It had been won for the past two years by Tom Morris, of Prestwick, and had he been successful at this competition, it was to become his own property. He was, of course, the favourite, but he was unlucky at starting, and he never made up the lost ground. The consequence was that he was defeated by two holes [sic] by his old opponent, William Park, of Musselburgh. There was a large turnout of professionals at this competition. The club was very unfortunate in so far as the weather was concerned, wind and rain being prevalent during the whole week.

1864

16 SEPTEMBER

Prestwick Golf Club – The annual autumn meeting of this club was held on Thursday last, when Lord David Kennedy was unanimously elected captain. Twenty-two competitors started for the medal contest, when Major Phillips came in the winner with 133 strokes. The major likewise carried off the sweepstakes.

The match among the professionals for the Challenge Belt took place on Friday and excited, as usual, no small degree of interest. Some fine golfing was displayed and at the close the game stood as follows: 1st prize, the belt and £6, Tom Morris 167; 2d, £5, A Strath 169, 3d £3 R Andrew, 175.

The office of Keeper of the Links having become vacant on account of the resignation of Tom Morris, who is removing to St Andrews, and who has done much to establish this favourite and scientific game in Ayrshire, it became necessary to appoint a successor, when Mr Charles Hunter, Prestwick, was the successful candidate – A Strath being only six votes below him.

On Saturday, a return match was played between the Perth James VI Club and the Prestwick St Nicholas Club, when the former club won by nine holes.

1865

14 SEPTEMBER

Domination of the Challenge Belt by Willie Park and Tom Morris was broken for the first time with Andrew Strath of St Andrews becoming only the third champion with a three-round aggregate of 162, a record score compiled in fine weather and two ahead of Willie Park. Tom Morris, now having returned to St Andrews and requiring a long journey to compete, was back in fifth place.

As a 19-year-old, Andrew Strath was the only player to break the Park/Morris domination of the first seven years of the Open. He was one of two golfing brothers from St Andrews. The younger Davie Strath was considered a better player, but never won the big prize. Andrew died at the age of 32 of tuberculosis. Strath Bunker, named after the brothers, is located to the right of the eleventh green on the Old Course.

Prestwick upgraded the status of the tournament by issuing players with official scorecards for the first time. Scoreboards for the benefit of spectators would not be introduced for another *62 years. Information was gleaned by word of mouth, often incorrect, or by approaching the players at the end of their rounds "to ascertain what luck had attended them".*

Incorrect information was at times given to players on the course, most notably in 1898 when it would play a part in Willie Park Jr losing on the final green at Prestwick to Harry Vardon.

Andrew Strath

1866

13 SEPTEMBER

This was Musselburgh's year with brothers Willie and David Park coming first and second respectively. One account suggests that golfers in Edinburgh and Musselburgh raised money to help with travel costs, thereby becoming pioneers in the practice of sponsorship. Scoring was on the high side on account of a strong wind.

Tom Morris Jr entered the Open for the first time at the age of 15. He finished 18 shots adrift. Two years later he would be unbeatable.

1867

SEPTEMBER (DATE UNRECORDED)

This was the fourth and last victory of Tom Morris, by two shots from his great rival Willie Park in gusting conditions which again resulted in high scoring. One account suggests that Morris was first in a race to borrow a "driving putter" from Colonel J O Fairlie, a club which kept the ball low in windy conditions and which he had previously used with great success. It seems that Park made the same request, but too late. Young Tom this time was fourth with three rounds below 60. Soon he would be posting unprecedented scores in the 40s.

A Strath, D Park, Bob Kirk, J Anderson, Jamie Dunn, Wm Dow, Willie Dunn, A Greig, Tom Morris, Tom Morris Jr and Geo Morris photographed in May 1867 at Leith Links during the Grand Golf Tournament for professionals

1868

23 SEPTEMBER

Young Tom Morris opened with a record 51, and lowered it in the third round with the first sub-50 score, a 49. The aggregate, not surprisingly, was also a record – 154. He was lifting the game to a new level. Old Tom this time had to bow the knee. He put in his best Open score only to be beaten by three shots.

1868, 1869, 1870, 1872
TOM MORRIS JR

The ultimately tragic Young Tom's first Open win in 1868 was achieved at the age of 17 years 5 months and 8 days and remains the record for the youngest winner. He is also the only player to have won four in a row. Having won the Challenge Belt outright in 1870 there was no competition the following year and he won in 1872, the first time the Claret Jug was the trophy. He won all four Opens at Prestwick where he learned the game.

He was the dominant player of his time and changed prevailing views about how the game should be played, using a rut iron, a small-headed club, for greater backspin on short approaches and applying topspin to his putts for a truer roll. He also employed an inward flex of his right knee for a stronger coil, a technique that has stood the test of time.

Young Tom, a dashing player, stood well back from the ball, waggling the club many times before his swing which was so full and vigorous that his Glengarry bonnet would often fall off.

After his fourth win he was dogged by ill health and was restricted to second place the next three years. Then, in September 1875, he and his father went to North Berwick to play Willie and Mungo Park for £25. The Morris pair won on the last green whereupon Young Tom was handed a telegram saying his wife was dangerously ill. A yacht was provided to cross the Forth, but before he set off he heard that his wife and newborn son were dead. The following Christmas morning Young Tom was found dead in his bed. He was aged 24. An autopsy revealed a burst blood vessel in his right lung. Others refused to believe the cause was anything other than a broken heart. Old Tom's comment was "If that was true I wouldn't be here either."

'Old Dow' Anderson's refreshment barrow on the Links at St Andrews, around 1900

1869

Young Tom created another record – the first hole-in-one in the Open, at the eighth in the first round. His 157 aggregate was still three shots higher than the previous year.

16 SEPTEMBER

Prestwick Golf Club – Yesterday the contest for the Challenge Belt came off over Prestwick Links, and created, as it always does, considerable interest. The competition is open to the world, and possession of the belt is coveted by all golfers. The trophy, which consists of red morocco, richly ornamented, is a fine piece of workmanship. Yesterday seven couples started in the competition. There was some fine play, but from the first it was pretty certain that young Tom Morris would prove the victor. The course is three rounds, or 36 holes. Young Tom made the first round in 50 strokes, doing the Station Hole in one stroke. He did the second round in 55 strokes, and the third in 52, and with the total of 157 strokes won the belt for the present year. Bob Kirk stood second in 168 strokes, and D Strath third in 169. Young Tom was also the champion last year, and should he repeat his performance next year he will retain the belt. His father, Tom Morris Sr, also won the belt two years in succession – in 1861 and 1862 – with the score of 163 each time; but in 1863 W Park beat Old Tom with the score of 168 strokes. The weather yesterday was very favourable for golfing and there was a large attendance.

1870

15 SEPTEMBER

Young Tom began his defence by completing the first hole, of 578 yards, in 3, holing out with a full iron shot, and went on to break the 12-hole record with a 47, one under fours. He followed with two 51s for a record total of 149. He was 12 strokes ahead of any other golfer. His dominant display gave him the three-in-a-row required to take custody of the Challenge Belt, marking the end of the first era of the Open.

*An 1859 golfing party, including James Wilson (clubmaker), Bob Andrew, Willie Dunn,
Willie Park, Allan Robertson, Tom Morris, D Anderson ('Dow') and Bob Kirk*

CHAPTER TWO

A CLARET JUG
FULL OF PASSION

THE CHAMPION TROPHY

The Challenge Belt, now in the custody of Young Tom Morris, was history. With no trophy to play for the Open was held in abeyance for a year while it was decided where to go from here. Prestwick Golf Club, who had run the first 11 Opens exclusively, felt the way to broaden its appeal was to take it to other courses. The Royal and Ancient Golf Club of St Andrews and the Honourable Company of Edinburgh Golfers, then based at the nine-hole Musselburgh course, accepted invitations to join forces. The rota was established as Prestwick, St Andrews and Musselburgh in that order, a system that would last for 20 years until the Honourable Company moved to Muirfield.

The trophy is the one that is still played for today, the collective organisers having learned from experience and removed the clause about permanent custody for three wins in a row. Otherwise the Open would be on its fifth trophy by now (Jamie Anderson, Bob Ferguson and Peter Thomson all fulfilled that requirement). It was a silver claret jug inscribed "Golf Champion Trophy" but one that by a strange irony the first winner, Tom Morris Jr, never actually got his hands on. It wasn't ready until the following year, though his name was engraved on it, back-dated. The Belt remained with Young Tom until his death aged 24. Then his father kept it, but before his death it was passed on to the R and A where it still is. To commemorate the 1985 Open, the 125th anniversary, two replica belts were made. One is in the Prestwick clubhouse, the other belongs to the winner that year, Sandy Lyle.

The Opens were run by the host clubs; the competition would not come under the full authority of the R and A until 1920 by which time it had become essential that the rules were regularised. They tended to vary from course to course, as witness the 1876 Open at St Andrews which was by far and away the most shambolic ever staged.

The passion with which the players pursued the great prize, however, was never in doubt and two cameos support this.

After Willie Campbell threw away the 1887 Open by taking five shots in a tuft of grass three holes from home and losing by three, Campbell and his caddie were seen in the Prestwick professional's shop "sitting on upturned buckets and weeping".

More spectacularly two years later was the action taken by Andra Kirkaldy when words were insufficient to express his feelings. Kirkaldy, a great character of his era and by various accounts a model of perfect etiquette on the course, but with rough-diamond tendencies away from it, was feeling sore after a play-off defeat at Musselburgh. He was mocked that evening by a fellow professional. What happened thereafter is best related in Kirkaldy's own words.

"By God, I couldna staun that. I grippit him by the arse o' his breeks and chucked him ower ma heid into tha watter and telt him tae gan fushin an droon himself."

Golf, and most of all the Open, mattered very much indeed.

1872

PRESTWICK

This was to be Young Tom's last win and his four-in-a-row has never been repeated. For the four championships Young Tom won he averaged 52 for the 12-hole round and the 149 he shot in 1870 was a record by eight shots for the 36-hole Open which ended in 1892 when it was extended to 72 holes.

However, the Glasgow Herald *had yet to get its head round the idea that the most important aspect of the Open was what the players did on the course. Greater prominence is given to the most aristocratic spectators who are named, an impressive list none the less which must have added to the prestige of the tournament.*

15 SEPTEMBER

Golf at Prestwick – The Challenge Trophy for the championship was yesterday played for the first time over Prestwick links. Money prizes were added to the successful players; and a medal, to be permanently retained, is to be given to the winner of the trophy in each year. The weather yesterday was not at all favourable, a strong wind having all day blown across the links.

There was a large muster of the members of Prestwick Club and other spectators who took great interest in the game. Amongst them were, Sir R Hay, Col Heneage, Capt Campbell of Craigie, Mr E A Hunter, Mrs Hunter, Miss Baird of Rosemount, Captain Macadam, Mr and Mrs Whigham, Mr J Pettigrew Wilson, Mr Gibson-Craig, Mr Chalmers, Bailie Wilson (Glasgow), Mr A Crombie, Mr Mure, Captain James, Mr Mitchell of Sauchrie, Col Hamilton, Mr Leighton, Mr Wauchope, Mr Roger Montgomerie, Mr W H Houldsworth of Coodham, Mr W Houldsworth (Mountcharles), Mr R M Kay, Rev James Rennie, Mrs Rennie, Rev A Gray, Mrs Gray.

The contest commenced at 10 o'clock when the following four couples started: – Young Tom Morris, St Andrews, and William Hunter, Prestwick St Nicholas; Old Tom Morris, St Andrews, and David Park, Musselburgh; Charlie Hunter, Prestwick, and W Doleman, Prestwick St Nicholas; David Strath, St Andrews, and Hugh Brown, Prestwick. Young Tom and Strath were the favourites. The game consisted of three rounds, or 36 holes – St Andrews rules.

In the first round Young Tom played very well but was unfortunate in his short putts, four of which he lost on account of the dampness of the grass. He also played well in the second round. In making for the stone-dyke hole, he struck a good ball off the tee, and got well over the Cardinal in two strokes. In playing his iron shot, however, he laid his ball close to the stone wall, so that it was impossible to play it for the hole. He then took his iron and played it against the wall, when it rebounded in the air and went over the wall. He then got a beautiful stroke with his niblick and laid it dead at the hole. In the remainder of the round he was more fortunate. In the third round he played beautifully throughout, until coming from the burn hole, where the wind caught his tee ball and carried it right into a bunker, which cost him three strokes. He played this round in 53 strokes.

Strath in the first round played a fine game but he was unfortunate in some of his long putts. In the second round, however, he was more fortunate, keeping up his play all round. In the third round he commenced very well, but after the second hole he played an unfortunate iron shot, which cost him three strokes; and in the last hole he lost one stroke in the water. Young Tom finished in 166 strokes, Strath 169.

Young Tom Morris was thus the winner of the trophy for the present year along with a medal to be permanently retained, and £8 in money.

1873

ST ANDREWS

Tom Kidd's winning total on the first Open to be played at St Andrews was the highest for the 36-hole Open, bizarrely so given the perfect overhead conditions. The preceding deluge is the explanation. There was no distinction in those days between casual water and water hazards. Players could lift out of water only under penalty.

4 OCTOBER

The annual competition to decide the championship of the golfing world came off today at St Andrews and was arranged to come off during the autumn meeting of the Royal and Ancient Golf Club of St Andrews to which it proved a most appropriate termination.

During the previous three days of the meeting, rain has fallen incessantly and up to Friday night the weather continued very unfavourable. Fortunately, Saturday, so far as weather was concerned, was everything that could be wished. The sun shone brightly from an unclouded sky, and there was scarcely a breath of wind to disturb the fair and sure swipes of the competitors. As much could not be said, however, for the green which was very heavy in consequence of the recent excessive rain, several portions of the course being pools of water.

As might have been expected, the favourite players were Young Tom Morris, the holder of the Champion Cup, and his rival Davie Strath, and it was expected that the coveted trophy would fall to either the one or the other. A large following accompanied them and their partners the whole day. Thirteen couples entered and the game consisted of two rounds of the green – 36 holes.

At the close Tom Kidd with rounds of 91 and 88 for a total of 179 strokes was the winner by one shot from Jamie Anderson (who is reported elsewhere to have taken a 9 at the Heather Hole in the second round). Young Tom was joint third with Bob Kirk on 183 and Strath fifth on 187.

Young Tom Kidd was accordingly returned champion for the ensuing year and besides the honour receives a money prize of £11.

Taken as a whole, the play may be characterised as indifferent, but this may be partly accounted for by the state of the green. The winner is a native of St Andrews and as a player is just coming to notice. He plays a strong game, but if deficient in any way it is when on the green.

1873
TOM KIDD

Tom Kidd is credited as being the first player to 'rib' an iron club to achieve better backspin. As a teacher he emphasised the importance of the set-up to a shot. He was said to have an ungainly swing but was an immensely long driver none the less. Whereas nowadays winning the Open is a passport to untold riches, Kidd, a caddie and manservant, as well as a player, was poor all his life and is said on several occasions to have been unable to travel further than the 12 miles to Elie for money matches because he could not afford the fare. He was 25 when he won the Open and died of a heart-related illness 11 years later.

1874

MUSSELBURGH

Musselburgh, the venue for six Opens, is steeped in history. It was a sixteenth-century haunt of Mary, Queen of Scots. In 1650 part of Oliver Cromwell's army camped on the links. Originally there were only seven holes but the course was extended to nine by the time the Open arrived. The adjacent racecourse came into being in 1816.

The holes had quirky names. The first (350 yards), an ancient burial ground, is called The Graves. The second (420 yards) became known as Linkfield, but was originally Barrack's Entry because it is opposite a road leading to army barracks. The third (500 yards) is Mrs Forman's, whose hostelry was behind the green. The fifth (360 yards) had various names, most popularly Pandy, an abbreviation of the notorious Pandemonium Bunker which was in play from the tee. The sixth (410 yards) is Bathing Coach, because one was located near the hole for many years. Much less appealing is the eighth (320 yards), The Gas, because of gasworks behind the green. The course was regarded as a fine test of golf and there were many who voiced concern when the Honourable Company moved to Muirfield and took the Open with them. With the increasing number of entrants, Musselburgh, as a nine-hole course, would not have survived much longer as an Open venue in any case.

10 APRIL

The competition for the coveted position of Champion Golfer was played yesterday afternoon at Musselburgh. The weather during the first of the game was dull and showery; but as the afternoon advanced, the rain took off and the weather was everything that could be desired. The links, especially the putting greens, were however rather heavy.

Play commenced about 12 o'clock. Sixteen couples entered. The game consisted of four rounds – 36 holes – and was well contested throughout.

The favourite couple were Young Tom Morris and Willie Park and a large crowd accompanied them during the day. In the first round, Young Tom's play, especially in the beginning holes, was wild, and he came to grief in several hazards. He, however, as usual, got into better form as the match progressed. His partner played well in the first round but failed to keep up his style.

The play of several others was worthy of note – specially Geo Paxton, R Martin, Jamie Anderson and W Thomson. It was, however, reserved for an outsider to carry out the trophy. Mungo Park, of Musselburgh, played a splendid game, doing the first two rounds with 37 and 38 strokes respectively. His score of 37 was the lowest with which the green was taken by any of the players engaged.

Tom Kidd, the ex-champion, occupies a fair position considering that he was to a great extent unacquainted with the green. Davie Strath, Young Tom's antagonist in the famous single of last summer, is pretty far behind, but it should be explained that he has not had any exercise for some months past in his favourite pastime.

During the last round the utmost excitement prevailed, and as each couple came in a knot of spectators gathered round them to ascertain what luck had attended them. When all had arrived, it was found that Mungo Park, Musselburgh, was first with a total score of 159 strokes. He was accordingly declared champion and besides retaining the cup for a year, receives a medal and also a money prize of £8. The next seven best scores likewise received money prizes from £5 to £1 in value.

[An important detail missed out from the report is that Tom Morris Jr, who had been in a strong position to win his fifth Open, missed a short putt on the penultimate hole, overshot the 170-yard Home Hole and finished two strokes behind.]

1874
MUNGO PARK

Mungo Park of Musselburgh, brother of Willie, was only an occasional Open player. He was a mariner who played golf at his many ports of call. He is said to have encouraged the start of golf in Argentina thereby providing an interesting link with a future winner, Roberto de Vicenzo.

After his seafaring days were over, Mungo Park became Keeper of the Greens at Alnmouth and had a great influence on another Open winner-to-be. Apprenticed to him there was none other than Willie Park Jr, his nephew. Mungo Park, who was 39 when he won the Open, seems to have been partial to a wee drink from time to time. He is said to have played a clergyman in a handicap match, for 10 shillings if he won and to remain teetotal for six months if he lost. Park holed a long putt at the last to tie. The man of the cloth offered a rematch the following day but Park replied: "No thanks, it's been ower near."

1875

PRESTWICK

At the age of 42, this was Willie Park's fourth and last Open win, 15 years after his first and nine years after his third. The same name, however, would reappear on the champion's cup 12 years later – his son's.

10 SEPTEMBER

The annual competition for the challenge trophy – open to all golfers – was played yesterday over the Prestwick links and drew a large field. General regret was expressed at the absence of the Morrises of St Andrews (following the death in childbirth of Young Tom's wife); but all the other leading players were forward. Thanks to the indefatigable keeper of the greens, the putting greens were in first-class order and everything was in favour of good play. Nine couples started.

The championship and £8 were gained by Willie Park, Musselburgh. The champion during the first round was in good form but in the second he came to grief at one or two of the holes, though in the third round he played a fine game. The ex-champion (Mungo Park) failed at the beginning of his first round but thereafter made pretty good play. D Strath was unfortunate on some of the greens.

1876

ST ANDREWS

The 1876 Open is reckoned to have been the worst managed ever. Prince Leopold, a son of Queen Victoria, had apparently held up the R and A's autumn meeting by arriving late three days earlier to drive himself in as captain. Having been cut back on playing time, members felt they were entitled to play on the Saturday as well and went off alternately with Open competitors. That made the course crowded not just with spectators but with players as well.

30 SEPTEMBER

The Autumn Meeting of the Royal and Ancient Golf Club at St Andrews was brought to a close on Saturday by the annual competition for the championship. The weather was showery and the greens in many places were very heavy while the links were so crowded by golfers as to interrupt play. Often, several of the couples had to stand waiting before they could play to the putting greens. Indeed, to this fact may be traced the unfortunate result of the competition. A total of 17 couples entered the competition.

The game was two rounds, or 36 holes. At the close it was found that Davie Strath and Bob Martin had tied on 176, but the former having, it is said, infringed one of the rules by playing upon the green before a previous couple had holed out, and striking one of the spectators. Objection was lodged and the matter has been referred to the Club Council. Meanwhile, the tie is to be played off today.

OCTOBER 1

The competition for the championship has gone in favour of Bob Martin, of St Andrews, who on Saturday tied with Davie Strath at 176 strokes for first place. Strath, however, it is said, infringed one of the rules by playing upon the green before the previous couple had holed out and the matter was referred to the Council of the Royal and Ancient Golf Club.

The tie was to be played off yesterday under protest, but Strath refused to do so and Martin walked over the course. Besides custody of the cup for a year, Martin gets a medal in memento of his victory and a money prize of £10. Strath is awarded the second prize of £8.

The tie between Tom Morris (St Andrews), Mungo Park (Musselburgh) and W Thomson (St Andrews) for the fourth prize of £3 was played during the early part of the day and went in favour of Morris. Park got the fifth prize of 32 and Thomson the sixth of 30 shillings.

The Glasgow Herald's *two brief reports raise more questions than they answer, and a fuller account is gleaned from Bobby Burnett's book* The St Andrews Opens.

Martin and Strath were both round in 86 in the morning, Strath having carelessly missed a two-inch putt in the process. In the second round he was further upset when his ball struck a spectator on the head. Still, he needed to play the last two holes in 10 to win, and the controversial incident occurred at the seventeenth. He played a full iron shot for his third and the ball landed close to the pin while players ahead were still putting. He holed out for a 5 and an objection was lodged by a player ahead. Meanwhile Strath, whose concentration must have been seriously affected, took 6 at the last to tie. Martin had finished ingloriously with a 7 and a 5.

The objection was referred to the R and A Council and Strath was told to play off before a decision had been reached.

There was much sympathy for Strath especially as many observers considered the only rule he had breached was one of etiquette and under the confusing circumstances of the tournament it was one that several others had broken also without being reported. However, in those days rules varied from course to course. The rule in force at the time at St Andrews read: "When two parties meet on the putting green, the party first there may claim the privilege of holing out, and any party coming up must wait until the other party has played out the hole, and on no account play their balls up lest they should annoy the parties who are putting."

It seems from this that Strath had clearly broken the rule. Burnett concludes: "Poor Strath must have known that once that rule had been invoked he would be disqualified. The fact that it had not been invoked on several occasions earlier in the day was irrelevant."

One question remains and that is the matter of Strath's second position seemingly being ratified. Perhaps the R and A felt that by not taking part in the play-off, Strath had suffered punishment enough.

Curiously, Martin's walkover was exactly that. The term survives in matchplay, and for sports other than golf, but the long walk is no longer required.

1876, 1885

BOB MARTIN

Bob Martin of St Andrews worked in Old Tom's shop, a touch of greatness obviously rubbing off on him. Self-deprecatingly he described his own flat swing as "like an auld wife cutting hay". It may not have won high marks for aesthetic beauty but it clearly worked in the low-scoring department. Later he helped spread the word of the links by travelling to Cambridge to instruct members of what was then the new university club. Before working for Old Tom he was employed by Jamie Anderson, who was to win the next three Opens, and club makers, Forgan.

I877

MUSSELBURGH

The annual competition for the custody of the champion cup, the winner of which is regarded as the champion for one year, was decided yesterday on the links of Musselburgh. The weather and green both favoured play. The entries were numerous, comprising the leading professionals from the golfing centres in Scotland. After an interesting and keen contest, the successful competitor proved to be Jamie Anderson, of St Andrews, who took the four rounds of which the game consisted with the excellent score of 160 strokes. In addition to the honour, Jamie received a money prize and a small medal in commemoration of his victory.

1877, 1878, 1879
JAMIE ANDERSON

Jamie Anderson, the son of "Auld Dow", a St Andrews caddie, ballmaker, greenkeeper and proprietor of a ginger beer stall which he would push about the links, won three Opens in a row, respectively at Musselburgh, Prestwick and St Andrews, giving him what was then a full set. He might have equalled Young Tom's four-in-a-row but didn't enter the hastily arranged 1880 contest because, he said, he was not given enough notice.

Anderson, who took up golf at the age of 10, once said: "As soon as the hole is within reach, I play to hole the shot." Move on eight decades or so and compare that with Arnold Palmer's snappier: "If you can hit it you can hole it." Anderson was rated a short driver but he frequently lived up to his dictum. In the 1878 Open he had the most spectacular finish of any Open, holing two long shots in finishing the equivalent of eagle, par, eagle, par, though such terms were unknown at the time.

He was a quick player, his pre-shot routine involving one look only at the hole and no waggles. He was rated the best iron player of his time and excelled in poor weather. Anderson, who worked briefly at Ardeer on the west coast before returning to St Andrews, was a role model for two young admirers worthy of note. They were J H Taylor and James Braid.

1878

PRESTWICK

This Open has to be a leading contender for the most sensational finish award. It may have been an era long before the advent of banner headlines and dramatisation of reports but there is a sense of exasperation at the way the thrilling clutch action is reported almost as an afterthought.

4 OCTOBER

Yesterday the annual competition for the silver cup which is the badge of championship among golfers came off on Prestwick links. The competition is open to all-comers and the Prestwick links yesterday presented an animated appearance. Early in the forenoon, upwards of 20 professional golfers and a few amateurs entered the lists, and 13 couples started.

The play was watched with keen interest. On summing up the cards it was found that Jamie Anderson, who won the competition at Musselburgh links last year, retained the honour, he having made the three rounds in 157 strokes. Some fine play was witnessed during the game.

Jamie Morris completed his first round in 50 strokes and looked the winner of the trophy while Jamie Anderson, the champion, in his last round, made the Burn Hole in 3 strokes and the Short Hole in 1.

The *Glasgow Herald*'s reporter might have made more of that last sentence. Anderson had needed to complete the last four holes in 17 strokes, the equivalent of level par, to overtake Jamie 'Jof' Morris. Anderson is reported elsewhere to have said at that point "I can dae it" and finished 3, 4, 1, 5.

To add to the drama, at the seventeenth Anderson overheard a woman spectator commenting that he had teed the ball in front of the markers before moving back to a correct place and holing out and thanking her with the words: "I am greatly obliged."

Bob Kirk still had a chance to tie but his putt at the last touched the hole and stayed out. He also missed the return.

1879

ST ANDREWS

English golfers were beginning to turn up in good numbers and if the Scots on this occasion were not worried, they should have been. In 11 years' time the silver claret jug would head south for the first of many such trips and a further 15 years on the Open itself would be staged in England.

27 SEPTEMBER

The annual competition for the Champion Cup was played on Saturday over the St Andrews Links and proved not an inappropriate termination to the great golfing meeting of the Royal and Ancient Club. There was an exceptionally large muster of players – as many as 46 entering – comprising the pick of Scottish golfers, professionals and amateurs. England also was not without her representatives. Hoylake sent George Lowe, Blackheath Manzie and Tommy Dunn appeared for Wimbledon while Jamie Allan had come all the way from the green on the sunny shores of Devon.

With such a field and the favourable circumstances, both of weather and green, it was evident that the play was to be close and exciting and that the score that would carry off the prize would be a very good one. Play began at 10 o'clock in presence of a large crowd of spectators.

The favourites were Jamie Anderson, the champion, Jamie Morris, who during the past few weeks has been appearing in fine fettle, Bob Ferguson who had beaten the champion in a recent match, and Jamie Allan who had lately been carrying everything before him. Crowds attached themselves to the couples in which they played. Allan was among the first to start and he left the tee with a fine swipe. His second landed in the burn, but he proved equal to the emergency. Rolling up his trousers he pluckily stepped into the stream and with a good iron shot placed the ball on the green. He was out in 41, but homeward bound his game rather fell off and shot 47 for a score of 88. Ferguson played indifferently and finished with rather a high score.

When Allan started the second round he had little or no attendance. This appeared from his play to be rather an advantage as he took 4 at each of the first four holes on his way to an 84 and a total score of 172.

The champion, Jamie Anderson, began expectations with a fine swipe from the tee. Steady play brought him a round of 84. In the second round he completed the outward half in 43. Homeward-bound Jamie took the first three holes in fine style. At the fourth he came to grief in a bunker, being compelled to take it out at the side. He was very unfortunate in his driving for the remainder of the hole and he only holed out in 7. At the fifth hole he experienced hard lines, just failing to hole. It became known here that Kirkaldy and Allan had both made scores it would be difficult to beat and Jamie's play was watched with keen and breathless interest by the ever-increasing crowd – which now numbered hundreds – as one mistake might deprive him of the lead he held. If he accomplished the remaining holes in 5 each he was again the champion, and he braced himself up for the task.

At the sixth hole after a careful survey of the ground Jamie holed out a fine long putt which called forth loud applause from the assembled multitude. He played the seventh and eighth holes in fine style and the last he accomplished in 4 for a round of 85 and a total of 169.

He accordingly won the championship for the third year in succession and as he retired from the green he was loudly and repeatedly cheered.

1880

MUSSELBURGH

9 APRIL

The annual competition for the Champion Cup took place yesterday at Musselburgh but excited little interest owing to public attention being occupied by the elections. Indeed, it seems not to have been generally known that the event was to take place and consequently resulted in the absence of several of the best professionals, St Andrews being represented only by the veteran Tom Morris. Great disappointment was expressed at the absence of Jamie Anderson, St Andrews, who has held the cup for the last three years but who was not made aware in time that the match was to take place. The cup was won by the deservedly well-known player Bob Ferguson (Musselburgh) who did the four rounds of the nine holes in 162.

From George Colville's Musselburgh Golf Story *we learn that Ferguson's victory was not straightforward. At the second hole in the first round he took an 8 visiting the road then hitting a telegraph pole. Later in the day at the same hole, Linkfield, which measures 420 yards, he was on the road again but holed out in 5 thanks to a single putt. However, he stretched away with a final round of 39.*

The effect of the short notice is illustrated by the dominance of home players. Only two out of the first 14 were non-Musselburgh players.

1880, 1881, 1882
BOB FERGUSON

Bob Ferguson of Musselburgh, was reckoned to be a man with iron will, his determination seeing him through in many money matches as well as his Open successes. He started as a tournament player by borrowing a set of clubs and won at Leith Links. Modesty with him was clearly a virtue, and his retort to a "gentleman player" who said he was unaware Ferguson, who he knew only as a caddie, actually played golf was: "You didn't inquire, sir."

Ferguson was expert at the putter shot from off the green and this club with a slightly angled face became known as a "Musselburgh iron". He was not infallible with it and the slack shot at the final green of the 1883 Open which led to him missing out on a record-equalling four wins in a row was his greatest disappointment. He was also highly rated with the cleek.

Three wins in a row, like Anderson, at Musselburgh, Prestwick and St Andrews in that order, might have made him immortal but it didn't make him rich. His victories won him a total of £22. He rose to the dizzy heights of Keeper of the Greens at Musselburgh where he also caddied for both professionals and amateurs.

Ferguson gave early notice of his potential by finishing third at Prestwick in 1869 when he was just 21.

After his 1883 agony, he did not compete the following two years at Prestwick and St Andrews, probably because the expense of travelling from Musselburgh was prohibitive.

1881

PRESTWICK

This was the day the Great Storm raged around Scotland claiming the lives of nearly 200 fishermen – 120 from the east-coast port of Eyemouth. The weather was also bad in the west, but it didn't stop the golf.

14 OCTOBER

The annual golf match for the Champion Trophy, open to all-comers, came off at Prestwick yesterday in the most inauspicious circumstances possible as regards weather. It was intended that a start should be made at half past 10 o'clock but it was delayed for an hour in the hope that some improvement in the weather would take place. Instead of this matters became if anything worse and at half past 11 a start was made. Eleven couples started. Bob Ferguson was the favourite and his play was watched with considerable interest. He played a fine game in the first round, holing it in 53 strokes. In the other two rounds he took 60 and 57 respectively. With this score he stood first, and won the trophy and the first money prize.

1882

ST ANDREWS

30 SEPTEMBER

The annual competition for the golf championship brought the autumn meeting of the Royal and Ancient Golf Club of St Andrews to a close on Saturday. It was fitting that after the gentlemen of the club had expended their strength on the three preceding days the professional players should have their innings also, for although the championship competition is open alike to amateurs as well as professionals, the latter have invariably proved the much larger portion of the field.

Better weather and a finer green could not have been wished for. The day was one of the best of the season – not too bright sunshine, with a moderate breeze which did not affect the flight of the balls.

The lowest scores at the end of the first round were: Bob Ferguson 83, Fitz Boothby and John Kirkaldy 86, Jamie Anderson and Tom Kidd 87. The second round was immediately commenced. Mr Fitz Boothby, continuing his fine play, went out in 42, returning with 47 for a total of 175 – fine play for an amateur.

Ferguson in the second round again played a very steady game. He was out in 42 – two strokes in excess of the morning. Homeward, Ferguson did the first two holes in 7 (4, 3), but at the Heather a 5 was again called for. The next hole was well played in 5, but in the Long and Ginger Beer holes 6s were required. As in the first round Ferguson drew to the left of the green among the rough grass in playing to the Dyke, but made up leeway with a good quarter shot and a fine putt to the hole, but took 5. For the last two holes he took 6 each for a homeward 46, a round of 88 and a total of 171

Jamie Anderson again took the first four holes out in 20, reaching the turn in 43 and with 45 had an 88 for 175. His playing partner, Bob Martin, 89 in the morning, was round in 86, also for 175. Tom Kidd was also higher than in the morning, taking 45 out and 48 in for a 93 and Kirkaldy an 89, but Willie Fernie improved with an 86 for 174.

Ferguson was thus the lowest scorer and accordingly became champion for the third year in succession. He played a steady and careful game throughout and it was observable that he made few mistakes and was seldom caught in any of the numerous hazards. Besides the medal he secured the first money prize of £12.

1883

MUSSELBURGH

If Bob Martin rode his luck in 1876 to win the Open with a 7, 5 finish and then won the play-off with a walkover, then Willie Fernie can beat that. He had a 10 with seven holes to play, tied for first place and came back from the dead at the final hole of the play-off.

16 NOVEMBER

Yesterday, golfers in the vicinity of Edinburgh mustered in strong force on Musselburgh links to witness the competition for the championship cup and medal. The weather in the morning was rather dull, but when play began about half past eleven, the air was clear and bracing. Later the darkness set in to such an extent that it was with difficulty the last drawn players could see the holes even at a very short distance off. Despite this the play of the tail end was exceptionally good and Bob Ferguson, who was in the second last couple, tied with Willie Fernie of Dumfries with a total for the four rounds, or 36 holes, of 159. Ferguson, who has held the position of champion golfer for the past three years, has therefore to play off with that rising professional today when a rare exhibition of the game is sure to be given.

There were 34 competitors yesterday, the Dumfries representative had on more than one occasion shown splendid form, but very few of those assembled to see the start followed him or any of the men as they left for play until Ferguson and his partner, Bernard Sayers, both local men, swiped off from the teeing place. The starting point was then almost immediately deserted and the large number who followed these two men were rewarded with some grand golfing.

Bob drove first and in three strokes was well on the green, but putted loosely and holed in 5. Leaving the Barracks Entry hole, he got lodged in furze but checked it

out in magnificent style holing out in another 5 while his opponent took 6. Mrs Forman's was reached with a capital 4 – Sayers getting bunkered on the journey and taking 6. By a nasty putt, Ferguson lost the Sea Hole by 4 to 3 but succeeded in getting home to Pandy in 4 and arrived at the very edge of the Bathing Coach hole in 4, but had to take another stroke to hole out. Both Sayers and Ferguson approached the Hole Across with their first strokes and Sayers had hard lines with his second, the ball just lying on the rim of the hole. Ferguson putted rather carelessly and took 4. The Gas Hole was taken by both in 4, but the Home Hole was taken by Sayers in 3 and Ferguson 4.

In the second round Ferguson began well but ere he got to Mrs Forman's he was one stroke to the bad as compared with his former round, and, losing another stroke going to Pandy, his chances, which on the first round looked rosy, did not improve. However, he reached home in 40. In his third round Ferguson was even less successful and consequently a good number of his followers left him and joined the ranks which had been following the Dumfries representative. Ferguson, however, notwithstanding that darkness was fast getting in, played a grand round and reached home in 38, making his total for the four rounds 159.

Fernie was in capital form and though he took no fewer than 7 at the second hole, came home with a register of 38. He improved on this in the second round, taking 37. After luncheon he fell of considerably and took 8 at Mrs Forman's having got badly bunkered and holed home in 40. The last round was more disastrous. Leaving home, he reached Barracks Entry in 5, but, driving loosely, his next stroke landed his ball in a bunker. Playing it out to the left, he got on to grass. He then drove, but his ball again fell into a bad bunker. In cleeking it out he drove hard against the sleeping banking and his ball rebounded on to grass. He then got a fair drive, but the hole cost him 10 strokes. He reached home in 44 strokes making a total of 159. Both players were cheered and congratulated when their scores were announced.

PLAY OFF

The play-off between Bob Ferguson and Willie Fernie resulted in a capital game in favour of the Dumfries representative by one stroke, his score being 158, one fewer than Friday. A drizzling rain fell during the whole of the first and last rounds but there was one of the largest assemblages of spectators. They were rewarded with a display of excellent driving, though the putting generally was poor.

At the halfway stage, Fernie was one shot up with rounds of 42 and 39 while Ferguson took 41 on each occasion. Ferguson took the third round in 37 to stand one up and the stage was set for an exciting final round.

In playing to the first hole, Ferguson landed badly in a bunker, Fernie's ball just resting on a ledge of another bunker. Bob by his niblick got nicely out of the sand and was well on the green with his third stroke, Fernie lying within four feet of the hole with a like number. Each holed out in 5. Linkfield saw no alteration in the respective positions of the players as Fernie showed really bad green play. Fernie, however, on going to Mrs Forman's, played a capital game and holed out in 4 while his opponent was unfortunate. His first shot landed close by the racecourse railing and in spooning out he landed the ball in a bunker. Though his next stroke landed on the green he took 5 to hole out. The game at this point was again all even. The Sea Hole was taken by Fernie in 3 by fine putting, while Ferguson took 4. Ferguson, however, pulled up at Pandy and they were even once more with five holes to play. Neither putted well at the Bathing Coach hole and each took 6. The Hole Across was taken by each in 3, although both shaved the hole with their second strokes. Both players reached the green at the Gas Hole in two, but Fernie took three puts for a 5 while Ferguson was down in 4 to go one up with one to play. Ferguson drove first and his ball went to the left of the hole while Fernie sent a beautiful shot on to the green about four yards to the right of the hole. Ferguson made a bad putt thus giving Fernie an opportunity of either of winning or drawing the game. The young one, however, by one of the cleanest and neatest putts of the whole game got in amidst tense excitement. Quietness having been restored, Bob played his third stroke which, had he been successful in holing, would have drawn the game. He, however, failed and Fernie was declared the champion and winner of the cup, medal and £8. Ferguson won £5.

1883
WILLIE FERNIE

Willie Fernie was born in St Andrews in the same year as Young Tom and so can be regarded as a late developer. Along with Jack Burns and Sandy Herd, both later to win the Open, he served an apprenticeship as a plasterer in Andrew Scott's yard in South Street before scraping a living from golf. He left St Andrews in 1880 to become greenkeeper at Dumfries, Felixstowe and Ardeer before going to Troon as professional. Fernie played in many big money matches and went on to play for Scotland against England in 1904. In later years he was in demand as a teacher and also a golf course architect.

James
Muir

George
Fernie

Jack
Simpson
Carnoustie (Winne

James
Cunningham

Andrew
Wright

William
Boyd

Andrew
Monaghan

James
Ray

Willie
Fernie

4 .

David   Charlie   Hugh   Archie   David
ton   Hunter   Kirkcaldy Simpson   Grant

Andrew   Tom   Willie   George   Ben
ll Kirkcaldy   Morris   Park   Sayers   Sayers

1884

PRESTWICK

3 OCTOBER

The annual match for the championship cup was played yesterday over the Prestwick links. As some of the best golfers in the country took part in the competition, considerable interest was manifested in the result and large numbers of amateurs had an opportunity of seeing some excellent golfing.

The belief was pretty general that the holder, Willie Fernie, would be ill to beat, but a few did not overlook the fine form of ex-champion Jamie Anderson, while Willie Campbell, Jof Morris and Douglas Rolland had also their admirers.

The weather was on the whole unfavourable and the strong wind was exceedingly baffling. The 28 competitors having been drawn in couples in order of starting on the previous evening, no time was lost in preliminaries.

On summing up the cards it was found that the championship had been gained by Jack Simpson of Earlsferry, who, playing a steady and faultless game, handed in the fine score of 160.

Jack Simpson was born in Earlsferry, one of six brothers whose names were later associated with Carnoustie where Robert Simpson was a renowned clubmaker.

1885

ST ANDREWS

3 OCTOBER

The autumn meeting of the Royal and Ancient Golf Club, and with it the golfing season at St Andrews, was appropriately brought to a close on Saturday by the annual competition for the golf championship. The muster of players was excessively large, no lower than 56 players entering.

In addition to the championship there were several money prizes under competition, subscribed for by the gentlemen attending the autumn meeting of the club, and before the play began the competitors had to declare whether they were simply competing only as amateurs or as professionals for the money prizes. Such men as Mr Laidlay, Mr Hunter, Mr Balfour, Col Boothby, Mr Goff, Mr L Ross, Captain W Burn, Mr Henry and Mr Ball, all declared themselves as amateurs, but several of the local artisan players entered the lists as professionals.

The entry was the largest that ever took part for the championship, and good play was anticipated. The conditions under which play was conducted were pretty favourable – the weather was fine and the greens in good order – the only thing that tended to prevent the lowest results being a stiff breeze from about west-north-west. The game was two rounds of the green – 36 holes – and play began punctually at 10 o'clock.

At the end of the first round Archie Simpson was lowest at 83, and Bob Martin second at 84. The second round was commenced after a short interval. Simpson made a bad start and took 6s at the first two holes, and he ran up his score to 27 at the Hole Across. His score out was 45. He returned with 44, total 89, which made him 172 for the two rounds. Martin in the second round going out made good work and scored 43. He had thus gained two strokes on Simpson, and had now one stroke of an advantage. Playing the first hole in, Martin somewhat missed the tee shot, but made a good long hit and got down in 4. Approaching the High Hole he carried away to the left and had the bank between him and the green. He reached it with his second, but made indifferent work on the putting green and took 5, and he had now two strokes of a pull over his rival.

With two fine drives he nearly carried the green at the Hole Across, laid a fine third about three yards from the hole, and holed out in 4. He had thus gained three strokes. Playing to the fifth hole he foozled his second shot and missing a putt, required a 6 to hole out, but still led by two strokes. The sixth hole was well played in 4, and he had 16 strokes for the last three holes to beat Simpson.

Playing to the Corner of the Dyke, he bunkered his tee shot and scarcely carried the green with his third shot. His fourth was short, but with a fine long putt holed out in 5. He had thus 11 strokes for the last two holes. Playing to the eighth hole he missed his second shot, and did not reach the green until four. He laid his fifth dead and was done in 6. With two fine drives and a beautiful third he laid himself almost dead at the Home Hole, but missed his putt, but had another shot to win, which he easily got down. For a round of 87 and a grand total of 171, one stroke less than Simpson. As he finished he was solidly applauded.

Throughout, Martin had played a strong, steady, and careful game, and his victory was well earned. On the occasion of his winning the championship at St Andrews in 1876 his scores were 86, 90 – 176; his victory this year being made with five strokes less. Simpson, who followed second, also played a fine game. He is quite a young lad, and gives good promise of future triumphs.

1886

MUSSELBURGH

Late arrival on the tee for the Open nowadays means disqualification. Tournament organisers were more lenient then, but there was a penalty. From this report we learn that offenders were sent to the back of the field.

5 NOVEMBER

Musselburgh, Friday – The match for the golf championship, open to amateurs and professionals, took place here today, and with it practically the season is brought to a close. This year there is £20 to be divided. Although the match is open to amateurs, they have never been able to wrest the honour from the professionals. The strain of playing 36 holes is perhaps too great for a gentleman whose presence on the golfing green is limited to hours of leisure, not to speak of the superior skill of the average professional. This year the number of amateurs was even smaller than usual. Out of a field of 42 there were only seven of them. The list, however, included Mr Horace Hutchinson, the champion amateur for the year, and Mr J E Laidlay, the winner of the recent tournament at North Berwick. It was hoped that Mr John Ball, of Hoylake, might take part in the contest, but he did not enter.

The draw took place in the Honourable Company's clubhouse shortly after nine o'clock and was remarkable for this that no two players of first rank were placed together. As a consequence the large gathering of spectators were at a loss whom to follow, and distributed themselves over several couples so that few of the competitors were embarrassed with the presence of a large following.

When play started, shortly after 10 o'clock, the weather was bright and promising. There was no indication of rain. The green was in first class order, although just a trifle bare. Traces of the recent race meeting were to be seen here and there, but, everything to be considered, Bob Ferguson (the three-times Open champion) was to be congratulated on the success of his work as greenkeeper. Before a round had been played heavy rain fell. This completely transformed the putting greens, and made competitors play a very different game. Some of them did not appear to observe the change, with the result that they always played short.

Bernard Sayers and William Thomson lost their position at the top of the list through the former being late, and had consequently to play last of all. This mishap cost them some trouble, for they had to finish their last round in the dark.

At the start it was thought that Mungo Park would make a good appearance against Willie Fernie, the winner of the recent match at North Berwick. The veteran, however, could not get into driving form, although on the greens he was most effective with his putter. His play was greatly admired by players of the old school, who still have great faith in the putter in spite of modern ideas. There is no doubt that if everyone could use the putter as Park does, it would be more largely in vogue.

When the fourth round was started it was impossible to predict the champion, so many players were all close upon one another. Willie Campbell was regarded with most favour, having registered three 39s. At the famous Pandy, however, he met his nemesis. The crowd refused to keep still, and Campbell amidst the constant movement drove off from the tee and missed his shot, the ball landing in the bunker. Although he got readily onto the turf again he once more bunkered, with the result that he took 7 to hole out. These two mishaps cost him the championship. The first good score finished was that of the veteran Bob Ferguson, who succeeded in doing the four rounds in 161 strokes. His game was as good as ever, only for the driving, in which he was rather weak. Like Mungo Park, he used his putter with great effect. Soon afterwards Willie Campbell made his appearance at the home hole with a total of 159. He was followed by David Brown and Willie Park, Jr. The latter in the fourth round played a magnificent game, his score of 36 being unequalled. His last putt, though played in presence of an immense concourse of spectators, was carefully and most successfully considered. To his partner, however, fell the honours of the day.

1886
DAVID BROWN

David Brown, known as "Deacon", was a slater from Musselburgh who won on home ground with a 36-hole total of 157, a record for the course. The fates were with him that day because he wasn't even entered for the tournament. In George Colville's *Musselburgh Golf Story* it

Brown, a comparatively unknown player, finished with a total of 157. He took 38 for the first round. In his second, however, he did not drive well, although on the greens he was very successful with his putter. The last three holes of the third round he took in eight, and of the fourth in nine, both excellent performances. Unlike many of his fellow competitors he was only once bunkered. Brown was left at the head of the list, and he accordingly became the champion for the year.

is related that Brown was sent for at the last minute to make up the numbers and came straight from his job in working clothes. He was given a bath and some clean clothes namely "a pair of striped trousers, a frock coat and a lum hat". He finished his third round 2, 3, 3 and his final round with three 3s.

This surprise win launched a golfing career. He was attached to the Malvern club in England and later went to America where he was attached for a time to the Boston club and lost a play-off to Willie Anderson for the 1903 US Open.

Brown was one of the pioneering Scots who made a great deal of money from golf in America. He also played the stock market but lost most of his wealth in the Wall Street slump of 1929. Soon thereafter he came back to Musselburgh in poor health and died a few weeks later.

1887

PRESTWICK

The Open has frequently given the lie to that overworn sporting expression "No-one remembers who came second". Who could forget Jean van de Velde's 7 at the eighteenth, incorporating a paddle in the Barry Burn, at Carnoustie in 1999 when he needed only a 6 to win, or Doug Sanders's missed short putt to win at the eighteenth at St Andrews in 1970. The Open, however, was littered with great disasters long before then and there is a bunker at Prestwick which immortalises the "terrible misfortune" of Willie Campbell in this Open. It is called to this day "Willie Campbell's Grave".

17 SEPTEMBER

Prestwick, Friday – The golf championship open to amateurs and professionals was played here today under conditions by no means favourable for a perfect exhibition for the royal and ancient game. Rain fell almost incessantly, and with a degree of intensity which not only drenched players and spectators, but, what was more distressing, rendering the links dull and heavy.

In addition to the difficulty with the ground the competitors had to cope with a cross wind of intermittent power, and that is no light matter on such a green. The course does not follow one line but is zig zag, so that after playing against the wind for a couple of holes you may find it at your back at the next. While speaking of the rain, this much must be said in its favour, that it made the putting greens very true, and gave players who could use the wooden club an opportunity of displaying their skill. Considering the state of the weather and the situation of Prestwick, the attendance of spectators was remarkably good. Play began at half past 10 o'clock.

Willie Campbell had practically a monopoly of spectators. Since coming to Prestwick this spring he has established himself among local golfers as a warm favourite, and at the start today he was regarded as the likeliest candidate for championships honours. Conscious of being in form, Campbell acquired just the degree of freedom which in golf assists largely to success. It could not be said that he ventured beyond the bounds of prudence, but he never lost a stroke by exercising too much caution. His first round gave him the record for the green, a circumstance creditable on such a day. In the second round he started fairly well, although he took 39 strokes against 35 to reach the ninth hole.

At the third hole from home he met a terrible misfortune. There is a bunker to be negotiated there, and, of course, two games are open to the player – he either must carry it or pass round the side. Choosing the former, Campbell took a strong drive. The ball, however, was left buried in the thick bent which fringes the top of the bunker, and Campbell was scarcely able to see it. He made a desperate effort to force it on to the green, but it proved futile, and five strokes were lost in the bunker. This misfortune cost him the championship.

When Campbell's chance of success disappeared in this way all attention was directed to Willie Park, Jr, who had Willie Fernie for a partner. Park's form is at present notorious. No golfer, either amateur or professional, has recently played with the same steady success. It is well enough known that he had a match arranged with Jamie Morris, of St Andrews, and that in view of it he engaged in regular practice at Musselburgh, where he attained a remarkable average. Today his game was perfect. No-one could detect a fault. In addition, he had the good fortune never to enter a bunker. His steadiness was such that in the second round he had not a single 6. When he finished with 161 it was at once seen that he would become the winner. The only other player at all threatening was Bob Martin.

Time after time he astonished onlookers with fine approaches and long, old-fashioned putts, reminiscent of the days of Tom Morris and David Strath. Martin however fell short of Park by one stroke.

The champion of last year, David Brown, played a remarkably fine game. Had he not bunkered at the third hole in the first round, he would have been well to the front. The green suited his style of putting well, and his long drives came in very profitably. There was disappointment over the performance of Willie Fernie. He knows the green, and should have given a better account of himself.

From this year's championship meeting amateurs ought to derive some consolation. One of their number stands fourth on the list and another tenth. The latter is Mr Horace Hutchinson, the amateur champion of this and last year.

1887, 1889
WILLIE PARK JR

Willie Park Jr can be regarded as the first Open champion to go on to establish himself as an international golfing entrepreneur, and many are the champions who have followed him on that road. His Open wins seem almost incidental, although his score of 155 at Musselburgh in 1889, when he tied with Andra Kirkaldy and went on to win the play off, remains an Open record for the course as it never came back there.

Park believed putting was the key to golf and was an avid practiser. He wrote a book *The Art of Putting* in 1920 to follow his first literary venture *The Game of Golf*, (1896)

After his apprenticeship with Uncle Mungo at Alnmouth, he returned to Musselburgh to work with his father and uncle laying out courses, then went on his own, helped by brothers Mungo and Jack. Before the turn of the century he had travelled extensively in America promoting golf and designing courses. He returned to England to lay out Sunningdale and Huntercombe, showing that the heathland around London was ideal for golf. He also designed Carnoustie, Formby and Gullane. Meanwhile, his international reputation was growing as he masterminded Vienna in Austria, Royal Antwerp in Belgium and Dinard, Evian and La Boulie in France. Later he was said to be working on 70 courses at a time in America with offices there and in Canada.

He is rated as one of the finest golf course designers in the history of the game. Against this background, his two Open wins seem a mere detail.

1888

ST ANDREWS

The field had the most noted of Scotch professionals, and a good few crack amateur players. The weather was bright and clear, with a high wind, but altogether the conditions were pretty favourable. The entries numbered 52.

On the conclusion of the first round, Willie Campbell, Prestwick, stood first at 84, Bernard Sayers, North Berwick, being second at 85; while W Leslie, Balfour D; Anderson Jr, St Andrews; Bob Martin, St Andrews; and Jack Burns, Warwick, came third at 86 each.

In the afternoon, Campbell was looked upon as the favourite man, but he did not maintain his forenoon's record, and fell away from his fine play, frequently made mistakes, and ran up his score to 90 strokes, and totalled 174. Bernard Sayers was two strokes better and held the favourite place until half the competitors had returned, when his score was touched by David Anderson, a local player. Later in the evening Jack Burns, Warwick, returned with an 85, which, with his first round of 86, gave him a total of 171, and this proved to be the winning score of the day, and he accordingly became champion golfer for the year.

1888
JACK BURNS

Jack Burns was better at golf than arithmetic. He won the Open only because an official spotted he had counted up his score wrong, much to the dismay of Ben Sayers and Davie Anderson who thought they had tied with him and would go into a three-man play-off. His total was one too many but as the scores at individual holes had been marked correctly the mistake could be corrected and Burns was duly declared the champion.

A St Andrean, rated as having a great all-round game, he was yet another plasterer to trade, but at the time of his win he was greenkeeper and professional at Warwick, later returning to St Andrews as a platelayer on the railway. In this occupation he is credited with a memorable *bon mot*. When asked about his form he would reply: "Never better – I haven't been off the line for years."

1889

MUSSELBURGH

8 NOVEMBER

Yesterday was the great field day of the year for professional golfers. The competition for the championship drew large numbers of the leading players to the Musselburgh links, where, in beautiful weather, with excellent green conditions, a most interesting contest took place.

Play was entered upon about half past 10 o'clock in the forenoon, but as the day wore on it became apparent that an earlier start would have been more satisfactory. Many of the players experienced diminished light during their last round, half a dozen actually playing in the dark before they reached the home hole between five o'clock and half past five. Hundreds of spectators were scattered over the links the whole day. Fortunately, the decisions for the cup were not interfered with in this way, as the likely men finished their play ere daylight waned.

The competition has resulted in a tie between Willie Park, junior, Musselburgh, and Andrew Kirkaldy, St Andrews, with the very creditable score of 155.

Willie Park's play is well known to golfers, and it will be sufficient to say that he was in good form, playing with considerable freedom, and very successful with his putting. A Kirkaldy, St Andrews, who is now one of the foremost golfers in the country, took the sixth place at last year's competition, and on other occasions has shown himself a skilful player. His style is not attractive, and one is rather surprised after seeing him play, to find the ball has been driven with such accuracy.

One of the amateurs (Mr Robertson) had a most interesting close to his day's play. His stroke from the tee reached the home hole in safety, thus accomplishing the remarkable feat of holing in one. It is worth mentioning as bearing upon the result of the contest today that Willie Park's last stroke from the tee came into contact with a gentleman's hat and was stopped certainly not further from the hole than it would have been with a fair field.

The tie will be played off at Musselburgh on Monday, commencing at half-past 10 o'clock.

PLAY OFF

The tie for the golf championship of Willie Park, of Musselburgh, and Andrew Kirkaldy, of St Andrews, was decided at Musselburgh yesterday over four rounds of the green – 36 holes in all, counting by strokes. The weather being favourable, there was a large turnout to witness what was undoubtedly the most important contest of the year.

After three rounds, Park was four strokes to the good. The last round commenced by Park missing a fairly easy putt, and thus giving away a stroke at the Graves. A half in 5 was the result of the play at the second hole. At Mrs Forman's, both men were loudly cheered for splendid putts, which secured a half in 4. After a run of another four halves, both playing a remarkably steady game, Kirkaldy was bunkered from a bad drive at the Gasworks, and virtually finished the match by acquiring 6 to Park's 4, the Home Hole producing a half in 3, Willie Park, by a majority of five strokes, won the championship for the second time. The Musselburgh player was warmly congratulated upon his success.

1890

PRESTWICK

The annual competition for the champion cup, open to both amateurs and professionals, has always appealed strongly to the sympathies of the public, and this year's contest which took place at Prestwick yesterday, may be said to have eclipsed all others in this respect. The reason for this was to be found in the strong representation of the amateur talent amongst the competitors. In no years since the institution of the cup in 1872 had the competition included three such distinguished amateurs as Mr John Ball, Mr J E Laidley, and Mr Horace Hutchinson. The professionals were also out in full force, not a single man of note, with the exception of D Rolland, being absent from the field. The list included previous champions in Willie Park Jr, Willie Fernie, and David Brown. Old Tom Morris, who gained the Champion Belt on four occasions, also took part at the age of 69.

For the first time in the history of the competition an amateur has asserted his supremacy over the professionals. Mr John Ball Jr, of Hoylake, who, in May last, won the Amateur Championship, yesterday defeated the strong field of professionals, and placed himself in the proud position of champion golfer of the world. This is another strong illustration of the proficiency in the game to which amateurs are now attaining, not only in this country but also in England. The champion of the national game of golf is neither a professional nor a Scotchman, but an amateur and an Englishman.

Mr Ball is all the more to be congratulated upon his victory. He is a very stylish golfer. Playing in an easy finished manner he never appears to press. He drives a very long ball, his approach play is usually pretty deadly, and mistakes on the putting green are few and far between. His play was remarkable for its steadiness. The card showed four 41s. Yesterday was not an ideal day for golf playing. The weather was fair and bright, but a strong wind which blew from the north-west interfered with the calculations of the players, and was responsible for the breakdown of not a few likely competitors. Those who started early had most to complain of in this respect. The first couple teed their balls shortly after quarter past 10 o'clock, and fully two hours elapsed ere the last couple started on their first round. So slow was the progress made the proceedings did not reach a conclusion until six o'clock that evening.

At the conclusion of the first round, Hugh Kirkaldy was seen to have an excellent chance of winning the trophy, but he threw away his chances in playing the first two holes in the second round, which cost him 13 strokes. Andrew Kirkaldy attracted a great deal of attention, and his chances altered greatly at different parts of the game. At the end of the first half-round his score was 43. He, however, finished the first round with the excellent total of 81 – the best score of the morning. In the afternoon he was first favourite for a time, but with no 3s, very few 4s, twelve 5s, and a 7 in his score it was seen that he was out of the running.

The next couple, Mr John Ball Jr, and Willie Campbell, were followed by a large contingent of the spectators. The end hole of the second round did away with Campbell's chance of the championship. He ran up an 8, and at the succeeding hole, after topping his drive, he tore up his card.

At the fourth last hole it became known that less than 21 for the remaining holes would secure Ball the championship. He soon put the matter beyond doubt – a 5 being followed by a 4, and then a 5 again for the second last hole left him with a 6 to win. The last hole he accomplished in 4, and was loudly cheered as the winner of the championship by three strokes.

1890
JOHN BALL

John Ball was the first of only three amateurs to win the Open (Harold Hilton and Bobby Jones are the others). Ball can be considered fortunate to be an amateur. In 1877, when he was only 15, he was fourth in the Open and accepted the prize of 30 shillings. However, he was allowed to remain an amateur on the grounds that he had been innocently misled.

Ball's father John owned the Royal Hotel at Hoylake and had golf right on his doorstep. The Amateur Championship was established at Hoylake in 1886 and from 1888 to 1912 he won that title a record eight times. It might have been more had he not taken a break from golf to serve in the Boer War with the Cheshire Yeomanry. Ball's style is described as a palm grip, a full swing and a mastery of half-shots. He won at Prestwick, but his defence at St Andrews the following year was noted for an 11 at the Road Hole. He was neither the first nor the last to founder there.

In 1890 he became the first golfer to hold the Open and Amateur titles in the same year, a feat only once repeated, by Bobby Jones in 1930, who also won the US Open and amateur titles that year.

Ball was a silent player who would acknowledge a good shot by an opponent with a nod of his head. He did not particularly enjoy the limelight. On his return by train to Hoylake in 1890 a welcome had been planned at Hoylake station from where, it was planned, he would be escorted to the Royal Hotel. When Ball heard of this he left the train at Meols, the station before Hoylake, and walked home alone along the foreshore.

1891

ST ANDREWS

St. Andrews, Tuesday – In the Open Championship at St Andrews today the professionals reasserted their supremacy over the amateurs. For the first time in the history of the competition Mr John Ball, Jr, the Hoylake crack, beat all comers at Prestwick, and a general impression prevailed that the days of the professionals at the top of the tree were numbered. But today's result must have disposed of any such idea. With the exception of Mr S Mure Fergusson, who was fourth, none of the amateurs came within sight of the winner.

The winner, Hugh Kirkaldy, is 23 years of age, and is the youngest of three brothers who have devoted the greatest part of their lives to the game. His great performance is the record score for St Andrews. The performance of the champion today is worthy of all praise. It was a grand exhibition of golf considering the weather, and the winning score – 166 – compares most favourably with 171 with which the championship was won on the former three occasions upon which it was decided at St Andrews.

The list of competitors was by far the most formidable. In no year since the institution of the match in 1872 have the entrants included so many distinguished amateurs, Mr John Ball, Jr, last year's champion: Mr J E Laidlay, the present amateur champion: Mr Horace Hutchinson, ex-amateur champion: and Mr H Hilton, Hoylake, who contested the final in the amateur championship this year, were included in the cream of the gentleman players who entered the lists. The professionals also turned out in large numbers both from Scotland and England, scarcely a green of any note not being represented. The list included previous champions in Willie Park Jr, Willie Fernie, Bob Martin, Jack Burns and

Davie Brown. Old Tom Morris also took part in the match for the thirty-first time. Of the 83 competitors, 43 were professionals and 40 amateurs.

The weather of the early part of the day was of the most wretched description. Rain had fallen continuously during the night, and when play commenced at nine o'clock was still heavily descending, while a very stiff breeze from the east made matters all the more uncomfortable. In the forenoon, fortunately, the rain cleared off, and with the exception of one or two heavy showers the weather remained fair during the latter part of the day. The wind was, however, very troublesome, and bothered the competitors considerably on the return journey.

It was fully half past 12 o'clock before the last of the couples left the starting point, and the proceedings altogether occupied about nine hours. In future years, it has been suggested that only those who do not exceed a dozen strokes more than the leader in the first round should be allowed to enter the second stage.

Hugh Kirkaldy's recent good form had made him a special favourite with the spectators. He soon showed that he meant to make a strong bid for championship honours. He was driving a very long ball and approached in magnificent style. Had he been a little steadier on the putting green he might have reduced his score, splendid as it was, by a few strokes. A long putt, however, gave him a splendid 3 for the End Hole, which was reached in the excellent total of 39. With the strong wind to contend against, Hugh played a remarkably steady game. On the return journey, after a 4 and a 3, he threw away a stroke at the twelfth hole by weak putting. At the fourteenth he was badly bunkered, and having to play back lost another stroke. The remaining four holes were admirably played, giving him a total of 83 for the round.

The expectation that this score would be excelled was realised, although W D More, the Chester professional, showed unexpected form. At the turn his card exhibited 40, and keeping up this form in returning, he upheld the honour of the Chester green by coming home only one in advance of Kirkaldy.

Andrew Kirkaldy, whose play of late had created a general feeling that he was out of form, showed that his hand had not lost its cunning by registering an 84. He went out steadily in 41 and returned in 43. Mr. John Ball, last year's champion, and Willie Campbell, who were expected to provide the most interesting play of the day, grievously disappointed the large body of spectators who started with them. Mr Ball threw himself entirely out of the competition at the Road Hole, which cost him no fewer than 11. A long brassie shot carried him into the road, where he lay so badly that after a couple of ineffectual attempts to extricate himself he was compelled to lift and lose a couple of strokes.

In the afternoon, Hugh Kirkaldy retained his form. On the green with his approach he holed at seven of the nine holes in the outward journey in 4, and turned with the splendid score of 38. Homeward, curiously, he took 5 to every hole. At the Short Hole he not only landed on the bunker, but also missed a short putt. At the Road Hole his approach just stopped within a yard or two of the face of the bunker, but he lofted beautifully on to the green and holed a good putt. Playing the last hole, Hugh was short with his second, and his third got a bad break on the green, compelling him to play two more. His figure for the round was 83, a similar score to that of the forenoon, making his total 166.

More did not play as well in the afternoon, and finished with 171 but both Andrew Kirkaldy and Willie Fernie were in grand fettle, and gave Hugh Kirkaldy a good fight. Andrew went out in the fine score of 39, but required 45 on the way home. He was left on the last green with a longish putt to tie with his brother, but he failed to get down, and took two more to reach the bottom of the hole. Fernie, although he failed to go out in less than 42, taking 7 to the High Hole, played a splendid game against the wind and returned with a like figure. He thus managed to tie with Andrew Kirkaldy for second place.

1891
HUGH KIRKALDY

Hugh Kirkaldy was the son of a miner who fought in the Crimean War. His brother Andrew (Andra) was better known but never won the Open although he did take second place to Hugh by beating Willie Fernie in a play-off. This was the first time two brothers had finished first and second in the competition for the claret jug although in 1866 David Park came second behind his brother Willie while playing for the Challenge Belt. Hugh's 36-hole total of 166 beat the previous St Andrews record by five shots. Andra had been runner-up on two previous occasions, was third three times and fourth twice.

Hugh was well liked by his peers but died young following a particularly bad bout of influenza which severely damaged his lungs.

The Oxford and Cambridge Golfing Society play annually for "The President's Putter", originally Hugh's putter.

Harry Vardon, Ted Ray, James Braid and J H Taylor at the
Glasgow Herald *1000 guineas tournament at Gleneagles in 1922*

CHAPTER THREE

LEGEND OF THE GREAT TRIUMVIRATE

THE WORD SPREADS

It was boom time for golf. Hundreds of new courses were being opened and not just in Britain. America was in the midst of a golf epidemic and to a lesser extent Europe, bringing new horizons for the top golfers, especially those with "Open champion" on their calling cards. No longer, like Old Tom Morris, would they be "solemnly handed the implements of their trade – a barrow, a spade and a shovel". As well as tournaments and exhibition matches, professionals were in demand as teachers and course architects to cater for a growing international appetite for the game.

Twice Open champion Willie Park Jr was involved in a big way. At one time he had 70 courses in America under construction in addition to others in Britain and the rest of Europe. Scots golfers moved not only south but west across the Atlantic, a brain drain that would return by the 1920s with a vengeance. Having taught the Sassenachs, Scots would now extend their missionary work to America and nurture a new breed of Open champion. That in a nutshell is why 1893 would mark the last Open won by a home-based Scot for 106 years, inconceivable though it would have seemed at the time.

While that monster was gestating, the Open remained primarily British and was about to witness the phenomenon of the Great Triumvirate of J H Taylor, Harry Vardon and James Braid. Among them they would win 16 of the next 23 Opens up to the outbreak of the First World War. In later life they would also be instrumental in founding the Professional Golfers' Association.

In the pursuit of longer hitting, another big development was looming, courtesy of an American by the name of Coburn Haskell who was about to invent the rubber-wound ball which would render the guttie obsolete. The Haskell ball became known as the "Bounding Billy" not just because it could be struck further than the guttie but also because it gave a reasonable result when hit less than perfectly. At first those who used it were called "bounders", an insulting term which is still used to describe those who bend the rules.

When the popular professional Sandy Herd used it to win the 1902 Open it opened the floodgates. Herd a bounder? Never. Just like the guttie succeeded the feathery in the 1850s, so the Haskell succeeded the guttie in the first decade of the twentieth century. Those who protested it was "nae gowf" were voices blown away in a strong wind of progress.

The status of the golf professional was rising fast, but as a general rule they still weren't allowed to sully the fine standard of company in clubhouses.

The Open was changing fast too. The last 36-hole Open had been played. Henceforth it would be over 72 holes and two courses in England, Royal St George's and Hoylake, would soon be on the Open rota. The number entering was another upward factor as was prize-money. In addition to entry fees, the halfway cut would soon be introduced. Many problems relating to crowd control and the size of field were still to be faced, but the modern Open was beginning to shape up.

1892

MUIRFIELD

For the first time the Open was played over the links of the Honourable Company of Edinburgh Golfers at Muirfield, coinciding with the move of the club from Musselburgh which had staged six Opens. It was the first time any championship had been played, anywhere in the world, over 72 holes, and the first time an entry fee had been charged. This was given favourable comment in The Golfing Annual as "a move in the right direction, and will go far to deter vain-glorious players from cumbering the field". Just as important, it boosted the prize fund. Two rounds were to be played on each of two days. Amateurs showed the way in the first round with Mr Horace Hutchinson leading with a 74 and the 1890 winner, Mr John Ball, in second place, one shot more. After the second round Mr Hutchinson's total was 152, giving him a three-stroke lead over Sandy Herd, Willie Park and Mr Ball. Ben Sayers was handily placed on 156 but Mr Hilton had slipped with an 81 to 159 and Hugh Kirkaldy had scored an 83 for 160.

23 SEPTEMBER

For the second time an amateur has secured the Open Championship, and, as on the first occasion, the victory has gone to England. It is a sad blow to Scotch professionalism to have an amateur beating all-comers, but it is all the more severe when an Englishman takes first place in the Scotch national game. To Mr H H Hilton all the more credit was due for his brilliant win yesterday. Under new conditions none but a steady exponent of the game had any chance of success, and therefore Mr Hilton only earned his honours after a most exhaustive test of his golfing ability. Twice within an ace of winning the Amateur Championship, he has been fully compensated for his disappointment by the victory over all-comers yesterday.

Although dull and cheerless in the morning, the weather

cleared up yesterday. The Right Hon. A J Balfour, M P, was again early on the links, and obliged the committee by doing active service as a marker for Mr Horace Hutchinson and John Dalgleish.

In the final round the only players who received any attention were Mr Ball, Hugh Kirkaldy, A Herd, Mr Hilton, and Willie Park. Playing as good a long game as he did in the forenoon, Mr Ball was loose in his putting and finished in 79 for a 308 aggregate. Hugh Kirkaldy, playing steadily, accomplished the first half in 38, and then stood two worse than Mr Ball was at that point. By taking the next three holes in 4 each the professional placed himself one stroke better than the amateur champion. He was left with a 5 at the home hole to beat the Englishman. After a fair drive and a good approach, Hugh, playing rather hurriedly, topped an iron shot clean into the bunker in front of the green. He recovered smartly, but failed to hole out in fewer than 6.

A Herd, who came in soon after, was running neck-and-neck with both Mr Ball and Hugh Kirkaldy. Like his fellow professional, he was left with 8 for the last two holes to beat the amateur or 9 to tie. He played the second last perfectly in 3. At the home hole, however, after being on the green in 3, he overran the hole, leaving himself with a fairly easy yard putt for a win. Playing without sufficient care he failed to get down, and with a 6 also tied with a total of 308.

All attention was now directed to the play of Mr Hilton and Willie Park. The former was left with a 76 to win. His outward half was negotiated in 38, leaving him another 38 for the homeward journey for a win. With 4s and 3s he accomplished the first six holes in 22. At the next he took 5, but recovered himself nicely with a 3 at the eighth, and had an 8 to finish to win. He very easily holed out in 6.

His victory was greeted with loud applause. Willie Park meanwhile was not playing a very brilliant game, and his chances had been discounted.

As the winner of the championship was not a professional, the first prize of £35 was withdrawn according to the rules, a proceeding which did not altogether please the professionals, who hardly seemed to understand the arrangement. Mr Hilton, as winner, received a gold medal. The Royal Liverpool Club, to which he belongs, receives possession of the cup for the year. In addition Mr Hilton received a plate to the value of £5 for having recorded the lowest score for a single round, *viz*, 72. The second and third prizes of £18 and £12 respectively were divided between Hugh Kirkaldy and A Herd, Mr Ball, as an amateur receiving nothing but the honour of dividing second place.

1892, 1897
HAROLD HILTON

Harold Horsfall Hilton was born in West Kirby, England. His parents and employer were opposed to him playing in the 1892 Open, but he went against their wishes taking the night train to Scotland leaving him time for just one day's practice.

He won the Open twice, the British Amateur four times and in 1911 he became the first and only Briton to win the US Amateur and the first player to hold the US and British Amateur titles in one year. His handicap at one time was said to be "plus 10".

His style was far from elegant and was described by Bernard Darwin as "a little man jumping on his toes and throwing himself and his club after the ball with almost frantic abandon". Rather in the style of Young Tom Morris, his cap would often fall off on his follow-through. Hilton, who died in 1942, was the first editor of *Golf Monthly*.

1893

PRESTWICK

A long spell of fine weather ended on the first day of the Open. "Umbrellas and mackintoshes notwithstanding the pelting rain soon drenched competitors and spectators alike," reported the Glasgow Herald. *The course was in fine condition but the rain had made the greens heavy and slow. A total of 72 players took part, six more than last year. These included 26 amateurs. Only two players broke 80 in the first round, J H Taylor with a 75 and Willie Auchterlonie with a 78. In third place was the amateur, J E Laidlay, who scored 80. J H Taylor had a disastrous second round of 89 while Auchterlonie had a steady 81 for a total of 159 and a three-stroke lead. Sharing second place on 162 were the amateur Mr John Ball, the 1891 winner, Hugh Kirkaldy, Robert Simpson and James Kay.*

Harold Hilton's defence came to an end at the twelfth hole, where the green was guarded by a wall. He got into heavy sand close to the wall and took a 9.

1 SEPTEMBER

The competition for the golf championship at Prestwick has resulted in the victory of the young St Andrews professional, W Auchterlonie. The Amateur Championship this year caused some surprise, when the youthful amateur, Mr P C Anderson, defeated a strong field of cracks, and it is remarkable that at the Open Championship another young player, also hailing from St Andrews, should come so unexpectedly to the front.

The natives of the great golfing centre of Fifeshire, and it may also be said of the world, were in high glee yesterday of this double victory. It shows that the love of the popular Scotch game is as strong as ever in the Cathedral City and that there is a young generation of golfers springing up well able to take the place of those who have so worthily upheld the credit of St Andrews in the past. The professionals are also to be congratulated

upon having again wrested the championship from the amateurs, although the winner was closely pressed by an amateur, Mr Laidlay.

The play witnessed during the two days was of the most brilliant description. Auchterlonie's performance is all the more creditable that it was obtained over Prestwick links which are admirably suited for testing to the utmost the ability of the golfer.

Aucherlonie's play all through was steady. He is a strong young fellow of 21 years of age, and plays all departments of the game equally well. Driving a long ball he perhaps excels in his brassie play, and uses his iron and putter with great precision. A member of a golfing family, having five brothers, all good exponents of the game, the champion is in the employment of Messrs Forgan & Sons, the St Andrews clubmakers. He has a local reputation as a prize taker in the St Andrews Club, and took part in the Open Championship at St Andrews two years ago, but this is his first venture from home.

Although dull and unpromising, the weather remained fair during the day, giving a light which just suited the golfers. In the circumstance, with but a trifling breeze, the competitors were afforded every opportunity of recording low scores. The improvement in weather also induced a much larger number of spectators. As the day advanced the trains from Glasgow and Ayr brought contingents of enthusiastic golfers, eager to be spectators of the finish.

All interest in the concluding round centred in the play of Auchterlonie, Kay, Mr Laidlay, Hugh Kirkaldy, Herd, Bob Simpson, and Mr John Ball Jr, beyond whom it was not considered necessary to look for the champion.

Auchterlonie again made an inauspicious start, taking a 6 to the first hole. Settling down with a 3 for the second hole, his subsequent play was of the steadiest character possible. A grand 3 at the Elysian Fields and an equally admirable 4 at the End Hole enabled him to finish the outward journey in 39. His homeward play was of the same careful character, a 43 giving him 82 for the round. To touch his grand total of 322 was a formidable task for the other competitors.

James Kay soon experienced a misfortune which greatly imperilled his chances. At the Cardinal he found his way into the bunker, where he lost three strokes before he managed to get clear. A 7 at the End Hole also tended to put him out of the hunt. He ran up the rather high figure for the round of 85, which brought his grand total to 327. Mr Laidlay required a 79 to equal Auchterlonie, and there were many who were confident that he would be equal to the task. A 7 at the Cardinal rather interfered with the accomplishment of the work he set himself to, and a 6 at

the End Hole still further discounted his chances. His score out was 41, three strokes worse than he took in the forenoon. He nevertheless played a dashing game homeward, and with a little luck might have equalled Auchterlonie's score. With 40 for the return journey, he totalled 81 bringing his grand aggregate to 324.

Herd, after an extremely bad start, taking 15 to the first three holes, played a splendid game. With a 40 out, he was in the position of needing 41 to complete his inward journey before he could tie with Auchterlonie. He played so steadily homeward that he was still in the hunt if he accomplished the last two holes in 7 – a by no means impossible task. A good drive to the second last hole, however, left him a bad lie, and in attempting to carry the green he landed in the bunker. A couple of strokes lost in clearing the bunker disposed of any chance he possessed.

1893
WILLIE AUCHTERLONIE

Willie Auchterlonie was one of a large family of talented golfers. Despite his ability as a player his main interest was the club-making firm he ran with his older brother David. In his sixties he was involved in the layout of the Jubilee Course at St Andrews when it was upgraded to 18 holes and later became honorary professional at St Andrews and honorary curator of the museum.

He was the last home-based Scot to win the Open till Paul Lawrie prevailed against the odds in 1999. Auchterlonie died in 1964 and in 1988 his son's widow presented his Open gold medal to the R and A.

1894

ROYAL ST GEORGE'S

For the first time the venue for the Open was in England, at Royal St George's in Sandwich, considered by many to be one of the best courses in the world. The decision to include Sandwich and Hoylake on the elite list of Open courses reflected the rising number of young English players taking part and acquitting themselves well. This year was no exception with an English player leading after the first two rounds. The entry of 90 competitors was the highest ever.

The Open rota was established, in order, as Royal St George's (Sandwich), St Andrews, Muirfield, Hoylake and Prestwick. Strong winds made scoring difficult. First-round leader Sandy Herd had an 83 and only two others managed 84, Willie Fernie and the Englishman, J H Taylor. After two rounds Taylor, having improved on his first round by four shots, was in the lead with a halfway total of 164, with Andrew Kirkaldy, runner-up to his brother in 1891, and Douglas Rolland one stroke back.

12 JUNE

Sandwich, Tuesday – For the first time in the history of the Open Championship the victory has been gained by an English professional, J H Taylor. The chief honour of the golfing world has gone at two previous gatherings to England; but on both occasions it was secured by an amateur. It is only of late years that the English professional of native growth has come to the front. The reason of this is not far to seek. When golfing greens commenced to become popular in England, the professionals were engaged from the north of the Tweed, and it is only now that the young Englishmen who were trained by their Scotch brethren are showing the benefit of their golf education.

The English golfers were proud of the victory of their champion, and the large contingent of Scotch exponents of the game who have assembled at Sandwich congratulated the winner just as heartily as if they had been born south of the Tweed.

Taylor's victory was by no means unexpected. Last year at Prestwick he was a favourite after completing the first round in 75. He fell off and finished tenth. That was his first championship meeting, so that he has attained premier honours very early in his golfing career. Taylor is 23 years of age, and learned his golf under John Allan at Westward Ho! He has been greenkeeper at Winchester for 18 months. With a three-quarter swing he drives a long ball, and approaches in deadly fashion with his iron, of which he has perfect command. He also putts very accurately.

The conditions were more favourable to those experienced on the opening day and it was rather curious that the scoring deteriorated. Perhaps this was due to the excitement which prevails amongst the competitors on approaching the conclusion of the contest. Play was recommenced at a quarter to 10 o'clock. The field was reduced in numbers by fully 20 players, who found that their scores on the first day had destroyed any chance they had of occupying a respectable position on the list. Amongst these were the erratic English amateur, Mr Hilton, and Mr Horace Hutchinson. As it was, 35 couples started.

With an 84 Ben Sayers increased his aggregate to 334. Fernie, who started the last round nine strokes worse than Taylor, played his best round of the competition. He went out very steadily in 40, but he fairly excelled this play by returning with another 40 over the longer portion of the course. With 80, he brought his total to 334, to be tied so far for third place. Rolland soon displaced them. The Limpsfield professional was in capital form, and by very steady golf completed the round in 82, taking 40 to go out and 42 to return. With an aggregate of 331 he defeated Andrew Kirkaldy by a single stroke.

It was now apparent that Taylor would be returned an easy winner if he maintained anything like the form he had shown in the earlier rounds. He very early dispelled any fears of a breakdown, finishing the half round in a splendid 37. This left him with 48 for the homeward journey to tie with Rolland. He played the next three

holes with steadiness, but at the thirteenth he threatened to spoil his score by getting beyond the fence, requiring a 7. He soon recovered his form, and playing without a fault completed the round in the capital score of 81. His aggregate reached 326, which easily placed him in possession of the championship. Taylor was loudly cheered by the large crowd on the home green when he finished his round.

1894, 1895, 1900, 1909, 1913
J H TAYLOR

JH Taylor was a strokeplay specialist, whose philosophy was to play steadily and not to take risks. After his second Open win at St Andrews, which followed an opening 86, Taylor wrote: "All was not over; I still had three chances remaining by which I might recover myself, and my second round of 78, third of 80, and the fourth and final of 78 counterbalanced my ill luck experienced during the first round."

Of that 1895 experience, he added: "It is a real, a very real question of steadiness and a capacity for controlling your nerves that is rendered a necessity for the playing of the proper game."

He took the title three more times in the next 18 years and in 1926 at the age of 56 he finished eleventh, the year of Bobby Jones's first victory. He also won the German Open once and the French Open twice. Taylor was the first of the Great Triumvirate to win the Open.

Born in Devon, near Westward Ho! in 1871, his father died when he was little more than an infant and he left school at the age of 11 to find work. He caddied at North Devon Golf Club and at the age of 20, by which time he had become an accomplished player, he became a greenkeeper and professional golfer. He worked at Winchester and later at Royal Mid-Surrey where he spent nearly 50 years before retiring in 1946, aged 75.

He was involved in setting up in the early 1900s the London and Counties PGA which later amalgamated with similar organisations elsewhere in England, Scotland and Ireland to form the Professional Golfers' Association. He was made an honorary member of the R and A, and in his eighties was president of Royal North Devon Golf Club. He was the last survivor of the Great Triumvirate, dying late in his ninety-second year in 1963.

1895

ST ANDREWS

By introducing an entry fee in 1892 it had been possible to establish a prize fund of £100. The winner, if he was a professional, received £30 and a watch worth £10. If he was an amateur he received a silver plate and no cash. The remainder of the fund was divided among the next 10 players with £20 for second, £10 for third and so on. Surprisingly, being at St Andrews, the number of entries was down to 76, including 18 amateurs.

After a long spell of fine weather there were frequent heavy showers in the morning making conditions difficult but these cleared away and the second-round scores were better.

The best score in the morning was that of Harry Vardon, who had an 80, one ahead of Andrew Kirkaldy and two ahead of his brother Tom Vardon and Sandy Herd. Two players were on 84 and two on 86, including the holder, J H Taylor.

After the second round, Herd had moved into the lead with a 77 for a total of 159 and Taylor had improved his position with a 78 for 164 and a share of second place with Andrew Kirkaldy. Four players, including the Vardon brothers, were one shot more and the top amateur was Laurie Auchterlonie on 168.

13 JUNE

After three rounds of the Open Championship at St Andrews this year Sandy Herd had taken a three-stroke lead over the reigning champion, J H Taylor, with Andrew Kirkaldy the nearest of the remainder, a further three strokes adrift. The play in the concluding round simply resolved itself into a match between Herd and Taylor. The Huddersfield professional, first to start, accomplished the outward journey in a rainstorm in 42. On the way home against the wind and the rain, he played a steady game, but still he failed to get down his putts. He was a trifle unfortunate in having an 85 for his last round.

Considering the weather, Herd's play was up to championship form. His aggregate of 326 left Taylor to score 81 to win. To cover the round in 78 under such circumstances was a remarkable feat.

Until the twelfth hole, his score was one over 4s. He was a trifle loose in going for the Long Hole, and then at the fourteenth a heavy and sodden green caused him, for the second hole in succession, to record a 6. At the fifteenth Taylor's approach play was scarcely up to form, but he retrieved himself by splendid putting and got down in 4, amid loud applause. A repetition of this play occurred at the Corner of the Dyke, which was also taken in 4.

Taylor now found himself in the comfortable position of 13 strokes in hand, with two holes to go, and he had simply to play a safe game. This he did to perfection, and, driving well clear of the Dyke, he again approached wide of the bunkers, and by keeping an open road to the green holed out in 5. The Home Hole he played out perfectly in 4, and won the championship on 322 with four strokes in hand. Taylor was carried shoulder high from the home green to the road amid loud cheering.

1896

MUIRFIELD

Sandy Herd shot a record 72 in the opening round. The course had been lengthened and such a score had not been thought possible. He led by five. Second on 77 was holder J H Taylor, with Willie Fernie on 78, Willie Park, Jr on 79 and Harry Vardon on 83.

In the second round Mr F G Tait had a 75, the best amateur score of the championship thus far. Taylor put together a solid 78 for a total of 155 to take the lead by one from Herd who slumped to an 84. Two players were on 157 and Vardon, although he improved on his first round by five shots, was still six behind Taylor.

11 JUNE

For the third year in succession Scotch golfers have been compelled to bow the knee to their English rivals, J H Taylor and Harry Vardon tieing for the Open. Taylor's success today, having won for the last two years, emphasises that he is one of the strongest golfers who ever lifted a club. It is only within the last three or four years that Vardon came to the front.

As both Taylor and Vardon are engaged in the North Berwick tournament tomorrow, it has been arranged that the tie should be played off at Muirfield on Saturday. Play commences at 11 o'clock, the conditions being two rounds of the course.

Most delightful weather favoured the concluding day's proceedings. The special train from Edinburgh again brought down a large contingent of spectators, and during the day interested golfers from North Berwick and the surrounding district made their appearance in considerable numbers. Play was resumed at 10 o'clock. The field was but slightly reduced, a number of competitors whose scores on the opening day made their chances utterly hopeless, persisting by their presence in delaying the conclusion of the competition. As it was, 31 couples started.

After three rounds the position was: A Herd 235, J H Taylor 236, B Sayers 238, D Brown 238, W Fernie 239, H Vardon 239, W Park 242, T Vardon 242, Archie Simpson 242, Mr F G Tait 242.

The play in the concluding round resolved itself into a contest among half-a-dozen players. Taylor was first to start and completed the first half in 40. On the way home no fault could be found with his form, steady golf giving him another 40, bringing his total for the round to 80. Thus early in the day Taylor provided the rest of the field with a grand total of 316, news that was rapidly circulated over the links.

For a time it seemed that Fernie, the veteran Troon player, would accomplish his object. The first six holes he took in one under 4s, and led Taylor here by three on his aggregate. At the eighth, however, Fernie found a bunker with the result that he took a 7. He finished in 80 – three more than the leader.

With Willie Park taking 88, it was left to another Englishman to produce a score that brought about a tie. Vardon, who settled down to a machine-like game in the forenoon, was again in grand form. His play all through was without a single mistake. He finished with a beautifully compiled 77, thus taking three strokes off Taylor for the round, and tieing with an aggregate of 316. Herd and Mr F G Tait were the only other competitors left in the running.

At the fourth hole Herd's hopes began to evaporate. A bad lie from his drive resulted in a pulled second into the rushes and a 6 was entered on his card. By the ninth his score had mounted to 42. He finished with an 85, four too many.

Mr Tait required a 74 to tie and so well did he play that six holes from home he required an average of 4s to accomplish his purpose. At the fourteenth he saved a stroke, and seemed in a fair way of maintaining the average at the long sixteenth, on the green of which he lay in three. It was here he may be said to have lost the opportunity, by running weakly to the hole. Though failing with his putt he might still have tied with a 3 and a 4, but a couple of 5s threw him into third place along with Fernie.

PLAY OFF

Another name falls to be added to the list of champion golfers. It is that of Harry Vardon, the young Scarborough professional, whose title to the honour he established today in the most satisfactory fashion. More brilliant golf than that shown by Vardon could scarcely be expected in a final tie, and it brought to recollection the magnificent display made by Mr F G Tait in the Amateur Championship. Taylor also played a grand game, the splendid tussle between the two Englishmen forming a fitting conclusion to a competition characterised all through by strong golf.

It only requires a glance at Vardon's scores to discover how thoroughly he deserves the honour. After an 83 for the first round, he settled down. For the next three rounds he took 78, 78, and 77. He maintained his brilliant form in the final tie with a 78 and a 79.

In the long game Vardon had a distinct pull over his opponent, and he more than maintained his advantage on the green, giving his putts every chance. In every respect he is a stylish player. He drives a long ball with an easy swing, plays his irons with great accuracy, and putts with confidence and precision.

Vardon went to the front at the second hole, and thereafter showed the way to the finish. With seven holes to go in the afternoon, he led by three. At the twelfth, he found an awkward lie in rough ground and did not care to risk the bunker. His opponent, on the other hand, went for it very prettily. This smart work gave a 4, a stroke less than Vardon. Matters began to look brighter for Taylor when Vardon drove his tee shot to the thirteenth hole into a bunker. His lie was all right, however, and after getting clear he had a grand run to the hole which secured for him a half in 4. The Short Hole was halved in 3, and perfect golf was shown at the fifteenth, splendidly taken by each in 4.

Success now almost seemed certain for Vardon for the long sixteenth hole was halved in 6. Taylor was left with the difficult task of taking a couple of strokes from his rival in the next two holes. At the seventeenth, Vardon indulged in a sensational piece of play by holing out a 12-yard putt for a 3. The feat was greeted with loud applause, which was heartily renewed when Taylor made a splendid, although unsuccessful, effort to hole out in the like.

Having three strokes in hand with a hole to go, Vardon played the safe game to the home green. After a good drive he kept a good bit short of the bunker, and lay safe for a pitch. Aware that his only chance of success depended upon a bold game Taylor put every ounce into his brassie shot, but it had not sufficient weight, the ball alighting hard under the face of the bunker. With the championship in his keeping Vardon played an easy shot to the green. All Taylor could do was to pitch out to the side of the bunker. He had now to play the odd from the far edge of the green. [The "odd" is an old matchplay term meaning one shot more than the opponent at that hole – the "even", equalling the opponent's score.] His effort was of no avail, and Vardon, playing easily, holed out in 5 to Taylor's 6, winning the championship by four strokes.

Before playing his last putt, Taylor congratulated his successor in the championship, and this was the signal for hearty cheers from the large crowd who formed a huge ring round the home green.

1896, 1898, 1899, 1903, 1911, 1914

HARRY VARDON

Harry Vardon was born in 1870 in Jersey, an unlikely birthplace for a man who would turn out to be one of the greatest players the game has known and one of the most influential in the development of the grip and swing.

A small course was developed near where young Vardon lived and he and some of his school friends started working as caddies and playing at an early age. He left school at 12 and when his brother Tom took a job in England as an assistant professional Harry went to help him, later moving to Bury St Edmonds and then to Ganton in Yorkshire as professional.

Vardon is regarded as the leading light of the Great triumvirate and he went on to win a total of six Opens, a feat unlikely to be repeated. He developed tuberculosis soon after winning his fourth Open in 1903 and this was a contributory factor in the period when Taylor and Braid were dominant.

It is an interesting aside that during the 21-year period when the Triumvirate won 16 Opens, on the five occasions when another winner emerged, one of the three was second.

Vardon is credited with inventing the famous overlapping grip, still favoured by the majority of golfers, but the truth is the grip had been used for some time before he adopted it, its most notable advocate being the highly successful Scottish amateur, Johnny Laidlay.

Vardon did, however, have some outdated views. For example, his advice was never to play without a coat, even on warm days. The coat, he believed "held the shoulders together" and did so even better when a player wore braces rather than a belt.

At his peak, Vardon played with just nine clubs at a time when there was no restriction. He believed this made for easier club selection. That view has relevance today as there are many who consider the current limit of 14 is too many. Harry Vardon died in 1937.

1897

HOYLAKE

The Open was at the Royal Liverpool's Hoylake course for the first time. Conspicuous by his absence was Old Tom Morris, unable to take part because of the illness of a close relative. He had taken part in almost every Open since its inception.

In warm sunshine, the first-round leaders were Mr John Ball from the home club and Sandy Herd with scores of 78. On 79 was another amateur, Mr F G Tait and another professional, David Brown. There were three players on 80, including the 1892 amateur winner, Mr H H Hilton, also a Royal Liverpool player.

In the second round, James Braid shot a 74 to lead with a total of 154, only one shot ahead of Mr Hilton who had a 75. Mr Tait was third on 158.

20 MAY

Hoylake, Thursday – For the fourth year in succession golfers have been compelled to look to England for an Open champion, although the Scotch players made a gallant effort. To Mr Harold H Hilton, of the Royal Liverpool Club, belongs the honour of being Open champion for 1897. There is no doubt that it has passed into worthy hands.

For many years Mr Hilton has occupied a prominent position in the golfing world. Upon three occasions he has forced his way into the concluding stage of the Amateur Championship, only to suffer defeat in the final round. But Mr Hilton's greatest feat previously was the winning of the Open at Muirfield in 1892. Two years previous Mr Ball had for the first time made the presence of the amateur in the Open Championship by a victory at Prestwick, and now for the third time the professionals have been compelled to bow their knee to the amateur brethren. Mr Hilton now occupies the unique position of being the only amateur who has twice won the Open.

His victory today was obtained by splendid golf, his total being 314. The large crowd, numbering between 2000 and 3000, gave Mr Hilton a most cordial greeting when he concluded his fourth round.

With the conclusion of the third round the best of the players stood in this order: J Braid, 236; Mr F G Tait, A Herd and G Pulford, 238; Mr H H Hilton, 239; and H Vardon and J H Taylor, 244.

Mr Tait was first to finish. He was in capital fettle and but for a mistake on two or three of the greens he might have reduced his 79 by a few figures. With a total of 317 he held a strong position, and by many experienced golfers it was considered that this total would scarcely be beaten. Mr Ball showed that he was distinctly off form by returning with an 87. It now became known that Mr Hilton, if he maintained the form in which he had started the concluding round, would easily capture the championship. It was a phenomenal opening with 18 for five holes. From this point he scarcely played so well, but on the return journey his play was above reproach. Playing every department of the game in the most deadly style, he came home without the slightest mistake in an average of one above 4s and beat Mr Tait's total by three strokes, but still, Herd, Braid, and Pulford had to be reckoned with.

Herd played steady, reliable golf; but, as on the previous day, he failed to beat 80. Braid was left with a 78 to tie with Mr Hilton. Out in 40, he came home in grand style. At the Short Hole he pitched grandly from the tee within holing distance, but missed a short putt. At the sixteenth tee he had 14 strokes for the concluding three holes to tie. He drove a splendid ball, and his second was a beauty to within 30 yards of the bunker. A strong pitch, however, sent his ball over the green and into the dip, and as his putt fell far short, the expectations entertained as to his success began to evaporate. A 6 here left him only eight strokes for the next two holes. His chances further diminished at the seventeenth, where a short approach led to a 5. By most people Braid's prospects were now settled, but he played up very pluckily to the finish. At the last hole, after a tremendous drive, Braid electrified the immense crowd by a magnificent cleek shot which laid the ball eight or nine yards from the pin .

As he settled down to play his putt the excitement became intense, and considerable sympathy was expressed when the ball just missed the hole.

Harold Hilton, winning the Open for the second time as an amateur

1898

PRESTWICK

A new rule was introduced this year which stipulated that anyone scoring more than 20 shots worse than the leader after two rounds would be required to retire with the proviso that at least 32 professionals should qualify. The dreaded "cut" had been introduced and among its first victims was Willie Auchterlonie, winner the last time the Open was at Prestwick in 1893.

Play started at 10am and went on until after 7pm, some of the players going round the course twice in the afternoon in fine weather. Old Tom was again missing.

Last year's winner, Mr Harold Hilton, and Willie Park Jr shared the honours in the first round with scores of 76, one better than T G Renouf of Silloth and James Kinnell of Purley Down. J H Taylor was on 78 with Harry Vardon, one stroke further back.

A 75 in the second round for a halfway aggregate of 151 kept Willie Park in the lead but Vardon matched his 75 to stay in touch, only three shots away. Taylor and Renouf went into the final two rounds five off the lead on totals of 156. A second round of 81 dropped Mr Hilton to fifth place.

9 JUNE

For the fifth year in succession golfers have been compelled to look to England for the Open champion. This year Harry Vardon again has come to the front with as brilliant a display of golf as has ever been witnessed in the championship.

The scoring shows a remarkable improvement upon that recorded over the Ayrshire links upon the last occasion of the championship being held there in 1893 when Willie Auchterlonie took first place with a score of 322. Upon the present occasion Vardon covered the four rounds in 307 – and the winning score of 1893 did not even enter the prize-list.

Tempted out of doors by the summer-like weather, spectators in large numbers travelled to Prestwick by the early trains from Glasgow.

There were only 43 out of the 76 starters left in the final stage today. Of these, 38 were professionals and five amateurs. At the conclusion of the third round Willie Park led with 229, and then followed Harry Vardon, 231; Mr Tait and J H Taylor, 233; Mr Hilton, 234.

Vardon was first to finish. He played an excellent nine holes out in 38. The return journey he started very steadily with two 4s. At the final hole he drove grandly, but he was rather weak in his iron play, and left himself a putt of three yards for a 3. He was however equal to the call made upon him, and holed out in grand style amid the long applause of the large crowd. With a total of 76 for the concluding round he brought his aggregate to 307. To equal this magnificent score required a great effort on the part of the other aspirants. Both Willie Park and Mr Hilton played on their top form but just failed. Park ran neck and neck with the Englishman nearly all the way home. Considerable excitement prevailed when it was found that they were on level terms at the fifteenth hole. Their scores remained equal at the seventeenth, and now Park's only chance for a tie was a 3 at the home green. His drive could scarcely have been excelled as it laid the ball on the edge of the green. There was nothing to complain of either in his run-up, which left him with a comparatively easy putt for a tie. To the general disappointment of the spectators, the putt ran past the side of the hole.

[Park's account of this putt in Colville's *Musselburgh Golf Story* is a contender for the best excuse in Open history. He relates: "I heard the cheer on Vardon finishing, and, standing on the eighteenth teeing ground, I asked if anyone could tell me what Vardon had done the last hole in. I was told by several it was 4. I hit a beauty straight down the middle, and with my approach, I laid the ball four feet off the hole. Examining the putt, I noticed that halfway between my ball and the hole was a little bit of yarrow weed, like the top of a carrot. I said to Fiery, my caddie: 'I have two to tie the championship: I will make sure of the tie, and we will have a fine match for it the morn.' There was the outside chance that, if I did bolt the ball at the hole . . . it would leave me a longer putt. So I made dead certain of the 4 . . . only to receive the disappointing news that Vardon had done the hole in 3, and had beaten me by a single stroke."]

The championship was almost in the grasp of Vardon. Mr Hilton, who earlier in the tournament had taken an 8 at the short fifth, the Himalayas, made a great effort to reduce his leeway, but failed by a couple of strokes. His 75 was the best round of the day.

Vardon on the tee at Cruden Bay, with a curious onlooker

1899

ROYAL ST GEORGE'S

There was a record entry of 98, including 21 amateurs, but for the third year in a row, no Old Tom. Holder Harry Vardon, took the first-round lead with a 76, one ahead of J H Taylor and Willie Park Jr and two ahead of James Braid. Jack White was on 79 and Ben Sayers on 81.

In the second round, Vardon went to the turn in an amazing 33, then had a 2 at the tenth. After that, the wheels came off. At the fifteenth he found deep rough off the tee and his first attempt to extricate himself went clean under the ball. His next effort found a bunker and he wound up with a 7. He played the back nine in 43 for a 76 and a total of 152 but still led by one from Taylor who also scored 76. Park and Braid were three shots further back on 156.

8 JUNE

Sandwich, Tuesday – The great English golfer, Harry Vardon, has accom-plished a feat which has only previously fallen to Scotch players. For a triple winner of the Open Championship in previous years, at least since the institution of the cup, golfers could point only to Jamie Anderson and Bob Ferguson; but now Vardon has equalled these performances and for the sixth year in succession golfers have been compelled to look to England for the Open champion.

At the completion of the third round Harry Vardon led with 233, and then came J H Taylor, 236; J Kinnell, Jack White, T Williamson, 240; A Tingey, J Braid, and Willie Park, 241.

In the afternoon attention was confined almost entirely to Vardon. Out in 34, he had every chance of breaking the record of the course, which this week was reduced to 75, but two or three bad holes spoiled his effort. After steady play at the tenth and eleventh, he got into the small bunker in front of the twelfth – an error that cost him a couple of strokes. Two raking shots brought him to the thirteenth, where he holed out nicely in 5. He visited the bunker, however, at the fourteenth, where another 5 was recorded, and he putted weakly on the fifteenth green for 6. After splendid play at the sixteenth, weakness on the green cost him 5 at the next. A similar fault gave him a 5 at the home green. He finished in 77, and as it was known that the aggregate of 310 could not be beaten, he was loudly cheered as the winner.

Jack White equalled Vardon's performance of covering the first half in 34, and excelled in the home-coming, covering the round in the splendid score of 75. This excellent work enabled him to run into second place with an aggregate of 315. To Mr F G Tait belongs the credit of heading the amateurs.

1900

ST ANDREWS

Old Tom Morris was present – performing the task of starter. It now seemed unlikely he would be seen again as a competitor. In the last Open at St Andrews in 1895, he recorded the total of 392, an average of 98 per round.

Even starting at 9am, one hour earlier than normal, it was still after mid-day when the last pair set off. Two players who had already won the Open title five times between them shared the lead after the first round. J H Taylor and Harry Vardon both scored 79 with Jack White and Willie Park on 80 and James Braid and Mr R Maxwell one shot further adrift.

In the second round, Taylor took a four-stroke lead, shooting a 77 for a total of 156 to Vardon's 81. In third place was Jack White on 161 with the amateur, Mr Maxwell, fourth on one shot more.

7 JUNE

St Andrews, Thursday – For the third time the honour of winning the Open Championship has fallen to J H Taylor. Today the Richmond professional carried off the championship in the phenomenal score of 309, compared with the score of 322 which gained for him the championship at St Andrews in 1895. Mr Hilton at Muirfield in 1892 covered the four rounds in 305, and Harry Vardon at Prestwick recorded 307, but neither of these courses presents the difficulties encountered at St Andrews. To play four rounds of the classic links in an average of just over 77 was a wonderful feat, entitling Taylor to the heartiest congratulations.

Showers and a cold north-easterly wind made conditions less favourable than on the opening day, but there were many spectators. J H Taylor and Mr J E Laidlay, and Harry Vardon and A Herd were the couples who monopolised their interest.

Owing to the operation of the rule that all the competitors who were 20 strokes behind the leader on the first day's play should retire there were only 44 competitors entitled to appear on the second day, 12 of them amateurs.

At the completion of the third round, J H Taylor led with 234; and then came Harry Vardon, 240; Jack White and J Braid, 243; W Park Jr, 244.

All interest centred in the play of Taylor. With a lead of six strokes on Vardon, it required only careful play to win for him the championship. Not only did he justify expectations, but he even surprised his friends by breaking A Herd's course record of 77. Taylor completed a most phenomenal round in 75.

His work was almost machine-like. He totalled 38 for the half round and at the tenth hole he lay in the hollow from the tee, but ran up splendidly and holed out a five-yard putt for a 3. To the Short Hole he drove straight and sure. He was rather short in running up and then missed a putt, taking 4. Splendid putting gave him the twelfth hole in 4, and the thirteenth he captured in a fair 5. At the fourteenth he was well on the green in 3, and got down a remarkable putt of fully 10 yards for a 4. The fifteenth was nicely taken in the same figure. With a grand approach, Taylor got down in 4 at the sixteenth, and in par play he holed out the Road Hole in 5. On the green in 2 at the eighteenth he finished up with a perfect 4, amidst loud applause.

1901

MUIRFIELD

There was a record entry of 101 including 19 amateurs and, with the fine weather, but a brisk westerly breeze, the number of spectators was more than usual.

Harry Vardon took the first round lead with a 77, while J H Taylor shared second place two shots back with James Braid, Willie Park and J Kinnell. Jack White was sixth on 82. Braid drew level with Vardon on a two-round total of 155 after shooting a 76 to Vardon's 78, while the others dropped further back, Taylor having an 83 for 162. White and Kinnell finished the day on 164.

6 JUNE

Muirfield, Thursday – A scene of great enthusiasm was witnessed this evening, when a Scotchman for the first time in the last eight years, won the Open Championship. Although entered from Romford, Braid is a thorough Scotchman, born 31 years ago at Elie.

His victory is by no means a snatch one. Braid has always been recognised as one of the strongest, if not the longest, drivers on the golf links, and also as a very accurate approach player. Doubts have frequently been entertained regarding his putting abilities, but these now ought to be dispelled. One of the strongest features of his play was the chance he gave the ball on the putting green. He acted fully up to the axiom "Never up, never in", and almost invariably, so confident was he of his putting powers, he got down his return putt.

Splendid weather concluded the final rounds, genial sunshine flooding the course. Between 3000 and 4000 spectators witnessed the closing rounds.

The large crowd who followed James Braid in the forenoon was a sufficient indication that he was the favourite. The close of the forenoon's play witnessed Braid leading with 229, followed by Harry Vardon, 234; J H Taylor 236; and the others far behind.

Braid's outward score of 40 was just a trifle high, and his 4 to open the second half should have been one less, as he was short in the run-up, and then off the line with his two-yard putt. Short in the approach and pitch, he left himself too much to do for a 5 at the eleventh then he missed a yard putt on the twelfth green. A nice 4 at the thirteenth revived the hopes of the spectators. To the fourteenth the Scotsman was badly bunkered off the tee with a long carry. He played the stroke beautifully, and hearty applause was raised when the ball, from a long putt, lay on the edge for 3. To the fifteenth he played short of the bunker, his pitch was strong, and he took 5. At the Long Hole, after playing short of the bunker in 2, he got down in 5. The long game to the seventeenth was played to perfection, but fears were entertained as to the result when he missed a two-foot putt for a 4. In approaching the home hole he broke his cleek with a magnificent approach, which reached the green, and he got down in 4. The total for the round was 80, bringing his aggregate to 309.

Vardon, out in 39, required to accomplish 36 on the return journey to tie. Excitement amongst the spectators was intense. The hopes of the English followers were disappointed when he topped his approach to the sixteenth hole, and got into the bunker with his third. He got out well enough, but was short with his run-up, and took 6 to get down. It was now evident that there was little chance of the championship returning to England.

1901, 1905, 1906, 1908, 1910

JAMES BRAID

James Braid, the only Scot among the Great Triumvirate, was born at Earlsferry, Fife, in 1870. He was the first to win five Opens. All were played in Scotland, one at Prestwick, two at Muirfield and two at St Andrews.

There were plenty of courses around Elie where he grew up and learned the game and by the time he was 16 he was playing to scratch. At that age his game inexplicably stepped up a gear. He wrote: "Without any alteration of my stance or grip or swing or any conscious effort of any sort on my part I suddenly within a week was exalted from being a short driver into a really long one. How it came about was a mystery to everybody, including myself."

Braid, who "was blessed with a serene disposition", worked for a time as a joiner. Such was his involvement with golf that when an opportunity arose in his early twenties he accepted a position in London where he could put his joinery skills to good use as a club maker.

His talent as a player soon became apparent and a match was arranged with the reigning Open champion, J H Taylor, which young Braid, despite his inexperience, halved. Soon afterwards at the age of 26 he became professional at Romford Golf Club in Essex.

Only 14 months separated Taylor, Vardon and Braid. Braid was the oldest, but in terms of Open success he was slow off the mark, the other two having won three times each before he finally triumphed in 1901 at Muirfield. By 1910, however, he had passed the others with five wins.

In 1904 he went to Walton Heath Golf Club with which he was associated for the remaining 46 years of his life, the last 25 as an honorary member.

Along with Taylor he was involved in the establishment of a professional golfing organisation in the London area which would later become the PGA, of which he became president.

He was involved in his later years in golf course design, his most famous being the Kings Course at Gleneagles, still one of the finest inland courses in Europe.

Highly respected as a player, course designer and ambassador for the game, he died in 1950. For many years he annually returned a score lower than his age, but failed by one at his last attempt when he was 80.

1 9 0 2

HOYLAKE

Sandy Herd was asked on arrival whether he had heard of the new rubber-cored Haskell ball. He hadn't, but in practice he was surprised to find John Ball outdriving him easily. Ball gave him a Haskell, an act of generosity which had a strong bearing on the outcome of the Open. Herd immediately gained 20 to 30 yards off the tee and used the Haskell in the Open, allegedly the same one for all four rounds.

By the luck of the ballot it fell to the Earl of Winchelsea to drive off the first ball, a fitting situation given that this was coronation year. The earl was the only nobleman in the record entry of 112, including 18 amateurs. Although he was rated a good golfer he scored a "no return".

In good conditions, Harry Vardon opened with a magnificent 72 – five better than Andrew Kirkaldy and Alex Herd. James Braid was a shot further back on 78 with E Ray and Mr H H Hilton on 79. Ray had a 74 in the afternoon for a total of 153 to move into a share of second place with Herd, while Vardon returned a steady 77 to stay four ahead. Braid had a 36-hole total of 154, one better than Kirkaldy and Mr Hilton. A total of 45 players made the cut, including nine amateurs.

5 JUNE

For the second year in succession the Open Championship has fallen to a Scotchman. After many hard fights Alexander Herd, one of the best known of the professionals, has at last reached the top of the race. Although now connected with Huddersfield Club, Herd, 34, is a thorough Scotchman.

Herd, who just missed winning the championship at St Andrews in 1895, is one of the most popular of the professionals. He received the heartiest of congratulations upon his victory from all the golfers on the course. His driving, in particular, was long and straight, and he approached with great accuracy,

particularly in the forenoon. His performance in the afternoon deteriorated, but allowance must be made for the strain of playing with the knowledge that victory was nearly in his hands.

The concluding rounds were interfered with by frequent heavy showers. The wind was also more troublesome than on the opening day. The principal subject of conversation this morning was the decided improvement which had taken place in the scoring compared with the championship meeting held in 1897. Then Braid led on the first day with 154 and there were only 10 competitors who accomplished the two rounds in 162. Yesterday no fewer than 25 finished with 162 or under.

At the conclusion of the third round Herd led with 226, followed by H Vardon, 229; T Vardon, J Braid, and J H Taylor, 234; and Mr R Maxwell, 235.

In the final round, Herd totalled 40 for the half round. After a good 4 at the tenth he made a sad mess of the eleventh, a weak pitch and loose putting losing him a couple of strokes. He showed steadier form at the twelfth which he took in 4, but again displayed indifferent form from the tee to the Short Hole. He sent the ball only 50 yards, and took 4. A couple of nice 5s followed. Then at the sixteenth two powerful strokes carried him over the green, causing him to take 3 to return. He putted out nicely for 4 at the seventeenth, but he was again too strong in his approach at the eighteenth, getting up against the paling, and losing a stroke. His aggregate was 307.

Vardon needed to make two 4s to tie with Herd. He drove magnificently to the seventeenth, almost over-running the green with his second, but a 4 was obtained. At the last hole he gained a lot of ground with his tee shot. His second struck the near side of the bunker and made the green, lying on the far side just too far to give any expectation of a 3 and a victory. He over-ran the hole with his third, and then steadied himself for the putt of a yard-and-a-half. The excitement was intense, Vardon failed to get down, and the crowd, although they raised a cheer, appeared to be disappointed.

Braid made a good effort to secure the 73 necessary to enable him to tie with Herd. After taking 40 for the outward journey, Braid came home in the extraordinary score of 34, and succeeded in tieing with Vardon for second place. To everybody's delight Mr R Maxwell, the popular Scotch amateur, accomplished a similar wonderful feat, he was also out in 40, and came home in a perfect 34. He led the amateurs with a total of 309.

1902
SANDY HERD

Alex (Sandy) Herd was born within earshot of the Old Course at St Andrews in 1868 and soon became a very fine golfer. He was much overshadowed at the time by the Great Triumvirate and may have been even more successful if he had been a more patient player. It seems he was always in a hurry. He tied for second place in the Open of 1892 at his first attempt, he was runner-up again in 1895 and he was one of only five players to wrest the Open from the three "greats" between 1894 and 1914.

Using the new rubber-cored Haskell ball, said to be the only player in the field to do so, he won the Open at Royal Liverpool in 1902, beating both Vardon and Braid by one stroke. In his 50s he was runner-up to George Duncan in the 1920 Open at Deal and continued to play competitive golf into his seventies, winning The News of The World Matchplay title when he was 58 and making his final appearance in the Open in 1939 when he was 71.

Herd was a popular player and Bernard Darwin, describing his pre-shot routine, wrote: "The number of waggles he takes is only exceeded by his friends."

1903

PRESTWICK

Another increase in the entry took the Open to what was described as "the almost unwieldy number of 127, including 23 amateurs".

In fine weather with a light breeze, the immediate post-guttie era produced a flurry of records. Harry Vardon nailed his colours to the mast early, playing the first nine holes in 35 and coming back in 38 for a record 73. Sandy Herd, the holder, equalled the record going out in 36 and back in 37. In joint third place were Vardon's brother, Tom and Tom Williamson on 76, with five players, including James Braid and Jack White, chasing on 77.

In the second round, Herd took 10 shots more than he had done in the morning. Vardon had a 77 for an aggregate of 150 and a four-shot lead over A H Scott of Elie who had two rounds of 77. Jack White with a 78 and W Hunter of Richmond, who had a 74, were on 155.

10 JUNE

Prestwick, Thursday – The Open Championship has again passed into the hands of English golfers. Today at Prestwick, Harry Vardon, who is claimed by most to be the greatest golfer who ever lived, carried off the championship for the fourth time. Not merely did he gain first place, but by accomplishing the most marvellous performance that has ever been known in connection with the competition, he lowered the record to 300.

Vardon excelled in all departments of the game, and with a score of 72, established a record for the course, and breaking the figures he put to his credit yesterday by one stroke.

With the third round finished Vardon led with 222, Jack White following at 229, A Herd and T Vardon came next at 232 each, with James Braid, Willie Fernie, Tom Williamson close up at 235 each. The crowd in the afternoon was about 2000.

Vardon's play was not so brilliant in the afternoon, but with a comfortable lead he risked nothing. Out in 37, at the tenth he had a soft lie for his second, and could not reach the green. Failing to get within putting distance with his approach, he took a 5. After a fine 4 at the eleventh, he carried the dyke in grand style and was hole high, but to the right, and buried in the bents. After two attempts to get clear he sent the ball over the green, and took a 6. Then followed four successive 4s and with the view of risking nothing, he played his second to the Alps short and then pitched to the green, holing out in 5. A 4 at the Home Hole gave him a total of 78, and an aggregate of 300. It was not considered lightly that the score could be beaten as to do it Jack White would have to do a 70; and Vardon was heartily congratulated on his marvellous performance.

His brother Tom played remarkably fine golf in the afternoon, and managed to run himself into second place. He took 37 each way.

1 9 0 4

ROYAL ST GEORGE'S

The entry was 144, including 18 amateurs, and the management committee of the Royal St George's Club took the view that two days would not give enough time. They decided, therefore, to play the competition over three days, with one round on each of the first two days and two rounds being played on the third day after the field had been reduced by the cut.

In dull, cold weather with a strong breeze from the north, R Thomson of Romford scored a 75 to lead by one from Harry Vardon and Mr J Graham Jr, with Tom Vardon, James Braid and J H Taylor all on 77.

The following day, Vardon moved into the lead with a 73 and a halfway total of 149, two better than Thomson and three ahead of Mr Graham, both of whom had 76s. In a share of fourth place on 154 were Tom Vardon and J Sherlock, while Jack White who had scored an 80 in the first round produced a 75 to improve his position to sixth.

10 JUNE

Sandwich, Friday – The honour of winning the Open Championship of the world has fallen to a Scotch golfer in the person of Jack White, of Sunningdale. From 1894 until 1900, the premier honours had been monopolised by the Englishmen. Today Jack White has not only brought back the championship to Scotland, but he has created a record.

He has been a regular attendant at Open Championship meetings. At the last one held at Sandwich in 1899 he ran into second place with 315 and last year at Prestwick he occupied third position with 308. Today he lowered the record of championship scores by four strokes.

Excellent weather favoured the proceedings. The players had every opportunity of breaking records, and this they did. To J H Taylor fell the honour of holding the record with 68, just beating a 69 half an hour before by J Braid.

At the conclusion of the second round yesterday there were 52 competitors, compared with 59 at Prestwick last year. After three rounds, Braid led with 226, followed by Jack White, 227; Harry Vardon, 228; Tom Vardon, and J H Taylor, 229; Mr John Graham, 230; Andrew Kirkaldy and R Thomson, 231.

In the fourth round, White received a large amount of attention, and it soon became apparent that he was to make a bold bid for the championship. His play outward was absolutely perfect. He covered the first nine holes in 32. His best hole was the fifth, which he took in 2. His homeward journey showed eight 4s and a 5, the latter being at the long fourteenth. He ought to have registered a 3 at the short sixteenth, but he pulled his tee shot into the rough, and lost a stroke. At the home hole he lay a yard in the rough from the tee. Out of a heavy lie he pitched nicely to the green, and ran his third to within a few inches of the hole. His total of 69 brought him an aggregate of 296.

While White was heartily congratulated, a 70 would have enabled Braid to tie, and as he had accomplished 69 in the forenoon, it was possible that he might repeat this performance. He covered the first half in 34. Homeward he started in fine style, and when he had obtained a 3 at the fifteenth, with a magnificent drive, a beautiful second, and a putt of six yards, he was left with 3, 4, 4 to equal White's score. To the short sixteenth, however, he was short in running up, and left himself with a two-and-a-half-yard putt for a 3. He just missed, and threw away his chance. After a weak pitch it took him some trouble to get the seventeenth in 4, and all now depended upon his play to the home green. He, however, failed with his putt of five yards, and had to be content with a 4.

White's only opponent now with any chance was J H

Taylor, who required to do 67 to equal White's score. He started in phenomenal fashion by taking the first three holes in 3, 3, 2. He reached the rough at the fourth and required 5, but played the first half in a total of 32. He was now left with 35 for the inward journey in order to tie with White. Right heartily did he set himself to his work. After a couple of 4s he carried off the twelfth in a magnificent 3, and proceeded in capital style to the fifteenth, where he found himself in the same position that Braid occupied. However, he ran up 4 for the short sixteenth, and after a good 4 at the seventeenth was left with a 3 for the home hole. He, like, Braid, reached the green nicely in a couple of strokes, and found his ball lying about eight yards from the hole. It was a nasty downhill putt and so well was it struck that the ball passed the hole by a hair's breadth.

1904

JACK WHITE

Jack White was born at Pefferside, East Lothian, in 1873 and started carrying clubs at North Berwick at the age of 10. He soon took a fancy to the game, watching players like his uncle, Ben Sayers, who so very nearly won the Open in 1888. As well as working as a caddie he became interested in club making and trained as an apprentice to Uncle Ben. He caddied for, among others, Mr J E Laidlay, when he won the Amateur in 1889 and went on to spend 25 years at Sunningdale where he earned a good reputation as a club maker.

He finished second in the 1899 Open and third in 1903 behind Harry Vardon and his brother Tom, the third time brothers had finished in the first two places. Then in 1904 he earned the distinction of being the first player to win an Open with a 72-hole score under 300. His total of 296 also included a round below 70, something that had not been achieved in previous years and equalled by only two other players that year, J H Taylor and James Braid.

He continued as a club maker for many years, one of the few in what was becoming a dwindling craft.

1905

ST ANDREWS

With 134 professionals and 18 amateurs, the Royal and Ancient had little alternative but to follow the precedent set the previous year at Sandwich and stage the competition over three days. Nearly two-thirds of the entries were from English clubs. The rule governing the halfway cut had now been changed to exclude those 15 or more shots behind the leader.

St Andrews was regarded as the most difficult venue on the circuit and this was reflected in high scoring. On the first day no-one broke 80. There was a four-way tie on that score, which was shared by Harry Vardon, J H Taylor, Sandy Herd and Walter Toogood. Nine players, including the French professional, Arnaud Massy, and James Braid shared fifth place on 81.

The best score on the second day came from one of the nine on 81, Rowland Jones from Wimbledon who shot a 77 for a halfway total of 158, two ahead of Braid who had a 79. Massy and James Kinnell finished the first two rounds on 161 with Herd and Vardon on 162.

The railway line at that time was not out of bounds, a situation that led to the most bizarre moments of the clutch action.

9 JUNE

St Andrews, Friday – For the second time James Braid occupies the proud position of being Open champion. His victory today was very popular, the crowd of several thousand cheering him heartily as he holed out the last putt. On account of high wind, Braid's aggregate of 318 exceeds that recorded by J H Taylor at St Andrews in 1900 by nine strokes. On account of the want of moisture, the greens were very keen.

At the conclusion of the third round J Braid led with 237, followed by Massy, J H Taylor and J Kinnell, 243; R Jones, J Sherlock, and A Herd, 245.

In the fourth round, Rowland Jones commanded a good

deal of attention, and spectators were rewarded by an excellent display. He went round in 78, and now took first position with an aggregate of 323. A Massy, as in the forenoon, returned 82, and followed close upon Jones with 325.

Taylor had to be content with 80 in the afternoon. Kinnell kept well amongst the leaders by covering the round in 81, his aggregate reaching 324. Ernest Gray did even better with 78, but previous high totals brought his aggregate to 325.

Followed by several thousand spectators, Braid began his fourth round at half past two and covered his outward half in 38. The tenth was also collared in its proper value of 4, but Braid missed a 3 at the Eden. His iron shot to the green ran to the brink on the far side. In putting downhill the ball struck the hole and stopped two yards beyond, but Braid made certain of a 4. At the twelfth green he again overran the hole and lipped it for 4. The next two were very finely played in 4 and 5 respectively.

Then Braid had a misfortune which might have ruined the chances of a man with less nerve and skill. His drive to the fifteenth was caught in a bunker. With a powerful stroke he got out but the wind caught it, and Braid was compelled to cross the railway fence to play his next shot. At the first attempt he got it back to the course, and, running up well, he holed out in 6.

Driving to the Corner of the Dyke he met with a like fate, bunkered, and then over the railway fence. This time the ball lay among stones. The crowd patiently waited for the swing of the club. Braid's only line for safety was below the green, and gaping bunkers lay to the left. After the spectators had been driven back Braid made a try. The club head came down hard on the stones, but the ball still lay between two sleepers. At the next try he sent it about

30 yards past the green. With a beautiful pitch Braid got to about 18 inches from the hole and secured a 6. It was a great performance.

The crowd then scampered away to the Road Hole, and awaited the arrival of the golfer whom they had all but crowned the hero of the hour. Making no mistake, he holed out in 5, and was left with a 4 at the Home Hole to complete the round in 81. Playing perfectly, he accomplished the needful, and the cheers which greeted his final putt were loud enough to convince even Braid that they heralded not the finish of a round but proclaimed him the winner of the championship.

Willie Smith, Ted Ray, James Braid, J H Taylor and Harry Vardon
pictured at Aberlady in 1912 in Mr William Guy's hire car

1906

MUIRFIELD

With an entry of 183, including 25 amateurs, the competition was again played over three days. James Braid still did not tee off on the first day until 5pm, one hour later than scheduled. Amateurs dominated on that first day. Mr John Graham Jr led with a fine 71, two ahead of George Duncan, the Scots international, Percy Hills from North Manchester, and two other amateurs, Mr R W Whitecross and Mr R Maxwell.

J H Taylor had a 72 in the second round to take the lead on a 36-hole total of 149, one ahead of Harry Vardon, who had a 73, and Mr Graham. Mr Maxwell and Duncan finished the day on 151 with Rowland Jones, one shot back and the holder, James Braid, four off the lead on 153.

15 JUNE

For the third time James Braid has carried off the Open Championship. With a total of 300, Braid today, by the aid of the rubber-cored ball, has reduced his total of 1901 by nine strokes. At the conclusion of the third round, J H Taylor led with 224, then followed Rowland Jones, 225, Harry Vardon and Braid 227.

Jones opened well with a 3 in the final round, but made mistakes from the second tee. He ran up 83 for the round. Then a change came over Taylor's play. By that time the sun was shining brilliantly, the wind had risen, and the greens had become very keen. The ex-champion was followed by several thousand spectators and reached the turn in 41. Beginning with a 3 on the inward half, the ex-champion gave his admirers some hope that his troubles had passed, but the end was not yet. His next hole was a 6. Getting into the side bunker to the right of the green, he pitched too well out and then displayed poor putting. He had a 5 at the twelfth, and dropping another stroke at the next hole by taking a 5, it seemed that Taylor was quickly throwing to the winds the honour which was supposed to be in his grasp. Another 5 at the short fourteenth added to the tale of woe, Taylor's tee shot dropping in the hazard in front of the green.

At the next, however, he holed out in 3. His playing partner, the Royal Liverpool amateur John Graham Jr who had been out in 39, was lying a clublength from the flagstick but slipped his second past the hole by a yard. At his next attempt the ball curled round the disc and jumped out, throwing away what was veritably the chance of a lifetime, for at that stage his aggregate was equal to Taylor's. Poor play was followed to the seventeenth, but in coming to the home green the ex-champion had a great second shot to within a couple of yards of the pin, and then holed a 3 amid cheers.

Expectations then ran high that Vardon might add to his championship honours. He was left with 76 to beat Taylor, but had to be content with a 78.

Braid, when he started off about four o'clock, had with him a moderately large gallery which soon swelled into a crowd of almost unmanageable proportions. He went out in 38 and needed the same score in to beat Taylor. Those who know the Walton Heath professional had no doubt of his ability to hold out to the end. A 4 at the fifteenth and a 5 at the long sixteenth left Braid with two 5s to win. There was a feeling of excitement in the air when he drove off to the penultimate hole. Getting a fine long ball away, Braid followed this up with a magnificent cleek shot which landed him on the green. He was left with a nasty downhill putt of 15 yards, and when Braid put the ball down there was an outburst of applause. In the comfortable position of having a 7 to win, Braid, after a fine drive, carried the bunkers guarding the green with his second. Running well up with his third, Braid, with a 4, won the championship with three strokes to spare.

1907

HOYLAKE

Non-counting qualifying rounds were introduced this year. They were played on the Monday and the Tuesday of championship week and the best 30, plus ties, on each day were eligible to play on the two days of the championship proper. Thus the Open had returned to a two-day affair but with reduced numbers. In the event 67 players qualified. Surprisingly, Jack White, Willie Fernie and Willie Auchterlonie failed. Braid, Vardon and Taylor, by now known as the Great Triumvirate, were safely through, as was the Frenchman, Arnaud Massy, Sandy Herd and amateurs, Mr John Graham Jr and Mr John Ball.

On the opening day, there was a strong wind in the morning and heavy showers in the afternoon. Holder Braid was in poor form and scored 82, Vardon did even worse with an 84. First-round leaders were Massy and W Toogood on 76, one ahead of Tom Williamson and two ahead of Tom Ball from West Lancashire and George Pulford of Hoylake. Taylor and W McEwan of Formby were on 79.

After the second round Massy with an 81 for a total of 157 was one shot ahead of Taylor and Tom Ball and two better than Pulford and Williamson.

21 JUNE

Hoylake, Friday – Arnaud Massy's victory was very popular. Ever since he came to this country he has been a great favourite with golfers, not only on account of his genial temperament but also for his beautiful style of golf. Born at Biarritz, France, 32 years ago, Massy picked up his golf while acting as caddie there. Brought to Scotland by the Hambro family, Massy spent several seasons at North Berwick, where he developed his game. He first appeared in the Open Championship at Hoylake in 1902, when he tied for tenth place with 320. Then at Prestwick in 1903, he stood thirty-seventh with 328, and

at St Andrews in 1905 he tied for fifth place with 325. Last year at Muirfield he was sixth on the list with 310. Massy won today with an aggregate of 312, J H Taylor coming second with 314, a position he has now occupied for four years in succession.

The position of affairs after three rounds was: J H Taylor, 234; A Massy, 235; Harry Vardon, Tom Ball, and G Pulford, 239.

In the afternoon Braid made an excellent effort to make up his leeway, and went out in the splendid score of 36. In the homecoming, Braid continued to play fine golf with 4, 4, 4, 3. At the fourteenth, however, he slightly pulled his tee shot, and, landing in the ditch, took 6. He finished steadily in 5, 5, 5, 4 for 76 and an aggregate of 318.

Taylor was followed by a big crowd when he started on his final journey shortly after two o'clock. The first incident of note, at the Long Hole, was of a disastrous character. Taylor skied his second shot, and landed in a bunker on the right. He pitched so well out that the spectators burst into a loud cheer, but their enthusiasm was short lived, for the ball dropped among rushes close to the green, and Taylor failed to dislodge it with his first attempt. His next try sent the ball spinning over the green, but he ran up well, and was probably thankful to see the ball at the bottom of the hole in 7.

He was out in 41 and began the homeward journey by giving away strokes he could ill-afford to lose. Slack again with the run-up, he scored a 5 at the tenth, and failing to carry the Alps, he required 4 for the next. His prospects were enhanced by a grand 3 at the twelfth, which he obtained by holing a putt of 15 yards. He threw nothing away at the Short Hole, being down in 3, but from this point, he ran up four 5s in succession mainly through slackness in putting. Going to the seventeenth, he missed his drive, and although he tried hard to hole a long putt for a 4 it did not come off. Finishing with a 4, Taylor had the homeward score of 39. This made his total 80 for the round, and 314 as the aggregate, which most people thought was likely to be beaten by the Frenchman.

Tom Ball gave away his chance with 81, but Tom Vardon ran into the prize list with a splendid 75, which gave him an aggregate of 317.

Massy, naturally, drew a large following. Turning in 38, he secured a grand 4 at the tenth, which atoned for the same figure appearing on his card at the Alps. The twelfth witnessed another 4, the proper value of the hole, and the next was taken in par 3. The crowd were now convinced that unless a serious mishap occurred, the Frenchman could win comfortably. After he played the fourteenth in a grand 4, allowing a 5 for each of the remaining holes he would beat Taylor.

A period of suspense ensued when with his second shot to the fifteenth, Massy's ball landed in a narrow bunker.

He had barely room to swing back a niblick. It was an anxious moment. Although the ball hit the face of the hazard it got over to the level, and Massy doubtless felt heartily relieved. Pitching well up he still had something to do for a 6, but was equal to the occasion. The requisite 5 was obtained at the sixteenth. Then came a 4 and the crowd pranced off to the home green.

Massy was over the bunker in 2, and had 4 strokes still in hand to win. He required only 3, putting with perhaps too much caution, particularly in the run-up, which stopped about four yards short. But the 5 was secured, and when the ball dropped into the hole a great cheer announced the first French victory in the greatest golfing event of the year. Massy was immediately surrounded and borne shoulder high to the clubhouse.

The prizes were presented by Professor A M Patterson, captain of the club, in front of the clubhouse. Massy, in response to cries for a speech, said he was glad to come from France to play such good golf, and exclaimed *"Vive l'entente cordiale,"* amid loud cheers.

1907
ARNAUD MASSY

Arnaud Massy was the first foreigner to dare to lift the claret jug. He learned the game at his home course at Biarritz where he showed talent using left-handed clubs as these were the only ones available. As well as playing in competitions he often caddied for British players who spent holidays there in the winter.

Eventually he was invited to go to North Berwick where Ben Sayers took him under his wing and introduced him to right-handed clubs. He had already won in France in 1907 against many of the current stars and his easy-going temperament kept him in good stead under pressure.

1908

PRESTWICK

After the qualifying rounds, the initial entry of 190 was reduced to a more manageable 65, including only seven amateurs. Notable failures were Jack White, winner in 1904, Willie Fernie, the 1883 winner, Tom Vardon and Andrew Kirkaldy, both former runners-up. Mr R A Lawson, the Amateur champion, also failed.

"Sensational Play" ran the headline and then: "After the interesting qualifying rounds the championship proper opened today with performances that are without parallel in the history of golf." The weather was dull but fine and calm, ideal for low scoring, underlined by the fact that 36 of the 65 qualifiers broke 80.

James Braid broke the course record in the morning with a 70 and less than an hour later Ernest Gray (Littlehampton) returned a 68. F Robson (Bromsborough) had a 72. Ben Sayers went to the turn in 33 thanks to brilliant putting but he finished on 74.

In the afternoon, Braid added a 72 to lead on 142 while the best Gray could do was 79 to lie second on 147. Sandy Herd and David Kinnell were one shot further back with Tom Ball on 149. The leading amateur was Mr John Ball whose total was 152. More than 5000 spectators turned out to follow their favourites, 44 of whom made the cut for the final two rounds.

19 JUNE

Prestwick, Friday – For the fourth time, James Braid has won the Open Championship. No greater victory was ever achieved or more richly deserved. It afforded not only striking testimony to Braid's remarkable golfing powers, but illustrated once again how brilliantly he can rise above misfortune at a critical stage.

It was while nearing home in the last championship he won at St Andrews that Braid played a ball from the Principal's Nose to the railway line, and was confronted with a difficulty that would have driven most golfers to despair. Today he had an experience at the famous Cardinal bunker which brought out once again Braid's faculty of rising above the stern trials which a champion is destined frequently to meet. To have finished the round in 79 after taking 8 there was a great performance, and when Braid went on his concluding journey he had the strong lead of six strokes.

In the end he returned the lowest card of the day, 72, and thus, with an aggregate of 291, broke the record of 296 made by Jack White at Sandwich in 1904, while the figures are nine below the aggregate with which Harry Vardon won at Prestwick in 1903.

By winning his fourth championship, Braid has equalled the feats of Old Tom Morris, Young Tom Morris, Old Willie Park, and Harry Vardon. In his early days Braid was complimented by Jamie Anderson, a triple champion of bygone days, on the way he could swing a club while yet a schoolboy. The famous old golfer told Braid he would be a champion some day if he persevered.

With a lead of five strokes, Braid entered upon his third round shortly after eleven o'clock. It is doubtful if ever in a championship he has had so anxious a time as he gave himself at the Cardinal. The trouble was traceable to a sliced tee shot, the ball landing in the rough about a club length from the banks of the burn. It lay in heavy grass, but to a powerful man the task of playing it over the Cardinal from a lie such as Braid had with a cleek did not appear to be insurmountable but the result was disastrous. The ball struck the sleepers and dropped among sand not more than a club length from the face of the hazard. Braid's object then was apparently to get out by all means, and distance also if possible. He made allowance for the height of the barrier, which he had to clear by taking a line as far to the right as was permissible without running the risk of more trouble, but the ball again struck the sleepers and rebounded into the field out of bounds. Dropping a ball in the bunker Braid tried once more to clear the obstacle, but for the third time he struck the wooden barriers. Happily the ball came straight back and far enough to give hopes of recovery with his next stroke. Over in five, Braid pitched to the green in six, but was left with a putt of three yards to obtain a seven. He missed it – no wonder – and at one marking, his card was augmented by eight strokes.

The position of the leaders at the end of the third round was: Braid 219, Tom Ball 225, Ray 225, Massy 227, Herd 227, Kinnell 228.

Braid was followed by a crowd of over 2000 in the final round. He took the first two holes in par figures. Going to the third tee Braid made certain that he would give himself every chance to successfully complete the fateful Cardinal. He drove a splendid ball, which dropped on the rising ground about 20 yards short of the hazard. With a perfect brassie shot he reached the green, the crowd waiting at the dyke signalling his success of the

stroke by applauding loudly. Braid from the distance of 10 yards almost had a 3, the ball coming to rest within two inches of the hole.

Out in 36, Braid gained further confidence with a splendid 4 against the wind to the tenth, which was wholly due to a brassie shot. The ball travelled low until it was over the ridge about 100 yards from the green, then it rose like a soaring bird, dropped and rolled to within three yards of the hole. Down in 4 and with a 4 at the eleventh, he greatly strengthened his position. He got a hint that Tom Ball had finished with an aggregate of 299, and that a 5 for every hole would enable him to win. In point of fact he covered the remaining six holes in an average of 4s.

Coming to the home green his tee shot landed in the pot bunker, but he pitched well on, ran up within easy holing distance, and going down in 4 completed the round in 72, the best card of the day, and was winner with a margin of eight strokes. Loud cheers proclaimed the achievement, and Braid was positively besieged by friends offering congratulations.

1909

ROYAL CINQUE PORTS

For the first time, the Open was played over the Royal Cinque Ports Course at Deal. In drizzly rain and a strong easterly wind 69 players survived the qualifying rounds.

Since 1894, the trio of Vardon, Taylor and Braid had won the Open 11 times and so it was no surprise when one of them emerged as halfway leader. Since both Vardon and Braid had won it four times it was only fitting that Taylor should be the serious contender this time with a two-round aggregate of 147, one ahead of C Johns (Southdown) and two ahead of Tom Ball. Johns had led on 72 after the first round, one ahead of J Piper (Eastbourne) and two ahead of Taylor but the latter's second round 73 had been enough to put him in the lead.

11 JUNE

Deal, Friday – The first Open Championship held over Deal course concluded this afternoon in a brilliant victory for J H Taylor of Mid-Surrey, who had an aggregate of 295. It was Taylor's fourth win in the great contest, and it placed him on a level with James Braid and Harry Vardon among modern golfers, and with the Morrises (father and son) and Old Willie Park among the giants of the links. There is a coincidence in this victory of Taylor's, for he had won his first championship in 1894 at Sandwich, when that course was introduced into the rota. No golfer will grudge Taylor the honour he has won. For 15 years he has been in the forefront of golf, and by his fine sportsmanship he has done much, along with Vardon and Braid, to raise the tone of professionalism in the game.

During this week Taylor has played almost perfect golf. Although the finish was not so exciting as it had been on many previous occasions, his victory was noteworthy, for his closest rival was Tom Ball, one of the rising stars of the young school. Taylor led by two strokes at the close of yesterday's play and he increased this advantage to four on the third round. He concluded by adding another two to his lead, winning comfortably by six strokes.

Taylor began his final round about half past one. The sun was still shining brightly, and the wind blew easily from the north. There were about a thousand spectators at the first tee when Taylor drove off. Although he had a margin of four strokes on Ball, he knew that he must not throw any strokes away and he was out in 39. He secured 4s at the tenth and eleventh, but at the Short Hole he pulled into the rough off his tee stroke, and that accounted for a 4. He made amends by snicking a stroke off par at the next green, where his approach lay four yards to the right of the pin. He holed the putt amid applause.

Taylor got a similar distance from the hole with his tee shot to the fourteenth, and missed a 2 by inches. With his approach to the fifteenth he got into the rough a few inches to the left of the green. His 5 at the next was the only such figure homewards. For the long sixteenth he secured a grand 4. Off the tee Taylor sliced a little, and landed in the rough, and although nine men out of 10 would have taken a cleek for the next stroke, Taylor played a brassie. There was some head shaking when he pulled the wooden club out of his bag, but Taylor's bold game was rewarded. He made a magnificent stroke, and reaching the green in two holed a 4. The seventeenth was a featureless 4, except for an abrupt exclamation by an onlooker, who thought Taylor's ball was to drop into the hole in 3.

Taylor seemed very self-possessed as he marched to the last tee. With his accustomed accuracy, he hit a perfect stroke, and his second, an iron shot, landed on the left side of the green about 20 yards from the hole. A large crowd had assembled to witness Taylor's finish. He may have been trying for a long 3 to cap his excellent display in a sensational manner; at any rate the ball ran fast and over the hole by seven feet. But he made no mistake about the next one; the ball travelled straight to its destination, and the crowd cheered heartily. Taylor raised his cap in acknowledgement, and was then besieged by friends. The famous professional had endured too many disappointments not to know that their congratulations might be premature, and he did his best to discourage them. Tom Ball, his closest rival, was already on the eighteenth tee, and for all that Taylor knew the West Lancashire professional might have a chance. As it happened, Ball could not possibly win.

The Golfing Diploma of 1910 with the Great Triumvirate of Vardon, Braid and Taylor in the centre

1910

ST ANDREWS

On the occasion of the Jubilee Championship at St Andrews, the headlines after the first day were dismal. "Unprecedented Situation. Thunderstorm and a Deluge. First Day's Play Cancelled." The storm had broken over the town about 2pm. Greens were flooded and holes were filled with water.

With 210 entries it had been decided to revert to a three-day event with all the players taking part on each of the first two days. Many of the 142 had already started and some had completed their rounds with good scores but the championship committee ruled the first round to be null and void.

Fortunately on the Wednesday the weather was fine and George Duncan, foremost of the school of young professionals, broke the Old Course championship record of 75 by two strokes. D M Wall (Dirleton) and R Thomson (North Berwick) were on 74 with two more on 75 and three on 76, including J H Taylor and James Braid.

On the second day Willie Smith of Mexico (an emigrant Carnoustie Scot who had won the US Open in 1899) broke Duncan's record with a 71 to take the halfway lead on 148, one ahead of Braid who improved on his first round by three shots. Duncan had a 77 to lie third on 150.

24 JUNE

St Andrews, Friday – James Braid won the Open Championship this afternoon for the fifth time, and thereby accomplished a feat without parallel in the annals of golf. It was a splendid climax to an altogether splendid tournament, distinguished by the highest quality of play ever seen on the historic Old Course of St Andrews. The record for the green has been twice lowered within 24 hours. That in itself is no mean contribution to the history of golf; but it pales beside the record now established by Braid who received a special jubilee medal.

In a field comprising the largest number of players who have ever taken part in a championship there were three men who had each gained the blue riband of golf four times – Vardon, Braid, Taylor. They had equalled the achievement of Old Tom Morris, Young Tom Morris, and Old Willie Park, and they were striving in this year of jubilee commemoration to excel their past performances. Despite the most brilliant attack that has yet been made by the younger school of professional golfers, the ambition of the Great Triumvirate has been achieved through Braid. Tonight he was the proudest man in St Andrews, and, escorted to the railway station by pipers and a cheering crowd, he left the Mecca in triumph.

Braid won with an aggregate of 299. This also sets up a new record for a championship over St Andrews, being 10 strokes better than the winning score made by J H Taylor with the gutta percha ball exactly 10 years ago.

The almost ideal conditions prevailing throughout the third round pointed to a keen tussle for the premier place. Smith went out of the running quite early by taking 48 strokes for the outward half, Duncan equalled the Mexico player's record of 71, and Braid, though doing splendidly, found himself two strokes behind the young Aberdonian at the end of the third round. The leading aggregates then were: Duncan 221, Braid 223, Herd 227, Ray 228, E P Gaudin 228.

Everything seemed to point to a grand tussle between Duncan and Braid; but while the former was struggling for a first championship, the latter was playing with all the confidence of a man who had come through the ordeal four times successfully.

Duncan's last round was 12 strokes worse than his third, due to a slight deterioration in all parts of his game, and accentuated by a change to less favourable conditions, which troubled him more than Braid. In the end Herd, by a fine effort, ousted Duncan from second place with an aggregate of 303, and Braid's victory was assured before he drove from the eighteenth tee.

Braid turned in 38 and opened homewards with a couple of 3s. By this time it was known what Herd and Duncan had done, and all that was required for Braid to win was to steer clear of disasters. As he drove off from the sixteenth, the experience of his last St Andrews championship must have recurred to his mind. He did not, however, drive on to the railway this afternoon, though the hole cost him one over. The Road Hole was taken in the par figure and when the danger zone was passed Braid had as many as eight strokes for the last hole to win. When he played his second to the green a wild rush was made by the crowd. Braid's third was about a yard from the pin, and when he missed the putt and took a 5 the crowd in their astonishment forgot for a moment to cheer. Then they realised it did not matter and they cheered for all they were worth. They surrounded Braid and he was borne from the scene shoulder high.

James Braid, Harry Vardon and Ted Ray

1911

ROYAL ST GEORGE'S

With 226 entries this year the championship committee of Royal St George's took the unprecedented step of deciding to play the first two rounds over three days, after which the field would be reduced to 73 for the final day. Unwittingly, greens staff cut new holes for the third day's play. Almost 80 players had already completed their second rounds and the remainder would therefore be playing under different conditions. With the assistance of James Braid, captain of the PGA, the players made a formal protest.

The championship committee, embarrassed at such a fundamental faux pas, *none the less deemed the scores should stand, taking the view that as organisers of the championship they had full jurisdiction over all matters. Many thought the R and A might have taken a different view given that one of the cardinal rules of strokeplay had been broken. (In the resultant play-off, another strokeplay rule was breached when the contest was conceded before 36 holes had been played.)*

The first-round leader was Mr E Blackwell (R and A) on 71, one ahead of Michael Moran (Royal Dublin) and J H Taylor and two ahead of George Duncan and J G Sherlock (Stoke Poges). Four-time winner Harry Vardon was on 74 together with three others.

Duncan leapt into a four-shot lead with a second round 71, ahead of Edward Ray, Taylor and Vardon, all on 148. Mr H H Hilton, Michael Moran and Alex Herd were two shots further back.

29 JUNE

Sandwich, Thursday – The contest for the Open Championship has been prolonged till tomorrow, Harry Vardon and Arnaud Massy having tied this afternoon for first place with the aggregate of 303. Rarely has the final stage of the tournament been so intensely interesting. When George Duncan at the end of the second round led

the field by four stokes a well-known golfer remarked that the only man Duncan had to fear was himself. The prophecy was fulfilled before he reached the turn this forenoon. When the final round began, the leadership was in the hands of Vardon, with the other three of the famous quartet – Taylor, Braid, and Herd – among his nearest rivals.

The position after three rounds was: Vardon, 223; Herd and Taylor, 226; Braid, Massy, Ray and Duncan 227; Mr Hilton, 228.

Vardon had whatever advantage lay in an early start. He reached the turn in 38, and coming back, he ran up 6 at the tenth through pitching into a bunker. On five greens he missed putts of less than two yards. In other respects Vardon's play was perfect. Teeing for the eighteenth hole, he was left to do a possible 4 in order to complete the round in 79, but again he took three putts. A hearty cheer proclaimed the fact that Vardon with an aggregate of 303 was regarded as a probable winner.

A flutter of excitement passed round the home green when it was found that Mr Hilton had covered the first nine holes in 33. Five holes from home Mr Hilton's score was still one below 4s, but, after two 5s, his prospects were darkened by an unfortunate tee shot at the short sixteenth. The ball landed in a bunker from which Mr Hilton pitched over the green, failing to lay his next dead. The hole cost him 5, as did the fifteenth. The Amateur champion could still tie with Vardon by taking 4 to the last hole, but he was left with a long run-up over uneven ground. The ball stopped within four yards of the pin. Mr Hilton made a good try to hole it, but missed.

Attention was now turned to Herd. Steady golf gave him an outward card of 36, and although he exceeded the par figures at several holes on the return half he had a very good prospect of leading the field. A stroke dropped at the sixteenth, however, made his task harder, but he had a splendid 4 at the next green. The wind was blowing stiffly against at the home hole, and Herd, pressing for a long shot, landed the ball in the rough, from which he had to play a niblick. Home in 3 with a cleek, he ran up to within a clublength of the flag, and was left to hole the putt to tie with Vardon. The ball touched the hole, but curled out.

Massy turned in 37 but at the fourteenth, a drive into the rough cost him 6. The next two holes were taken in par value, and with eight strokes for the remaining two holes he would have beaten Vardon. Massy, however, failed to reach the seventeenth green in 2, and holing out in 5 the prospects pointed to a tie. Massy deliberated between playing a driver or a brassie for his second shot to the home hole, and ultimately taking the brassie made a beautiful stroke, which landed on the green. Running up from about 15 yards Massy missed the hole by a few inches, and tied amid hearty cheers.

The leaders had still to reckon with Braid, and when the news spread abroad that the champion was out in 36, although he had missed three short putts, the crowd following him was speedily augmented. The newcomers arrived in time to see Braid throw away his chances. A badly sliced approach at the fourteenth was the beginning of the end. A 6 there was followed by a pulled iron shot to the fifteenth, a weak run-up, and another 5. Taking 4 to the Short Hole, he gave away his last chance.

Finishing in 78, Braid was two strokes behind the leaders. Duncan was next with a chance but, out in 40, he had to do the almost impossible score under the conditions of 35. He never looked like it, and eventually finished in 79. Taylor, who was out in 37, required only a 39 in to upset the tie. Two holes settled the matter. Approaching the twelfth, Taylor played a faulty mashie shot into the bunker at the side of the green, and the hole cost him a 6. The Long Hole also cost him two more than the par value. His drive went into the long grass, and it was all that he could do to get back to the fairway. He could not get home with his third, and over-running the green with his next, the hole eventually was a 7. Taylor's chances were then gone.

PLAY OFF

In the first round of the play off a 6 at the fourteenth and a 7 at the seventeenth by Arnaud Massy led to Harry Vardon taking a five-stroke lead with 18 holes to play. Early in the second round Massy pulled a couple back until Vardon took a birdie 3 at the fourth and went further ahead.

The play-off ended prematurely on the seventeenth. When Vardon put his second shot safely on to the green Massy recognised his task was hopeless. As the play-off was strokeplay the full 36 holes should have been completed, but the Frenchman strode up to Vardon, hand outstretched, and congratulated him on his victory amid cheering from the crowd.

1912

MUIRFIELD

There was controversy over the re-introduction of non-counting qualifying rounds to eliminate players who were considered by some to have little or no chance of ever winning the title but who, by their presence, were prolonging proceedings. The total field was divided into three groups and each played a two-round competition the week before the Open. By this method it was possible to revert to a two-day championship.

In the first championship round the leaders were Edward Ray with a 71, one ahead of George Duncan, with Harry Vardon on 75 and James Braid on 77.

Duncan collapsed to a second-round 79 while Ray shot a solid 73 for a halfway total of 144. The holder, Vardon, closed the gap to three with a 72, while James Braid also made up ground with a 71 to be only one behind Vardon.

25 JUNE

Muirfield, Tuesday – The Open Championship meeting ended this afternoon in a brilliant victory for Edward Ray, one of the famous school of golfers who hail from the Channel Islands. Entering on the third round of play with a lead of three strokes, Ray held his advantage and won with the splendid aggregate of 295 – five strokes lower than the score by which Braid won at Muirfield in 1906. The players who were in the best position to challenge the leader finished precisely in the order in which they stood at the close of the second round, Vardon, after a great final effort, having 299, Braid coming next with a 303, and Duncan fourth with 305.

Muirfield, the scene of Mr Hilton's first triumph in the Open and of the first of that long line of victories gained by Vardon and Braid, now witnessed the crowning of another golfer who had justly earned the title of champion. Ray, at 34 years of age, is not one of the young

school, but it is only within the past five years that he has come into the front rank. In the six successive rounds his scores have been: 77, 76, 71, 73, 76, 75. These figures, showing an average of under 75 per round, are testimony to the sustained excellence of Ray's golf.

The dominating feature of Ray's golf is his tremendous power. He stands over six feet in height and is solidly built. Every ounce of his bodily weight is hurled behind the ball in the prodigious strokes he makes either with wooden clubs or irons. Ray would be the first to admit that he is not a graceful player. His swing lacks the beautiful rhythm of Vardon and Duncan; its power alone impresses. And yet it would not be easy to name a golfer with a more delicate touch than Ray. Over the past five years Ray has occupied fifth place in the championship on three occasions.

The concluding proceedings of the Muirfield meeting attracted over 5000 people, the largest crowd that ever assembled on the green of the Honourable Company. Delightful weather prevailed.

When Ray started on his final round at half past one o'clock there were over 5000 spectators on the links, the majority of whom elected to follow the leader. A critic remarked that the big Jersey man seemed "as nervous as a kitten when he teed up for his first stroke", but he quickly proved that he had full command of all his faculties.

Ray is an inveterate smoker, and the pipe, which he lit after luncheon, was never out of his mouth (except to be refilled) until he holed out on the home green. The opening was perfectly steady and he reached the turn in 38. It was reckoned that another 38 would bring him victory and he started back with six straight 4s. There was some doubt as to whether Ray would play the bold or the safe game at the long sixteenth, where he encountered a head wind. He drove well up the fairway, and after consultation with his caddie he drew a heavy iron from his bag. Looking again at the menacing cross hazard, he selected a lighter club to make sure that he would keep short of the bunker; but he hit hard, and the ball rolled into the sand. It lay well for an easy pitch, and Ray had a safe 5 after playing his niblick stroke. The seventeenth was taken in a perfect 4.

Some minutes elapsed before Ray could drive to the home hole, the vast crowd forming a line from the tee to the putting green. Ray struck one of his best, and the ball lay nicely for an iron approach. Still there was danger ahead, and a timid player might have quailed at such a moment when the great prize was within his grasp; but Ray

seemed perfectly at ease and sent the ball soaring high to the green. It dropped about 10 yards to the right of the flag. Ray mopped perspiration from his forehead but did not linger. He gave the ball a chance to go down in 3, and then with a putt of 12 inches sent it into the hole. The crowd broke into loud cheers, for although the winners of 14 championships were still trying to make up the leeway it was well known that none of them or any other rival could beat Ray's magnificent aggregate of 295 which he had just completed by holing the final round in 75.

The new champion, though not yet officially proclaimed, was immediately surrounded by his friends, some of whom, greatly daring, hoisted the burly Jersey man shoulder high and almost collapsed under the weight before others came to the rescue.

1912

TED RAY

Born in the Channel Islands in 1877 Ted Ray's name was as closely associated with the links at Ganton near Scarborough where he was employed for many years as it was with the pipe which was rarely out of his mouth during play. He also had an appointment at Oxhey, a course near London.

Like many of his contemporaries it was his misfortune to be at the height of his career at the same time as the big three of Taylor, Vardon and Braid, who overshadowed almost everyone for more than 20 years. He had several top 10 finishes in the Open in the early 1900s, including third to James Braid at Prestwick in 1908 before finally taking the title. He became the second of only three British players to win both the US Open and the Open, the others being Harry Vardon and Tony Jacklin.

He was said to be a resourceful player when confronted with difficulties. On one occasion owing to a curious mistake his name was engraved on the Leeds Cup a day before it was played for; but Ray was equal to the emergency.

He continued to play in the Open into his mid-fifties and was runner up at Prestwick in 1925 at the age of 48. He was captain of the first British Ryder Cup team in 1927.

1913

HOYLAKE

Two non-counting qualifying rounds were again played the week before the Open. Play on the first day of the championship was delayed for an hour while greens staff removed flood water from the eleventh green, caused by three hours of rain. Conditions thereafter were tolerable and despite a strong wind, the scoring was generally good.

The first round was closely fought with three formidable players tied for the lead on 73, the holder, Ted Ray, J H Taylor and Sandy Herd. After the second round Herd had dropped out of contention and the leader on 147 was Ray with Taylor a close second on 148. Michael Moran (Royal Dublin) was two shots further back.

24 JUNE

Hoylake, Tuesday – By the ample margin of eight strokes, J H Taylor won the Open Championship this afternoon, with an aggregate score of 304. Starting a stroke behind the leader, Edward Ray, he beat last year's champion by four strokes in the third round with a score of 77 against Ray's 81. Having got in front, Taylor played steadily on the final journey, and when he completed it in only two strokes more than in the morning, his victory was assured, for Ray, playing about nine holes behind him, had done nothing to gain the leading place, and eventually finished in 84. Not since Braid won at Prestwick in 1908 has the winner's aggregate been as many as eight strokes better than the next best.

A storm of wind and rain swept over the course for two hours after play began, and although the rain eased after that, the wind continued to blow hard from the west. Taylor experienced both, but Ray played his last two rounds in fair weather.

That the champion should have completed his aggregate with scores of 77 and 79 under conditions so testing is high testimony to the quality of his golf. Taylor was never in serious trouble. His play through the green was very steady, and but for a considerable slice of ill luck in putting he would probably have returned an aggregate of 300. Though it exceeded that by four strokes, Taylor's 304 is three better than Herd's winning total over the same course in 1902.

Apart from Ray, the new champion had nothing to fear from any of the other competitors. Vardon, still putting feebly, threw away his chance of making up the leeway, and tied for third place at 313 with Michael Moran, who took 10 to the first hole in the morning, but finished with a brilliant round of 74, while the next place was shared at 315 by McDermott, the American champion, and T G Renouf, Manchester.

The most surprising feature of Taylor's success is that it was maintained after he had almost failed to qualify for the last two rounds. He made the final list of 65 players by the "skin of his teeth" with a qualifying score of 156, which was the limit on Friday. All's well that ends well, however, and Taylor confessed this afternoon that his victory realised the summit of his ambition, for it placed him equal with Braid and Vardon as the winner of five championships.

Starting his final round in the presence of over 1000 spectators with a useful lead of three strokes over Ray, Taylor had a mediocre start and his outward half was 41. On the tenth green he was unlucky when his ball jumped out of the hole after being in for 4, but he had the Alps in a fine 3 through laying the ball dead with his aluminium putter from the grassy ledge to the right of the green. When he just missed a 3 at the twelfth the crowd expressed their sympathy with exclamations of "Oh!" but after a 3 at the Rushes, Taylor had some reward for his run of ill-luck. Off a long iron stroke his ball popped into a pot bunker to the left of the fourteenth green, but it jumped out and lay in good ground. Taking a mashie he dropped the ball on the edge of the green about 35 yards from the hole. Then it ran along and trickled into the hole for another 3 amid great cheering. The shot gladdened Taylor's heart but the end was not yet, as at the next green Taylor's approach putt was so weak that he failed to get down in 5. He pitched rather briskly to the sixteenth green and the putt for 4 with which he was left was a six-yarder. Like many more, it came near enough to provoke disappointment. After a steady 4, Taylor turned to the last hole. His drive was off the line, and the ball landed in a hollow among thick grass. Probably Taylor knew then that he had something to spare, for he played short rather than risk getting into the cross bunkers from his heavy lie. He pitched too far in three, but chipped back close enough to secure a 5. The more exuberant spectators broke into cheers for Taylor, who was then surrounded and congratulated, but he reminded his friends that their expressions were premature.

Braid, who had waited patiently for the arrival of the champion, squeezed through the crowd to reach Taylor, but with the handshake Taylor remarked: "Wait a bit, Jamie, wait a bit". It was soon known, however, that nobody could come near Taylor's winning aggregate of 304, to which his last round had added 79.

1914

PRESTWICK

There was a link with the first Open Championship held here at Prestwick 54 years ago. Of the original eight competitors there was only one survivor – club professional Charlie Hunter.

Many players criticised the long time lag between qualifying rounds the previous week and the actual championship. Huge crowds came to Prestwick for the final practice day in temperatures reaching 90°F, causing concern about difficulties with crowd control.

The Great Triumvirate inevitably headed the list of contenders with Harry Vardon slightly more favoured than the others. Exactly 100 players qualified to do battle over 72 holes and the first tee-off time was brought forward to 8am.

Vardon returned a first-round 73 to take the lead by one from J H Taylor, James Braid and E Whitcombe. In the second round, Vardon's 77 for a total of 150 was just enough to keep him one stroke ahead of a little-known professional from West Drayton, James Ockenden, who, when asked about his previous Open experiences, said prophetically that the best he had achieved was "four steady 80s". He closed with "steady" rounds of 83 and 80 to finish seventh. Taylor was third at the halfway stage on 152.

19 JUNE

Prestwick, Friday – After one of the greatest contests in the history of the game Harry Vardon this afternoon won the Open Championship for the sixth time. By the luck of the ballot it fell to Vardon and Taylor to play together in the last two rounds. A disastrous 7 at the fourth hole in the afternoon completely turned the fortunes of the players, and from that point Taylor went on to lose and Vardon, in his forty-fourth year, went on to win his sixth championship.

The final round was played in the presence of the largest crowd ever assembled on a golf course, more than 10,000,

and intense excitement prevailed. All of them wanted to see Vardon and Taylor play the last decisive round, but it was with the utmost difficulty that one could see what was happening. The presence of so large a concourse of people and the keenness of the fight undoubtedly affected the men who were the central figures in it. If the golf did not reach a superfine standard in the closing stages of a great struggle it was at least of a very thrilling character.

The final round started with Taylor on 226, two shots better than Vardon and six better than Mr Jenkins. Abe Mitchell, R G Wilson and Tom Williamson were on 233.

The spectators formed almost a solid wall from the left of the teeing ground to the hill in front of the first green when Taylor drove off on what proved to be for him a disastrous last round. Excitement was intense, and the players seemed to be as jumpy as the crowd. Vardon went one shot further behind at the first with a 6 to a 5. Unsteady putting at the short hole resulted in a couple of 4s.

Something happened then to upset Taylor, and it had far-reaching effects. While he was on the point of driving to the Cardinal a photographer within a few yards clicked his camera. Taylor slightly pulled the ball, got over the bunker with his brassie, but was not quite home. Vardon, on with two beautiful strokes, got back the point he had lost by holing a 4. The Burn Hole wrecked Taylor's prospects completely. Owing to the enormous crowd it was impossible to see precisely what happened, but afterwards he was practically a beaten man. He sliced from the tee into the bunker by the burn side, pitched up to the bank, and then fluffed the ball into water. Dropping another, which ran in also, he was allowed to drop again (without penalty), pitched it over the green, and finally holed a 7. Vardon, with a steady 4, thus found himself suddenly hoisted into the position of leading by a stroke..

Taylor was clearly shaken and poor putting cost him another stroke at the Himalayas where Vardon had had a lucky rub by striking a spectator with his tee stroke. At the end of the outward half Taylor was lagging three strokes behind, having taken the abnormally high score of 44, compared with 39 by Vardon.

Play at the next two holes extinguished the last flickering hope, for Vardon had both in 4, and Taylor taking 3 putts at the tenth and missing a two-yarder at the eleventh after pitching well out of a bunker was now 5 strokes to the bad. Taylor pulled back one shot at the thirteenth but lost it again at the fifteenth when he overran the green

and took 5. Taylor was again five strokes to the bad, with only three holes to play, but he picked up a useful 3 at the sixteenth as the result of a beautiful chip shot, and as Vardon had a bad lapse in putting and took 5 the difference between them was reduced to three. Vardon made no further mistakes by holing 4s at each of the remaining greens. Taylor had 4s also.

When Vardon holed his last putt for a total of 78 there was a round of applause, but no jubilant shouts of acclamation, for there were still competitors in the field, but struggling in vain as events ultimately proved. Taylor cordially congratulated Vardon, for they are very good friends, and Vardon left the green showing not the slightest trace of excitement or of exultation.

Bobby Tyre Jones

CHAPTER FOUR

UNCLE SAM'S SHOWTIME

AMERICAN SEA INVASION

As a result of the First World War, six years had elapsed since Harry Vardon won the last Open. The era of the Great Triumvirate was over and a new one was about to begin that would shake British golf to the core. Enter showman Walter Hagen, one of the most outrageous characters in the history of golf. Enter Bobby Jones, the greatest amateur golfer of all time. The first American invasion was under way and the Open Championship – open to the world – would never be the same again.

From 1920, when Hagen became the first native-born American to win the Open, the claret jug would sail west across the Atlantic in 11 out of 12 years. America, which could sustain full-time tournament players and near enough year-round golf, was showing the way. British professionals, downtrodden by upper-class tradition, hidebound by club jobs that restricted play, as well as a comparatively poor climate, could barely compete.

There was a hitherto unseen affluence and bombastic confidence. The fashion-conscious Hagen, refused admission to the Deal clubhouse on his first visit in 1920, parked a Daimler outside and had a picnic. Two years later when he won at Sandwich, he is said to have given his prize-money to his caddie before travelling by Rolls Royce to Southampton where he caught a liner for his first-class journey home.

After Hagen, came the quieter and more modest Bobby Jones who in 1930 won the Open, US Open, Amateur and US Amateur titles, the so-called Impregnable Quadrilateral. There were others – Jim Barnes, Gene Sarazen and Densmore Shute. The question of whether the Open, which they referred to as the "British" Open, was worth winning at all in comparison to the US Open was raised, before Britain's own golfing aristocrat, Henry Cotton, made a stand, notably in 1937 when the field contained the American Ryder Cup team.

That contingent, however, was the exception. Into the 1930s the number of Americans fell away, the Great Depression meaning ever fewer could afford the long journey. More British names began to be engraved on the claret jug.

Jones is considered the last master of hickory and from that point the fundamentals of the golf swing changed. Equipment was to make another big advance with the introduction of the steel shaft which The United States Golf Association legalised in 1924, with the R and A following suit five years later.

This shaft reduced the amount of torque or twist of the shaft in the swing. With hickory compensation had to be made for torque with a late wrist adjustment before impact. With steel this was not so necessary with the result that the ball could be hit harder with greater confidence, and the Americans were ahead of the game in that department.

The Open was changing too. Whereas host clubs had been responsible for running the Open, the R and A took full control from 1920. The Open became too big for Prestwick which staged its twenty-fourth and last Open in 1925 while Royal Lytham and Carnoustie made their debuts.

1920

ROYAL CINQUE PORTS

In the first post-World War Two Open and only the second to be staged at Deal, the brilliant golf of Abe Mitchell and the lapses of George Duncan, the favourite, and the American, Walter Hagen, twice winner of the US Open, were the outstanding features of the first day's play. Duncan had good scores to the turn each time and then, as had happened so often in the past, it all went wrong and he ended the day 13 shots behind the leader, Mitchell, who shot 74, 73 for a total of 147. Sandy Herd, who led the first round with a 72, fell away with an 81 but held on to equal second place with the American Jim Barnes on 153. The leading amateur was Lord Charles Hope on 159.

1 JULY

Deal, Thursday – Never has the Open Championship provided such a turn of fortune as we witnessed here today. George Duncan has confounded critics. He is laughing last, and therefore laughing much the best. No-one can rob him of the halo which he deserves for these wonderful rounds today.

To be sure he was helped to his wonderful victory by the almost undreamt-of collapse of Mitchell. Duncan was 13 strokes behind him overnight. He might have levelled up the matter in 36 holes. It was a thousand chances to one against his doing it in one round, but the almost miraculous happened. Even a 71 and a 72 would have availed him nothing had Mitchell played two steady rounds. One fancies Duncan did not go out to win this morning but, like a good Scot, to get into the prize-list. He was a careful golfer, with the burden of the strain of things thrown off his shoulders, and because of that everything came off, but he did the same again this afternoon when once again things mattered. The fourth round was the real test, and, having passed it with flying colours, let us greet this new-born Duncan with a cheer. He has been for years our uncrowned champion. He has mastered himself at last. He always had the golf.

Mitchell's breakdown is past understanding. He, not Duncan, was supposed to be the man of iron nerve. His nerve today was as flabby as a schoolgirl's and his tragic start the most dramatic thing the game has seen for many a day. He began 13 strokes ahead of Duncan. He finished four strokes worse. The triumvirate were completely beaten, but the "Old Guard" was to the fore still with Sandy Herd, the oldest of them all, finishing second. It is 20 years since he won. He will probably never have another chance like this.

In a strong south-west wind, Duncan had five 3s in the first half, and his longest putts were three and five yards. He played the first nine holes in 33 including a wonderful 3 at the third (476 yards). Now he started out on his second half and for a few brief minutes it looked as if his ill-luck dogged him still. He pulled his drive and had a very difficult approach to stay on the green. He overran it and lay below the green, but he chipped up firmly and lay beside the hole. With one to play, he had 4 for a 69. Then for one brief hole his luck was out. He was driving when a man strayed over the line of play. A steward shouted in the middle of the swing. Duncan pulled his drive, had a bad second, put his third over the green and took 6.

Few had any doubt as to Mitchell's ability to stand the test. Yet he broke down utterly. He dropped shots at all of the first four holes but the fifth was the crowning hole in his downfall. Mitchell topped his drive into a bunker. He was lying well, and meant to get a long shot out, but he failed to clear, and played out with his third. Then he pulled into the rough, put his fifth across the green, and the end of a very sad tale was a horrible 8. He never played so badly again, but he had thrown his chance away. He got a 2 at the short eighth, but, starting with a hooked tee shot to the ninth he took a 6 and was 44 to the turn and came home in 40. His 84 gave him the same aggregate as Duncan.

Duncan clinched matters in the afternoon by putting up a round of 72. He was out in 34 and with a 4 at the last would have repeated his morning round of 71 but his drive was lying badly, and he was lucky to jump the ditch with his second. The bad shot visibly upset him. He completely duffed his pitch and it looked as if his 5 had gone, but he layed his next one dead and holed his putt. Home in 38, his aggregate of 303, though within the reach of some, was never touched.

The veteran Herd went to the turn in 37 and played home against the wind like a hero. With three holes to play, he could have tied with 5, 4, 4. It was the Sandwich Open of 1911 over again when Herd, playing the last hole, had a 4 to win and a 5 to tie with Vardon. That day he took a 6 and went out. Today he had his chance again, but disaster tragically overwhelmed. He sliced his drive, got out on to the fairway, but lying badly, took a wooden club to carry the green. He did not get the ball away. It found another bunker, and the hole was a tragic 7. It said much for Herd's real golfing temperament that he finished with two 4s. His round was 75 and he came in second. A very worthy performance for the oldest man in the field.

Mitchell also failed, but he was a different Mitchell from the player of the morning. A 76 then would have changed the face of matters. Now it came too late to do him any good. This has been Duncan's greatest year with wins in The Glasgow Herald tournament at Gleneagles and the Daily Mail tournament at Westward Ho!

1920
GEORGE DUNCAN

George Duncan was a man in a hurry and was nicknamed "Miss 'em quick Duncan". He was rated the fastest player of his era and his autobiography is entitled *Golf at the Gallop*.

He was born at Methlick, near Aberdeen, in 1883 and by the age of 17, having rejected an opportunity to play football for Aberdeen, he became professional at Stonehaven. He soon emerged as a fine naturally talented if temperamental golfer. By the time he was 30 he had twice beaten James Braid in the British Matchplay Championship, the second time in the 1913 final. He played in his first Open in 1906 and finished in the top 10 seven times in nine attempts before the First World War interrupted the championship and his career.

He was easily recognisable not just because of his speed of play but also by his dapper appearance, often taking to the links wearing a bow-tie.

Among his triumphs were the Irish, French and Belgian Opens and he played in the first three Ryder Cup matches, including, as captain, in the victorious side of 1929. Like a surprising number of his golfing contemporaries he lived to a very good age and died in 1964.

1921

ST ANDREWS

One of the warmest days of the year with a welcome fresh breeze greeted the start of the twelfth Open to be staged at St Andrews. Overseas players made their mark with three Americans and a Frenchman in the first seven after two rounds.

Jock Hutchison, an ex-St Andrean now hailing from Atlanta, USA, led after the first round with 72, closely followed on 74 by the holder, George Duncan, the Frenchman, Arnaud Massy, and the Cornish-born American, Jim Barnes. Hutchison had been struggling on three over 4s after seven when he had a hole-in-one at the short eighth and promptly followed it with an eagle at the ninth where he drove to within a yard of the hole.

After two rounds, Hutchison led on 147, one ahead of Ted Ray who had a 72 and Barnes. Sandy Herd, Massy, Duncan and another American, George McLean, shared fourth place on 149. Bobby Jones, playing with Hutchison, was leading amateur with rounds of 78 and 74, having come back in his second round in 35. This match at one stage was followed by almost 3000 spectators.

25 JUNE

St Andrews, Friday – Only an amateur, but a brilliant one at that, stands between us and an American win. One by one today our great bulwarks, as we thought, against the invaders from overseas failed us, and Mr Roger Wethered in a last-ditch encounter with Jock Hutchison will fight the matter out tomorrow. That this brilliant young Oxonian should be our last remaining hope out of a field embracing all our best professionals reads like a fairytale, a phantom of a dream, but that is the sober fact which emerges from the most remarkable day of golf that any of us can remember.

Mitchell, the hot favourite, was hopelessly out of it overnight. I saw him this morning before he went to play, a rather pathetic figure looking out wistfully at the crowd down at the first green. It was the crowd which went to follow the fortunes of Hutchison the overnight leader, and these same fortunes form a dramatic story to which only Duncan's at Deal, a year ago, can yield a parallel.

This morning Hutchison's sunny smile had gone, and, as he threw his overnight lead to the winds with both his hands, missing putt after putt on four successive greens, you felt that whatever the American attack might be he would have no further part in pushing it home. He had 79 this morning.

Mr Wethered is 23 and captained Oxford in 1920. He was third in The Glasgow Herald amateur tournament at Gleneagles a year ago. He is of course the brother of Miss Joyce Wethered.

Today there was again a great burst of heat, and hardly a breath of wind. The crowd was probably 8000. The leaders at the end of the third round were: Barnes and Herd, 222; Kirkwood and Massy, 223; Williamson, 224; Wethered and Hagen, 225; Hutchison and Kerrigan, 226; Duncan and Havers, 227. Mr Wethered, in his third round of 72, called a penalty on himself after he accidentally stood on his ball.

The sensation of the afternoon was the great round of Mr Wethered in 71. He had four 5s in the first six holes. The seventh was the regulation 4, then came a string of five successive 3s. He turned in 38, drove the tenth and twelfth greens (both over 300 yards), and went on like a hero to the home hole, for even the Road Hole he had in 4. He had a 4 for a 70, and, as it turned out, that would have given him a win outright, but he misjudged his second, and it dropped on the face of the bank and rolled back. In the end he had still a three-yard putt for his 4, but he ran the ball past the hole a couple of inches, and missed the greatest thing of his life.

Duncan's great feat at Deal last year came very near to repetition by Hutchison. He was back again this afternoon to the brilliant Jock of yesterday. Even was he better, for he equalled the record of the course with a wonderful round in 70.

There were might-have-beens in Mr Wethered's round, but Hutchison had his too, for he had putting lapses at the fourth and then again at the ninth. At the first of these he missed a putt of not more than a foot, and then having driven the ninth (303 yards), and laid his ball nicely to the right of the pin, he took three more to get down. Against these he holed a seven-foot putt on the seventh green for a 3, then at the eleventh, where in the morning he had a 5, he laid his tee shot nicely on the green and holed a five-yard putt for a 2. At the sixteenth he got down one of six yards for a 3.

PLAY OFF

The Championship Cup is leaving these shores for the first time since Arnaud Massy won in 1907. It was almost a foregone conclusion after the position we were in last night. But we hoped against hope that Mr Roger Wethered might strike again his yesterday's form.

Hutchison played with his ribbed mashie to great effect all day. I was told he sharpened it up this morning before he started. He certainly made it a "stop-em" club, for long full approaches dropped on the greens, bounded, then pulled up almost in a yard if, indeed, they did not bite into the turf and jump some inches back. That apart, he had streaks of putting madness. He had five 3s in the morning and three in the afternoon. Over the whole day Mr Wethered had only two. Hutchison had the longest hole on the course, the fifth, in 3 this afternoon, and that was by the first of three long putts which broke the heart of the young amateur.

What Mr Wethered did yesterday and again today in a last desperate effort to beat off the American attack has covered himself with imperishable glory, and the special cheer he got for himself when it was all over this afternoon was a very hearty one. The cup will leave this country on Saturday next, when Hutchison and most of the Americans sail in the *Mauretania* from Southampton.

1921

JOCK HUTCHISON

Born at St Andrews in 1884 Jock Hutchison played at the St Andrews Golf Club before emigrating as a young man to America where he continued to develop his golfing talents. It is ironic that when he came "home" (he always regarded St Andrews as his home) and won the 1921 Open he did so as an American citizen and took the trophy to the States with him, the first American to do so.

Before that he had achieved a number of high finishes in US majors, including being twice runner-up in the US Open, runner up in the inaugural US PGA Championship in 1916 and winner of that event in 1920. Another player who continued to compete for many years, he made a token appearance at the Centenary Open at St Andrews at the age of 76, intending to play only nine holes but completing the course in 82 shots. He lived into his nineties and died in 1977.

1 9 2 2

ROYAL ST GEORGE'S

After the qualifying rounds, 80 players emerged to do battle over Royal St George's. James Braid did not survive the weeding out process. George Duncan, Ted Ray and Jim Barnes scraped through.

Strong winds prevailed on the first day resulting in high scores. First-round leaders were J H Taylor and Ted Ray on 73 with Gustavus "Gus" Faulkner, of Pennard (father of 1951 champion-to-be Max), on 74 and a group on 75 including the Cornish American, Barnes.

In the second round, the US Open Champion of 1914 and 1919, Walter Hagen, came in with a 73 to take the lead on 149, two ahead of George Duncan, Taylor and Barnes. Four others, including Percy Allis and the holder, Jock Hutchison, were on 153. Mr Roger Wethered (R and A) was the leading amateur on 154.

23 JUNE

Sandwich, Friday – In a fairly wide experience of championship golf I have never witnessed anything so dramatic as the failure of George Duncan on the last green here tonight. "Old Glory" was flying at topmast; Walter Hagen led the field. Bunched up at the top beside him were two other Americans, Barnes and Hutchison, not pure-breds like Hagen but still Americans. All our big men had failed us. Taylor, the veteran, had done his noble best, but Taylor is 51, and the battle in these days is to younger men. But Ray and Mitchell, of the men we thought our bulwarks, had let us down, and up beside Taylor at the top were unknown golfers.

But there was still Duncan left. He required a 68 to tie. He was the one man in the world who could do it. This morning he had played very careless, off-hand stuff and for a last hope of Britain he cut a rather pitiful figure. This afternoon he was last man out. By that sort of wireless telegraphy which operates during a big golf tournament we heard he had gone to the turn in 34.

Even that was received without a thrill; no man, not even Duncan, could play those big holes back in 34. It had never been done this week; it could hardly be done when so much depended on it. We underestimated Duncan. The next we heard was that he was coming to the home green and required a 4 to tie. He was lying in the middle of the fairway off his drive, behind him and grouped round the green the biggest crowd of the week, numbering perhaps 2000. His second, played with a brassie, finished just off the green to the left. Here was a chance of achieving, even for Duncan, immortal fame. He walked down the fairway leisurely, and at the green surveyed the putt. The ball lay in rough grass about 20 yards to the left. Duncan took a straight-faced iron, and with hardly any more than normal care he played a run-up shot. In such a crisis it is hard to criticise, but Duncan had hardly hit the ball when it was seen to be hopelessly short. It was smothered by the grass, and went little more than halfway on its journey. The crowd groaned. Duncan threw his club down in disgust, and took his putter. He had still a six-yard putt with which to tie. Surely ever since the game was played it was "never up, never in". Duncan again addressed the ball, and hit it with that sweeping, persuasive stroke which is his putting manner. Again we saw he was short. "On, on" shouted several excited people as it drew up 12 inches short. Duncan for once wore his emotions on his sleeve. He looked utterly dejected as he holed the last tiny putt. The crowd was stunned; there were faint efforts at a cheer, but we could not cheer. Duncan walked off the green, people shook hands with him and clapped him on the back, telling him what a splendid fight he had fought, but it was useless to try to cover up the tragedy.

Hagen was regarded from the first by many as the most dangerous of the Americans. "As a patriotic Briton," said Mr Bernard Darwin early in the week, "I don't like the look of him." Hagen is 30, and won the American Open Championship in 1914, and again three years ago. He is one of the longest drivers here, as he is the best of putters, and he is a very desperate fighter. He had booked his passage, as had the other Americans, in a liner which leaves Southampton for New York tomorrow, and he came as near as may be to having to give up his cabin.

On a wild day, with a stiff wind blowing until the evening and sheets of rain falling at intervals, Hutchison set the pace in the final round with a 76, which gave him an aggregate of 302. He was playing extraordinarily good golf, and but for one supreme disaster at the fourth, where he took 7, he would tonight have been still Open champion.

Then Hagen brought in a card of 72, which gave him an aggregate of 300. His long game was the most impressive thing you could picture, straight as an arrow and as far as any man here could hit. If there was a weakness it was a tendency to leave himself a good deal to do on the greens, but he hardly ever failed to get down. He turned in 35. At the twelfth he holed a three-yard putt for a 3. This was where he got ahead of Jock. Then with the rain coming down in sheets Hagen carried on almost on the same

high plane. He dropped a stroke at the thirteenth, where his second found a bunker, but he had a wonderful 4 at the long Suez Canal. Here his second hit the bank in front of the canal. Then taking his brassie Hagen played a "whale". It was a low-flying shot which drew up five feet past the pin, and Hagen holed the putt. When he got to the final hole he needed a 4 for a 71 to take a three-stroke lead. With two shots played he was lying to the left, a grand 20 yards from the pin. He surveyed the putt carefully, then ran up four yards short and failed to hole out in 4, but a 5 was good enough, and Hagen was warmly cheered by the big crowd.

Barnes, like Hutchison, had his own particular "if", for if he had not taken a disastrous 6 to the short third, the Sahara, he would have been champion tonight. From this tee he played his spoon shot too low. It caught the face of the bunker and dropped into the great sandpit, and he spent two shots in getting out. When he came to the seventeenth tee, James Braid told him that he had to do two 4s to tie. He got the first and from the last tee Barnes hit a good drive. He took a spoon for his second and pushed it out to the rough just at the side of the green. Here you have the worst of possible pitches, and Barnes' ball ran merrily across the green among the feet of the crowd. He had a 15-yard putt over difficult country, but finished three yards short. He holed the putt for a round of 71, an aggregate of 301, and equal second place.

1922, 1924, 1928, 1929

WALTER HAGEN

"Who's gonna be second?" was one of Walter Hagen's most famous and prophetic sayings. He won two US Opens, four Opens and five US PGA Championships, four in a row from 1924 to 1927. The Masters, first played in 1934, came along too late for him.

Hagen was born in Rochester, New York, in 1892, into a family of German descent. He had five sisters but no brothers. His father was a railway worker and as a boy Hagen earned his pocket money as a caddie at Rochester Country Club. In his teens he worked with the professional there and eventually fell heir to his job at the age of 19. Two years later he finished fourth in the US Open.

He had a reputation for high living which may have been exaggerated with his blessing and he was happy to promote that image. "I don't want to be a millionaire, I just want to live like one".

Refused admission to the clubhouse at Deal during the 1920 Open because he was a mere professional, he parked a Daimler outside and had a champagne lunch. As Henry Cotton would do later he did a great deal to promote the cause of the professional golfer.

He practised a great deal but in contrast to his high-living image, he played down his dedication to the game. He was a showman with a sunny outlook on life and the dictum: "Don't forget to smell the flowers along the way." But he was much more than that. He dominated the game in Britain and America during the 1920s and made a huge contribution to the lifestyle of the professional as we know it today. He died in 1969.

Walter Hagen (left) pictured with George Duncan

1923

TROON

British stock went up with a jump after the qualifying rounds for the first Open to be held at Troon. Four out of 10 American entrants had failed to make the grade including US Open champion Gene Sarazen, while Jim Barnes and last year's winner, Walter Hagen, had only just survived. On the downside Harry Vardon, now in his fifty-third year, and Mr Roger Wethered failed. A total of 88 had qualified to contest the championship proper, most British stalwarts coming through "with some conviction".

The first day was fine, if a little breezy, with a west wind "raising white horses in the Firth". The crowd was estimated at 10,000 with more expected on the second day. Charles Whitcombe had a first-round 70 to lead by three from Arthur Havers, while Robert Scott of Glasgow scored 74 and holder Walter Hagen a 76.

At the halfway stage, 25-year-old Havers and 27-year-old Whitcombe were leading on 146 with Hagen one shot back. Gordon Lockhart (Gleneagles) was on 149 and Robert Scott on 150. A total of 54 players made the cut for the final two rounds.

15 JUNE

Troon, Friday – The Open Championship was brought to a finish tonight, and from every point of view the most satisfactory finish we could have had. We have met the American menace and beaten it, and we have opened the select circle of Open champions to a new generation of British golfers. Tonight we hail with pride a very worthy champion in Arthur Havers.

Havers was 25 on Sunday. Nine years ago on this same old Troon course he qualified at the age of 16. Three years ago – Duncan's year – he tied for seventh place, and the next year he was fourth. He is a big, handsome, strapping fellow, and a rare good golfer, who was marked out two years ago for the very highest honours. Starting this morning as joint leader with C A Whitcombe, he was the one of these two men who showed a stout heart at the pinch. When he displaced MacDonald Smith this afternoon he set the pace with an aggregate of 295, which was only once in danger. Hagen made a gallant fight, and went down with his colours proudly flying, but the 74 he needed to tie was just a stroke beyond him.

A south-westerly wind in the morning threatened rain, but it never came. Later it veered round to the north-west and blew hard for a brief spell.

The afternoon was one big thrill after another, as man after man fought to secure a position at the top. Smith went out in 35 and started home with a couple of 4s. This promised the setting of a very hot pace, but it did not quite materialise, though it was sufficiently hot to beat everybody excepting two. He came home in 40 for a round of 75 and his aggregate was 297.

Joe Kirkwood had a great chance to win, but he threw it away with both hands by a disastrous start and finish. He was only two under 5s for the first five holes. Then he struck a purple patch and played the next seven holes in four under 4s. But his troubles now began and he ended with a card of 78 for 298 and fourth place.

Then Havers came in, and there was a fine inspiring scene at the end, for he beat the leading score, displacing the American-Scot and setting up an aggregate which Hagen and all the rest of the field could not touch. His opening was like a winner – six holes in level 4s – then he dropped a stroke at the next four. Next is the hardest part of the course – "Tattenham Corner" the English players call it – and with the wind now blowing its hardest it was easy to get into trouble. But he picked up a stroke with a 3 at the eleventh, and after a bunker visit at the short fourteenth he came to the last, requiring only a 6 to lead.

He pulled his drive a little and, playing his iron, he found the bunker to the left. Out anywhere he was safe. He made no mistake and got the hole in 5. He received a fine hearty cheer with 76 for the round and an aggregate of 295. Havers was received as a likely winner. He was besieged by autograph hunters, and the cameramen got busy.

It was now a quarter to six. Hagen needed to come home in 36 to tie but three 5s between the tenth and sixteenth meant he now required two 3s. He got one of them at the seventeenth, though he had to pitch dead from the right to get it. Then came the big thrill of the afternoon. Round the big home green the crowd stood in thousands. Hagen's drive was well up the middle. He played a full iron against the wind. It carried slightly to the right and dropped right in the middle of the bunker. The crowd rushed for places round the green, but were held up by stalwart stewards and policemen, and the last scene went forward within a human frame of perhaps 10,000. Hagen walked up to the green. A wonderful man this, you felt, fighting to the last ditch when just three days ago he seemed completely down and out. Photographers crouched down beside the bunker to snap the vital shot. Hagen studied his problem well and played, but finished four yards short.

Robert Scott Jr, Glasgow, led the amateurs with 307 with Cyril Tolley next at 312.

1923
ARTHUR HAVERS

Although one of the lesser known Open winners, Arthur Havers was a talented golfer as early as 16 when he qualified for the Open. At the age of 25, just five days after his birthday, he became the only Briton to win the Open between 1921 and 1933, a period when Americans dominated, taking the trophy 12 times until Henry Cotton broke the mould in 1934.

Few Britons travelled far between the wars but Havers bucked that trend visiting America, Europe and Argentina. In America he beat Bobby Jones over 36 holes and Gene Sarazen over 72.

He played in the first Ryder Cup Match in 1927 when the Americans had a comfortable victory. In 1932 at Sandwich he was again in contention at the Open, going into the final round in second place behind Gene Sarazen after shooting a course record 68 in the third round. Alas, he started badly in the final round and closed with a 76 which dropped him into third place.

Havers employed an open stance tending to produce faded shots, but he was a long hitter and noted for his accuracy with wooden clubs.

1924

HOYLAKE

At the age of 53, J H Taylor led the qualifiers by four shots with rounds of 72 and 70. At the other end of the age scale, the 22-year-old American, Gene Sarazen, qualified at his second attempt having failed last year at Troon. A total of 83 players qualified.

Sarazen began disastrously with an 83. Although he improved with a 75 in the afternoon, he was 11 shots behind the leader, Ernest Whitcombe. The older brother of the better known Charles, he had equalled the course record of 70 in his second round to take a two-stroke lead on 147 over J H Taylor. One stroke further back on 150 was Walter Hagen.

27 JUNE

Hoylake, Friday – Walter Hagen won his second Open Championship here tonight with an aggregate for four rounds of 301. It was an exciting finish, though not quite so thrilling as when he last won at Sandwich and so narrowly failed last year.

Hagen had played such accurate golf at the last few holes that he could hardly fail to win. He had struggled hard all the way round in the late afternoon, for he was the last of the men to start who were really in it. He had taken 41 to the turn, and knew then that he must go home in 36 to beat the aggregate of E R Whitcombe. He had the last five long testing holes to play, and to only one could he take a 5, and just in that way he did it, though when his pitch scampered over the eighteenth green and only a 4 would do we had visions of a tie. But he pitched up, and without a tremor nobly holed the putt.

It was an amazing performance for a man who looked on Monday night, just as at Troon last year, to be in direct jeopardy of even qualifying. We must now surely hail him as the greatest fighter and the greatest golfer in the world, for his record in these last three championships is

to win outright twice and to be beaten by a stroke in the intervening year. Nothing is more certain than this 32-year-old will be a thorn in the side of British golf for many a day. So for the third time in four years the cup makes the transatlantic trip.

George Duncan, our greatest British hope, failed, as he has done before. Having got out in 37 he must have had great hopes, but he played an appalling inward half of 44. Then Whitcombe, after an outward 43, made a great recovery, and with an inward 35 he took the lead by a couple of strokes with an aggregate of 302. He got a tremendous cheer when he finished, and was surrounded by congratulating friends, who hailed him as the champion. "No, not yet," protested Whitcombe. He was right.

This was setting Hagen a stiffer proposition. With only 303 to do to win, a 79 would do, and we knew Hagen could do that, but a 77 was a horse of an entirely different colour. We knew by then that he had taken 41 for the first nine holes and was told he required a 36 to win. Hagen continued his back-to-the-wall fighting golf. He got out of bunkers and holed good putts, and when I caught him up he was bunkered from the tee at the short thirteenth, but he got his 3. So now he had to go home in one over 4s to win, and there is not a harder finish to any course in the world. He just got through the rushes at the fourteenth hole, ran up dead, and got his 4. Two magnificent shots with his driver and he was on to the fifteenth (440 yards) in the teeth of a hard north-west wind. Again his 4 was safe. He took his 5 at the sixteenth. It is 480 yards and it takes two of any man's best to get home. Now he had two 4s to win, and the seventeenth, though shorter, might easily be a 5. He drove right up the middle, as he had done at the last three holes, and his iron shot was on the pin all the time. He putted and almost got a 3, ran two feet past, and got another 4. The last is a hole of 400 yards with a big cross bunker right in front of the green. Excitement was at fever heat. The crowd must have numbered 7000. I have never seen it so big on the Hoylake course. They scampered wildly for places to see the last vital putts. Hagen's second went through the green. He walked up to his ball. There was no more collected man in all the crowd. He chipped it up. It was short by just five feet, and he had this putt to win. From where I watched him, wedged in a corner of the crowd, it seemed as if he had mis-hit the ball, but in it rolled.

Hagen smiled a big smile, pitched his putter to his caddie, received the little man's congratulations, and the next I saw was Hagen being affectionately embraced by his wife, a little lady in a light brown dress, who had rushed in with a crowd which surrounded her husband. The crowd who had cheered as the ball dropped, cheered again as they saw Hagen throw his arms round his little wife. Then he was carried shoulder high to the clubhouse.

There was a flow of oratory there, with a vigorous cornet-player adding musical honours to all the cheering, speeches by Hagen and J H Taylor, Mrs Hagen again embracing her husband, with more cheering, and still more cheering when she kissed the great John Henry.

1925

PRESTWICK

This was the twenty-fourth and last Open at Prestwick. James Braid failed to make the main event, the second time he had been eliminated in qualifying. Exemptions, which would not be introduced until 1963, would have enriched these early Opens. Only three Americans took part but two of them dominated the opening day. Jim Barnes set a course record of 70 in the morning and followed up with a 77 for a 36-hole score of 147. His compatriot, Carnoustie-born Macdonald Smith, who had opened with a 76, set the course alight in the afternoon, breaking the hours-old record with a 69 to take the halfway lead on 145. Archie Compston, from Manchester, was the nearest home challenger on 151 with three more on 152. Ironically, Smith apparently thought the milling crowd didn't want him to win because he was an American whereas they were willing him on because they regarded him as a Scot.

One player who did not enjoy his afternoon round was George Murdoch of Troon Municipal. He started with a 14. Having found a disused bunker under the bridge behind the green, instead of taking a penalty drop, "he just kept banging away at the ball until he had played himself hopelessly out of it".

26 JUNE

Prestwick, Friday – James Barnes, of New York, won the Open Championship here today with an aggregate of 300. Though the final afternoon furnished one of the most dramatic surprises in the long history of the championship, there were no thrilling closing scenes such as we have had in the last few years. Barnes holed out on the eighteenth green early this afternoon, and not a soul in the vast crowd thought of greeting him as champion. There is always a thrill in seeing a great man playing the last stroke to win the biggest golfing prize in the world. Barnes played his, and no-one, not even I imagine, Barnes himself, knew what it implied.

The dramatic thrust which Mac Smith made yesterday afternoon was completely eclipsed by his own surprising failure this afternoon. He had a 78 to win when he went out for his last round. He had done 76, 69, and 76 in his three earlier rounds, and no-one had a doubt but that he would easily do it. But the "breaks", as the Americans call them, began early in the round. He had only six strokes over 4s to play with. By the time five holes were played, three of them were gone. The accuracy of his irons had departed. He still drove well, but he couldn't play his seconds, and he got into trouble at every other hole. Worst of all he lost his fine touch on the greens. I think the crowd troubled him a lot.

He took 42 to the turn. The great prize, he must have felt, was slipping from his grasp. He started home with a string of 5s. The task before him became more and more hopeless. At the fifteenth he took a 6, and that sealed his doom. He had to do then 3, 3, 2 . It was not impossible. Indeed he got the Alps in 3, but he took 4 for the other two, even missing a putt on the last which would never have troubled him in any of his earlier rounds. Smith walked off the last green a sad and dejected looking man. It required no vivid imagination to picture the scene had it been otherwise. There was a feeble attempt at a cheer, which Smith acknowledged with a wan smile. In the crowd I saw Mrs Smith, who had faithfully followed her husband's fortunes throughout the week, take him consolingly by the arm. My mind flew back to the contrast at Hoylake and the little excited lady rushing out from the crowd to embrace her husband after Hagen had holed his putt.

Compston and Ray had just failed by a putt to tie with Barnes, and rumour now got busy with Mitchell. We heard all sorts of stories about the wonderful things he was doing, but the bold fact in the end was that Mitchell took 77, and with an aggregate of 305, finished fifth.

It is a victory for America certainly, and the cup will make its fourth transatlantic trip in just five years. But there is this consolation, that Barnes was born and bred and learned his golf in England.

The crowd was variously estimated, but generally it was put at round about 15,000. All day overladen trains emptied themselves at the adjoining Prestwick station. They behaved themselves, for the greater part of the day, admirably, though towards the end they assumed proportions which would have been beyond the wit of any band of stewards completely to control.

Compston, following Barnes, drove the last green, and he had a putt of about a dozen yards for a 2 and a tie. He threw his massive form on the ground, and studied the putt as if, gifted with second sight, he knew all that it imported. Confidently he hit the ball. It had just the right line, but it fell off at the last, and drew up two inches to the left of the hole. Had it gone down, as things turned out, we should have had a 36 holes tie tomorrow.

Ray had the same chance at the last to tie with Barnes, and of all the said "might-have-beens" of this week's championship the saddest was Ray's today, for on the ninth green he took four putts from the edge. Playing an uphill putt, he went two-and-a-half yards past, ran past again a little over a foot, and missed the tiny putt.

Responding to the demands for a speech, Barnes said: "Many years ago I caddied for James Braid and J H Taylor when they won Open Championships and I said to myself that I would win this championship some day and I've won it today."

1925

JIM BARNES

Jim Barnes was born in Cornwall in 1887 and emigrated to California in his late teens. He soon established himself as a golfer of some standing and was nicknamed "Long Jim", partly because of his height (he was over 6ft tall) and partly because of his length off the tee.

He had many victories during a highly successful career in the States, including the first two US PGA Championships in 1916 and 1919 (the First World War cancelled out two years) and the 1921 US Open which he won by two strokes from Walter Hagen and F McLeod.

The Open which he won at Prestwick at the age of 38 was the twenty-fourth and last to be played at the course which had been the venue of the first 12 Opens. Only St Andrews has been the venue more often, reaching 26 with the Millennium Open.

1926

ROYAL LYTHAM AND ST ANNE'S

A total of 117 golfers, including 13 Americans, qualified for the first Open to be played over Lytham. The competition reverted to the three-day format, in which one round would be played on each of the first two days, after which there would be a cut and those who survived would play two rounds. This format would remain for 40 years. The cut was set at 14 shots behind the halfway leader.

The headline told the story of the first day all too clearly: "Bad Day for British Golf". Five Americans led after the first round with scores ranging from Walter Hagen's 68 to the 72 returned by amateur and current US Open champion Bobby Jones.

After the second day, there were Americans in the first six places. Jones, bookie's favourite at 3-1, was joint leader on 144, alongside Hagen and Bill Mehlhorn. The nearest home players were Archie Compston and T Barber of Cavendish, six shots adrift of the leaders.

24 JUNE

St Anne's, Friday – Robert Tyre Jones, to give the new champion all the honours, has been held by many to be the greatest golfer, paid or unpaid, in the world. By his triumph here today, in company of the world's best golfers, he has definitely established himself as that. He has a record in the post-war golf of his own country which is without parallel in the world, and to that brilliant record he has now added the greatest of all golfing honours.

There was a big atmosphere with great crowds rushing about wildly in the last few hours to witness the final scenes, yet there was a strange lack of thrill about it all. In any circumstances, patriotic Britons could not be expected to get violently excited. British golfers had been hopelessly out-played. It was just as if the American Open Championship were being played in Britain. While

the fight may have been intriguing, as the cup was to go to America once more, making five times out of six, respectable British citizens were not going to lose their heads as to whether it went in charge of a man from Grand Rapids or Atlanta.

There was perhaps a shade of sympathy with the amateur, but his winning was as tranquil a business as the championship history of the last 20 years has ever furnished. The last green provides the setting, but the drama was not there, and as Jones holed out this afternoon after a terrific fight for the lead with Al Watrous he was not hailed as the champion, for Hagen could yet win.

Hagen had gone out in 36 and had to come home in the same. With a hard north-west wind in his teeth at many of the holes it was no soft proposition. But at Hoylake Hagen's case was, if anything, worse, and we remember how he fought like a lion and just won. Today he slipped a stroke here and there and when he took 4 at the short fifteenth hole he required two 3s and a 4 to tie. Having got none of them when he came to the last he was in the desperate case of requiring to hole his pitch to tie. Instead he was right over in a bunker at the back. Hagen even smiled as he failed to get out with his first. In the end he took his first 6 in the championship.

Abe Mitchell, who played the best golf of the day when it was too late, led the British players with an aggregate of 299. Archie Compston, the one man who might have made a fight for Britain, was disqualified for playing from out of bounds.

Jones and Watrous, paired together, were both out in 36. Jones said afterwards that he felt the personal duel aspect of the partnership He was desperately near to cracking, he said, but he showed no outward signs of the strain.

With two holes to play he was all square with Watrous, and he had still to get in front. He got one of his strokes by the greatest shot of the championship.

The seventeenth is a dog-leg hole of 411 yards with big sandhills waiting to trap the pulled drive and Jones got in. Watrous from the tee was in the middle of the fairway. Jones walked from his ball to the fairway and carefully surveyed the ground. Watrous, whose shot it was, went over and had a look at Jones's lie to weigh probabilities.

Watrous just got to the edge of the green. Now Jones had to get the green. He took a No.4 iron and with the courage of a lion hit a magnificent shot on to the middle of the green. Watrous, shaken by this shattering blow, took three more, and now for the first time in the round Jones was in the lead. The last hole saw Jones one more stroke ahead. Watrous, still in shock, pulled his drive. He got a bunker, played from that into another, and in the end took a 5 to Jones's 4.

1926, 1927, 1930
BOBBY JONES

Robert Tyre Jones, born in Atlanta, Georgia, in 1902, grew up and practised law there. He was never a professional golfer but in a short career he became the greatest amateur the world had ever seen.

Bobby, as he was known to his fans – plain Bob to his friends – was the last of the greats who used hickory clubs. He rarely stepped on to a course with fewer than 16 (the limit of 14 came into force in 1938). He had a "Carnoustie swing" having been taught by emigrant Stewart Maiden who came originally from the Angus coast. The swing was marked by a full shoulder turn and well-timed wrist snap to compensate for the now eliminated factor of torque.

The son of a lawyer, he was not a healthy child and his father, himself a keen golfer, introduced him to the game to provide a tonic. He played his first full round of golf at his father's club when he was seven years old. He won the club championship when he was 13 and at 14 entered the US Amateur Championship and survived the first two rounds. After the First World War, in 1919, he reached the final of the US Amateur Championship. He reached six finals and won five. He won his first major, the US Open, in 1923 and between then and 1930 he won the US Open four times, the Open three times, the British Amateur once and the US Amateur five times, the only golfer to win all four of those titles in one year (1930). He is pictured here with the trophies and his biographer O B Keeler (right).

Even at the height of his success he rarely played in tournaments other than championships. He was a private individual and did not enjoy being in the limelight. After 1930 he effectively retired from competitive golf "with no more worlds to conquer".

His ambition was to establish an exclusive golf course where he and his friends could indulge in a friendly fourball away from the admiring but intrusive public. The result was Augusta National in which he played a major part in the design with the help of a wealthy business friend and the skill of Dr Alister McKenzie, a Scots doctor turned golf course architect. The inaugural invitational tournament held in 1934 turned out to be the first Masters as we now know it.

He was an invalid from 1946 with a serious spinal problem and never played golf after that. In 1958 he received the freedom of St Andrews and was pronounced an honorary burgess and guild brother of the city, the first American to receive this honour since Benjamin Franklin almost two hundred years earlier. He died in 1971.

1 9 2 7

ST ANDREWS

Qualifying rounds were played on the Monday and Tuesday of the same week as the championship. Vardon, Taylor and Braid were among 108 contenders, as was Sandy Herd and Cyril Tolley of Royal Liverpool, who led the field on 144.

It was one of the most international gatherings thus far with players from Australia, France, Holland and America. Two overseas players, both amateurs, led after the first day. Bobby Jones, last year's winner, equalled the course record of 68 set by George Duncan in 1922. The Australian amateur champion, Len Nettlefold, took second place with a 71. Six players shared third place on 72 – the American, Joe Kirkwood, two Scots and three Englishmen.

After the second day, Jones took a 72 and a two-stroke lead on 140 from a little-known Englishman, Bert Hodson (Newport), who had rounds of 72 and 70. A 19-year-old former public schoolboy who had turned professional just one year before was well placed on 145 in his first Open. His name was Thomas Henry Cotton.

For a change there were only two Americans in the top 12 at this stage. The field was exactly halved to 54 by the cut which claimed Vardon as one of its victims.

15 JULY

St Andrews, Friday – Bobby Jones today further established his right to be acclaimed the greatest golfer, paid or unpaid, in the world. He has this week scattered all records to the winds. He has broken 70 on the Old Course for the first time in the Open. He has lowered by six strokes to 285 the championship aggregate, which has stood since Braid won at Prestwick in 1908, and the American Open Championship aggregate record held by Chick Evans since 1916. Now he has done what nobody but the old triumvirate have done since the days of Bob Ferguson and Jamie Anderson and the Morrises – won

the Open in successive years. He already had a record in post-war golf, including the winning of the British and American Opens in one year, which was unparalleled in the world. His phenomenal performance today has crowned a golfing career which, for a young man of 26, belongs to the world's romances.

Jones won by six strokes. It was still a big and excited crowd which witnessed the finish. Jones did a morning round of 73, a little ragged, like his round of yesterday; but with a fine steady finish for an aggregate of 213, he led the field. His nearest challenger four strokes behind was Fred Robson, Coombe Hill, who had scored 69 in the third round.

Jones was dressed again in his grey pullover, and he went through the ordeal of this trying day calmly and, I need hardly add, modestly. He took the good luck with the bad all day with the same good humour. It was estimated that 12,000 stood round the last green watching Jones give the knock-out blow for the second time to British professional golf.

The great crowd formed itself into a human frame stretching from the back of the green down to the Swilcan and round the last tee. Every window and balcony overlooking the course was crowded. The players drove off, and there was a wild rush for places to watch the pitches. Seymour, Jones's partner, played, and there was a premature breakaway by the crowd. An army of stewards performed prodigies of valour, and back the crowd had to go. Jones, in the best Hagen manner, meanwhile sat down beside his ball, and patiently waited until he had a clear course.

At long last Jones played, and before his ball had dropped there was another wild stampede. On and on the crowd surged right to the edge of the green, threatening to trample Jones's ball which lay in the dip. At last the stewards stemmed the wild onrush, and Jones for the first time this week played from the dip. Andra Kirkaldy stood at the pin, where he has stood faithfully all week.

The ball climbed the slope, ran on something like 20 yards, and drew up on the side of the hole. It might as well have gone in. There was a big cheer and another when Jones tapped in the ball.

Kirkaldy was the first to congratulate him, and characteristically he waved him aside until Seymour had played. Jones waited till his partner had holed out. The cheers broke out again, the crowd rushed the green, and

Jones was swallowed up, to appear again when he was "chaired". And so he was carried off the green holding aloft his trusted putter which had served him faithfully all week. The day's play might then have been at an end. Everybody knew that the championship was won by a handful of strokes, and players still out were largely left to themselves.

The presentation of the cup was deferred till late in the evening. A great cheer went up when Jones announced that he was not going to take the cup out of Scotland, but would leave it in the custody of the R and A, to which he was granted life membership.

Bobby Jones – practice makes perfect for the world's greatest amateur

1928

ROYAL ST GEORGE'S

A week before the Open Walter Hagen played a scheduled 72-hole exhibition match with fellow Open champion Arthur Havers, who, in rounds of 67, 66 and 70, beat the American by 18 and 17. The result signalled great hype about the wonderful state of British golf. Hagen never once complained and chatted happily to the gallery as he was being trounced. He posed smilingly for photographers, warmly congratulated Havers, then was driven away in his customary Rolls Royce to begin his practice for the Open.

Jose Jurado, the Argentinian champion, led the qualifiers, scoring a record-equalling 69 over the St George's course.

The Americans, who have provided six winners in the last seven years, were again to the fore after the first round with Bill Mehlhorn at the front on 71, Gene Sarazen next, one stroke more, and Hagen equal fourth with a 75. Jurado was on 74, while British hopes George Duncan and Archie Compston and Leeds professional Sid Wingate were tied with Hagen.

On the second day, Jurado set the pace with a 71 for a halfway total of 145 and a three-stroke lead over Hagen and Sarazen. Havers shot 80, 74 and was nine shots adrift. A total of 52 players were left to do battle on the final day.

11 MAY

Sandwich, Friday – Walter Hagen tonight won his third Open Championship with an aggregate of 292. It is an amazing record, stamping him as the greatest golfer in the world, after his countryman, Bobby Jones. And what a commentary it is on the Moor Park fiasco of last week. The American bogy, we were told, had at last been laid and British golfers started favourites here this week.

Yet this man, who had played hardly any golf before he came over, having been engaged on "movie" work at Hollywood for several months, rushes across the Continent, catches his boat, and two days after he lands gets the beating of his life. He takes it like a sportsman, and, after a week's practice here to get his game tuned up, wins the championship out of a field of over 270 of what we must suppose are the world's best golfers.

It is an amazing business. Paying a courtesy visit to the press tent when it was all over, Hagen confessed that without taking anything from the other boys he never won a championship with less confidence than in this. "I never," he said, "was master at any one time of any one shot in my bag. Now that is a peculiar thing to say," he added. "But I don't think anyone in either country realised how little golf I have played before coming over here. I won simply by trying to avoid trouble, and, of course, I like the course, having won the last time we were here. I hate annoying you in this way," he said, "but I am really coming back as long as I can get my passport." Americans have now won seven out of the last eight championships; and watching some of the men today who started out as British hopes, Mitchell and Duncan in particular, it required a sturdy optimism to see an end to the sequence.

Hagen came to the home hole and ran a putt for a second 72, setting up an aggregate which might or might not yet be beyond the reach of the men on his heels. He could not throw his putter in the air as he did at Hoylake. So we gave Walter a hearty cheer, and went out to see how things were going with Compston and Sarazen. At the sixteenth, the short hole, we met them both.

Compston came down, his long hair flying in the wind, but so terribly serious that I did not like the look of him. Clearly he had his back to the wall, yet he did look the part of Britain's last ditch defender. "Does anyone know how Compston stands?" someone shouted. Someone did. "He requires a 2 and two 3s." It was not impossible, but it revealed a desperate case. Still Compston never gave up fighting. His tee shot lay eight yards from the pin. He studied the putt with characteristic thoroughness, and as the ball ran down there was a shout you could have heard at Sandwich. Still that left two 3s and Compston's second lay at the back of the seventeenth green, quite 10 yards off. Yet very nearly did he get the ball down. His line was good, and as it ran straight for the hole there was an excited shout "Go in" but it drew up three inches to the right of the hole. That was the end. So back we went for Sarazen. He too, we found, required two 3s to tie for his putt for a 2 at the short sixteenth just failed to get down. He took a 4 at the seventeenth, and he, too, just failed like Compston. Jurado cracked, and with a round of 80 finished equal sixth, Mehlhorn added a 77 to a 76.

Hagen got to the turn in 36, helped by a 2 at the eighth.

Almost he had a 2 at the short hole coming home, and now requiring two 4s to make him tolerably safe, he played a magnificent shot to the seventeenth hole. It covered the pin, and lay one yard off, but Hagen missed. A hysterical girl laughed, though it might have been for Hagen a dark tragedy. At the last the 4 was just for a moment in doubt. His second, played with great care, drew up at the bottom of the green, but Hagen laid the ball a yard from the hole, and without a tremor put down the putt.

His Royal Highness the Prince of Wales who had followed Hagen for most of the final round, just one among the crowd, handed over the cup. He expressed the hope that the Americans would continue to come, and, as they said in America, give us the opportunity of "putting it over".

1929

MUIRFIELD

The Open returned to Muirfield for the first time since 1912 with a big turnout of Americans. First-round honours were taken by a young British golfer, Percy Alliss, professional at Wannsee, Berlin, and father of eight times Ryder Cup player and commentator-to-be Peter. Alliss had a record 69 to lead two of the American challengers, Diegel and Jim Barnes, by two shots. Walter Hagen, the holder, out in the worst of the weather, had a 75.

For the third time the record came under fire. Playing in the second round with Henry Cotton, Hagen set the course alight with a 67, also establishing a new mark for a single round in the Open. Cotton, whose solid 73 had been made to look mediocre, was first to offer his congratulations.

Diegel, with a 69 for a total of 140, led Hagen by two shots and Abe Mitchell by four with Alliss, who had a 76, on 145. At the halfway stage eight Americans were in the first 11.

10 MAY

Muirfield, Friday – So Walter Hagen has successfully defended the championship with a total of 292, exactly his aggregate of a year ago. It is truly an amazing feat, stamping him as the greatest golfer in the world. Should one qualify that by adding "after his own countryman, Bobby Jones"? It is so hard to say that any man who did this course in the wizard score of 67 and followed it with two rounds of 75 in a raging wind has a superior anywhere.

Hagen has now been over for eight championships since the war. At Deal in 1920 he finished so far down that we thought he was a joke, a man over merely to show us how a professional golfer could dress. At St Andrews the following year he was equal sixth. In the six championships in which he has competed since he was four times winner, second once and third the other year. The day is the story of the brilliance of one man and the failure of all the others. Hagen played with masterly self-confidence. He laid the real foundations of his triumph by his wonderful round of yesterday. The crowd rushed and scrambled after him in his second round today, yet it was in the morning that he really won. At 12.30 to be exact it was, humanly speaking, all over bar the shouting. Hagen had gone round in 75. In the conditions it was as magnificent as his great record round of yesterday.

I had a chat with Hagen the other night and learned from him something of his philosophy of life. It is a very happy one – that whatever you do in life you must get some fun out of it. "Whenever I cease getting fun out of this game of golf," he said, "I quit".

Leo Diegel failed because he could not play his seconds in the wind. Just with that shot Hagen won. For he played some of the most glorious iron shots imaginable, shots that required not only a perfect technique, but playing to those closely guarded greens, the courage of a lion. Diegel cracked at the critical period this morning and had 82. Mitchell, after a great start, took four putts on the thirteenth green, and finished on 78. Alliss was better, but still not good enough. Hagen at the interval had a clear lead of four strokes.

In the final round Hagen was at the eighth in three under 4s. Then for the second time in the championship he took a 6. His second lay close to the wall and Hagen, who always carries a left-handed club in his bag, pitched the ball on to the green, ran six yards past and missed the putt. That took him out in 35, a wonderful half in such conditions and his best nine holes of the day. The crowd was wildly excited, though there was really nothing at stake. Hagen could, it then seemed, go on turning out par figures to the crack of doom. Now he had equalled the feat of the great Bobby Jones with a six-stroke win.

1930

HOYLAKE

In late April, Bobby Jones, his wife, and O B Keeler, his biographer and close friend, sailed to Britain on the Mauretania to play in the Walker Cup at Sandwich and then at St Andrews in the Amateur Championship, the only big title he had not won. It had already been suggested that he could win the Amateur and the Open, then return to America and claim their two equivalents. He won the Amateur, and so this Open was stage two of his unprecedented and ultimately successful quest. The qualifying rounds were led by two Britons, Archie Compston on 141 and Henry Cotton on 143. In the first round of the championship, Jones was on schedule by setting an amateur record for the Royal Liverpool course with a 70 to share the lead with Cotton and another American, Macdonald Smith. Jim Barnes and Fred Robson (Cooden Beach) were on 71. In the afternoon there was a thunderstorm. There were no hooters in those days to announce suspension of play but even so it was surprising that Cotton, Barnes and MacDonald Smith played through it. Cotton had been five under 4s with five to play but just failed to take the outright lead.

Jones and Robson both had second-round 72s giving the American a one-stroke advantage on 142. In third position was Horton Smith on 146 with Compston and four Americans one shot worse. Cotton had a disappointing 79 for a total of 149. Under the new halfway cut rule, the best 60 plus ties went through. George Duncan failed to join the 61 who succeeded.

20 JUNE

Hoylake, Friday – There were no thrills at the finish and no drama, no final scenes such as St Andrews staged so well when Jones won the Open there three years ago. A crowd of between 3000 and 4000 followed Jones this afternoon, confidently believing they were bringing in the winner. At the end the crowd did not make much of a demonstration. There was a cheer, of course, and Jones

was hailed as the winner even then. As he marched off the green and through the crowd three policemen formed themselves into a bodyguard, a gesture copied from St Andrews.

The real thrills were in the morning with the great fightback of Archie Compston to wrest the lead from Jones. The stage seemed set then for a terrific fight in the afternoon between these representatives of the rival golfing nations.

Diegel was not then thought about at all. Yet Compston, as the Americans expressively have it, blew up in the afternoon. It was past comprehension how he could play so badly now. When half a dozen holes were played you knew he was right out of it, and Jones, who started 4, 3, looked to have the cup again in his hands. But he had a disastrous 7 at the eighth. Though he nobly played for a round of 75 and an aggregate of 291 he had not yet won. Diegel had started the final round two strokes behind. He turned in Jones's figure of 38, and with only five holes to go he was on level terms. Jones did them in one over 4s, five of the most testing holes in the world, two of them over 500 yards.

At the first of them Diegel dropped the one stroke he had to play with, and when his drive to the sixteenth was bunkered and he took three to reach the green it was almost over. His long putt drew up five feet short. Diegel walked up to the putt with a smile and missed. The crowd could hardly believe their eyes. Yet there was Diegel, standing with his arms thrown out in a gesture as who should say: "Did you ever look on such a thing!"

Jones is not the first man to win the Amateur and Open Championships in one year. One man did that 40 years ago, and he was marking score cards here this week – the great John Ball.

1931

CARNOUSTIE

For the first time, the Open was staged over the Carnoustie Links and fittingly an ex-Carnoustie boy now the American, Macdonald Smith, runner-up in last year's US Open, set a record 71 over the championship course on his way to becoming leading qualifier.

Joint leaders at the end of the first day were Henry Cotton, Johnny Farrell from America and T Twine of Bromley, all on 72. The Scots-born American, Tommy Armour, was fourth with a 73. Gene Sarazen was one shot further back.

After two rounds Cotton was still in front on a total of 147, which he shared with the Argentinian, Jose Jurado, who equalled the course record in his second round. Close on their heels were four Americans, Armour on 148, Farrell one shot more, with Sarazen and Joe Kirkwood on 150 alongside Twine. A total of 66 players made the cut for the final day.

5 JUNE

Carnoustie, Friday – It seems tonight about three days since, at half past nine this morning, I saw Henry Cotton drive off on a round that was to shatter British hopes. In between there has been such a welter of play and such strange pranks played by fortune as I can hardly recall on any championship occasion. The morning round saw favourites crash, and men who had almost been given up come right into the picture. Even the ultimate winner played such a round as seemed to import his end.

Ten men were separated by three strokes. It was the openest of Open Championships. Even Armour's mark of 296 looked sure to be beaten by Jurado. But in the supreme crisis Jurado, like all the others, cracked.

Armour's triumph must have seemed to him like a dream. I saw him hole out on the eighteenth green after a great round of 71, but hardly anyone gave him a thought. The real drama of the day was Jurado's failure. Today's

placid return of the conqueror reminded me of Prestwick six years ago, when Barnes holed out in what proved to be the winning aggregate, and nobody took any notice. Percy Alliss had come near it, and but for getting out of bounds at the last would have tied. Macdonald Smith should have gone even nearer. He came right back into the picture this morning with a round of 71. But in the crisis he took 5, 6, 5 to the last three holes when with Armour's finish he would have won outright

Cotton cracked in the morning and was little better in the afternoon. Havers, Farrell, and Sarazen had all been left with too much to do. There was still Jurado, playing like a hero and looking every inch a winner but I believe Mr Bernard Darwin in a broadcast talk last night expressed his fears about Jurado standing the racket. He is such a slight figure of a man, though he must have wrists of steel, and his 73 this morning seemed to suggest that his heart was in the right place. He had a three-stroke lead over the field, and for 15 holes this afternoon he fought with a lion's courage. Ten thousand people scampered over hills and bunkers after the little man.

He had gone to the turn faultlessly in level-par 36. Jurado wavered a bit after the turn. He dropped a shot at the tenth and another at the thirteenth and, worse still, the famous Spectacles took toll of a 6. Then a bunker from the tee at the short sixteenth, and Jurado must have begun to wonder if the great prize was slipping. But there was an explosion out, a six-yard putt, and a tremendous cheer at the 3. Jurado now had a 4 and a 5 to win outright.

The seventeenth is a hole of 428 yards. With a following wind, it is played with two irons, the first on to the island. Jurado underclubbed and when the great crowd had scampered to their places waiting for the pitch, they saw Jurado dropping a ball behind him. He had failed to carry the burn. Still, all was not yet lost. But the third shot was tragic. Doubtless shaken by the penalty stroke, Jurado cut the shot which he played with a spoon and it made straight for the bunker. He had still a chance with a four-yard putt, but he was two inches off. So now it had to be a 4 at the last to tie. It was not a two-shot hole with the wind blowing so hard, but there was always the pitch. The crowd, thrilled and excited in the last degree, lined the fairway on both sides, 15,000 I am sure. Jurado played short, though he had tried to carry the burn in the morning and lost a penalty stroke which now would have been worth a ransom. With 3 played, he was four

yards off, but again he just failed. He had left the last green in the morning, his face wreathed with smiles. Now a sad, dejected figure walked off, but taking with him the sympathy of every man, woman, and child in the crowd. Armour won with just the aggregate James Braid predicted, 296.

Armour's triumph was achieved with the Prince of Wales on the course, though His Royal Highness saw very little of the new champion's play, for Jurado was his man all day. There could have been no-one more disappointed on the course when Jurado crashed than the prince.

1931
TOMMY ARMOUR

Born in 1895 in Edinburgh where he learned his golf on Braid Hills, Tommy Armour was one of many Scots to seek their fortunes in America. He won three majors, the other two being the US Open in 1927 and the US PGA in 1930. He also won the Canadian Open twice. He was an American citizen by the time he won the Open.

Soon after his 1931 success at Carnoustie his game went into decline, particularly his putting. He is said to be the first player to complain of having the yips. He eventually retired from tournament play and became a highly successful teacher and author of golf instruction books.

One of his better known pupils was Babe Didrickson Zaharias, renowned American Olympic gold medallist in athletics, who after taking up golf went on to win many events including the US Women's Open three times.

1932

PRINCE'S, SANDWICH

For the first and also the last time, the Open was played over the Prince's course rather than the St George's layout and Eric McRuvie, a Scottish Walker Cup nominee, set the course record with a 69 during qualifying.

Gene Sarazen led with a 70 after the first round, one ahead of Macdonald Smith, with three Englishmen, Charles Whitcombe, Percy Alliss and W H Davies, sharing third place on 72. Tommy Armour, the holder, opened with a 77.

Day two dawned bright and breezy with the wind rising and falling and setting different problems for each group of players. Sarazen shot a record-equalling 69 for a halfway total of 139, three ahead of Alliss, who had another 71. Davies, Whitcombe and Archie Compston were all two shots further back. Armour recovered with a 70 to take a share of sixth place on 147 with Smith.

10 JUNE

Sandwich, Friday – It is the simplest championship story that I have ever been called on to tell. There was just one moment shortly after Gene Sarazen had set out on his final round when our pulse quickened as Arthur Havers dropped a bombshell with his third round of 68. It seemed at the time to make a tremendous difference, for it cut down Sarazen's lead of eight strokes to four. Sarazen had finished with an aggregate of 283, a record for the championship, which beat Jones's total in 1927 by two. It meant that Havers required a round of 70 to tie.

Havers was out in 37. Coming home, several long putts touched the hole and slipped past. Had they dropped, the championship might have been a different story. So Havers having failed, the day's story becomes simply one of the brilliance of a little, stockily-built American in a green pullover, swarthy of skin, telling of the Italian blood in his veins. He started life as a New York caddie and now represents another of golf's romances as he stands tonight Open champion.

Sarazen never looked in the morning like doing anything but shutting the door on all the other players. There were strokes dropped in the second half near the end, but when a three-yarder went down on the sixteenth green, leaving him two 4s for another 69, he was virtually champion.

Sarazen never wavered. He was superb to the turn with just one faltering 5 at the eighth. He looked as if he could go on getting par figures to the end of time, but after the turn he fell from his high estate. He dropped strokes at two of the first three holes after the turn, and he was off the green in two at the next. But he chipped on and sank the putt. Then came the hole and the putt which put all doubts at rest. His tee shot to the short fourteenth lay 10 yards wide of the hole. Sarazen putted uphill, and the ball, catching the side of the hole curled in. There was a great cheer, and Sarazen, with an amusing gesture, blew a kiss to the ball as it lay in the hole.

After three 5s, Sarazen drove to the last. It was again long and straight, and, with a fine No.3 iron shot, he laid his second shot on the green some six yards from the hole. He rolled the ball up and tapped in the putt for a final round of 74. There was quite the cheer which greets the undisputed champion. In a neat little speech when the cup was put into his hands, he said, his face wreathed in smiles: "I am the happiest man in the world and my only regret is that my wife is not over with me this trip to share my happiness."

1932
GENE SARAZEN

When Eugenio Saraceni realised he would make a better golfer than a musician he changed his name to Gene Sarazen. Born in 1902, the son of an immigrant Italian carpenter, he worked with his father before becoming a caddie and taking up the game which was to dominate his long life. He had a reputation for being tough. As he said: "You had to be when you were Italian."

Only 5ft 4ins tall, he seemed to be starting at an enormous disadvantage and yet, by the time he was 21 he had won three majors. His career went into decline and it was almost seven years before he re-emerged as a force in world golf. In 1923 he came over for the Open at Troon and failed to qualify. "I'll come back," he vowed, "even if I have to swim across."

In 1930 he narrowly missed winning the US PGA Championship and it was about this time that he invented the sand wedge by soldering lead on to the sole of his niblick. After his 1932 Open win (he won the US Open the same year) he went on to take the US PGA Championship in 1933. In 1935 at his first attempt he won the Masters, thus becoming the first player to win all four professional majors, a feat which has been repeated only by Ben Hogan, Gary Player and Jack Nicklaus.

Bobby Jones said of Sarazen: "When the wand touches him . . . he is probably the greatest scorer in the game." He is well remembered for his "shot that went round the world", holing out with a No.4 wood for an albatross (or double eagle) 2 at Augusta's fifteenth en route to that 1935 win.

He still had that magic wand 38 years later. In 1973 at the age of 71, making a token appearance in the Open at Troon, where ironically he had failed to qualify 50 years before, he holed his tee shot at the eighth, Postage Stamp. The following day in the second round at the same hole he had a 2, holing out from a bunker. Who needs a putter? Gene Sarazen died in 1999.

Walter Hagan, Sam Whiting, Gene Sarazen and Jock Hutchison, with Joe Kirkwood behind, pictured in San Francisco

1933

ST ANDREWS

W Nolan of Portmarnock set an Old Course record of 67 to lead the qualifiers by four strokes with a total of 138. Percy Alliss failed to qualify.

The last nine Opens had been won by Americans and again they were well to the fore after the first round. Walter Hagen set the pace with a 68 to lead by two from Ed Dudley, Cyril Tolley (Royal Eastbourne) and T R Fernie (Royal Lytham & St Anne's). There were three on 71, including Nolan, and five on 72, including the holder, Gene Sarazen. Densmore Shute, runner-up in the US PGA in 1931, was on 73.

A British bid came from Abe Mitchell in the second round with a 68 to sit in third place on 142. Hagen led having added a 72 for a total of 140. Second was Dudley who had a 71. Also on 142, was a young Scots professional, F Robertson, of Dumfries and County. Only five shots separated the first 12 players who included five Americans. Shute, who had another 73, was six shots behind.

On Wednesday evening, a tribute was paid to Old Tom Morris and his son, Young Tom, by members of the US Ryder Cup Team. Led by their captain, Walter Hagen, and headed by a bugler, they marched to the old cathedral grounds and laid wreaths on their graves.

7 JULY

St Andrews, Friday – (Transmitted direct by teleprint machine from the golf course at St Andrews to the *Glasgow Herald* office.)

The most amazing Open Championship of recent years, if not the most amazing of all time, has left us tonight with two American players, Craig Wood, Hollywood, and Densmore Shute, Llanerch, tieing for first place with aggregates of 292. Thus has ended a day of astonishing swings and changes of fortune, a day in which British hopes of a victory soared to the clouds only to be dashed.

From the simple issue of the whole field in pursuit of Walter Hagen, who had led by one from Ed Dudley and by two from Abe Mitchell and Fred Robertson, the championship developed into the complication of at least 13 players having a real chance in the last round.

Hagen's collapse had its foundations in a disastrous fourteenth, the Long Hole, on which he topped a brassie shot into one of the smaller bunkers, known as Hell's Kitchen, and spent seven shots before he holed out.

For this final setting the Old Course was in one of its most tantalising moods, with a stiff east wind which made the homeward journey a grim test of steadiness of nerve and swing.

Thousands witnessed the final failure of Britain's last but biggest hope, Sydney Easterbrook, the tall young professional of the Knowle Club, Bristol, who only 10 days ago had been his country's mainstay in just as tight a finish to the Ryder Cup match.

Wood had finished before Easterbrook had reached the ninth hole. The American's aggregate of 292 had left the British player to make a score of 75 to become the champion. It was the greatest chance of his life, and for a long time he seemed likely to do it. An outward 37 and 3s at the tenth and eleventh holes had given him a fairly wide margin.

His last few holes compare in sheer, stark collapse with any of the great failures of the past. He played like a man bewildered and beaten and at the last hole, when his lead was so far squandered that he was left with a 3 merely to tie, he pulled his approach wide to the grass bank near the foot of the steps. When he tried to hole that chip he was hoping for little short of a miracle, and it did not happen.

These last holes of Easterbrook's will remain long in the

memory. The first indication of the strain of his position was at the Hole O'Cross. He half-topped an iron shot into a bunker to run up a 5, and then at the Long Hole his brassie shot, none too well hit against the stiff wind, was caught in the Kitchen Bunker. He was lying well in the sand and came out cleanly, only to throw the chance of recovery to the winds by being very short with his pitch. He reached the green in 5 to take a 7.

He now had to do 4s all the way to win. A two-yard putt for a 4 beat him at the fifteenth. He got one at the sixteenth after cutting his approach and being saved from going out of bounds on the railway by his ball striking a fence post. At the seventeenth, he ran on to the road and came to rest on the grass verge on the far side. He pitched up well, but missed a lengthy putt.

Shute and Wood are in a unique position in that one of them will break a tradition by winning the championship on his first visit to this country. Shute had ploughed a lonely furrow all day, but when the news spread that he required par figures for the last three holes to get in ahead of Wood pandemonium broke. The crowds rushed to meet him at the sixteenth, and arrived as, from a hollow, he had a long, uphill putt which finished two yards past the pin. He missed the return, took a 5 at the Road Hole and a 4 at the last. His four rounds are a great tribute to his steadiness, each of them 73.

Wood, who is Hollywood's professional and its newest "star", crashed in on the leaders with a magnificent 68 in the third round. He was hitting the ball a tremendous distance, and downwind his tee shot to the long fifth finished in the bunkers near the green, a distance of almost 400 yards.

Out in 36 in the afternoon he looked as if he had shot his bolt, but he struggled on tenaciously. After dropping a stroke at the twelfth by three – putting and taking 5 at the thirteenth, he cut his tee shot to the fourteenth close to the dyke. The ball lay in the rough, but he tried to play a spoon. His daring shot did not come off, and he landed in Hell's, that dreaded pit. However, he got out well, pitched on, and holed a putt of about 10 yards for his par 5.

With another cut drive against the wind at the fifteenth he landed in a small forest of whins. Luckily his ball had finished in the only clear space in yards around; but he did not make the best use of it, for after playing three strokes he was still short and ran up a 6. At the seventeenth, he hooked wildly over the second fairway. He just missed the road, chipped up well, and holed his putt for a 5.

He finished with a 75, tied for the championship with Shute on 292.

PLAY OFF

Densmore Shute, USA, is the new Open champion by virtue of his win over his compatriot, Craig Wood, in the replay today over 36 holes. Shute's aggregate was 149 and Wood's was 154.

It did not seem to matter much from a British point of view who took the trophy back to America. At the start there were only about 250 spectators, and there could not have been more than 2500 round the last green to acclaim the champion. It seemed that American supremacy was being rubbed in, in a way which was more difficult to bear than if one man had romped away from the whole field.

There is no doubt, however, that the Championship Cup is in the hands of a very fine golfer. Shute, aged 20, from the Llanerch club in Philadelphia, has gained the added distinction of having won at his first attempt. The telegraph wires between this country and America hummed with detailed hole-by-hole reports of the progress of the play.

Wood lost four strokes in the first two holes. He misjudged his approach to the first green and was caught in the Swilcan Burn. In the spirit of determination which characterised Leo Diegel's similar effort the previous day he took off his shoes and socks, rolled up his trousers, and waded into the water. The ball came out well, but he did not profit by his courageous stroke, as he was very short with his run-up and took 6, as he did at the second after his tee shot was bunkered.

Time and again Shute was left yards behind from the tee, but just as often, when the two balls reached the green, Wood was playing first. Shute was three ahead after 18 holes with a 75 to a 78.

Shute in the second round was out in 36 against Wood's 39. Shute's lead of six at the turn mounted to seven when

Wood fluffed a pitch at the High Hole, swung back to six when he was bunkered, and again became seven when Wood missed a putt of less than a yard on the thirteenth.

Wood did cut off two by taking the Long Hole in 4 and with Shute three-putting the fifteenth green, but the big advantage never seemed like being lost.

1933
DENSMORE SHUTE

Densmore (Denny) Shute's Open victory was the perfect tonic. The week before in the Ryder Cup at Southport he had three-putted the final green – sending his first putt strongly past the hole – to lose by one hole to Syd Easterbrook and gift the cup to Great Britain. Two putts for a halved match would have left the overall match a draw, with the Americans, as holders, retaining the cup.

His father was a professional to a Devon club for many years before going to America, where his son was born in 1904. Denny spent more time working as a club professional than he did on the tour which in those days was not lucrative. In 30 years on the tour, however, he won 15 tournaments and developed a reputation as a magnificent long-iron player.

In 1931 he was runner-up in the US PGA Championship and won the title in 1936 and 1937, the last man to take it in consecutive years. Despite his lapse in 1933, he had a good Ryder Cup record. He was elected to the PGA Hall of Fame in 1957.

1934

ROYAL ST GEORGE'S

The sixty-ninth Open was marked by the lowest qualifying score so far of 152, and Henry Cotton reduced the St George's course to a championship record of 66, three better than George Duncan in 1922 and Jose Jurado in 1928.

Cotton, attached to the Waterloo Club in Belgium, led after the first round with a 67, the lowest first round score in the history of the championship. Second on 70 was F Taggart (Wilmslow) followed by a group of six on 71 which included Charles Whitcombe and the holder Densmore Shute, the only American in the first 24. Taggart had only 21 putts in his round and had holed three chip shots.

In the second round Cotton lowered the record again to 65, creating a further three records in the process. It was the lowest single round for the championship, his halfway aggregate of 132 was the lowest by seven shots – the previous best being Sarazen's 139 at the Prince's course in 1932 – and his lead of nine shots was the highest ever at the halfway stage. Alf Padgham was second on 141 with Shute, Joe Kirkwood and Charles Whitcombe on 143.

29 JUNE

Sandwich, Friday – The Open Championship of 1934, famous for its record-shattering achievements, closed tonight in a turmoil of excitement and thrills with the victory of Henry Cotton, the first British professional to win in 11 years. His aggregate of 283 was five strokes ahead of that of Syd Brews, the South African, who made a late bid with magnificent rounds in today's gale of 70 and 71. For a championship which seemed as good as over yesterday when Cotton had spreadeagled the field the finish was almost incredible.

Instead of a cut-and-dried affair for Cotton it became a nerve-racking ordeal in the heat of the closing stages, with the man who had held an apparently invincible lead reduced to a state of almost nervous prostration, throwing away strokes in the final round with lavish and trembling hands until danger actually confronted him.

In the last round Cotton faced two mighty factors – his own temperament and a fierce gale which tore over the course from the north. When he started on the third round it was obvious that the magic of his inspiration was dulled, but, scrambling at times and at others producing a worthy shot, he finished in the fine score of 72. That gave him a lead of 10 strokes over Joe Kirkwood, the American, who had jumped forward into second place with a score of 71.

The start of his fourth round was disastrous, and as hole after hole cost him a stroke more than it ought to the position became ominous, and finally menacing when Brews crashed a magnificent shot up to the last green and holed the putt for a round of 71 and an aggregate of 288. By this time Cotton had played 10 holes in a total of 45, and the long journey of the inward half – dangerous holes in the wind – in front of him. His tremendous margin was away. A repetition of his outward half was almost to be expected from the strained way in which he was playing.

He had started by shanking his iron short to the first hole, taking 4 to reach the green, only to get down a three-yard putt for his 5. He followed that by hooking his tee shot to the second deep into the rough, where four or five hundred people searched for it for about three minutes before they found it lying half-buried. Slashing at the ball with a heavy niblick, Cotton again pulled the shot, but his next was on the green and a brave five-yard putt saved the situation. His long game had completely broken down, his drives had lost their straightness, and for the next nine holes not one of his shots to the green reached their mark. In that spell came the only 6s he had taken throughout the championship, utterly bad holes at the fifth and seventh, where, after being in trouble from tee to green, he took three putts.

The tenth, eleventh, and twelfth holes saw no arrestment of this collapse, as each was struggled in 5s, but the thirteenth, today the most difficult hole, broke the spell. Here he brought off his first really confident shot, a difficult pitch over a bunker, and down went the putt for a fine 4.

From that point on the championship was won as Cotton's shots began to line up in their old style. But it was all too easy to visualise, as he stood on the thirteenth tee, a totally different picture from the scene of boisterous enthusiasm which greeted him as champion on the last green where four or five thousand spectators rushed wildly forward eager to congratulate and carry shoulder high the man who after 11 years had won the Open Championship for Britain.

1934, 1937, 1948
HENRY COTTON

Sir Thomas Henry Cotton's contribution to golf cannot be over-emphasised. Today's players owe a great deal to his efforts to raise the standing of the game and its exponents. Unlike many of his contemporaries he was not from a "cloth cap" background, having been born in 1907 into a prosperous family. His father, a successful businessman, sent him to public school, no doubt expecting him to study law or some other "respectable" profession.

Young Henry had other ideas, and it must have been a shock to his family when he declared his wish to become a golf professional, which he did at the age of 17. Three years later he was ninth in the Open at St Andrews and, at the age of 22, he played a vital role in the British Ryder Cup victory at Leeds. Throughout his career he was determined to raise the status of the professional golfer and to this end he made tremendous progress.

With his distinctive three-quarter swing, he was a perfectionist on the course and if he missed a putt he felt he should have holed punishment would sometimes be to hit himself on the head with his putter.

He also broke the domination of the Americans in the Open when he won in 1934, keeping the silver claret jug on this side of the Atlantic for the first time since 1923. His second round record of 65 that year, which stood until 1977, gave birth to the Dunlop 65 golf ball and his 36-hole total of 132 remained an Open record for 58 years until Nick Faldo shaved two off that total at Muirfield in 1992. Cotton won the Open again in 1937 and 1948 as well as numerous other championships around Europe but World War Two undoubtedly deprived him of many more important victories. He was Great Britain's Ryder Cup captain in 1939 and 1953.

He was an extremely supple man. Even in his sixties he could lie on his back and raise his feet over his head to touch the floor behind. At his peak he was noted for the practice technique of repeatedly swinging a club into a car tyre to build up tension in the forearm and back.

He wrote many fine books on the game, had a long-running weekly newspaper golf column and later became involved in designing and building golf courses including his favourite, Penina in Portugal. He was knighted in 1987, the first and only golfer to be so honoured. Sadly, he died a few days before the formal ceremony.

1935

MUIRFIELD

Two 28-year-olds led the qualifiers – last year's winner Henry Cotton and the up-and-coming Englishman, Richard Burton. "A storm of rain of almost cloudburst intensity" marked the first day of the championship, but Cotton began his defence with a 68, one ahead of Macdonald Smith and a young Ryder Cup player, Alf Perry. Apart from Smith the main challengers were, for a change, home players with no fewer than 14 on Cotton's trail on scores of 72 or better. The nearest other American was Henry Picard, one of those on 72. Eric McRuvie was leading amateur on 70, a score he shared with Alf Padgham and Ernest Kenyon.

Smith's challenge faded with a 77 in the second round, but Charles Whitcombe came in with a 68 to take the lead with a halfway total of 139, three ahead of Cotton, who had carded a shaky 74, and Padgham. There were huge crowds. The Cotton game alone attracted at least 5000 spectators. Perry, Kenyon and William Branch were all within two shots of Padgham and Cotton. No American or other "invader" was in the first six at that stage.

28 JUNE

Muirfield, Friday – A remarkable round of deadly spoon shots and brilliant putting today won for Alfred Perry, the 30-year-old Leatherhead (Surrey) professional, the greatest honour in golf – the Open Championship title.

In the third round, carried through in brilliant weather, he created a record of 67 for the reconstructed Muirfield course, and completed the fourth round in 72 to give him an aggregate of 283, which equals the lowest ever in the championship. The other occasions on which this figure was returned were last year by Henry Cotton and in 1932 by Gene Sarazen.

After a third round of pulsating excitement, the final scene was shorn of a great deal of its interest by the collapse of many of Perry's nearest rivals, particularly Cotton, who could do no better in his third round than 76 and 75 in the final round.

Still, when Perry won he had a wonderful reception. From tee to green the fairway at the home hole was lined with spectators four and five deep. After having stormed the long seventeenth in a perfect 4 he was left to play the eighteenth safely to make his position as champion secure. A well-placed drive, second to the green, and a sound approach putt allowed him to hole out easily for his 4.

With an almost nonchalant touch of his cap he acknowledged the rousing cheers of the crowd, and turned to leave the green when he was stopped by the deposed champion, Cotton, who congratulated him. "I had the breaks in these two rounds today. That's why I won," said Perry modestly when he had escaped from the throng of admirers into the quiet of the clubhouse.

Although he was not regarded as one of the leading challengers to Cotton at the beginning of the week, Perry has such an extremely sound record that on reflection one wonders why his chances were not more favourably regarded. His swing is exceptionally fast and flat. He is inclined to be short from the tee, and in the fairly stiff west wind of yesterday he probably played more second shots with wood than any other competitor.

One of the really great shots of the championship was one he played at the fourteenth in the last round. He had hooked his drive enough to bring the ball close to a bunker on the edge of the fairway. It was lying on the down slope in such a way as to make a shot to the green almost impossible.

Instead of clipping the ball on to the fairway with a lofted iron, Perry walked up to it with his spoon and a determined look. He did not know how the others were faring, and he was dropping no strokes if he could help it. He went for the long shot to the green, and played it magnificently to reap the reward of a 4.

Putting with a Diegel-like left arm and a tendency to waggle frequently when addressing, he was regularly pushing the ball right up to the hole-side. It was only according to the law of average that some of these putts went down.

His last round started humbly with a "gallery" of two caddies and a marker, and he reached the fifth hole ordinarily enough in level 4s. But after that somebody saw him drop an eight-yard putt on the sixth green for a 3 and joined him. Several people saw him hit a perfect tee shot five feet from the seventh hole and snatch a 2, and their applause when he dropped in another eight-yard putt for a 3 at the long eighth hole brought the crowds flocking round. When he holed out for a 4 on the ninth green for an outward half of 32 he was trailing in his wake a crowd of several thousands.

He dropped a stroke at the tenth hole, made it up by holing out from two yards for a 2 at the short thirteenth. When he had taken his par 3 at the sixteenth there were visions of a new record. But in that Perry disappointed them, for his second shot to the seventeenth – where he did not rely on his spoon – was short and trapped and he had to be content with a 5. He took his 4 with comfort at the last for victory by four strokes.

1935
ALF PERRY

Alf Perry, aged 34 when he won the Open, was a surprise winner against the favourites Henry Cotton and Americans Henry Picard and Lawson Little. He had been associated with golf all his life, beginning as a boy caddie at Coulsden in Surrey and then being apprenticed to James Braid at Walton Heath. Later he had an appointment at Malmo, Sweden, before returning to his Leatherhead post. He played in the British Ryder Cup team at Southport in 1933. Perry had a highly individual swing and grip and he was blessed with a good short game. In the Jamie Anderson mould of half a century before him, he played to hole the shot when within range and rarely played safe.

1936

HOYLAKE

A spectacular storm with thunder and vivid flashes of lightning resulted in the first qualifying round being declared null and void, thus delaying the start of the championship proper by a day.

At the end of the first day 50 players, almost half the field, were within seven shots of the leader, W J Cox of Wimbledon Park, who scored a 70. On one stroke more was the Scot, James Adams, with the Scottish amateur, Jack McLean, sharing third place on 72, equalling the amateur record, alongside Reg Whitcombe and W H Davies. One stroke further back were Henry Cotton, Gene Sarazen and Alf Padgham.

At the halfway stage 18 players were separated by only four shots. Cox was still in the lead alongside Adams with an aggregate of 144, one better than Cotton, Padgham, Richard Burton, Marcel Dallemagne, the French champion, and the millionaire amateur, Francis Francis. The nearest American was Gene Sarazen on 148.

26 JUNE

Hoylake, Saturday – In a finish which was crammed with excitement, thrills, suspense and torments, Alfred Padgham, the 30-year-old Sundridge Park professional, won the Open Championship on this famous old course today with an aggregate of 287. James Adams, the young Romford professional, formerly of Barassie, finished in second place with 288 and Henry Cotton shared with Marcel Dallemagne, the French champion, third place with an aggregate of 289.

By this success Padgham has crowned a brilliant sequence of wins. Commencing last September by winning the matchplay championship, he has taken four professional events in a row and won a total of over £1400 in prize-money. For the championship this year he was the form horse, both in view of this season's success

and his previous record in the championship. In 1932 he took fourth place, fifth in 1933, third in 1934, second in 1935, and is now first this year.

No greater climax could have been provided. To picture the scene one must visualise the Hoylake course with its surround of fashionable dwelling-houses bathed in brilliant summer sunshine. Immense crowds have come down from Liverpool for the day.

Padgham, Cotton, Adams, and Sarazen are all specially fancied. The passage of these and other leading players is punctuated by sporadic outbursts of applause, which crackle over the course from all its corners like machine-gun fire. In just one of these scenes the champion of the year plays his last stroke. At the time we do not know that he is the champion, but by holing a three-yard putt on the home green for a 3, a score of 71, and an aggregate of 287 Padgham has given every other competitor in the field a tremendous task.

One of these is Adams, the burly, happy-go-lucky Scot, who, just as the mighty cheer heralds Padgham's putt, holes a good 4 on the sixteenth green. At that point he requires level 4s for the last two holes to tie. To the seventeenth, for which the line is to be taken on John Ball's home, he plays a perfectly placed and long drive, goes boldly but too directly for the pin with his approach and with a fall of the ground to the left, the ball swings out, and to the accompaniment of a gasp of dismay from the onlookers drops into a bunker. Rubbing his chin in a gesture of disappointment and annoyance, Adams takes a long time to decide how to play the next difficult shot, but not a soul is impatient. When he pitches out the ball little more than two yards from the hole there is a cheer which must echo across the Mersey.

The Scot, the first for many years to be so near to the

greatest title in the game, again studies the shot carefully, bends on his knees, and swings his putter at imaginary balls until he feels it is working just right. He stands up to the ball, putts, and again there is that horrified gasp as the ball skims round the lip of the hole and stays out.

Adams in this moment of strain and excitement makes the most gallant effort to retrieve the position I have ever seen. To the home green with its vast circle of spectators he pitches firmly and directly on the line, but the ball runs on until it is finally 10 yards at the back of the hole. The Scot takes the line quickly, hits the putt surely and firmly, and stands back in an attitude of expectation. Every person in a position to see is certain that he has got it. The early beginnings of a cheer ripple round among them, only to die away to a groan of sympathy as the ball hits the back of the hole and, for no apparent reason, stays out. It is an extraordinary piece of luck's give and take.

The next man to come up on the heels of Adams is Cotton, who has reached the turn in 36 strokes and requires 36 home to tie, having at the end of the third round held a one-stroke lead over Padgham. All his career, even in his brilliant moments, Cotton has never seemed to be the big golfer for the big occasion. He indicates that once again by his finish, because while he takes both short holes in 3 each he is bunkered and takes 5s at the tenth, twelfth, and fourteenth, thus requiring to do the last four tremendous holes in one under 4s. It was too much to ask of him. He takes his 4 at the fifteenth after being twice in the rough, but the necessary 3 is a long way off, and he finally runs out of the count when at the seventeenth he pulls into the rough and misses his putt for a 4.

Dallemagne has started his last round with the extraordinary figures of 3, 3, 4, 2, so off we rush to watch him, and we find him holing out the thirteenth in 3 to stand four under 4s. The big Frenchman, like Cotton, requires to finish one under 4s to the end to tie – a tremendous task, and one which a 5 at the long sixteenth makes impossible.

Now only Sarazen remains, smiling, debonair and happy as he marches with his gallery to the thirteenth to come again into the chase with a five-foot putt for a 2. The smile vanishes and a look of grim determination takes its place. But his bid does not last, for, like the rest, he has to break 4s, and when he takes three to reach the green at the fifteenth the task has become well nigh impossible.

The leading amateur position was taken by the South African player, AD Locke, who scored 72 and 74 to give him an aggregate of 294, seven behind Padgham.

1936
ALF PADGHAM

Alfred Harry Padgham was born at Caterham, England, in 1906. He had a natural swing, considered by Vardon to be among the best and likened by some to that of Sam Snead. His game around the greens was sound but his putting could be inconsistent. He said he pictured a putt like a drive in miniature and stood upright with his hands away from his body.

Between 1932 and 1938 he was in the top 10 in the Open every year, winning in 1936, and during this period he had a number of other important successes, including the Irish, German and Dutch Opens. He died in 1966.

1937

CARNOUSTIE

The Americans were back in force for a trip that included the Ryder Cup at Southport and Ainsdale the previous week. The USA won 8-4 and there were fears that a run of three British Open wins in a row might come to an end. There was an ominous start when Americans claimed the first five places in qualifying – Horton Smith, Gene Sarazen, Sam Snead, Byron Nelson and Walter Hagen.

Although an American led after the first round their threat did not materialise. Ed Dudley who led with a 70 and Densmore Shute on 73 were the only ones in the first 16. Four players shared second place on 72, W McMinn (Fairhaven), holder Alf Padgham, William Branch and Reg Whitcombe.

After the second round, played in near perfect conditions, the lead moved into British hands when Whitcombe returned a 70 for a two-round total of 142, two ahead of brother Charles, and Dudley. Henry Cotton was still in the hunt with a halfway total of 146, alongside Padgham and Shute who, ominously, had another 73 as he did at St Andrews.

9 JULY

Carnoustie, Friday – The excitement surrounding Henry Cotton's brilliant finish at Carnoustie today to win his second Open Championship and turn back the strongest American challenge faced by British golfers for several years was the natural outcome of a situation which had been gradually working up all day on this course of many terrors.

It had started in a dismal forenoon of continuous rain when Reginald Whitcombe, who had led overnight, held his position with a third round of 74 and an aggregate of 216. Still two strokes behind him was his brother, Charles, also with a round of 74, and while the leading American, Ed Dudley, had fallen back with 78, Cotton had advanced with a score of 73 and stood at 219.

Reginald Whitcombe was first of that group out in the afternoon. The course was a tremendous test by now. Heavy with the rain that still fell, the mood of the field was such that little over par had a chance. It was obvious as soon as Whitcombe's club had slipped in his hand and caused a 6 to go on his card for the seventh hole. His outward 39 made his position dangerous, and more so when he took the same number to come back for an aggregate of 292.

By this time Cotton had overtaken him in having holed the second in 3 with a putt of some eight yards and having passed the long sixth in one under 4s. Perhaps the big, excited crowd, to whom he had to appeal twice for quietness and room to play, had some effect on him, because he was not just catching all his drives, and he had to pull out wooden club seconds. Some of these were beautifully hit, but at the fifteenth he tried to 'bump' a half spoon out of the rough, and he did not quite catch it and was short. For once his chip shot did not yield par, as it did at both the sixteenth and seventeenth holes. At the latter he pushed the shot among spectators and struck one of them. I do not think, however, that his lie was any better or any the worse. On the last green a 10-yard putt for a 3 was valuable, giving him a 71 and a total of 290.

C Lacey made a good effort to catch Cotton with a 72, a very gallant performance on top of his earlier round of 70. Shute had ruined his chances in the third round by taking 5 to the seventeenth and 6 to the eighteenth, when the burn caught his shot. But the man who had the chance was that perennial champion chaser, Charles Whitcombe, the Ryder Cup captain.

Whitcombe required 73 to tie. He was not considered the man to crack, but this time he did, though partly because of the weather. The rain streamed down like steel rods.

Nothing could keep the clubs dry and nothing could keep the water from gathering on the greens.

During the finishing holes of Whitcombe's round the championship committee spent an uneasy half hour. Word had come from the course that several of the holes were unplayable. I saw Percy Alliss and W J Branch standing forlornly on the first green looking at a hole which was submerged. Others sent in an SOS to the committee, who ordered greenkeepers to set to work.

Right heroically did those men work with shovels and brooms – with anything that would clear away the water. And they kept the holes clear, and the championship went on. It was just at the time that Whitcombe, one over with five to play, was making his bid. No matter what the rain was like the crowd had to see this. Out they streamed again in thousands, but by this time Whitcombe was in the toils. His driver, in spite of being carefully guarded and wiped, was wet as he addressed the ball on the fourteenth tee, and it slipped as he swung. He got the ball away, but not far enough to get over the Spectacles and that was a 5.

Another desperate drying process was carried out at the fifteenth, but again, the club slipped, and there was another bad drive. From his lie he put the ball into a bunker, failed to reach the green in three, and his championship aspirations died.

Henry Cotton, on the way to his second Open Championship

1938

ROYAL ST GEORGE'S

The qualifying rounds were played in torrential rain resulting in high scores. It was left to James Braid at the age of 68 to keep the by now not-so-great triumvirate flag flying.

A fascinating day's play in the first round, marked by unpredictable weather varying from flat calm to squally showers, left six players including the Scots, John Fallon and James Adams, leading on 70. Keen competition was underlined by seven players on 71 and a large group of well known faces on 72, including Tommy Haliburton and Jack McLean. Only two strokes separated the first 20 players.

J J Busson added a 69 to his first-round 71 for a two-round total of 140 as did Richard Burton. With W J Cox adding another 70 to his first round of the same score there were three players tied on a halfway total of 140. James Adams and A Gadd were on 141 with Reg Whitcombe on 142.

8 JULY

Sandwich, Friday – The Open Championship was battered by a hurricane into a tremendously thrilling finish here this afternoon, when R A Whitcombe, the youngest of the three famous brothers, won with 295 after a tense duel with the Scot, James Adams, and after Henry Cotton had failed to catch up with probably the greatest round of his career.

To bring up the proper atmosphere of this fierce and furious finish one must imagine all the little windstorms of the past final championship days rolled up into one great big blast, which screamed across the course with a fury that had even the rigid flagpoles in the holes bowing almost to the ground before it. Sand flowed from bunkers like smoke from a fire, the players staggered with uneasy balance and with water streaming from their eyes, and the big marquee, in which is housed golf traders' exhibits, gave up the struggle and fell flat to the ground.

Thousands of pamphlets and posters were flying wildly over the fields.

When play started there were 37 competitors and all had a chance. When the first round today was over heavy toll had been taken. The order of precedence was: R A Whitcombe who had done a magnificent 75 for an aggregate of 217, Richard Burton on 218, James Adams 219, Padgham 221, Perry 222, Busson 223 and Cotton and Rees 224.

Ted Ray, James Braid, and myself discussed the prospects. They both confessed that it was the worst final championship day in their memory for wind, its nearest rival being in 1913, when J H Taylor won at Hoylake. They agreed, too, that the par of the course had risen from the humble 69 of the qualifying rounds to something approaching 80.

To Whitcombe and Adams as partners came the task of setting the pace. Right in a flash, Adams was given his chance, for on the very first green Whitcombe was almost whipped off his feet by a sudden gust and for the second time that day was driven to taking four putts. He must be the only golfer who has taken four putts twice in one day and still won the championship.

Then Whitcombe began to play those long and wonderfully controlled iron shots low and fast along the ground, using the wind with skilful hooking and slicing to get his distance in a way that Adams afterwards confessed to me he could not equal. They gave Whitcombe a row of 4s to the ninth for a 39 out against 38 by the Scot, who was then only one behind.

The homeward half was a thrilling affair. The crowd had grown to the biggest I have ever seen on this course. The strain of even keeping the ball in play could be sensed by the extreme caution of both players, who weighed up every stroke with care. Adams, usually happy-go-lucky, was grim and determined. Whitcombe, no doubt holding in mind that tragic day at Carnoustie last year when he started out three strokes ahead of Henry Cotton on the last round and was overhauled and beaten, was deadly cold. He had himself as well as his shots under control. He showed this by chipping up at the tenth, eleventh, twelfth, and thirteenth holes stone dead for the par 4 each time, while Adams dropped shots at three of these giving Whitcombe a lead of four with only five holes to go. As they cover the most difficult stretch on the course anything, we felt, might happen. And happen it did.

Whitcombe saved himself by chipping dead out of a bunker and taking a 5 out of the fourteenth (520 yards). Then Adams, after his partner had run a long approach dead for a 4 at the fifteenth, chipped right into the hole for a 3. The Scot slapped his tee shot with new hope in his heart right into the middle of the sixteenth green, while Whitcombe was short and bunkered. He got out into another, and the hole was 5 against 3 by Adams, who now was just one stroke behind.

Adams drove well at the seventeenth and thought that another shot with the driver would make it. It was a magnificent shot, but there was a trace of draw on it. Round the ball whipped in its dying moment and dropped into a bunker. It lay in its own plug mark. There was no chance to get on the green, and the hole was a 6, two worse than Whitcombe, who again employed that pawky run up to get the ball so close that he could not miss. The Scot finished with a 4 for 297 to Whitcombe's 5 for 295.

Richard Burton could do 76 to win and we followed him until he took 42 to the ninth. Then we chased after Padgham, who was doing well until he sliced out of bounds at the fourteenth and had an 8. All over the course it was a case of crash after crash.

Then came the sensational news that Henry Cotton, who, requiring a 70, a completely impossible score, was three under 4s after holing the twelfth in 3. But the wind whips up again, there is rain with it, and the thirteenth becomes a 5, the fourteenth a 5, the fifteenth a 5. Now he has 3, 4, 4 to do to tie. But it's too much. He is bunkered to the sixteenth, and it is 4, and the seventeenth, with an impossible 3 to play for, becomes a 6 when he pulls his drive into the rough. That finishes it. He holes his 4 at the last for a truly wonderful, if losing 74.

1938
REG WHITCOMBE

Reginald Whitcombe was the youngest of three golfing brothers, the others being Charles and Ernest, whose father was a gamekeeper at Burnham. They learned their golf on the shores of Somerset and by various accounts Reg was least talented although he made those who said that eat their words with his Open win at the age of 40. His short, uncomplicated swing was ideally suited to the strong winds of the final round at Royal St George's when scores went soaring into the 90s. Charles was rated most talented but his best Open finish was third in 1935.

1939

ST ANDREWS

Percy Alliss scored a record 69 in qualifying on the New Course while the Irish amateur, James Bruen, did the same on the Old and then emulated Alliss on the New for a qualifying total of 138.

The first day of the championship was punctuated by thunderstorms and relentless rain, yet four players shared the lead on 70 – Max Faulkner, J J Busson, Richard Burton and the newly turned professional, South African Bobby Locke. There were five players on 71, including the young Welsh professional, Dai Rees.

After the second round the leader was Burton, one of the game's longest hitters and a member of two Ryder Cup teams. With an aggregate of 142 he was closely followed by M Pose, Argentinian winner of the French Open, on 143, and Scots international, John Fallon, on 144. There were six players on 145, including Locke and the 1935 winner, Alf Perry.

Henry Cotton, followed by a crowd estimated at 5000, appeared set to take the lead when he reached the fourteenth at five under 4s. Crowd control was non-existent and may have contributed to his poor finish. He came in with a 72 and a halfway score of 146, four off the lead.

7 JULY

St Andrews, Friday – Given the chance of scoring 72 in a 'tearing' St Andrews wind this afternoon to keep the Open Championship from America, Richard Burton, professional at Sale, Lancashire, with one of the biggest efforts ever made by a British player, won the title with the truly magnificent score of 71. His final aggregate score of 290 for 72 holes beat that of Johnny Bulla, Chicago, USA, by two strokes.

At four o'clock this afternoon it seemed certain that once again the trophy was destined for an Atlantic crossing in the company of Bulla. Coming right up from the back of the field, the American had pieced together two wonderful wind-beating rounds of 71 and 73, and his aggregate of 292 was ominously good under the conditions.

A dozen players, roughly, had some sort of chance to beat him but the task of each was cruelly difficult. John Fallon, the Scot, had the best chance of all. He had taken the leadership at the end of the third round on the 215 mark, four better than Bulla, but by the time each had reached the turn the margin was gone.

Martin Pose, the Argentine player, put on a brave face in spite of one of the unkindest cuts – he was penalised two shots in the third round for grounding his club on the grass verge beyond the green at the Road Hole, unaware it was a hazard. With four holes to go he had to finish in the par of 4, 4, 5, 4 to lead. Pose's challenge put the "gallery" out after him in full cry, a seething, jostling, excited mob, who, I am afraid, completely put the slim South American off his concentration. He did a solemn procession of 5s with three putts on every green.

Then came the almost incredible news that Burton, who is 6ft and a mighty hitter and who has failed in the past in a high wind, had reached the ninth in 35 strokes. It meant that he could take 37 back and still win. With the fiercest of slices, he sent the ball from the tenth tee right across the ninth fairway into the heather. He made a brilliant recovery and got a 4. Then he played a magnificent tee shot to the High Hole and holed out from five feet for a 2. The next three holes were played safely in par. The fifteenth was a 4 as he pulled his second shot wildly to the left and had to putt from the far edge of the big double green, an approach of nearly 50 yards. A wild cheer of encouragement went up as he put the ball about three yards from the hole, and a wilder cheer of triumph followed when he holed out confidently.

In such trying circumstances, I should say that Burton was as cool as ice at this point, even when from the sixteenth tee he pulled very badly, almost into whins. And even when, after just clearing, he chipped so dreadfully short that the ball escaped the Wig Bunker and disaster by inches. That made it a 5, and now he had to do the par of 5, 4 to win.

He played the seventeenth simply as a 5, placing a long second shot short of the green in the proper place on the right, and chipping it, almost it seemed casually, three yards past the hole. A 4 was all that was needed now. By this time crowds had deserted every other player as Burton drove from the last tee, a tremendous ball that landed 10 yards short of the green. It is safe to estimate that 10,000 people looked on.

Calmly, and with no studying or careful addressing of the ball, he pitched on to the green three yards directly behind the hole, and then walked up and holed the putt for a 3. That was the championship won. Burton could scarcely acknowledge the cheers. He was so exhausted by his winning battle against the wind that he had almost to be carried by two police constables into the R and A clubhouse.

1939
DICK BURTON

Richard Burton had his first taste of golf, if you could call it that, hitting cotton reels with a walking stick on waste ground in Darwen, Lancashire, where he was born in 1907. He became a powerful player and was rated the longest driver in Britain.

His unique claim to fame is that, having won the 1939 Open, he retained the title for a record seven years until 1946 when the competition was resumed after World War Two when he served with the Royal Air Force. In some ways he was unlucky not to have had a chance to improve his record while he was at his peak, but he had his own view on that.

"Unlucky?" he exclaimed. "I came through the war didn't I, and that's a lot more than many did who were at St Andrews that day."

CHAPTER FIVE

WIZARDS FROM OZ – AND AFRICA

THE SOUTHERN HEMISPHERE ARRIVES

The word crisis might be too strong, but if ever the Open went through one this is it. America continued to lead the way in just about every respect and if the Open was to maintain credibility as the world's premier golf tournament then it was essential that the leading Americans played in it. Even with the option of air travel, it still required great commitment for Americans to make the journey and when Sam Snead won the first post-war tournament he found that his prize-money did not even cover expenses. It would be 1955 before serious steps were taken to address this problem.

There was an international field with South African Bobby Locke and Australian Peter Thomson coming solidly to the fore, but the status of the tournament was measured annually by the quality of the American entry. With the exception of 1953 when Ben Hogan made his one and only appearance it was generally thin on the ground. Hogan at least recognised that his career would be incomplete without an Open success. Having achieved that, however, he never returned.

Locke and Thomson tallied four and five wins respectively but did little to alter prevailing views in America about the Open. The simple reason was that neither could win the US Open which was assuming such a high world championship status of its own that the "British" Open was regarded by many as second rate. The concept of the modern four majors was embryonic. In 1953 Hogan also won the US Open and Masters, but he could not win the US PGA because it clashed with the Open.

Such a view nowadays is unthinkable, and with hindsight the American opinion at that time could be regarded as parochial given the kind of back-dated canonisation that goes with the territory of being Open champion. American absence was a loss to the Open but it could be argued as a mutual one.

In the history of the Open, by far the longest of what are now regarded as the four majors, this era can be regarded as a short one. By the late 1950s the status was rising again, much of the credit going to Keith MacKenzie, secretary of the R and A for 35 years until 1983. Prize-money rose from a total of £1000 in 1946 to £3750 in 1955 and to £7000 in 1960. Live television coverage arrived in 1957 when, for climactic assistance, the leaders would go out last for the first time. The rota was extended to include Royal Birkdale and, fleetingly, Royal Portrush.

1946

ST ANDREWS

In the first post Second World War Open, Sam Snead, familiar with lush, tree-lined fairways laced with water hazards, took his first look at the great links and thought it was an old, disused golf course. He quickly learned otherwise.

There was a strong overseas challenge. Norman von Nida of Australia led the qualifiers with a total of 145 while Snead was fourth on 149.

In the first round of the championship proper, Bobby Locke took the lead with a 69, followed by von Nida and Henry Cotton, both on 70, with Snead lying one shot further back. Henry Cotton scored a second 70 to take the lead at the halfway stage on 140 while Snead also shot 70 to lie in second place on 141. Welshman Dai Rees scored a course record, 67 to be one shot back with Locke still in contention on 143.

5 JULY

St Andrews, Friday – After a break of 13 years the Open Championship cup is going back to America – this time in the possession of Sam Snead, a lean, sunburned Virginian of 34 years of age, who hits a golf ball with such a whiplash of powerful wrists and over such distance that he is known in America as "Slamming Sam".

He won the Open this afternoon on the Old Course of St Andrews, however, without the need for any huge hitting. He was so far out in front of the field as he played the last few holes that when he stood on the eighteenth tee somebody said he could play his putter all the way to the green and still win. Snead took only four more strokes in a cool and perfectly played finish. His winning round of 75 – his highest of the three days – left him four ahead of his nearest challengers with an aggregate of 290.

Another American, Johnny Bulla, and A D Locke, the South African, shared second place at 294. The nearest British golfers were another stroke behind – Henry Cotton, D J Rees, and C H Ward bracketed in fourth place with yet another "invader", the little Australian, Norman von Nida.

Snead has only once before played in the Open. He was ninth when Cotton won at Carnoustie in 1937. He had never played at St Andrews until he came here a week ago. He was told that he would not like the Old Course at first, but that it would grow on him. His verdict was: "That's about right. It has a lot of character and it has been different every time I've played it." Snead is flying back to America on Tuesday to resume the round of open tournaments there, in which he is this year's third highest money-winner.

A great last-green crowd of some 8000 people cheered the winner as he holed out, acknowledging a complete golfer with a truly American precision and power. But for them – and for Britain – it was a melancholy finish. Not since 1933, when Densmore Shute won at this same St Andrews, has anyone but a home golfer taken this championship. It was not the American win that was melancholic so much as the way in which British golfers lost. They had promised so brilliantly at the halfway stage.

Rees struck his first tee shot this afternoon so badly that it would have gone out of bounds had it not struck a spectator and rebounded on to the fairway. His next shot went into the Swilcan Burn, like Cotton's, and with three putts he had opened with a heartbreaking 7. He reached the turn in 42 and thereafter, there was only one flash of the lost Rees brilliance. At the Road Hole, the seventeenth, he hit such a magnificent second shot, drawing in along the length of the dangerous, narrow green, that he nearly holed out in 2. He had merely to knock the ball in from a short distance to get an eagle 3

[The Road Hole then was a par-5; it was later changed to a par-4]. It was this that gave him the last-green chance to tie for second place.

Even Snead nearly fell a similar victim to the first hole. His opening drive of the last round finished only about a foot from the fence which marks out-of-bounds, and the hole cost him a 5. His winning round had no need to be a masterpiece by then, for one after another came reports of windblown scores at the turn. Besides Cotton and Rees, Bulla had taken 39 and Ward 40. Only Locke was keeping up his challenge with 36.

Snead himself felt that St Andrews wind, and when he took 40 strokes to the turn the prospect that had seemed set fair for him had widened into one where anything seemed liable to happen. Snead confessed later, too, that he never steadied in the wind till he put in a good putt on the tenth green for a birdie 3. That was the turning point. From there on Snead was cool and masterly again, and the only fault in a fine run home in 35 was a slip with a 5 at the sixteenth – the point at which he heard what he had to do to win.

Locke, on the way in, lost the accuracy of level 4s in the wind, and his challenge faded in missed short putts that made him throw his head back in despair. Bulla, similarly afflicted, and taking a series of practice putts in vain on many greens after holing out, never got his head up throughout the round. On the last green, like Cotton, he missed one finally from two feet.

In the minor distinctions of the last day the Scottish Professional champion, William Anderson, of Murcar, Aberdeen, was leading home Scot, sharing fourteenth place, and did the best outward half of the windy last round with 35 strokes of finely controlled golf.

The first amateur was an Englishman – R K Bell, the Lancashire champion. Andrew Dowie, of St Andrews, who led the amateurs until this afternoon, fell back with a last round of 83.

1946
SAM SNEAD

"Slammin' Sam" seems a misnomer, conjuring up as it does the image of a big strong golfer knocking the ball 300 yards using brute strength and little more, when the truth was quite the opposite. When Sam Snead drove a ball 300 yards he did so with one of the most elegant and natural golf swings ever seen and he revived British interest in American golf with the era of Jones, Hagen and Sarazen fast fading into history. Snead was an athlete. He was extremely supple and even in his sixties he could perform his famous trick of kicking the top of a doorway.

Samuel Jackson Snead was born in Ashwood, near Hot Springs, Virginia, in 1912. He was the youngest of five children and was raised in the backwoods of Virginia where he is said to have started hitting a golf ball with sticks which he had carved roughly to the shape of a golf club. He was encouraged and helped by an older brother,

obtained some old clubs and began to develop the swing which would win him more than 80 official US tournaments and around double that number worldwide. He became a professional in 1934 and in his first year on the PGA Tour (1937) he won five times and finished runner-up in the US Open, the only major he failed to win. He was runner-up four times. He won the US PGA Championship three times, the Masters three times and the Open once, in 1946, the only year he entered while at his peak. He was not a fan of playing in Britain nor, for that matter, anywhere outside America. He played in seven Ryder Cup matches, twice as captain, and in 1969 was non-playing captain.

Snead was instrumental in getting the US Seniors Tour off the ground and won the US PGA Seniors title six times. His near perfect swing never left him but his putting eventually gave him serious problems which he tried to solve in odd ways including adopting the croquet style which was later outlawed.

1947

HOYLAKE

Playing in warm sunshine in the second qualifying round, the Australian, Norman von Nida, scored a course record 69 to lead the qualifiers on 139 with Arthur Lees two shots back and Johnny Bulla on 142. American Frank Stranahan was leading amateur in a field of 100 qualifiers.

After the first round, the joint leaders were Henry Cotton and the Scot, L B Ayton, on 69 equalling the record. Stranahan was third on 71 with the Irishman, Fred Daly, and three others, including the Belgian, Flory van Donck, sharing fourth place two shots further back.

A total of 40 players qualified for the final day's play with Daly in the lead on 143 after a 70. Cotton, who had an uncharacteristic second-round 78, and S L King shared second place on 147 with Richard Burton one shot further back. The overseas challenge was represented by van Donck and von Nida on 149 and 150 respectively.

4 JULY

Hoylake, Friday – F Daly, of Belfast, was hailed here tonight as the new Open champion. The first Irishman ever to win Britain's supreme golfing event, he had an aggregate of 293 for 72 holes, and led an international field by a single stroke. The tension at the close can seldom have been equalled in this event, Daly, aged 35, achieving his success by holing a putt of 10 yards on the last green almost nonchalantly. F Stranahan, the US amateur, and R W Horne, of Hendon, were joint runners-up.

As the best of the overseas challengers to finish and the only amateur in the field, Stranahan late in the day received a great ovation all to himself. While both Daly and Horne played in ideal calm conditions, Stranahan had to fight nearly all the way over the windswept links. Desperately carrying on his late struggle against the kind of wind which makes Hoylake one of the most feared courses in the world, Stranahan kept the crowd on tenterhooks right to the finish. He had a 2 to do at the 408-yard last hole – impossible, everyone knew – but he nearly brought it off by placing his iron shot only nine inches from the flag.

At the end of the third round only five strokes covered the first 19 players. Daly, who started the day four shots to the good, had lost them all with a 78 and shared the leadership with three others – T H Cotton, A Lees, and the Australian von Nida.

Even the morning round had its piquant flavour of uncertainties. Rees, for instance, badly needed a 4 at the last hole, and took a 5 when he missed from two feet, his reaction being to throw the ball disgustedly into the nearest bunker. Padgham, wanting two 4s, ran up two 5s instead.

Now came the last round. The day was still grey and windless when the American, Bulla, walked on the first tee as the opening performer. Scoring under conditions like these was bound to be low, despite the stress of the critical round, and low it was. Bulla did a 71 for an aggregate of 297, but he was partnered by the Australian-born W Shankland, who played magnificently, and finished finally in fourth place with a 70 for 295. With 13 holes behind him, Shankland was six under 4s, but he came to grief by doing the fearsome Hoylake finish in 5, 6, 5, 3, 5. Those last five holes have featured in every Hoylake Open and fate seems to have ordained that the man who wins must do them in not more than 21. Like Hagen in 1924, Jones in 1930, and Padgham in 1936, Daly completed them in exactly 21.

Daly made only one real mistake in going out in 38 when at the eighth he pushed out a brassie shot and took a 6. Then, putting well, he started back 3, 3, 4, 3. With two great wooden shots he had a 4 at the fourteenth. Two other 4s followed, and then his morale received a setback when, at the seventeenth, he was in the rough and then putted three times for a 6. All now depended on his steadiness at the home hole, and rising nobly to the occasion, he holed his 10-yard putt, and was carried shoulder-high from the green.

Just in front of Daly was Horne, the joint runner-up, who was going down the sixteenth fairway three under 4s, and, it seemed, all set for victory. But he finished 5, 5, 4, being in two bunkers at the seventeenth, and had a 71.

Interest switched to Cotton. At this stage he had completed the first half in 36, and the wind was rising. He had a 6 at the tenth, but he could still do a 72 to tie with Daly. A tussle with the wind, now blowing fiercely, saw him in the rough all the way at the seventeenth, where he had a 6 which put paid to his chances.

Rees appeared to be out of the question. Those who remember his 7 at the first hole at St Andrews last year will be less surprised at the 8 he took at the first hole this afternoon, the inevitable penalty for being twice out of bounds. As for von Nida, whose last round of 76 kept him out, his crowning mistake was to take four shots from the edge of the fourteenth green – he required three putts from a range of three yards. Though dressed in Montgomery fashion, with a black military beret and a polo-necked cardigan, he had no command over his putter.

There remained only Stranahan, fighting the wind grimly, his hair tousled, his lower lip protruding in determination, and he wanted a 4 and 3 to tie for the first place. The American was beautifully home in 2 at the seventeenth, but he took three putts for a 5. That left him with a 2 as his only hope at the last hole, and, to his credit, he nearly did it.

By popular choice there could not be a better champion than Daly. His cheerful way has warmed all hearts to him here tonight, and everyone liked the way he received the trophy saying: "This cup is going to have a change of air, and the change will do it good."

1947
FRED DALY

Born at Portrush, Northern Ireland, in 1911, Fred Daly was a caddie at the age of nine at Royal Portrush where he learned the game. By the age of 17 he was the professional at Mahee Golf Club. He was a genial character who would whistle to himself as he walked the fairways always with a spring in his step. He reached his prime at 30, winning often in his native Ireland but, like so many others, lost the opportunity to capitalise on his talent due to the intervention of the Second World War. After the war he had a successful period into his early forties, starting with his Open victory at Hoylake in 1947. Over the next five Opens he was runner-up once and third twice. He played in four consecutive Ryder Cup matches from 1947 to 1953 winning three matches and halving one in a total of eight outings – a good record at the time for Great Britain.

On the green he was noted for making as many as a dozen ghost strokes over the top of his ball before finally putting.

Fred Daly – 1947 Open winner

1948

MUIRFIELD

Henry Cotton was back in form, leading the qualifiers with a two-round total of 138. Then in the championship proper he opened with a 71 and followed up with a course record, 66 for a halfway total of 137 and a lead of four strokes. C H Ward of Little Aston and S L King (Knole Park) were on 141 with the nearest overseas challenge coming from the Belgian, Flory van Donck, on 142.

2 JULY

Eleven years after his first success Henry Cotton yesterday won the Open Championship at Muirfield with an aggregate for 72 holes of 284 – one more than Alf Perry's winning total over the same course in 1935. Cotton put himself in a winning position with his rounds of 71 and 66 on Wednesday and Thursday and although he required 10 strokes more for the two rounds yesterday none of his challengers could make up the leeway and he won by five strokes. Fred Daly made a grand effort to hold his title and did well indeed to finish second.

Cotton, at 41, played as well this week as he has ever done. He told me last night that he thought his American trip this year had tightened up his game and had more or less given him a new lease of life. Although he gave his challengers a chance yesterday with his third-round 75 he still held a lead of two strokes and his final round of 72 on a cold and stormy afternoon practically assured him of his third championship three hours before the end of the day's golf. Cotton holed out on the last green minutes after Ward, one of the most likely players to catch him, but who shot a 74 to finish six behind, had driven from

the first tee. So there was little drama for the huge crowds.

At the end of the third round, Cotton led at 212, followed by Padgham (214), King, Vicenzo, Lees, and van Donck (215), and Warren, Daly and Ward (216). Ward left himself in the running by holing his tee shot at the thirteenth, his ball hitting the pin about nine inches from the ground on its first bounce and dropping into the hole. Hitting the ball vast distances from the tee and putting better than he usually does, Cotton had an unruffled afternoon round, which meant that only an exceptional effort by one of the challengers could catch him. Although he frequently left himself quite a bit to do because of erratic approach putts, he holed out confidently, and only at the last hole did he show the slightest sign of strain. There he was bunkered at the side of the green and made a really poor recovery effort failing to get clear with a shot which looked suspiciously like a socket. His second attempt was much more like the thing and he got down from four feet for a 5.

That left Padgham to do a 70 to tie, and he made his task almost impossible by taking 14 shots for the first three holes. Lees and Vicenzo could not get the necessary figures. King was only two strokes behind Cotton with nine holes to play, but a 6 at the tenth followed by a 5 put him out of the hunt. Those failures allowed Daly, with a steady round of 73, to creep into second place.

The American Army officer, Captain E C Kingsley, and Mr Mario Gonzalez, from Brazil, shared the position of leading amateur on 293.

1949

ROYAL ST GEORGE'S

Irishman Harry Bradshaw led the qualifiers on 139, closely followed by Bobby Locke and the American, Johnny Bulla, twice an Open runner-up and runner-up in this year's Masters.

In the first round, James Adams, the Wentworth-based Scot, took the lead with a 67. Bradshaw and Roberto de Vicenzo were on 68 with seven others on 69, including Locke, who had missed five putts of five feet or less. After the second round with the leaders bunched closely together, one of the smallest fields of just 31 played the final two rounds.

S L King (Knole Park) led on 140, two ahead of Max Faulkner and W Shankland and three ahead of de Vicenzo and Richard Burton. Frank Stranahan and Bulla were on 144, along with five others, with Locke on 145.

8 JULY

The elegant platform erected outside the Royal St George's clubhouse at Sandwich for the presentation of the Open Championship trophy cannot be utilised until tonight for yesterday A D Locke and Harry Bradshaw tied at 283, a score which equalled the championship lowest aggregate. There was not a stroke between them all day. Each had 68 in the morning and shared leading place with Max Faulkner, and each scored 70 in his second round while Faulkner took 74.

The replay over 36 holes today will present an interesting contrast to personality as well as in golfing methods. Locke, sphinx-like always, is the stylist, whereas Bradshaw's golf is in keeping with his jovial character – almost slap-dash compared with the laborious method of most present-day professionals. Locke, who is 31, four year's Bradshaw's junior, will doubtless remain favourite, but the Irishman is not one to be overawed.

Everything contributed to make yesterday one of the most pleasant and most exciting last days in the history of the championship. After a dull morning the sun came through around midday, and the crowds rolled up in the afternoon in even greater numbers than had been expected.

Bradshaw, in the second couple off, played as if he was enjoying a Saturday afternoon game on the course at Kilcroney where he is professional. He did not waste time walking 50 yards forward to study the lie of the land nor did he crawl about the green in the fashionable manner before putting. He told me afterwards that he had decided to "go for everything", and he did so to such good purpose that he went to the turn in 33 perfect strokes – six 4s and the regulation 3 at each short hole. He had the misfortune to see three successive putts on the tenth, eleventh and twelfth greens lie on the rim of the hole. He took those bad "breaks" philosophically and went on playing faultlessly until the fourteenth. There, with the green within reach of a No.2 or No.3 iron, he hit his second shot right on the head and breathed a sigh of relief when the ball bounced over Suez Canal 100 yards away. However, a 5 there was one too many and he gave himself no chance of getting the stroke back by skying his drive to the long fifteenth. His 5, 3, 4, 4 was the strict par finish and the round of 70 for an aggregate of 283 meant that his challengers had plenty to do.

Locke, four holes behind, gained a stroke by going to the turn in 32. He carried with him into the second round the confidence given by seven pitch-and-putt holes in the morning. Right away he holed out from 15 yards at the second and those missable putts of two yards went down at the fifth and eighth. The stroke was gained from Bradshaw when a three-yarder dropped in at the ninth for his fifth 3 to that point. It was quickly lost, for he took three putts on the tenth green, and with a repetition of

Bradshaw's 5 at the fourteenth and fifteenth he needed the par 3, 4, 4 finish to tie.

By this time he knew what he had to do, and there was tension when he left his approach putt two yards short of the sixteenth pin. He missed the second and with it apparently his chance of the title. Still without the slightest expression on his face he placed his second shot eight feet from the seventeenth hole and stroked in the putt. He was just short of the eighteenth green in two, but he pitched to the hole-side and gave himself another chance of achieving his greatest ambition.

"I am going to need this right hand tomorrow," he remarked, as he refused to shake hands with the many spectators who wished to congratulate him.

Only Faulkner, King and Ward were in the reckoning then, and they more or less threw their chances away by taking 36, 37, and 36 respectively for the comparatively easy outward half. With a fine last round of 69, however, de Vicenzo headed these three and took third place again.

PLAY OFF

The rounds of 67 and 68 with which A D Locke gained a clean-cut victory in the play off for the Open Championship on Saturday must rank among the greatest. I can recall no parallel in this country, and it is doubtful if even in low-scoring America anyone has ever played so brilliantly with so much at stake.

Harry Bradshaw kept pegging away, but his efforts to make an impression on the South African were about as successful as trying to move a mountain. It was a case of a skilled workman opposed to a master craftsman and though Bradshaw, with rounds of 74 and 73, lost by a dozen strokes, he was by no means disgraced.

It was disappointing that only a few hundred spectators were present to enjoy a golfing feast. Locke was a master of the situation from the start. The precision of his play never faltered in a first round of 67, a score which included 17 par figures and one birdie at the famous Suez Canal hole (the fourteenth). The hole had cost him a 7 last Wednesday, but on Saturday after Bradshaw had pulled his second into a bunker Locke placed a No.4-iron shot 18 inches from the pin.

That gave him a three-stroke margin, and he increased his lead to six after errors by Bradshaw. Another putting lapse at the seventeenth put Bradshaw seven behind on the first round. Locke gathered identical figures for the first 13 holes of his second round. Bradshaw by starting 6, 5 and taking a 5 at the fifth had fallen 11 strokes behind, but he got his first taste of blood by holing a three-yard putt for a 3 at the ninth. A pitch close to the hole at the eleventh gave him his second and last success. The only break in the machine-like precision of Locke's golf came at the fifteenth, but the 5 there was written off when he holed his longest putt of the day for a 3 at the seventeenth.

The champion will be at Troon next year to defend his title. He is 31 and since the war has played the American circuit with a greater measure of success than any other "foreigner". His Open victory is the realisation of a life's ambition.

1949, 1950, 1952, 1957
BOBBY LOCKE

Arthur D'Arcy Locke was born in Germiston, South Africa, in 1917 but was never known as anything other than Bobby in the golfing world. It is believed he called himself Bobby in deference to his hero, Bobby Jones.

At the age of 14 he became the South Africa boys champion. At 16 his handicap was down to scratch and two years later in 1935 he won both the South African Amateur Championship and the South African Open. In 1937 he repeated this remarkable feat and also finished top amateur in the Open, won by Henry Cotton. He turned professional in 1938.

He played with what appeared to be a vicious hook but managing almost invariably to land his ball on the spot on the fairway he had chosen. Short irons also moved from right to left and some say he even hit his putts with a draw. Putting was his strongest suit and he possessed an uncanny ability to have the ball drop into the hole just as it ran out of steam, seldom long or short.

He was one of the first truly international golf stars, winning regularly in South Africa, America and Europe. On his first tilt at the US Tour in 1947 he won four events and finished second on the money list. He won the South African Open nine times, the Open four times and won Opens in Canada, New Zealand, Ireland, France and Germany. A serious car crash in 1959 effectively put an end to his golfing career.

1950

TROON

The qualifying rounds started with a bang as Flory van Donck broke the course record with a 65 while Bobby Locke did the same at Lochgreen with a 68. Johnny Bulla from America led the qualifiers on 140.

After the first round of the championship Arthur Lees led with a 68, one shot ahead of Ernest Whitcombe and, more ominously, holder Locke. Only 35 competitors qualified for the final two rounds with Dai Rees leading on 139 and Locke two strokes behind.

7 JULY

With a record aggregate of 279, four strokes better than the previous best, A D Locke (South Africa) retained the Open Championship yesterday at Troon – an achievement equalled in modern times only by Bobby Jones and Walter Hagen. On one of the greatest days of golf ever seen in Britain Locke played with monumental calm and unvarying precision. He amply bore out the testimony of every worthwhile critic that he was the best golfer in the field.

Since the championship started it has been more or less a question of who was to be second. Locke got his bad round over on Thursday – no more than 72 – and everyone who knew his finishing power realised that he was halfway to his second title. While others faltered during the dangerous third round, Locke handed in a 70 which made him joint leader, and his 68 in the afternoon when the strain was on was too good for those who were within the firing line.

Only de Vicenzo threatened to make Locke's task difficult and it would have been a travesty had he won. I doubt very much if anyone who has ever been within sight of winning a championship has played such erratic golf and escaped punishment so consistently. The Argentinian set

a hot pace, for his aggregate of 281 was two strokes better than the record and it meant that Locke had to do 69 to win. The champion reached the turn in 33, but with the wind against him – from the north-west for the first time this week – the inward half was a severe test. He dropped a stroke at the twelfth, but got it back a couple of holes later and the par finish gave him a two-stroke advantage. During the day 70 was broken 11 times and another championship record was created in that every one of the 35 players had aggregates under 300.

De Vicenzo set the standard – of scoring, not of play. He used an iron club from the tee more often than not, but even that expedient did not keep him out of the rough. In an outward half of 33 he was off the fairway from five tees, but his deftness in recovery and a wonderful touch on the greens saved him. He got a 3 at the eighth despite a penalty. There he pulled his tee shot into a bunker and was lying so badly up against the far bank that after consultation with his partner, Max Faulkner, he decided to deem the ball unplayable. It may be that he regarded the spirit of the rules rather cavalierly, but he went back to the tee and almost holed his second shot. (The penalty for an unplayable lie then was distance only – today he would also have incurred an extra stroke). He had, however, to suffer sometime for his waywardness and it was that wild tee shot – again with an iron – that cost him a 6 at the twelfth and a bad second shot which cost him a 6 at the next.

Faulkner, who had started the round one stroke behind had 4, 3 for these holes and when he had a 4 to de Vicenzo's 5 at the fifteenth, the pair were level pegging. But the Argentinian, showing no signs of uncertain Latin temperament, hit two long wooden shots to the side of the sixteenth green and followed up the 4 there with an eight-yard putt for a 2 at the seventeenth. Faulkner lost two strokes there and his 283 was good enough for only equal fifth.

Five couples behind, Locke was carrying on sedately, hitting every shot down the middle and holing the occasional putt. He holed from three yards at the second and two yards at the long sixth to beat par each time and, out in 33, was nicely placed to win. He took three putts for the only time in the day on the twelfth green and left himself the strict par finish to win. When he put down a two-and-a-half-yard putt for a 2 at the fourteenth the championship was in his pocket.

The only player with a chance to catch him then was Rees and the little Welshman gave himself the chance with an outward half of 33. Like Locke, he dropped a stroke at the twelfth and from that point found the strain too great. A magnificent last round of 66 enabled F R Stranahan, the Amateur champion, to wipe out the memory of his original 77, and to finish first amateur and first American. Locke, a very proud man to have joined Jones and Hagen in the gallery of immortals, gave a piece of advice to which all golfers should pay heed. "Some temper has been shown here this week," he said before receiving the trophy, "but everybody got an object lesson yesterday when I thought I had put myself out of the tournament by taking 6 at a par-3 hole (the fifth). I went on hitting the ball and forgot it. Temper never got anyone anywhere."

South African Bobby Locke at St Andrews

1951

ROYAL PORTRUSH

This eightieth Open Championship coincided with the centenary celebrations of Prestwick Golf Club, the birthplace of the Open. For the second year in a row course records were set on both courses in the first qualifying round. Arthur Lees, a Ryder Cup player, scored 69 at the championship course of Portrush while Norman von Nida and Tom Haliburton each scored 68s at Portstewart.

In the first round of the championship, being played in Ireland for the first time and, to date the only time, the leaders were James Adams of Wentworth and von Nida on 68, two ahead of Dai Rees and the Australian, Peter Thomson, followed by Bobby Locke and Max Faulkner on 71, and Flory van Donck on 72.

In the second round most of the leaders frittered away strokes and Max Faulkner with a steady 70 for a halfway total of 141 led N Sutton of Leigh by two shots with the ever-present Locke on 145 and still regarded by many as most likely to take the title.

6 JULY

For once conquering his uncertain temperament, M Faulkner at Portrush yesterday won the Open Championship by two strokes from the Argentinian, A Cerda, with the rest of the field trailing behind. The win was as deserved as it was unexpected, and but for a great effort by Cerda, Faulkner would have won by a wide margin.

Rounds of 70 and 74 gave him an aggregate of 285, which meant that Cerda, the only man by then with a semblance of a chance, needed a 68 to tie. The Argentinian made an exciting finish possible by going to the turn in 34, and after dropping a stroke at the tenth, holing putts for birdies at the twelfth and Calamity, the short fourteenth. But the effort of playing the testing last three holes in 4s was too much for him. He hooked his drive against the boundary fence at the sixteenth, scrambled his way to the green in 4, and holed out in a 6 which allowed Faulkner to relax in the clubhouse.

By his victory, Faulkner, whose career has been as varied as his taste in dress, has realised the second of two ambitions. When he was 12 he decided that he wanted to play for Britain in the Ryder Cup and win the Open Championship. Now he says he does not care if he never hits another ball – he will be happy to go fishing and work on his father's farm in Surrey. Farming is Faulkner's job nowadays for, since leaving T H Cotton at Royal Mid-Surrey, he has been unattached. He was playing assistant with Cotton after having been professional at a nine-hole course at Selsey, owned for a period by his father. Max will be 35 this month.

Only Faulkner of the overnight leaders played well yesterday, when scoring generally was very ordinary on a perfect golfing day. His third round of 70 gave him an aggregate of 211 and a six-stroke lead over N Sutton and Cerda, with the holder, A D Locke, J Panton, F J Daly and H Weetman well behind at 219.

Not since 1934 when Cotton led by nine with two rounds to play had the championship developed into such a one-horse race at that stage, but there was always the possibility that the incalculable Faulkner might once again have a breakdown in concentration that has frequently prevented the realisation of his ambition.

Faulkner has gone to all sorts of lengths to win the Open – dieting and working out a plan whereby he might reach the peak of physical condition at the right time – but his best effort was to tie for fourth place at Troon last year. This year, without any special preparations, he won handsomely by mastery over nerves rather than clubs. He illustrated his new-found composure in the final round by holing from over a yard at the first, third and fourth – putts that a year ago one could confidently have gambled on his missing.

His 37 to the turn more or less ended the contest, for there was not the slightest sign of the strain that he must have been feeling. He then played from the turn to the fourteenth in perfect par. Who can blame him for dropping two strokes at the difficult last four holes? He had the courage left to gain one from par with a magnificent pitch to the seventeenth green and although he finished with a 5, his aggregate of 285 left only Cerda with a chance.

After his heartbreaking 6, the Argentinian finished in 70 and headed C H Ward, whose last-round 68 was the day's best return, by three strokes.

The decisive defeat of Locke, who shared sixth place, has raised the status of the championship. Had he won for the third successive year, the American reaction would undoubtedly have been that the Open is not worth entering. Now they will have to think again.

One must spare a thought for N G von Nida, who has been a welcome though sometimes aggressive competitor here regularly since the war. He tore up his card in the final round yesterday after taking 43 to the turn and then announced that he would not be coming back. "They've finally convinced me that I'm finished," he commented rather sadly.

1951
MAX FAULKNER

Max Faulkner was born in 1916, the son of Gustavus "Gus" Faulkner, the professional at Pennard in South Wales. The young Faulkner quickly came to the fore after the Second World War making effective use of a strong physique and a natural swing with a wide arc.

Not only was he a very talented player but he was also one of the game's flamboyant characters turning up at tournaments in colourful eye-catching outfits. Even from a distance, you could not miss him. On the final round of his Open success Max was wearing canary yellow plus-twos, matching socks and shoes and a blue-and-white striped shirt. Sometimes he had strange clubs as well. He was forever experimenting with new putters, very often making them himself.

He tempted providence in 1951 by signing a golf ball, on request and against his own better judgment, "Max Faulkner, 1951 Open champion" before he set out on his final round. The act was witnessed by Henry Longhurst who wrote that he immediately distanced himself from Faulkner lest fate deal him retribution by association. Faulkner had nightmares about doing this for years afterwards. The incident has been exaggerated over the years and stories that he cavalierly signed autographs in that manner before the final round are not true.

As well as the Open, he won the PGA Matchplay and Dunlop Masters which together with the Open is a unique trio. He won the Spanish Open three times, played in five Ryder Cup teams and was on the winning side at Lindrick in 1957. Faulkner raised a great deal of money for charity and gave a series of exhibition matches in Britain in aid of Cancer Research.

1952

ROYAL LYTHAM AND ST ANNE'S

Qualifying rounds again produced excellent scoring. Harry Weetman returned a record 68 at Royal Lytham while Harry Bradshaw set a record at Fairhaven with a 65. Gene Sarazen, aged 50, came home in 31 for a 69 and John Panton equalled Weetman's 68 to lead the qualifiers on 134.

In the first round proper Fred Daly broke the record again to lead on 67, one shot ahead of Peter Thomson and two ahead of Bobby Locke. After two rounds Fred Daly had increased his lead to four with a 69 for 136, with Bobby Locke on 140 and Peter Thomson on 141.

11 JULY

St Anne's, Friday – British golf suffered a setback today when A D Locke (South Africa) won the Open Championship for the third time in four years with an aggregate of 287. Locke, who was so unsuccessful in competition against the Americans this year that he retired after qualifying amongst the tail-enders in their Open, started the day four strokes behind F J Daly (Belfast), the winner in 1947. However, in a high wind and rain he illustrated beyond dispute that he has the better of our professionals, in control as well as in temperament.

Daly, whose overnight lead had placed him in an apparently strong position, was pipped at the post for second place by a wonderful last round of 70 by P W Thomson (Australia), who needed to play the last three holes in 10 strokes to tie with Locke – and just failed.

It is unfortunate, but true, that Locke's victory will tend to confirm the modern American belief that it is no longer worth crossing the Atlantic to compete in what we can have less justification than ever now for claiming to be the premier golf event in the world.

Having made my views clear on that point, it is only fair to concede that Locke played golf of very high quality in most testing conditions. Although he would be the last to suggest it, Locke may have suffered additional strain from the knowledge that a complaint had been made by a fellow competitor about his deliberate play. I refuse to call it slow play when uncontrolled spectators were responsible for at least 90% of the time-wasting in a morning round taking three-and-a-half hours.

Before he started his second round of the day he was warned by the championship committee that the complaint had been made. At all events, Locke's movements on the green lacked their usual deliberation and his putting some of its inevitability.

It must have been annoying to be held up for practically every stroke in the uncomfortable conditions in the morning, but Daly, the player with the best chance of all, had no complaints on that score. Indeed, it was a spell of uncertainty after the turn, when he dropped four strokes to par in three holes, that prevented his maintaining the four-stroke advantage with which he started the day. With that millstone round his neck he took 42 strokes for the inward half and his 77 gave him a 54-hole aggregate of 213.

Locke, too, had his adventures, but his pre-eminence in the art of holing out enabled him to compensate for the few long-game errors inevitable in the conditions, and advanced to within one stroke of the Irishman with a 74. After one hole of the final round he had made up the leeway, by the third he was ahead and, although he dropped a stroke at each of the last two holes, his victory was not seriously threatened.

It was in the morning principally that the home players lost their chance. John Panton persistently dropped strokes by using his putter instead of a pitching club from just off the green and a 5, 5, 6 run from the fifteenth to the seventeenth put him out of the hunt. H Bradshaw took 40 for the inward half, and others confirmed a long-standing apprehension about their ability to last the pace.

It was left to F Bullock, the Glasgow club's professional, to illustrate that good scoring was not impossible. His praiseworthy 72 might have been two strokes better but for the fact that he was bunkered at the last two holes, dropping a stroke each time. Bullock had been too far behind, however, and at lunchtime the championship seemed to have developed into a straight fight between Locke and Daly, with Thomson five strokes behind, the leader.

Locke, the first off, quickly got into his stride with a five-yard putt for a birdie 3 at the third, and his progress to the turn in 34 was ominously competent. When, after a series of par figures, he was one under 4s on the seventeenth tee one felt that one could congratulate him then. Even the great can falter, however, and Locke missed a two-foot putt on the seventeenth green and then failed to hole out in two from just off the last green. Nevertheless, he had set a difficult target – one which I was convinced Daly could not hit after playing the first six holes. He had been in four bunkers and was two over 4s by that time, but he played the next seven holes in 4, 4, 3, 4, 5, 3, 4, and was in the chase again. Alas, he was bunkered once more at the fourteenth and dissipated his chance by hooking into thick rough at the next and running up a 6.

It seemed to be all over bar the shouting then until word reached the clubhouse that a 3, 4, 3 finish by Thomson would mean a play-off. It was too much for him, but he had the satisfaction of holing a six-yard putt for a 3 on the last green to edge out Daly.

J W Jones, an English internationalist, was leading amateur with 302, a score that might have been several strokes better had he been shown even the merest courtesy by the large crowd following him and Locke and wishing only to see the latter.

1953

CARNOUSTIE

The qualifying rounds produced records on both courses. Bobby Locke had a 65 on Burnside and John Panton a 69 on the Championship course. Ben Hogan, twice winner of the US Masters and three times winner of the US Open, playing this year in the Open for the first time, scored 32 to the turn on the Burnside course and carded a 70. Locke led the qualifiers with a total of 136 while Hogan, with a 75 on the Championship course, finished nine strokes further back on 145.

The first round proper was played in high winds and occasional rain and hail and Frank Stranahan's 70 led from Eric Brown on 71 with Hogan tied for seventh place alongside Fred Daly, both with solid 73s. After two rounds the lead was held jointly by Eric Brown and Dai Rees with totals of 142, one ahead of Roberto de Vicenzo and two ahead of Thomson, Stranahan and Hogan.

10 JULY

Carnoustie, Friday – Timing is all important in golf. All good golfers have it in the execution of their strokes, but only the great can time their supreme effort with the same perfection. Ben Hogan, the greatest golfer who has played in this country since Bobby Jones himself, did just that here today when with final rounds of 70 and 68, he won the Open Championship at the first attempt. His 72-hole aggregate of 282 placed him four strokes ahead of an international quartet – D J Rees, F R Stranahan, P W Thomson and A Cerda. The holder, A D Locke, was eighth at 291.

Hogan has more than lived up to his American reputations as "Mr Golf" and "Little Ice Water", and he won the admiration and praise of the most educated golf audience in the world by his deportment and play. While Scottish crowds were just as hopeful as anyone of hailing a British victory, they felt that Hogan's success was thoroughly deserved and rounded off a distinguished career.

No film scenario writer could have thought out a more dramatic story than that unfolding this day. With Rees and a Scot, E C Brown, narrowly leading a host of international celebrities there was promise of great doings. Promise was amply fulfilled as most of the leaders faltered only slightly, but enough for Hogan to step in despite a personal example of the toughness of the Carnoustie finish. Needing two 4s for a record 68 and a two-stroke lead with one round to play he cut his second to the seventeenth, recovered indifferently, and then took three putts.

A 70 put him on the 214 mark with R de Vicenzo, who played superbly for 71 but had no luck on the greens. A stroke behind came Rees, Thomson and A Cerda, who created a record of 69 and came back into the reckoning. Brown, with a tragic inward half of 40, dropped back to 217 along with Stranahan, and Locke became virtually "the former champion" by falling five strokes down with an indifferent 74.

We felt rightly that the champion would come from the first five and the draw gave the large but well dispersed and controlled galleries a wonderful opportunity to watch progress. Rees followed Vicenzo and Cerda followed Hogan, and one could take in either pair at one time. Morning drizzle gave way to sunshine and a light breeze and the stage was set for the drama.

Stranahan was the pace-setter, taming for the second time the fierce Carnoustie finish. Out in 37 he seemed unlikely to make a challenge until over the last six holes his putter engineered wonders. He holed from three yards at the fifteenth and 10 yards at the eighteenth, and at each of the others got down with a pitch and putt. That spell brought an inward half of 32 and enabled him to equal Cerda's record of 69 and post a total of 286.

Behind him, Vicenzo threw away his chance with a run of 5, 5, 3, 5 from the long sixth, and Rees after opening with birdies at the first and fourth threatened to crack when a badly cut drive cost him a 6 at the sixth. The perky little Welshman has a big golfing heart, however, and he sensed that he might yet come back when he holed a 10-foot putt for a 2 at the eighth. Out in 35 he dropped a stroke at the tenth, but recovered it immediately with an eight-yarder for a 3. He equalled par for three holes more, then he lost the chance of leading Stranahan by missing holeable putts at the fifteenth and sixteenth.

That put two on the 286 mark and only Thomson, Hogan, and Cerda could reach or surpass that target. Thomson with par for every hole but the sixteenth where he missed the green from the tee, made a triple tie. Neither Cerda, who failed to live up to the promise of a 4, 3, 4, 4 start, nor Rees could do any better.

The championship to all intents and purposes was Hogan's and how majestically he finished. A steady start was electrified when he ran down a chip from off the fifth green and from that point, as if he knew he was sure of victory, he played more powerfully and purposefully than at any other time.

In the morning he had occasionally been behind his Scottish partner, Hector Thomson, from the tee but not now. He cracked two mighty shots to within 10 yards of the green at the 567-yard sixth and ran up to his 'dead' distance of a yard. Par for the next three holes took him to the turn in 34 and he set his seal on the championship by following a delicate run-up to the twelfth with a five-yard putt for a 2 at the thirteenth.

He did falter momentarily by being short with his second and then with his pitch to the fourteenth, but made no repetition of his morning seventeenth-hole lapse and smiled as the crowd, massed down both sides of the eighteenth fairway, roared their approval of his victory. Few players can have earned the distinction of rounding off an Open win with a record.

A final word: the Royal and Ancient owe Hogan a hearty vote of thanks. His presence has attracted the largest crowds that one has seen at a championship. The title may have gone to America again but R and A finances have benefited sufficiently to sugar the pill.

At the presentation ceremony Hogan closed his speech of thanks with the comment: "I don't know when I'll be back, but I'll try to make it next year." [He never came back.]

There will be arguments about the respective merits of Hogan and Jones, but at least the Texan can claim that not even Jones won at the first time of asking.

1953

BEN HOGAN

William Benjamin Hogan was born in Dublin, Texas, in August 1912, the son of a blacksmith. His father died when Ben was barely 10, leaving the family in dire straits. At the age of 12 young Ben began to caddie at Fort Worth Country Club and was soon playing. Although naturally left-handed he had to play right-handed as he had no access to left-handed clubs.

He became a professional in 1931 but barely made a living until 1938 when he finally won his first tournament. After that his constant practice began to pay off and in the early 1940s he was arguably the most successful golfer in America and possibly the world. He worked hard at changing a natural and sometimes damaging draw into a fade. He pursued perfection all his life and some commentators said he almost achieved it.

His obsession with technique was supported by a positive attitude. His wrote: "My suggestion is that before each shot you be positive and don't change your mind. Think over your shot and your choice of club. Then make it." He said that every time he failed to follow this advice he made a poor shot.

After a spell in the armed forces during World War Two he returned to golf and by 1948 had won two US PGA Championships and his first US Open as well as a host of lesser competitions.

In 1949 he was seriously injured when his car was in a head-on collision with a bus. He threw himself across his wife, Valerie, to protect her and in doing so saved himself being impaled by the steering column. The seriously injured Hogan was told he would never walk again. Sixteen months later he won his second US Open by which time writer Grantland Rice had commented: "His legs weren't strong enough to carry his heart round." The following year he won the US Open again and his first Masters.

He won the Open only once because he played in it only once and in the same year took the US Open and the Masters, the first golfer to hold three majors at the same time. Jack Nicklaus would achieve this in 1972 when he won the Masters, the US Open and the US PGA Championship. In all, Ben Hogan won nine majors.

For all his determination, he was a withdrawn character who rarely spoke either on or off the golf course, but he did have a sense of humour. "The perfect round of golf has never been played," he said. "It's 18 holes-in-one. I almost dreamt it once, but I lipped out at the last. I was mad as hell."

Hogan won his last tournament at the age of 47 and continued to compete occasionally until he was almost 60. He died in 1997.

1954

BIRKDALE

For the first time in several years there were no new records set in the preliminary stages. Norman von Nida led the qualifiers and Eric Brown, who fared so well at Carnoustie last year, failed to qualify.

After the first championship round, two Britons shared the lead with another in third place. S L King and T W Spence both had opening 69s while N Sutton had a 70. Peter Thomson, who was sixth in 1951 and has been runner-up the last two years, was on 72. After two rounds only five shots separated the first 20 players. Spence was the halfway leader on 141 with Antonio Cerda of Argentina on 142 and S L King, S S Scott, Dai Rees and Peter Thomson all on 143.

9 JULY

Southport, Friday – P W Thomson (Australia) completed a remarkable record today at Royal Birkdale, when, after having been runner-up either individually or jointly for the last two years, he won the Open Championship with a 72-hole aggregate of 283. Lying equal third two strokes behind when play began, he had rounds of 69 and 72 and prevented what appeared to be an inevitable tie by leading S S Scott (Carlisle City), D J Rees (South Herts) and A D Locke (South Africa) by a single stroke.

One of the most exciting championships found a worthy victor in Thomson, to whom golf's premier prize has come at the early age of 24. Small, but strongly built, he plays without fuss or fetish

It is a tribute to his control over himself under severe strain that knowing what was required of him he had two birdies in the last five holes and would have made the margin wider had he not missed a five-foot putt on the last green. Thomson had shared the lead at the end of the third round with Scott and Rees, while Locke lay two strokes behind. Thomson's 71 meant that Locke, in the second

last couple, needed 69 to tie, and, great-hearted competitor that he is, he almost succeeded. One feels that justice was done to Thomson when the South African's putt from 15 yards slid a foot past the hole.

Excitement mounted as the leaders more or less matched strokes all the way. Scott, the first off, went away as if playing a Saturday afternoon friendly instead of facing the biggest test of his career. Short with his pitch to the first, he holed from two feet without a tremor and reached the critical sixth without having faltered. He followed a fine drive with a magnificent wood club second to the green, but one could almost feel the silence when he sent his approach putt four feet past.

If there were doubts about his composure he removed them by sending his ball across a bad left-hand bias into the middle of what must have looked a very small hole. After that he set himself some awkward problems but found the answer to them with his pitching clubs.

Out in 35, he did not drop a stroke until the short thirteenth where he putted too boldly down and missed the return. But again he made certain that his rivals would have to work hard to overtake him by chipping well from 20 yards off the eighteenth green and holing a shortish putt for his 4, a round of 72 and an aggregate of 284.

The first challenge came from Rees, who reached the turn in 36. Fortune was kind to him at the twelfth, where after two crooked strokes he put down a 10-yard putt for a 4, but his finish under pressure was a surprising mixture of good and bad. Indifferent wooden club seconds to the fourteenth and sixteenth gave him no chance of birdies but in between he holed a two-yard putt for a 3. Another of four yards went down at the seventeenth leaving him requiring a 4 to lead Scott. A great roar from the crowd massed round the last green greeted a second shot which ran a little too far and up a slope at the back. His chip broke badly to the right and the putt from two yards dropped below the hole.

Thomson, whose caddie, Timms, carried last year for Ben Hogan, had kept to the pattern by reaching the turn in 35. A putt for a 3 at the tenth touched the hole and he maintained his par course with a neat little chip from a hillside to the left of the eleventh green. Then he sent an approach putt racing four feet past the twelfth pin and missed the return. So, after a par 3 at the thirteenth, he was back on the same mark as Scott and Rees at that stage. But where they had faltered he gained strength and splendid recovery work won the day. At the long fourteenth, he was in the rough all the way to the green but pitched well and holed from six yards for a birdie 4.

Going for the green at the 520-yard sixteenth, he hooked into a bunker but blasted his way out so successfully that putting was a formality. And so the last hole where another bunker visit and that missed putt gave Locke an outside chance.

The South African made up no leeway with an outward 35, but a birdie 3 at the fifteenth put him in a position to challenge. He failed to make the necessary birdie at the sixteenth, missing from two yards, and his second shot to the last green asked too much of his putter.

The young Tasmanian, P Toogood, carried on the Australian tradition and at the same time gained some recompense for his unsatisfactory defeat by J B Carr in the Amateur Championship, by beating F R Stranahan by four strokes for the leading amateur place.

1954, 1955, 1956, 1958, 1965
PETER THOMSON

Peter Thomson's record in the Open was awesome. At his first attempt, at Portrush in 1951, he came sixth and the following two years he was runner-up behind Bobby Locke (1952) and Ben Hogan (1953). In 1954 at the age of 24 he won at Royal Birkdale and followed this up with wins at St Andrews and Hoylake in 1955 and 1956, the only player to win three times in a row in the twentieth century. The following year he was second again to his arch-rival, Bobby Locke, and in 1958 he took the title for the fourth time. In 20 Open appearances from 1951 to 1970 he finished in the top 10 no fewer than 17 times

He was so dedicated that when he walked along the street he practised assessing distances to the next lamp post and then pacing it out to check if he was right.

Peter Thomson was born in Melbourne, Australia in 1929. In 1948 he was leading amateur in the Australian Open. He turned professional the following year. In 1950 he finished second in the Australian Open and won the New Zealand Open for the first of nine victories in that event over a period of 20 years. In 1951 he had the first of his three successes in the Australian Open.

Then he looked for new worlds to conquer and began to travel, but at a price. In his 1968 book he reflected: "Three times a year I say goodbye and my small son weeps and says he doesn't want to go to school. He doesn't know why and it tears my heart so that I wonder why I am doing it to him and whether it is worth the anguish."

Although he had many more successes following his four Open wins it was not until 1965 that he took the Open for the fifth time, only the fourth golfer to achieve this. In some ways that triumph was his greatest as the field included many Americans, including the defending champion, Tony Lema, with whom Thomson was paired in the final round, thus dispelling the suggestion that his success had been due to lack of competition.

During his career he won many more championships including Opens in three European countries and three Far East countries. He was a truly international champion.

At the age of 45 he seemed to be on the verge of putting serious golf aside for good. He dabbled in politics, even stood for Parliament and was only narrowly defeated, and he became involved in golf course design, largely in Japan, but also in Scotland near St Andrews where the new Duke's course bears his signature.

In 1982 he decided to take the Americans on again in their own backyard, by trying his luck on their Seniors tour, and with considerable success. His best year was 1985 when he won nine events and almost $400,000. He is an honorary member of the R and A.

1955

ST ANDREWS

In the first qualifying round the record of 69 for the New Course was broken twice. Irish Walker Cup player, J B Carr, set the mark at 67 only to see this equalled by Harry Weetman and then shattered by F Jowle of Edgebaston who returned a 63. The previous record of 69 was held by Irishman J Bruyn and Percy Alliss, whose son Peter would also score 67. The two-round qualifying score of 148 was also a record.

In the first round of the championship only Eric Brown, Dai Rees and S S Scott of Carlisle City broke 70, all three carding 69s. Henry Cotton and five others, including Jowle were on 70, with the holder, Peter Thomson, and 10 others one stroke further back. Only four strokes separated the first 44 players. After 36 holes three players shared the lead on 139, D F Smalldon (Cardiff), Eric Brown (Buchanan Castle) and Peter Thomson. J Fallon of Huddersfield equalled the Old Course record of 67 to finish on 140.

8 JULY

St Andrews, Friday – If a writer of fiction made his hero win even a local tournament with a 7 and a 6 on his final card he would be accused of drawing too heavily on the imagination. Yet that is what P W Thomson (Australia) did today in the greatest golfing event of all, the Open Championship, which he won for the second time in succession with a 72-hole aggregate of 281.

The tremendous self-control of this young man of 24 enabled him to ignore what to most golfers would be irretrievable disaster and go on to beat an Anglo-Scot, J Fallon (Huddersfield), by two strokes, with a Birmingham professional, F Jowle (Edgbaston), third at 284.

Thomson thus achieved equal distinction, with R T Jones, W Hagen, and A D Locke who, in modern times, have won the championship in successive years. It is little

wonder that he described the Old Course as a great course which "has been very kind to me twice". He became British matchplay champion here last October, and on that occasion, too, Fallon was his runner-up.

After three rounds Thomson, at 209, led by a stroke from Jowle, with Brown, Weetman, and Jacobs at 212. Fallon and Locke were together at 213. Hopes were high that if not a Scottish at least a British victory might be recorded. Fallon fairly set the cat among the pigeons by reaching the turn in a spectacular 31. One was inclined to discount a failure from only a yard at the ninth, but as Fallon began to find the tide turn against him coming home it became apparent how vital that miss might be. Luck was against him at the eleventh, where his tee shot finished in a heelmark in Strath bunker, and he took two strokes to recover. He retrieved some ground with a good chip to the twelfth, but a tendency, suggesting fatigue, to push his shots on the stretch in against the wind cost him 5s at the fifteenth and seventeenth, and he took 39 for the inward half. A door which had looked like being closed and safely bolted swung slightly ajar.

Brown, 37 to the turn and taking 5 at the eleventh, and Weetman, out in 39, gave themselves no chance of knocking upon it, but Jowle, after an indifferent start, brought himself back into the reckoning with birdies at the sixth and ninth and an outward half of 35. Like those who had gone before, however, he found the long inward half against the freshening easterly breeze too much and he could not better Fallon's 39 home. Locke, too, found the four-stroke leeway too much.

Thomson started like a champion, holing a three-yard putt for a 3 at the first but trouble came at the 567-yard fifth, where he was bunkered and took four to reach the green. That meant a 6, but Thomson has the knack, as highly developed as any great players of the past, of treating misfortune lightly and it was readily forgotten when a huge putt dropped for a 2 at the eighth. Out in 35, he must have felt that his first initial at least was on the cup already when he started back 4, 3, 3, 4.

But Thomson had that second trial to face before success was his. His drive to the fourteenth hooked into the cunningly-placed Beardies, his third found the Grave, about 100 yards from the green, and five strokes had gone before he was at putting distance. Was it, after all, to be a tie? Thomson, himself, gave the answer by stroking in his putt from eight feet for a 3 at the fifteenth, and from there with a 5 permissable at the Road Hole, it was plain sailing.

1956

HOYLAKE

Holder Peter Thomson and rising South African Gary Player led the qualifiers on 140. In the first round of the championship the first player out, D F Smalldon, an assistant to his father at Cardiff, scored a 68 which remained the lowest of the day. E Bertolini of Argentina was in second place on 69, with Thomson one shot further back.

Fierce wind and rain in the morning of the second day ruined the chances of many of the players who were out early. Thomson, fortunate to go out when the weather had abated, took the lead on 140 after scoring another 70 with Bertolini and de Vicenzo only one shot behind.

6 JULY

Hoylake, Friday – P W Thomson today became the first golfer in this century to win the Open Championship three times in succession. Normally one of the most relaxed players I have ever seen, the young Australian this afternoon was tense and drawn. In a fiercely competitive age Thomson has led, in turn, fields of 349 at Royal Birkdale, 301 at St Andrews and 360 here.

His margin this time was three strokes giving him the advantage over F van Donck (Belgium). R de Vicenzo was third for the third time since the war, G Player (South Africa) fourth, and J Panton (Glenbervie) leading British professional in fifth place on 292.

After 54 holes Thomson held a three-stroke lead at 212 over van Donck, who came into the picture with a splendid 70. Only these two were really involved then, for E Bertolino (Argentina) was five behind Thomson, and T H Cotton, who will soon be 50, lay fourth at 219.

Van Donck gave himself the most worrying of starts to the last lap by playing his second shot out of bounds at the first hole, but some gallant recovery work and brave putting earned him a card of 74 for an aggregate of 289. Thomson, it seemed, had the easy task of returning 76 for victory. Knowing what lay ahead of him, the champion spent most of his lunch hour resting, but even this sensible preparation did not bring him mental ease. Two over 4s after five holes, his concentration was disturbed by an amateur photographer on the sixth tee and he hooked out of bounds. That was his first test and he met it nobly, recording a 4 with his second ball. He struggled occasionally coming home, but covered the last five holes in two over 4s and with a round of 74 led van Donck by three strokes.

Van Donck played with fine courage and gave Thomson a fair target to aim for by coming home in 36. The champion, unusually timid with his short shots, gained only one stroke in the first three holes and could do no better than 37 to the turn against van Donck's 38.

His position became alarmingly insecure when he missed a four-foot putt on the tenth green. After a superb long iron shot to the next – a championship winner if ever there should have been one – he failed from two feet, but he scored par then until the end. He said afterwards that the task had given him greater anxiety than at any period last year when his winning margin was a stroke less.

De Vicenzo, whose driving was no more certain than when he was runner-up at Troon six years ago, had six 3s in his final round of 70, but only another Argentinian, A Cerda (68, 73), had a better aggregate over the last 36 holes than Panton. The Scot, who was one of those who were denied any chance of winning by the tricks of the weather on Wednesday and Thursday, recorded his best performance in the Open in many years of entering.

1957

ST ANDREWS

The US Open champion, Cary Middlecoff, got off to a bad start in the first qualifying round, carding a 75 on the New Course, but his 73 on the Old Course ensured him a place in the championship. Bernard Hunt and Bobby Locke led the qualifiers on 137.

After the first championship round the lead was shared by two Scots, Eric Brown and L B Ayton, on 67, with Bruce Crampton of Australia on 68 and four others, including Bobby Locke, one shot further back. Going into the last two rounds Eric Brown retained his lead with a 72 for 139, while Flory van Donck moved up to second place with a 68 for a total of 140 and Crampton and Locke stayed in contention, four off the lead.

This was the first year that the leaders went out last after 36 holes, coinciding with the first year the close of the championship was shown live on television.

5 JULY

St Andrews, Friday – A D Locke (South Africa) won the Open Championship on the Old Course here this evening with the magnificent 72-hole aggregate of 279. He was three strokes ahead of P W Thompson (Australia), who had won the championship in the three previous years, and four in front of E C Brown (Buchanan Castle) the Scottish professional champion, who finished third. Locke has equalled the record of Walter Hagen in the period between the wars in winning the Open four times. His aggregate this week equalled his own record low figure of 279, achieved at Troon in 1950.

It was 6.15 on this glorious summer evening when Locke, having played one of his best approaches of the day to the home hole, stroked his final putt smoothly in for a 3 and an easy victory. The foundations were laid in the morning when he started two strokes behind Brown. Playing in the second last couple – Brown and F van

Donck (Belgium) were the final pair – he completed the inward half in 32. Locke was now three in front.

What had promised to be a close finish gradually became a championship dominated by the bulky South African, who throughout the week has strolled through his rounds, expending the minimum of energy, a model of the perfectly relaxed player. When Thomson gracefully accepted the condolences of the crowd shortly before 6pm – the bush telegraph had spread the news that only a catastrophe for Locke could prevent his winning – the unrehearsed ceremony of welcoming the 1957 Open champion by the enthusiastic throng began.

Several thousands of people surged on to the fairway, encouraged, one suggests, by the sight of a group of policemen carrying ropes. The ropes served the purpose for which they were probably intended and reasonable peace and quiet was restored.

Locke by this time was studying the line of his third shot to the green, knowing that two 5s would beat Thomson's 282. The first was child's play and he drove over the road across the final fairway with all the nonchalance of the composed victor. Then came that beautiful lofted pitch to the home green, the ball nestling on the lush turf barely a yard from the hole.

Watching the scene of grandeur from the balcony of the St. Andrews New Club pavilion, the almost cloudless azure sky meeting the deeper hue of the sea, the beach in the distance where only the smallest of children, it seemed, had stayed in preference to the Old Course, the thousands of spectators in their summer clothing, and Locke an imposing figure in his navy blue plus fours and white cap, shirt, stockings, and shoes, I thought of only one imperfection – that Locke was not in the final couple. Locke holed his putt as Brown, half a mile behind, was gradually being pressed in by a further multitude of people, even though he had scant chance of overhauling the South African.

When Brown and van Donck drove from the last tee the gallery spread out over the width of the course, cast discretion, stewards, and police to the wind – of which by the way, there had been merely a puff throughout the day – and came plunging up the fairway, leaping the Swilcan Burn with few casualties and being, with difficulty, stopped by a large body of stewards, given moral encouragement by several policemen, from making it impossible for the two players to complete their round.

Brown failed with his putt for a 3 which would have enabled him to tie with Thomson for second place. The final stroke of the day and the championship was over, and the masses gave the home player a reception they would undoubtedly have trebled had Locke indeed been the one to close the proceedings.

Perhaps even more gratifying from a Scottish point of view than Brown being third in the prize list is the excellent performance of W D Smith (Prestwick) in gaining joint fifth place with 286. He and another Scot, K P Galloway (Royal Mid-Surrey), were the only amateurs who qualified to take part in the final day's play. Smith finished three strokes ahead of C Middlecoff, one of America's and possibly the world's finest professional players.

Eric Brown of Scotland – 3rd in the 1957 Open.

1958

ROYAL LYTHAM AND ST ANNE'S

In ideal conditions with barely a breath of wind Peter Thomson, complaining that he was suffering from hay fever, had 11 birdies in his first qualifying round of 63 over Royal Lytham and St Anne's. He then added a 70 for a qualifying record of 133, beating John Panton's 1952 aggregate of 134.

In the first championship round Thomson returned a 66 to lead by one from Christy O'Connor and by two from Henry Cotton, Gary Player and Max Faulkner. On day two the early lead was taken by Argentine champion L Ruiz who went out in 30 and returned a 65 for a halfway total of 136. O'Connor replied with a 68 to take the lead on 135, while Thomson showed uncharacteristic inconsistency in a 72 which dropped him into third place, tied with Welshman Dave Thomas on 138.

4 JULY

St Anne's, Friday – P W Thomson (Australia) and D C Thomas (Sudbury) have tied for the Open Championship and will play off over 36 holes here on the Royal Lytham course tomorrow. Each totalled 278 for the four rounds proper of the championship – a record aggregate for the event. After one of the most exhilarating finishes possible Thomson and Thomas beat by one stroke E C Brown (Buchanan Castle), the only Scottish player who qualified for the final two rounds, and C O'Connor (Killarney).

In the warmth of a sunny evening some 10,000 spectators had a breathtaking experience. Just after six o'clock Thomson and Thomas drove from the last tee, each needing a 4 to beat the aggregate of Brown, who for almost an hour awaited the late challenge he knew was inevitable. What an extra agony of waiting it was for Brown, for he had caught a bunker on the left of the fairway with his final drive, taken three to reach the green, and then used three putts for a soul-destroying 6. Brown had leaped into the reckoning in the third round

with a 65 featuring an inward 30, and began the last circuit of the course only three strokes behind Thomson, the leader, on 205.

Thomson was only 10 yards behind the mighty-hitting Thomas with his drive from the last tee but he played the shot of a champion to the green, his pitch of some 140 yards almost touching the flagstick and rolling three yards on. Thomas's second just missed a bunker on the left, finished on the cut grass surrounding one of the smoothest greens I have ever seen, and had a putt of fully 15 yards.

He tackled his task bravely, gave the ball every chance, and left himself only some 18 inches beyond the hole. Then Thomson studied his slightly downhill line. Success here and the title, one imagined could be his – could and not would, for the only other couple to come in, O'Connor and L Ruiz (Argentina) had, after merely moderate outward halves, returned to the fray, as the turmoil behind the two T's indicated. They too needed the par 4 at the eighteenth to oust Brown.

Thomson struck his putt and sitting in line with him, I knew the ball was fractionally off the target, but the second putt needed but a back-of-the-hand flip. Thomas had to hole his little putt to ensure a tie and this he did to a tumult of applause.

But all was far from over. No sooner had the fairway been cleared for O'Connor and Ruiz than speculation began again; would either obtain the 3 that has so often been achieved this week on the 279-yard hole. Alas for both each drove into a bunker and, whereas O'Connor cleared his ball on to the fairway but still over 100 yards short of the green, Ruiz took two strokes to escape the sand and three more to reach the green.

O'Connor played his approach as if he appreciated that

he had to hole it to win the championship for his ball shaved the hole but ran on 16 feet. Hush turned to a clamour of condolence as the beautifully struck ball grazed the edge. We retired somewhat dazedly then. So on to tomorrow and the first Open play-off since 1949.

PLAY OFF

Generations of the future are most unlikely to see such a golfer as P W Thomson (Australia), who on Saturday at Royal Lytham and St Anne's won the Open Championship for the fourth time. Having beaten D C Thomas (Sudbury) by four strokes in a 36-hole play-off for the 1958 championship, Thomson became Open champion for the fourth time in five years.

Thomson will be but 29 next month. Such is his mastery of the game that it is probable that he will establish an almost incredible record in the Open Championship. There is no weakness in Thomson's game and he has a temperament second to none.

I am certain that he will consider his latest success far and away his greatest. First, throughout the week at St Anne's-on-Sea, he was in nothing like the best of health. Thomson is a martyr to hay fever and the clammy, damp weather took its toll of him. Few golfers can have coughed and sneezed so often during a championship. Furthermore, the treatment he had brought him out in rashes. Secondly, the galleries at St Anne's were restrained in their applause when Thomson was the centre of attraction. British golf spectators can be pardoned for supporting their fellow-countrymen in the Open – they have had little to console them in recent years – but at times they become fanatically partisan.

Thomas of the magnificent physique gave the man, who had been his mentor on several occasions, a real fight. On Friday he started two strokes behind Thomson his partner on the final round, and caught him. On Saturday morning in the first 18 holes of the play-off he was four strokes behind after seven holes. He was still that margin in arrears after 13 holes. Yet at the end of the round he was but one stroke behind, with a 69 (34, 35) to his opponent's 68 (31, 37).

Thomson, consistently outdriven, was not once tempted into trying to emulate Thomas's wooden shots from the tee and he played his iron clubs with almost uncanny accuracy. And in the first half of the morning round he putted as meticulously.

Thomas was bunkered from the tee at the first hole in the afternoon and went to two down with a 4 to a 3, but he won the next two holes to be all square, having at the third played a second with an iron of surpassing excellence for a birdie 3. After eight holes, however, Thomson again led with a 4 to a 5, Thomas failing with a putt of little more than a yard, and by the eleventh the Australian was again four ahead. It was too much to expect that Thomas would again neutralise that leading margin. Thomas completed the second 18 holes in 74 (35, 39) for an aggregate of 143 and Thomson in 71 (35, 36) for 139.

1959

MUIRFIELD

Peter Thomson, the holder, won the qualifiers' prize of £50 with rounds of 71 at Gullane and a record 66 at Muirfield. Amateur Joe Carr scored a 64 at Gullane to beat the previous amateur mark of 68 and the professional record of 67.

The first-round leaders in the championship were Fred Bullock (Prestwick St Nicholas), and A F Stickley from Ealing, both on 68. Antonio Cerda was third with a 69 while three players were on 70, S L King (Knole Park), Michael Bonallack and the Belgian, Flory van Donck. Gary Player, runner-up in the US Open in 1958, was well down the field with a 75.

In the second round, Fred Bullock added a solid 70 to take the halfway lead on 138, while van Donck also had 70 for a total of 140, two ahead of Bonallack. Player had a 71 to stay in touch.

3 JULY

For the eighth time in succession and the eleventh time since the end of the Second World War the Open Championship has been won by an overseas golfer. The 1959 winner is G J Player (South Africa), whose final aggregate here at Muirfield was 284 – two ahead of that of F van Donck (Belgium) and F Bullock (Prestwick St Nicholas).

Van Donck and Bullock, the last pair on the course, drove from the last tee each needing a 3 to tie with Player, and the milling crowd fairly revelled in the exciting prospect. Appetites had been whetted on the previous green, where both were through with their second shots. Van Donck was some 15 yards away from the hole and on the slope of the bank behind the green. He played the little pitch superbly. A gradually increasing roar urged the ball to the hole but it stopped short by six inches. Bullock then used his putter from 12 yards and was much too strong, but he holed the two-yard return and the crowd went almost mad with joy.

Bullock, joint leader after one round, leader by two strokes at the half-way stage, and again joint leader after the forenoon's third round, squandered his chance by driving into a bunker on the right but van Donck hit straight down the middle. The Belgian's iron shot of some 200 yards was also dead in line with the flag but it finished on the fringe of the green nearly 20 yards from the hole and at 6.35 on this blustery evening the championship was Player's as van Donck rolled off the line.

Three-quarters of an hour earlier S S Scott (Roehampton), another professional of vast experience, had had the same task of covering the last two holes in seven strokes to tie, but a poor drive at the long seventeenth led to a 6. Player of the garish garb – this week he has been resplendent in crimson, yellow, and black, and today in white cap, black sweater, salmon-pink slacks, and shoes of red, white and blue – played magnificently in the strong west wind. Not a drop of rain fell on the final day and the sun shone for long periods but the wind caused sore travail.

Player was four behind the joint leaders after the third round. The young South African's morning 70 was a fine score, but in the afternoon he romped away.

Out in 33, he was four under 4s at the twelfth, where he holed a six-yard putt and scampered after the ball as it dropped. Having put his tee shot at the short uphill thirteenth only three yards from the hole he rattled in this putt too. So now he was five under 4s and although he took the par 5 for the long fourteenth he played another glorious iron shot from the tee at the last short hole of the course (the sixteenth) and putted unerringly from just four feet for a 2.

At the seventeenth a record round of 65, as well as the

championship was in sight. He played a little chip from the bank behind the green four yards short and one wondered then if disaster was to befall him, for before he played he saw fit to address a photographer and some spectators regarding their movements as he addressed his ball. "I beg of you," said Player, "I'm playing for my living; I ask you from the bottom of my heart not to move." Player's face was like thunder as he studied the putt but he showed great relief when this putt, too, rolled into the hole.

At the last hole (427 yards) Player drove into the first of the three bunkers on the left of the fairway, took three to reach the edge of the green, and three putts from there and a 6 which had him literally in tears. Player's round finished at 4.20 in the afternoon and he preferred not to remain at the course and suffer the two-and-a-half hours of strain and stress which he knew would be his lot.

At 23 he is the youngest player this century to win the Open and if he can eliminate the irascible side of his temperament he should have a future rich in financial gain and fame. He is no more that 5ft 6ins but he is compactly built and he hits the ball as far as most of his taller, burlier rivals, and what a persistent attacker of the hole he is. A golf course is as much an enemy to Player as any golfer.

Midway through the afternoon we had hopes that a Scot would win the Open – and a Scottish amateur at that. R R Jack (Dullatur), broke the amateur record for Muirfield with a 68 in the morning and was only two behind the joint leaders when he set off on his final round. In the afternoon he had little luck on the greens, where he putted boldly and well and was two under 4s as he went to the ninth tee. But his drive from there gave him a half-buried lie in the rough to the right and his second shot merely moved the ball diagonally across the fairway into further trouble.

The 6 that ensued practically ended the possibility of an amateur winning the championship, although M F Bonallack (Thorpe Hill), a Walker Cup colleague of Jack's, kept the effort going well into the afternoon. Bonallack, playing in the second last couple, needed a 3 at the last hole to tie with Jack for the silver medal, but he put his drive in the bunker where Bullock was to land 15 minutes later.

J Panton (Glenbervie), who tied with Jack on 288, might have achieved the success so many of the crowd wished, had he putted as well as he played the rest of his golf. Too often, however, Panton could not make even two putts suffice. A touch of the killer instinct of Player would have made an open champion of Panton ere now.

1959, 1968, 1974

GARY PLAYER

"The more I practise the luckier I get," was Gary Player's quick, apt and truthful response to a spectator who suggested he had been lucky after he played a particularly good shot in difficult circumstances. And practise he did with a dedication seldom seen in the past, and with astonishing results. His record over a career spanning 40 years has few parallels.

Gary James Player was born in Johannesburg, South Africa, in 1935 and, unlike most highly successful golfers, did not take up the game until his middle teens. He had an instant "feel" for the game, taking a job as an assistant professional in 1953.

Three years later he won the South African Open, the first of 13 wins in that event and, in 1958, he won the first of seven Australian Opens.

His first major came in the Open at Muirfield in 1959 and by 1965 he had added the US Masters, the US PGA and the US Open, only the third player to win all four, a feat which would later be equalled by Jack Nicklaus. In all Player took nine majors, the last being the US Masters at the age of 42, and just failed to win all four twice – he won the US Open only once.

He had a determination to win, perhaps unequalled before or since, and he spectacularly demonstrated this on two occasions. Playing in the World Matchplay Championship in 1965 against Tony Lema, he came back from seven holes down after 19 holes to win at the first extra hole and went on to take the title, the first of five. Then in 1978 he went into the final round of the US Masters seven shots adrift of Hubert Green. He went to the turn in 34 and came back in 30 for a 64 and his third US Masters title.

He was the first golfer to take fitness seriously. He became a fanatic, doing weight training and press-ups by the hundred and he strictly regulated his diet, avoiding alcohol and tobacco amongst other things, even tea and coffee. It paid off handsomely and enabled him to continue to play at the highest level longer than most and to achieve enormous success on the US Seniors Tour.

Player had a 15 minute wait before the presentation of the trophy

CHAPTER SIX

THE BIG THREE

AMERICAN AIR INVASION

Arnold Palmer fairly burst on to the Open scene in the early sixties and gave the ailing Open the shot in the arm it so badly needed. He was the charismatic US Open champion of 1960 whose go-for-broke style had captured the imagination. He also recognised the place in world golf of the "British" Open and his example led the way for a steady trickle then a flood of leading Americans whose travel problems were easing in any case with the arrival of jet airlines.

There were other influences. South African Gary Player, who had won the Open in 1959, played his part by taking the US Open in 1965. When Jack Nicklaus arrived, third in 1963, second in 1964 to fellow-American Tony Lema, twelfth in 1965 and finally winner in 1966, the Open, with the full support of the Big Three, was back on course. Against that quality of player an Open champion's credentials were beyond reproach. Then the stakes were raised even higher by the arrival on the scene of Tony Jacklin.

Jacklin's triumph in 1969 was the first of British vintage for 18 years and when he added the US Open the following year it was the catalyst for a whole new era in British and, indeed, European golf. In addition to raising the ambition level of his countrymen, there was a rush of sponsors hungry to be associated with the success and keen to inject money into tournament golf.

Meanwhile, John Jacobs, the first PGA tournament director-general, was busy consolidating the commercial interest sparked by Jacklin by founding the European Tour, which separated from the PGA parent body in 1975.

The European Tour, which fell into the guiding hands of Scot Ken Schofield, went from strength to strength offering top professionals for the first time a means of earning a living without needing to be tied to club jobs.

If it was Jacklin who lit the blue touch paper, then it was Mr Swashbuckler himself, Severiano Ballesteros, who exploded into a display of colour. His feats would not only lead to a rise in prize-money to a level that hitherto existed only in dreams but also raise European golf to a standard that would give the superior Americans the fright of their lives.

More changes were taking place in the Open. The prize fund rose from £7000 in 1960 to £200,000 in 1980, the first four-day Open was staged in 1966, two more courses were added to the Open rota, Troon in 1962 and Turnberry in 1977, and there was another significant alteration to equipment.

There were two legal sizes of ball, the 1.62ins and 1.68ins diameter. The Americans, typically, were ahead of the game. The USGA had legalised the 1.68 in 1931 while the British felt the 1.62 was better for the tight links fairway lies. There was more to it than that, however. The small ball could be played with a wristy, flicking action, a throwback to the hickory club style, while the larger ball demanded a more firm arm action of which British players, in the face of regular international defeats especially the Ryder Cup, had become belatedly aware.

In 1974, the R and A made the larger ball compulsory. The small ball's day was over and in 1990 it became illegal at all levels right down to club golf.

1960

ST ANDREWS

It was 100 years since the first competition for the Challenge Belt was won at Prestwick by Willie Park Sr with an aggregate score of 174 for 36 holes. After the first qualifying round when Peter Alliss opened with a 66, Willie Auchterlonie, the R and A professional and the 1893 champion, was in pensive, sad mood when he said: "It shows you what they've done to the Old Course". Last year's winner, Gary Player, led the qualifiers on 135 with Christy O'Connor on 137.

Playing in the cold and rain, Roberto de Vicenzo took the first-round lead with a 67, with F de Luca of Argentina and Kel Nagle of Australia on 69.

In the second round Vicenzo scored another 67 for a halfway total of 134 to move seven ahead of all but Nagle who matched his 67 to stay within two shots. Arnold Palmer, bidding to match Ben Hogan's achievement of winning three majors in one year, was on 141 along with S Miguel of Spain, five shots behind Nagle. Seven Scots amateurs qualified for the last two rounds.

8 JULY

Not since 1933, when British professional golfers had only one representative in the first six of the Open Championship, have they failed as they did in the centenary event which ended on Saturday on the Old Course, St Andrews, with victory for K D G Nagle (Australia). Four other overseas golfers and two British amateurs were in the first eight.

The leading home professional was B J Hunt (Hartsbourne) and he became joint third, four strokes behind Nagle. He began the final round nine strokes behind and therefore with no hope of winning. Consequently, comparatively free of stress and strain, he scored 66, which equalled the record established by P Alliss (Parkstone) in the first qualifying round.

G B Wolstenholme (Sunningdale) who, having reached the turn in the final round in 31, had an outside chance of becoming the first amateur to win the Open since R T Jones in 1930, and J B Carr (Sutton), the Amateur champion, finished ahead of all but Hunt of the British professionals in the field of 47. Three other amateur players, all Scots, D A Blair (R and A), R R Jack (Dullatur) and A M Deboys (Taymouth Castle), were eight, 10 and 12 strokes respectively inferior to Nagle.

This is a shocking state of affairs. The professionals who complain that the rule whereby prize-money offered for a place occupied by an amateur is not awarded will have little sympathy from the golfing public.

Nagle won the championship with his putter, though it is fair to say that he played the Old Course intelligently and respectfully, probably because of the advice he received in practice from his Canada Cup partner, P W Thomson. Nagle was rarely off the correct line in his long game: he merely completed with his putter what he had started with his driver and his irons.

Nevertheless, there can rarely have been a more unlucky runner-up than A Palmer (United States), who finished a stroke behind the Australian. Palmer expended at least a dozen strokes more than Nagle on the greens during the four days. Yet he did not putt badly. The fact is that the Australian Open champion holed many putts of distance and the American Open champion remarkably few.

Palmer had been seven strokes behind R de Vicenzo (Argentina), the leader after two rounds. When the final round began, Palmer with a 211 aggregate, was four strokes behind Nagle, and two behind de Vicenzo. All three went to the turn in 34, Palmer and his partner, S Miguel (Spain), being the couple in front of Nagle and de Vicenzo, the last partnership.

Playing the 453-yard seventeenth, Palmer was only two strokes behind Nagle and had a lead of one stroke over de Vicenzo. The American went for the hole with his second shot, though he had seen Miguel run through the green and go down the bank. Palmer's ball just failed to hold the green and he was left with a shot at the foot of the bank close to the road, similar to Miguel's.

The Spaniard tried to chip up the bank, but did not manage to gain the putting surface. But Palmer, unperturbed, used his putter and played a superb shot to

within two feet of the hole. Palmer achieved a birdie 3 on the final green watched from afar by Nagle. The Australian, by this time having played safely to the hollow short of the seventeenth green, had left his putt seven feet short. Here, indeed, was a test of nerves. But he maintained his reputation. And the duel was almost over. A fine second shot to the eighteenth – the ball stopped only a yard from the pin – was cheered to the echo by the vast crowd. Nagle had two putts for victory and the championship was over.

1960
KEL NAGLE

Kelvin Nagle, born in Sydney, Australia, in 1920, worked as an assistant professional in his teens and became a full-time tour professional after the Second World War but made little immediate impact on the tournament scene. In 1949 he won an Australian professional event but little else. His long game tended to be erratic and his putting was also inconsistent.

As he matured, he changed his style and began to sacrifice distance for accuracy and he worked on his

putting, all to good effect. When he was 36 he won the first of seven New Zealand Opens between 1957 and 1969. In 1959 he took the Australian Open.

His real claim to fame is his success in the Centenary Open at St Andrews in 1960 which Arnold Palmer was determined to take in order to emulate Ben Hogan's feat of winning the US Masters, the US Open and the Open all in one year. Palmer took Nagle all the way to the seventy-second hole. In a career spanning 30 years Nagle also won the French and Canadian Opens and the World Seniors title twice.

1961

ROYAL BIRKDALE

In the first qualifying round, Bob Charles, the New Zealand left-hander, scored a record 66 and led the qualifiers after adding a 70 for 136. His record was equalled by J S More of Carlisle City. After the first championship round three players shared the lead on 68, holder Kel Nagle of Australia, Harold Henning of South Africa and the Welshman, Dai Rees. Three others were on 69 and six were on 70, including Arnold Palmer.

Scoring in the second round deteriorated. Both Rees and Henning slipped to 74s but still retained the lead with a 36-hole total of 142, one ahead of Nagle who had a 75 for 143 and of Palmer who moved closer with a 73, also for 143.

14 JULY

Though there was a terrible downpour for an hour in the middle of the day, the weather at Royal Birkdale on Saturday relented sufficiently for the Open Championship to be decided. Indeed, for over three hours in the afternoon several thousands of people were able to appreciate in comfort the duel between A Palmer (United States) and D J Rees (South Herts).

Rees, who is in his forty-ninth year, and who twice before has been joint runner-up, fought a splendid rearguard battle. He might well have been discomfited by taking a 7 at the first hole in the morning and a 6 at the sixth in the afternoon, but he plugged determinedly on.

Palmer won the title with an aggregate of 284 by a stroke from Rees. The American's was a more comfortable margin of victory than bare figures indicate. When the final round began he was a stroke ahead of Rees, three ahead of C O'Connor and four better than N C Coles. He was also six ahead of his partner K D G Nagle (Australia), the defending champion, who, having taken 40 for the last nine holes of his third round, had ruined his chance. Long before Rees played the final stroke of the championship, a four-yard putt for an eagle 3, the steadiness of Palmer had blunted the challenge of all.

On the inward half he was concentrating on not dropping strokes. Nevertheless he repeatedly shook his head as he left approach putts short. Only twice in the last 18 holes did he succeed with a putt of distance. At the sixth, after he had been bunkered from the tee and Nagle, short in two, had pitched into the hole from 50 yards for an eagle 3, he got down from eight yards. At the fifteenth Palmer played the decisive stroke – the shot of a champion. His drive was only a yard off the fairway on the right but the ball was on a bank and in deep, clinging willow scrub, but he blasted the shot on to the green 150 yards away.

As Palmer played the tee shot at the short seventeenth well-nigh perfectly, Rees in the last match was achieving a second successive birdie and became two over 4s to Palmer's one over. Again Palmer left the putt – this time of only four yards – short. When he was safely on in two at the last, and Rees away in the distance had in his turn got only a par 3, the championship was settled. Rees would have had to hole his second at the 470-yard eighteenth for an albatross to force a tie.

There was marked improvement in the performances of home golfers. Only Nagle and Thomson as well as Palmer of the overseas players finished in the leading nine. Coles struck a blow for the younger players and E C Brown (unattached), who was joint fifth, returned to the form of which we know he is capable.

Even before the championship began, everyone stood in awe of Palmer, who is now as greatly respected as a golfer as Hogan. The more often he visits this side of the Atlantic the more welcome he will be for this son of a greenkeeper – a groundskeeper as Palmer himself describes his father – is in his unassuming way a great gentleman.

1961, 1962
ARNOLD PALMER

Arnold Palmer's enormous popularity, and the crowd phenomenon that became known as "Arnie's Army", had much to do with the "go for broke" attitude which often resulted in a series of brilliant shots and sometimes deep trouble. Watching Palmer at work was never dull, and there was always the prospect of his trademark hitch of the trousers to signal a charge.

Peter Dobereiner wrote of Palmer: "He played bad golf better than anyone else, before or since." We could all identify with Arnie's occasional wild tee shot, landing him in a near impossible situation. What we couldn't do was conjure up the miracle shot that almost invariably followed to give Palmer a chip and a putt for another easy par. If he was on a charge he would just hole the chip for birdie. He once said, in a throwback to Jamie Anderson's dictum of the 1870s: "If you can hit it you can hole it" – and that was his philosophy at the height of his career.

Arnold Daniel Palmer was born at Latrobe, Pennsylvania, in 1929, the son of the greenkeeper at Latrobe Country Club. He was swinging cut-down clubs at the age of three and his father taught him the basics well. By the time he entered high school he was already an accomplished player.

He went to Wake Forest University on a golf scholarship in 1947 but dropped out without a degree and spent three years with the US Coastguard. After a brief spell as a salesman he turned professional in 1954 after winning the US Amateur that year. The following year he won his first tournament as a pro, the Canadian Open. He was on his way.

In 1960, having won the US Masters for the second time and the US Open, he headed for the Centenary Open at St Andrews, hoping to emulate Ben Hogan and take all three in one year, but it wasn't to be. He lost by one stroke to the Australian, Kel Nagle.

The following year he was back and took the title at Royal Birkdale and in 1962 at Troon he got his revenge for his defeat at St Andrews. He won his second Open with a record total of 276, six shots ahead of Nagle who was second.

In all Palmer took four US Masters, the US Open once and the Open twice, as well as nearly 60 official US tour events and numerous other tournament wins worldwide. He was the first golfer to earn a million dollars and the first to have his own plane. He went on to revitalise the American Seniors Tour when he joined it in 1980 and started winning all over again.

His tally of majors may not look impressive given his enormous talent but he came close so many times, being runner-up once in the Open, twice in the US Masters, three times in the US PGA which eluded him and four times in the US Open.

But it is for the impact he made on the game as a whole for which he will be remembered. His cavalier style of play, his rapport with the galleries and his general demeanour on the course, which coincided with a much wider TV coverage than hitherto, brought the game to life for a whole new public, many of whom had previously known little or nothing about the sport.

Perhaps even more significantly for the game he played a big part in re-establishing the Open to its rightful place as the most important golf tournament in the world.

1962

TROON

As so often happens in the Open the first round leader at Troon this week was virtually unknown. K A MacDonald (Hankley Common, Surrey) had scored 80 in the second qualifying round and was drawn to play with Arnold Palmer in the first round proper. He must have been more than a little daunted by the size of the gallery which turned out to follow them, but he rose to the occasion and compiled a 69 (equalling the course record set by Sam Snead two days earlier) while Arnie scored 71. MacDonald had a Scottish grandfather but was himself born in England.

In the second round, amateur Charlie Green from Dumbarton, put paid to the hopes of 12 golfers including Gary Player and Gene Littler. Last player to finish as the sun went down, he carded a 75 for an aggregate of 151 to become the fifty-first player on 153 or better. As it had been decided that a maximum of 50 players and ties would contest the last two rounds 12 players on 153 were eliminated. These included the only remaining four amateurs, guaranteeing Charlie would win the silver medal.

13 JULY

Troon, Friday – Arnold Palmer (United States) won the Open Championship for the second year in succession here tonight on the Old Course. With his most impressive combination of power and skill he so spread-eagled the rest of the field of 39 final qualifiers that his aggregate of 276 was six strokes better than that of second-placed K D G Nagle (Australia) with whom he played his final two rounds. Palmer's total was also 13 strokes superior to the aggregates of joint third-placed B G C Huggett (Romford) and P Rodgers (United States). Not only was Palmer's aggregate a record for the Open but his margin of success equalled the greatest since the end of the First World War achieved by two other Americans, R T Jones in 1927 and

Walter Hagen in 1929. Not one in 20 of the crowd, which I estimated at 15,000, saw the final putts. When Palmer, most fittingly as the finest golfer of the week, holed the last putt – for a birdie 3 to equal Nagle's – only the prompt action of the police enabled the players to reach the clubhouse. Even so, Nagle, who I felt had the benefit of what partiality the crowd had displayed, was borne on the shoulders of a cheering mass and gained the sanctuary of the clubhouse through a window.

On a glorious sunny morning, Palmer, two strokes ahead of Nagle, broke the 7045-yard course record of 69, made earlier this week by E C Brown (unattached), S Snead (United States), K A MacDonald (Hankley Common) and P Alliss (Parkstone), by two strokes. In doing so he increased his lead to five over Nagle and eight over R J Charles (New Zealand).

Palmer holed a five-yard putt for a birdie 3 at the second in the final round and became six strokes up overall. As in the morning he holed a longish putt, this time of six yards at the fifth for a birdie 2, whereas Nagle again missed the green and took 4. By the turn Palmer was almost incredibly for an Open Championship nine strokes ahead of the only player who at the start of the final round had a semblance of a chance of challenging him seriously.

At the Railway Hole (485 yards) Palmer's advantage in length with both wood and with the long irons was again apparent and the American's birdie 4 put Nagle 10 strokes behind. As the crowds surged up hill and down dale and all over the flat, too, and sorely tried the players as well as the police and stewards, Palmer lost a little of his concentration and Nagle rallied by holing putts of three feet, seven yards and 12 yards for birdies at the fourteenth, seventeenth and eighteenth. Palmer missed the green at the fourteenth and took a 4 and Nagle had reduced the deficit to a level which I am certain Palmer considered fairer than the 10 which applied little more than an hour earlier.

The American played the five rounds here on the Old Course (including one qualifier) in 76, 71, 69, 67, 69. The improvement from first round to second was ominous.

Huggett, the leading British player, is 25, and at no more than 5ft 5ins the smallest golfer who takes part in the professional tournaments. He has some slight connection through his father with Troon for Huggett Sr was an assistant to the late J G Hutcheson of Troon when he was at Porthcawl. Huggett's father, who came up to Scotland to see this week's play, won a wager of £20 to £1 that his son would not reach the first 10.

1963

ROYAL LYTHAM AND ST ANNE'S

Peter Thomson and Phil Rodgers led with 67s in the first round, Thomson scoring 29 on the front nine, as did Tom Haliburton from Wentworth. Bob Charles, the New Zealand left-hander, had a 68 and Kel Nagle a 69. Arnold Palmer, the winner for the last two years, had a disastrous start, shooting 76. Play on the first day was watched by ex-King Leopold of the Balkans and his wife, the Princess de Rothy.

In the second round Rodgers followed his 67 with a 68 for 135 to lead Thomson (69) by one and Jack Nicklaus, who had a second round 67, by three. Nagle had a 70 for 139 and Charles a 72 for 140. Palmer recovered with a 71 to qualify. There were only three Britons in the first 11, Tom Haliburton, D MacDonald and Christy O'Connor.

12 JULY

St Anne's, Friday – P Rodgers (United States) and R J Charles (New Zealand) tied for first place in this year's Open Championship here tonight at Royal Lytham and St Anne's, where five years ago there was a similar result. In continuing fine, sunny weather, the wind of the eve of the championship having almost vanished, this pair of great contrast in style and temperament aggregated 277. They will play off for the first prize of £1500 and second of £1000 over 36 holes tomorrow at 10am and 2.30pm.

In just such a furore of excitement as five years ago, when no fewer than five players had a chance of winning, Rodgers and Charles, the last couple in the field, played their final tee shots in the sure knowledge that each needed the par 4 at the 389-yard hole to beat J W Nicklaus (United States) who some 20 minutes earlier had finished 5, 5 for an aggregate of 278.

The mightiest man in the field had overclubbed at the seventeenth after a stupendous drive and duffed a little pitch over the mound at the back of the green, and at the last he had driven into the bunker on the left-hand side of the fairway that possibly cost Brown the championship in 1958.

Many more people saw this late evening's climax than those who had a view of the finish five years ago, for the excellent stand accommodation on either flank of the last green can take at least 4000. The favoured places were packed, of course, and the milling crowds along the chestnut fencing added their several thousands more as Rodgers, the specialist in wise-cracking, and Charles, the most silent of golfers, drove safe and straight down the ribbon of fairway. Charles, the tall, thin left-hander, was first to play the second shot and he made the front of the green and no more; the square-built Rodgers played his iron shot a little more than 12 feet from the hole. Charles put his 20-yard putt barely four feet past, and Rodgers, at this moment at least the favourite to win, left his putt some 18 inches short. He did not mark his ball but putted out, and amid gasps of incredulity and to his momentary consternation his ball ran right round the rim of the hole before it dropped. Thereupon as the crowd roared their appreciation Rodgers doffed his cap and immediately covered the hole and shouted: "I'm afraid it will pop out." There followed a moment to savour as Charles lined up the most important putt in his life. The huge crowd was now soundless and even almost motionless; one could almost hear 10,000 hearts beating. And then the acclamation of all as Charles struck his putt with deadly accuracy.

PLAY OFF

R J Charles (New Zealand) won the Open Championship on Saturday amid no great acclamation. The gallery who watched the last strokes of the 36-hole play-off with

P Rodgers (United States) was no more than a couple of thousand, and for them there had been a gradually increasing feeling of anti-climax.

The two players had tied at the eighteenth hole on Friday when excitement was at its peak and when the crowd was at least three times as large as it was on Saturday, but long before they approached the hole at the clubhouse on the evening of the play-off the Open had been won; there remained only the question of the size of the margin.

The championship was won by eight strokes by the first left-handed golfer and the first New Zealander to succeed, Charles having aggregated 140 (69, 71) and Rodgers 148 (72, 76). It was won by such deadly putting as has ever won the Open; it is not unfair to Charles to state that almost throughout the first round he was the inferior player up to the green. Of Charles's 69 strokes in the first round on a warm, sunny day on which the wind was the merest breeze only 26 were putts; Rodgers, on the other hand, used his putter 33 times.

It was to the American's great credit that he did not crack before he did against such an automaton on the greens. Rodgers lost stomach for the fight only after he had made a heart-warming rally in the afternoon which was baulked once again by putting. His interval deficit of three strokes was quickly increased to five when he bunkered his tee shot at the first and missed from four feet at the second, but Charles pulled on to the railway line at the third and took 6 to the American's 4.

Then came Rodgers's great effort. At the fourth he surprised and delighted himself by holing a 12-yard putt, but he profited not, for Charles also gained a 3 with a five-foot putt. Still, two holes later the deficit was only one, for Rodgers achieved two more 3s. He holed from six feet at the fifth after Charles had been too strong with a 25-yard putt, and he played by far the better second at the sixth – Charles slightly hooked into long grass – and got down from four yards.

Just as it seemed that Rodgers was to gain command came the beginning of a quick end for him. He hit a cracking drive at the long seventh, and when Charles sliced his tee shot away out over the spectators' rope fence the American was favourite to draw level at least. Charles had a most favourable lie, however, in the tramped-down rough and was able to play his second well down the fairway. Going for the green at the 553-yard hole, Rodgers bunkered his shot 40 yards short and to the right and shanked his third into another trap high up in the hillocks and the hole cost him 6 to Charles's 5. The end came, I feel sure, at the very next hole. Rodgers, still perkily confident, put down his second long putt of the day – one of 16 yards downhill – but his inscrutable opponent replied with an equally sure putt from 10 yards. Rodgers visibly wilted thereafter. Charles scored only one birdie during the rest of the round – he had yet another single putt, his fifteenth of the day, this time from eight feet, at the tenth – yet he drew away by six more shots.

Long before the end the gallery had rapidly dwindled. Charles, who is so gloomily silent and undemonstrative as to make one wonder if he gains any enjoyment from his golf, did not improve matters by answering the applause he received with an almost lethargic flourish of his putter which did not rise higher than his chest; he might have just won the local monthly medal. Nevertheless, one feels that in these barren days for British golf, Charles would be a most popular fellow.

1963
BOB CHARLES

Born in Carterton on New Zealand's North Island in 1936, Robert James Charles learned to play golf left-handed when his parents gave him an old set of left-handed clubs. Being left-handed, he would later quip, "is a big advantage because no-one knows enough about your swing to give you advice".

He soon became a successful amateur and when he was 18 he won the New Zealand Open. He remained an amateur for another six years after which he won three more New Zealand Opens between 1966 and 1973. He has also won the Canadian Open once and the Swiss Open twice as well as several US tour events and a number of other tournaments in Europe and South Africa. Always a steady player, perhaps his greatest asset was his putting, considered to be one of the best ever. His greatest triumph was the Open of 1963 at Royal Lytham where he tied with the American, Phil Rodgers on 277 and went on to decisively win the play-off, the last time it would be decided over 36 holes.

Bob Charles joined the US Seniors Tour in 1986 and enjoyed huge success, earning more money than he ever did on the regular tour. He won the British Seniors Open in 1989 and again in 1993.

1964

ST ANDREWS

In the first round high winds made for high scoring, the leaders being Christy O'Connor and J Garaialde of France on commendable 71s. Bob Charles, the holder, shot 79 as did Peter Thomson, while Gary Player had to settle for 78. Peter Alliss and Neil Coles had 83s.

After the second round the American, Tony Lema, runner-up to Jack Nicklaus in last year's Masters, had established a two-stroke lead over Harry Weetman with rounds of 73 and 68 to the Englishman's 72 and 71. Bruce Devlin of Australia and O'Connor were one shot further back on 144.

10 JULY

St Andrews, Friday – A Lema (USA) gained a remarkable victory in the Open Championship here this evening at his first attempt with a 72-hole aggregate of 279 which gave him first prize of £1500. He was five strokes ahead of J W Nicklaus, the former US Open and Masters champion. Among his immediate rewards is a place in the world television series, which is contested in America in the autumn by the winners of the Open championships in Britain and the United States and the holders of the American Masters and PGA titles.

Lema's victory climaxed six weeks of extraordinary achievement. In June he won three out of four circuit tournaments in America and finished sixth in another. He took a less prominent part in the US Open championship in Washington but came here because he felt his current form was good enough to allow him to do justice to or enhance a growing reputation.

An exhausting transatlantic journey brought him to St Andrews after lunch on Monday and allowed him only two practice rounds over a course which has the reputation of needing years of experience for one to acquire even a moderate knowledge of its variable moods and subtleties. Fortune was on Lema's side in two important respects. His first round of 73 was scored when Wednesday's gale had not reached its full force. And Nicklaus's difficulties on the greens yesterday made the task of pursuit almost impossible.

Yet Lema quickly revealed that he had a simple, compact method which would be unlikely to allow disasters to creep into a good round in the making and had possibly the most graceful style seen here since Littler. His temperament, which used to have the reputation of being suspect under pressure, is now well disciplined, and he above all displayed a sophisticated outlook to the problems he had to solve in conditions which were entirely foreign to him. He must, however, have owed a great deal to the knowledge of his caddie, "Tip" Anderson.

The crowds came early this morning, the sea sparkled in the sunlight, and a hard wind from the Guardbridge end promised absorbing watching and demanding careful shotmaking. With several British players in close contention an expectant air was abroad. In the event the day belonged entirely to the two Americans as they fought it out together before large and excited galleries.

Nicklaus, nine shots behind Lema after 36 holes, responded bravely with a third round of 66, which equalled the record for the course. His long game retained its accuracy and power, but for the first time this week his putting worked for him and it saved him time and time again, notably over the closing holes, where underhit pitches left him a long way from the hole.

There was only one moment during the morning when it seemed possible that Lema would be caught. As Lema was walking up the sixth fairway with a score of three over 4s, Nicklaus was moving homewards on the adjacent thirteenth with the bright red figures of 5 under revealing the extent of his thrust. It speaks volumes for Lema's courage and determination that from that point on he played the course in seven under 4s.

That gave Lema a lead of seven strokes, the greatest number after 54 holes since T H Cotton led the field by 10 shots in 1934 at Sandwich. Nicklaus was at that moment standing on the first tee and to his credit, he never relented. While Lema rested, Nicklaus played the first nine holes in 34, recovering well from a 5 at the fourth and a 6 at the fifth with birdies at the eighth and ninth. He also came home in 34 for his second round of under 70 of the day.

Lema started his last round in an atmosphere of silence and anti-climax, the crowd probably realising that the conclusion was now foregone. Lema left them in no doubt that he could turn the thought into hard fact. He began with three cast-iron 4s, slipped a stroke at the fourth, where he was short for the second time today, and took three putts, but he was home with a No.4-wood shot at the 576-yard fifth hole from an awkward stance in the rough although the ball lay on the fairway.

Soon Lema was safely through the Loop with four more 3s on his card. In his four rounds he played these six holes, where the seeds of great rounds are so often sown, in 6 under 4s. Naturally, as he had so many strokes in hand his concentration eased and he dropped a shot at the fourteenth and took a 5 at the Road Hole for the first time in the championship.

The air was almost completely still and the wind a whisper after its strength earlier in the day when Lema drove up the last 20 yards short of the green. The crowd engulfed the fairway and were pressed back to allow Garaialde, Lema's partner, to play his approach. Then Lema chipped up through the Valley of Sin to within a yard of the hole – one for the gallery indeed.

It was some minutes before Lema was able to struggle through the cordon of spectators, and then, after Garaialde had holed out, Lema quietly knocked the putt into the centre of the hole for his 3.

Seconds later the ball flew from his hand far across the first fairway. He went to receive his trophy and it was not long afterwards that we were enjoying his pleasant custom of providing champagne for the press when he wins.

1964
TONY LEMA

"Champagne" Tony Lema seemed to have it all when he began winning tournaments on the US Tour in 1962. He was young, handsome and had an elegant swing, which seemed destined to bring him many victories. True to his promise he would open champagne in the press tent after each victory, hence the soubriquet.

Lema was born in 1934 in Oakland, California, the son of a Portuguese labourer who died when Lema was three. Tony was a caddie before serving with the US Marines in Korea, after which he took a job as an assistant in the pro shop at San Francisco Golf Club. He turned professional in 1959. Then in 1962 he came to the fore with three victories on the US Tour. The following year he lost the US Masters to Jack Nicklaus by just one stroke.

In 1964 he entered the Open at St Andrews. It was the first time he had seen a links golf course and had time for only two practice rounds. He did, however, have one advantage. Arnold Palmer who was not playing that year had recommended he use his caddie, Tip Anderson, which he did. According to Lema afterwards, he just did what Tip told him to do and it was enough to give him victory over Jack Nicklaus by five shots.

The following year he led by two after two rounds but the title went to Peter Thomson. In that year he also suffered at the hands of Gary Player during the World Matchplay Championship when Player came back from being seven holes down after 19 holes to win at the thirty-seventh. Despite these disappointments 1965 was a good year for Lema. He had a highly successful Ryder Cup, winning four of his five matches and he was second on the US money list behind Nicklaus.

The future looked bright for "Champagne" Tony. He had the talent and the temperament to win. He had one major under his belt and he was popular with the press, the galleries and his fellow professionals. He may even have been the player many thought could break the domination of the new triumvirate of Palmer, Player and Nicklaus.

But it wasn't to be. In 1966 Tony Lema and his wife, Betty, were killed in a plane crash.

1965

ROYAL BIRKDALE

Tony Lema, the holder, led after the first round with a five-under-par 68, one ahead of Irishman Christy O'Connor and two ahead of Arnold Palmer and 43-year-old J B Carr (Sutton), the British Walker Cup captain. Carr's round was described as a "box of tricks". At the fifth he had shanked his second into a bunker and promptly holed from there for a 3. Then at the thirteenth after another poor second he holed out with his wedge for another 3.

In the second round, Bruce Devlin moved up to share the lead with Lema on 140 with Brian Huggett of Romford on 141 alongside Palmer. Eric Brown, O'Connor, Carr and four-time winner Peter Thomson were one shot further back, Thomson having recovered from a first round 74 with a 68.

9 JULY

Southport, Friday – P W Thomson (Australia) this evening became the first player of modern times to win five Open Championships. He made this achievement at Royal Birkdale, where in 1954 at the age of 24 he gained the first of his titles. Thomson won with a seven-under-par total of 285 by two strokes from B G C Huggett (Romford) and C O'Connor (Royal Dublin) who had totals of 287.

Thus Thomson laid aside all criticisms that his four other victories were achieved without the full might of American golf ranged against him. This time A Palmer and J W Nicklaus were never in contention after the third round and G J Player (South Africa), the US Open champion, having made an indifferent start, retired after the third round because of a painful neck.

Only Lema, fighting hard to keep his grip of the trophy, advanced the challenge from across the Atlantic but he fell to superior golf on a day of bustling wind. When Lema took three putts on the last green for a 6 Thomson, who tapped the ball in with the back of his putter for his first victory, was left with three putts, which he did not use, to take the title and first prize of £1750.

After the third round the overnight traffic jam had thickened. Thomson took over first place on 214, with B J Devlin (Australia) and Lema, leaders at the halfway point, next on 215. O'Connor, de Vicenzo and Palmer lurked menacingly on 216. S Miguel (Spain), L Platts (Wanstead), Nagle and Huggett rounded off a powerful and cosmopolitan challenge.

The first to lay claim to the limelight was B J Hunt. He seemed on the point of setting a good target when he came to the seventeenth needing two 4s for a 69, but he missed from two-and-a-half feet there and bunkered his drive at the last and two 5s and a total of 289 opened the door.

A long way behind came the star performers. It soon became clear that Thomson and Lema were the main protagonists, but de Vicenzo and Huggett fired an occasional 3 and O'Connor was moving steadily along so that these three kept the two others constantly looking over their shoulders.

O'Connor was first up with a 71 to pass Hunt's target. Sound putting supported the occasional sag in his driving and O'Connor finished determinedly with a 2 from six feet at the fourteenth and 4s at the last two long holes. With a 3 at the eighth, de Vicenzo had the prospect of a low outward half, but four putts at the ninth for a 6 after he had driven something like 50 yards from the green were a blow. But a 3 at the thirteenth, where he holed from seven feet, was one of three in a row. Had he not driven poorly at the closing holes the story might have been very different.

Then came Huggett, a small, burly figure with the

temperament of a bull terrier. A No.2 iron to four yards at the fourth gave him a 2, and he turned in 35. A 3 at the dog-leg tenth saved the 5 he had at the thirteenth, where he took three putts, and having gained a birdie at the long fifteenth, where he pitched to five yards, he survived two bad second shots at the seventeenth and eighteenth, bravely holing from five feet at the last for his 4.

Just as this event was greeted by a tremendous cheer from the packed galleries, Thomson was driving from the last tee. Both he and Lema hit magnificent shots, but whereas Thomson's second shot rolled to within seven yards of the hole, Lema, who has never quite been sure of judgment of the shot through the narrow entrance to the green, pulled his into a bunker.

This had been a tremendous struggle, Thomson out in 34 to Lema's 36, led by three shots. But with strict par figures at the twelfth and thirteenth Lema reduced the lead to one, and when Thomson missed after a fine shot to five-and-a-half feet at the fourteenth and Lema who was short of the hole in two, putted in from five feet for his 3, the outcome hung in the balance.

The next two holes were shot for shot, but Thomson got the break he needed at the seventeenth, where Lema drove to the right, hooked into the crowd, and was glad to make a 5. Thomson's putt for a 3 at the last hit the hole and stayed out, but that did not matter, for Lema sadly relinquished his title by taking four shots from the greenside bunker.

1966

MUIRFIELD

This Open marked a departure from the previous practice of playing 36 holes on the third day. Henceforth, the Open will be decided over four days, one round each day finishing on Saturday. The reasons were to make it possible for the top 55 and ties to play the last 36 holes, to increase revenue with an extra day's gate money, and to make the tournament more suitable for television.

Jack Nicklaus, already with five majors including three Masters and who was second at St Andrews in 1964 to Tony Lema but who still hasn't won the claret jug, took an early lead in the first round with a 70, tied with J Hitchcock. Scottish amateur R D B M Shade scored 71 to lie third. (Ronnie's father is said to have given his son the initials R D B M hoping that he would live up to them and hit the ball "right down the bloody middle", as indeed he was doing here.)

By the end of the second round Nicklaus had a one-shot lead on 137, one ahead of Peter Butler who had a best-of-the-week 65. Two shots further back on 140 were Kel Nagle, Harold Henning and Phil Rodgers with Shade among those on 141.

When Phil Rodgers took 40 to the turn in the third round he seemed to be falling out of contention. He came back, however, in 30 for a total of 210 and Nicklaus bogeyed each of the last five holes, finishing on 212, having dropped nine shots to Rodgers over the back nine. Sanders was a shot further back while Palmer and Welshman Dave Thomas were on 214. Shade remained leading amateur.

9 JULY

Until last week J W Nicklaus had won almost everything worth winning in golf both as an amateur and as a professional except the Open Championship. At Muirfield on Saturday he filled that nagging gap with a final round of 70 and an aggregate of 282, as sooner or later his prodigious talents had to allow him to do. It was no easy victory as in the middle of the third round Nicklaus's measured step was suddenly disturbed, but this time he did not surrender his lead, and bravely though D C Thomas and D Sanders set their joint target of 283, Nicklaus recovered his balance and strode on to a most fitting triumph.

No-one in the history of the game has achieved so much in as little time as Nicklaus. Now he has drawn in the final side of the great modern quadrilateral and joined Sarazen, Hogan and Player as winner of the Open championships of Britain and America and the US Masters and PGA titles. Nicklaus, however, has won them at a younger age, 26, and in a shorter space of time, less than five years, than the others.

On two of his four previous attempts to win the Open Nicklaus finished third at Lytham and second at St Andrews. There was no doubt about his golfing ability and competitive courage, but misgivings did exist that he might be unable or unwilling to accept the need to damp down his power and master British conditions and the smaller ball by hitting his shots on a lower trajectory, making the ground do some of the work for him.

Nevertheless, at the 56 holes during the championship when technically it would have been possible for him to take his driver from the tee, Nicklaus used it only 17 times, and this strategic and coolly detached approach resolved itself handsomely for him in the final round. For example, he played iron shots to the ninth and tenth, covering in nine shots holes which cost Palmer 11 and Rodgers 12. Nicklaus made certain of his figures with four more superbly struck and flighted long-iron shots.

No praise can be too high for Thomas, the solitary British player in the thick of it to the end. Two noble strokes through the wind to four feet at the first for a 3 put him in great heart to sustain his pursuits right round the course. On his day Thomas is the most impressive driver, perhaps in the world, and when, as on Saturday, his putting stroke also is working well the combined results are infinitely worth watching.

His round of 69 was equalled by Player but was the lowest of those in contention. If he looks back on it with any regret it can only be because he did not make the most of a holeable putt at the sixteenth, where his tee shot struck the flagstick, and then when he caught the top of a

bank at the seventeenth with his second shot and took 5. With two shots fewer at these holes, the title might have been his. The wonderfully easy way he hit his second to 15 feet at the last also was not rewarded.

Sanders, for the second successive day, did not have his inelegant but extremely efficient method completely under control with the result that his progress was again a high-class scramble. During the championship he was unable to break 70 but he did produce the most consistent four rounds, at least in their appearance on paper.

1966, 1970, 1978
JACK NICKLAUS

The record books tell the story. Jack Nicklaus, to date, is the most successful golfer the world has ever known and his achievements are unlikely ever to be surpassed. Two US Amateur Championships, six US Masters titles, four US Opens, five US PGA Championships and three Opens in a 27-year period from 1959 – 18 professional majors and 20 in all.

Jack William Nicklaus was born in Columbus, Ohio, in 1940, the only son of a pharmacist who enjoyed his golf and Jack, as a young boy, would sometimes be allowed to tag along. The seed was sown and when Jack was 10 he had lessons at the Scioto Country Club. He practised a lot and at the age of 16 he won the Ohio State Open.

When he won the US Amateur in 1959 he was the youngest player for 50 years to do so. In 1960 he was runner-up to Arnold Palmer in the US Open while still an amateur and the following year won the US Amateur again. He turned professional at the end of that year and just six months later he beat Palmer in a play-off to take his first major, the US Open. He was not at that time the most popular golfer in the world. Many of Arnie's Army resented this overweight upstart kid with the crew cut who had unseated their hero and it is to Nicklaus' credit that he withstood this attitude with a dignity and grace beyond his years. The pair became lifelong friends.

The bitterness soon subsided, however, as Jack matured and grew his hair and it began to emerge what a truly great golfer he was and, more importantly, a fine sportsman and ambassador.

Nicklaus won numerous prestigious tournaments worldwide but perhaps less well known is the fact he won the Australian Open no fewer than six times. As a measure of his consistency at his peak, he was Open runner-up seven times in addition to his three wins. He played in six Ryder Cup sides and was non-playing captain twice.

He now devotes a great deal of time to course design and has been very successful on the US Seniors Tour. Not surprisingly he is an honorary member of the R and A.

1967

HOYLAKE

At Hoylake, where the Open was being played for the tenth and last time, four players shared the lead on 69 after the first round. They were the holder, Jack Nicklaus, Tony Jacklin, Harry Weetman and R R W Davonport (North Hants). Bruce Devlin of Australia and Harold Henning of South Africa were on 70 with six more players on 71, including Gary Player and the popular Argentinian, Roberto de Vicenzo.

Devlin and Nicklaus, shared the lead after two rounds on 140, one stroke ahead of the unlikely quartet of Vicenzo, Lionel Platts, J M Hume, the Scottish-born professional at Formby, and F S Boobyer.

In the third round Player shot a record 67 to temporarily take the lead on 210. Shortly afterwards Vicenzo repeated the feat for a third-round total of 208 and outright lead.

15 JULY

As all the world must know by now Roberto de Vicenzo (Argentina) came at the age of 44 into his rightful inheritance at Hoylake on Saturday. On a tide of brilliant golf and welling, vibrant emotion he prised the Open Championship title from its reluctantly yielding holder, Jack Nicklaus (USA), with a 72-hole aggregate of 278.

And so a dwindling dream became a joyous reality to be cherished and warmed like a glass of fine old brandy, by victor and onlookers alike. "You could cry for the old boy," said Peter Thomson and another multiple champion Henry Cotton, was almost beside himself. It was that kind of day.

Every golfer is a Walter Mitty. "This for the Open" instead of half a crown at stake is a favourite illusion; it was a fact for Vicenzo. On the seventy-second green he had three putts for the title. The first stopped inches away and as the next disappeared the cheers which had accompanied Vicenzo on every step of his triumphal

progress exploded into the sunlit sky, past the barriers of mere encouragement and enthusiasm.

Afterwards, Nicklaus, with the cool detachment which belongs to the completely self-assured, said: "He is one of the lucky ones. An awful lot of fine golfers have tried for 20 years to win a major championship and never succeeded." True, but it was a remark which took little account of the general affection for Vicenzo. Perhaps with the exception of Arnold Palmer, no other professional inspires such unalloyed affection. The two men are much alike in the appeal they command.

Until last week, however, Vicenzo's charming resignation to every setback, bred perhaps by the fatalism of the Latin, compelled the unwelcome belief that he lacked by a hair's breadth that resolve which sets the champion apart from his fellows. After all, since Vicenzo turned professional at 17, having been a caddie in Buenos Aires since the age of 10, he has won some 30 national championships and 140 tournaments round the world. In the last two seasons he has earned thousands of dollars in the States, but always the major titles escaped him.

Six times he finished third or better in the Open. In 1957 he led in the US Open by a shot with nine holes to play. But something always went wrong and one feared for him on this occasion, leading before the final round by two strokes from Gary Player and by three from Nicklaus – about the most exposed situation there could be and especially so for a golfer whose temperament under extreme pressure had been proved unreliable.

He gave us hardly a moment's worry. Vicenzo clearly was in a happy frame of mind, and his swing, the power and graceful rhythm of which is equalled at their advanced years in durability only by Snead and Boros, scarcely faltered. When it did, exquisite chip shots put matters right, but the shaping of his shots to the challenging flagstick positions was masterly, his driving grew longer and straighter, and his holing out, often suspect before, was invulnerable. His natural authority cracked the labouring Player, his partner, by the eleventh. That left Nicklaus as the sole challenger and he was still three behind with five holes to play. "Good boy," murmured Vicenzo as Nicklaus took 5 at the long fourteenth and he followed with the 4 which was its truer par all week. "I feel better now."

Vicenzo pitched into a bunker at the fifteenth and the margin was back to two. Then at the sixteenth, Vicenzo

not merely struck but dismissed from his presence with a spoon a towering shot across the out of bounds to within 20 feet of the hole. That shot really set all fears at rest. Nicklaus, however, is never one to quit and he implacably birdied the last. But with two careful 4s Vicenzo's triumph was proclaimed.

The British cause again proved fruitless, but eight players in the first 20 provided an honourable consolation and the performances of Clive Clark and Tony Jacklin, aged 22 and 23 respectively, were surely not misleading signposts to the future.

1967
ROBERTO DE VICENZO

Roberto de Vicenzo was born in Buenos Aires, Argentina in 1923 into a poor family. He was only 15 when he became a professional golfer and began an incredible career, winning the Argentine Open when he was 21 and going on to win more than 200 tournaments. The majority of these successes were in Argentina and South America but he also won the national Opens of five European countries and won several times on the US Tour.

When he won the Open at Hoylake in 1967 aged 44 years and 93 days, he was the oldest player to have done so in exactly 100 years, Old Tom Morris having done it at Prestwick in 1867 at the age of 46 years and 99 days. Soon after joining the US Seniors Tour, de Vicenzo won their US PGA Championship and in 1980 he took their Seniors Open. He is an honorary member of the R and A.

Ironically for such a prolific winner he will forever be remembered for a tournament he lost, the US Masters of 1968 when he tied with Bob Goalby only to discover, after signing and returning his card, that his playing partner had given him a par 4 at the seventeenth when in fact he had scored a 3. The 4 he had signed for had to stand and he lost by one shot. Eighty years earlier, in the Open of 1888, Jack Burns was more fortunate when he signed for a score which was one shot too many. In his case it was only the arithmetic that was wrong and the mistake was corrected to give him the title.

1968

CARNOUSTIE

The British contingent made a good start this week. After the first round, Michael Bonallack, the Amateur champion, and Brian Barnes were in a share of the lead on 70 with two other Britons, Peter Mills and Maurice Bembridge on 71. Bob Charles, Billy Casper, Tony Jacklin and a young Irishman, Paddy Skerrit, were all on 72.

In the second round, Casper shot a record 68 to lead by four shots on 140 from Barnes, Jacklin and Charles with Gary Player, Jack Nicklaus and Skerrit one shot further back.

Casper stumbled in the third round to a 74, allowing Charles and Player, both scoring 71, to close the gap to one and two shots respectively going into the last round. Nicklaus was two shots further back while Bonallack remained leading amateur on 221.

13 JULY

Gary Player won the Open Championship for the second time on Saturday at the Carnoustie course, resisting the pressing challenge of Jack Nicklaus his partner in the last round. Player walked a tightrope stretched over disaster. He could have slipped up through faults of his own making on a course of uncompromising difficulty or been pushed aside by rivals in or out of sight. Player did not move to victory with the massive self-assurance of Nicklaus nor in the cavalier way of Arnold Palmer. That he kept his balance was a triumph of will, concentration and application and although his total of 289 gave him the prize by only two strokes, it was one of the most clear-cut of his career.

All season in America Player has scored well without being able to win. Inconsistent putting was at the root of the trouble and it was renewal of acquaintance with an old and trusted friend which most contributed to his victory. He took three putts only twice in the championship and his holing out from six to eight feet during the last afternoon was brilliant. Not far behind in importance was Player's achievement in avoiding the worst kind of trouble. He never had a 6, and if the spoon he hit to two feet for a 3 at the fourteenth was the shot that won the title, the stroke would have been valueless without these other qualities he brought to his game.

In the stiff, blustery wind one competitor, Brian Barnes, broke the par of 72 and one other, Al Balding, equalled it. Neither were in contention and those who were must have calculated that the winner would be who could stay closest to the card. And so it proved. Of the four most likely to succeed Player with a birdie at the sixth and the wonderful eagle at the fourteenth, and Nicklaus who had a 4 there, alone scored below par at any hole. Bob Charles, joint second with Nicklaus, and Bill Casper, who was fourth, did not have a birdie between them in the last round.

In a real sense then the course not the players was the overwhelming factor of the championship. Except on the second day, when Nicklaus and Casper broke 70, no-one came near to dominating it. Tight target areas, great length and innumerable hazards made an iron fist of it; the wind which blew for three of the days clothed it in a steel glove.

Nicklaus might well have won had he been prepared to use his power more frequently instead of trying to finesse his way round the course, as others also did. His drive out of bounds at the sixth was costly for he was able to make 4 comfortably with the second ball and he took three putts at the short eighth but his play coming home, and especially his driving was immense. His tee shot on to the sixteenth green was one of the great strokes of the championship and by keeping the pressure bearing down on Player he made the finish more gripping than it otherwise might have been. In seven Opens Nicklaus has had one victory and four times had the second lowest aggregate: he has also proved himself to be one of that comparatively rare breed who can accept failure to win graciously.

Charles plays a muted game and it has become something of a cliché to describe him as one of the great unwatched. He hit a dreadful drive into a bunker at the third, went into another and took 6, otherwise he played well and outscored Casper, with whom he played the last 36 holes, by seven shots.

Casper, who seemed halfway to victory when he led by four strokes after two rounds, lost touch with his putting on Friday and never regained the confidence on the greens he had shown in making his record score of 68. He drove fractionally out of bounds at the fourteenth and

another 6 at the last cost him second place. Tony Jacklin on whom high hopes rested, committed a suicidal 7 at the seventh where he drove out of bounds. Eric Brown with six 3s in his score of 73, re-emphasised his liking for the small ball and led the Scottish party on a total of 299. Michael Bonallack, the British and English champion, duly took the amateur award, for which he was the only qualifier.

The final thought on a memorable week is that Carnoustie is infinitely worth restoring to the championship roster. Quite apart from its stature as a course its general suitability for staging the complex event which the Open has now become is the equal of any and better than most. And, just as important, events at Carnoustie are always well supported as the crowds this week have demonstrated.

1969

ROYAL LYTHAM AND ST ANNE'S

Bob Charles who won here in 1963 demonstrated just how much he likes the Royal Lytham course by shooting a record 66 in the opening round. Tony Jacklin and Hedley Muscroft from Moor Allerton shot 68s while Miller Barber of the United States had a 69.

In the second round, Charles maintained his challenge with a steady 69 but saw his lead cut to one when Christy O'Connor broke the day-old record with a 65 for a total of 136. The young Jacklin had a steady 70 to stay in contention.

Charles and O'Connor slipped in the third round with 75 and 74 respectively to be tied for second place on 210, while the 25-year-old Jacklin turned in another 70 to take a lead of two shots going into the final round.

12 JULY

Tony Jacklin made the golfing world his oyster on Saturday when he won the Open Championship at Royal Lytham and St Anne's by two strokes with a total of 280. He is only the ninth British professional in five decades to take the title and his achievement will bring him rewards far above the record first prize of £4250 and beyond the dreams of any of his predecessors.

At 25 Jacklin has an attractive personality and as the first British winner for 18 years he is in pole position to convert his triumph into considerable wealth, as much as half a million dollars according to his manager, Mark McCormack.

Jacklin gives much of the credit for his capacity to win to the experience he has gained in the hard school of American professional golf. After another year's toughening process there was no sign this time of the collapse he endured last year at Carnoustie. Perhaps his example will have the same effect for British golfers as Roger Bannister's four-minute mile had for athletes.

Jacklin has won three tournaments after having led as he went into the last round, but this was a new kind of ordeal. With his own hopes and those of a multitude of spectators resting on his shoulders Jacklin, not unnaturally, was highly nervous at the start of the last round but he kept his feelings under iron control. He made certain he did not swing too fast and only two drives missed the fairway. He holed only two putts of any length and his sand play was again in wonderful order. Twice in the last round he was down in two from bunkers.

Thus Jacklin passed the test which scores of British professionals have failed, with flying colours. Although there were no Americans in the first five after three rounds six were in the first 12 and this was the strongest representation from the United States beaten by a British player since 1937, when Henry Cotton overcame the full might of an American Ryder Cup side at Carnoustie.

Of course there was the gnawing fear that Jacklin, two strokes in the lead as the final round began, would not be able to protect his advantage against this challenge, strengthened by the closer threat of three former champions, Peter Thomson, Roberto de Vicenzo and Bob Charles.

Lytham has established a history of producing winners who benefit from the mistakes of others, but this time the pattern was broken. No-one could build up and sustain a charge from behind Jacklin and at least one reason may have been the challenging positions of the flagsticks. The wind was less gusty than before yet none of Jacklin's pursuers could do better than 72, one over par, which was Jacklin's own final round.

Jacklin, with long putts at the third and fourth, made a better start than the others and bought himself valuable insurance against any further setbacks, and the overcast afternoon was brightened by only the occasional vociferous acknowledgement for a holed putt. Apart from the welcome, heard in the distance, given to the procession of players as they came towards the packed stands around the last green it must have been one of the quietest of final days in an Open Championship.

But not of course at the climax, when Jacklin, with a wonderful flourish rifled a long straight drive over the treacherous bunkers at the last and struck his second shot inside that of Charles, his partner and closest pursuer, to make certain of victory. First Charles then Jacklin missed their putts but by then they were merely completing the formalities.

Peter Tupling won the amateur medal adding an unnecessary but satisfying credit to his credentials for selection to the Walker Cup side, which will be announced today.

In total the attendance of 45,845 was some 6000 down on last year's figures at Carnoustie, but that was expected. The management and presentation of the championship by the Royal and Ancient and the host club were, however, unsurpassed, especially in the supply of scoring information on the course. This reached a new degree of sophistication and is without question the most comprehensive of any system yet devised anywhere in the world.

1969
TONY JACKLIN

Anthony Jacklin was born in Scunthorpe, England, in 1944, the son of a lorry driver. His father introduced him to golf when he was nine and he soon decided that his future lay in the game. He wanted to be the best in the world and he quickly demonstrated that he just might have the talent.

He won the Lincolnshire Boys' Championship at 13, played for the English boys' team against Scotland when he was 15 and at 16 won the Lincolnshire Open. The leading professional was nine shots behind him. In 1962 he became an assistant professional at Potters Bar Golf Club and the following year won the Sir Henry Cotton Rookie of the Year award. A year later he won the British assistants' title.

By 1969 when he won the Open at Royal Lytham he had already won the Dunlop Masters – scoring the first televised hole-in-one in the process. In America, where he had gone to develop his game in the toughest company, he won the Jacksonville Open in 1968 and was regarded by many as the next superstar. This seemed to be confirmed when in 1970 he became the first Briton in 50 years to win the US Open and only the second Briton ever to win both the Open and the US Open, a distinction which still stands.

The weather contributed to his unsuccessful defence of the Open title in 1970 at St Andrews, where he reached the turn in the first round in 29 and birdied the tenth before a thunderstorm stopped play. He finished with 67 and eventually came fifth. In 1972, however, it was Lee Trevino's cruel chip into the hole at the seventeenth in the final round which proved his undoing and Trevino went on to win. Trevino had chipped in at the same hole in the third round and also at the sixteenth.

Although Jacklin won a number of European events thereafter his experience at the hands of Trevino had given his confidence a severe blow and he never seriously looked like returning to his earlier form.

His contribution to European golf was far from over, however, and in 1983, as non-playing captain he led the European Ryder Cup team to defeat by only one point, their best performance since their win in 1957. Jacklin, who crucially had persuaded the disillusioned Severiano Ballesteros back into the fold, insisted on first class travel and the best of everything for his team, to remove feelings of inferiority to the Americans who had been existing that way for years. In 1985 he led them to victory at The Belfry and two years later to their first ever win on American soil. After retaining the Trophy in 1989 with a drawn match he stood down as captain.

He was awarded the OBE after his US Open success and is an honorary life president of the British PGA.

1970

ST ANDREWS

A violent thunderstorm on the first day caused severe flooding and resulted in the suspension of play with 38 players still out on the course. Neil Coles had already posted a record 65 while last year's winner, Tony Jacklin, out in 29, was eight under after 13 but had just found trouble at the fourteenth, with a cut second shot into whins when the weather intervened. Jacklin eventually finished with a 67.

After the second round Lee Trevino was in the lead with a total of 136 with Jacklin and Jack Nicklaus one behind.

Prime Minister Ted Heath turned up to give Jacklin his support in the third round, accompanied by Reginald Maudling and another of his cabinet colleagues, William Whitelaw, who just happened to be Lord President of the Council and captain of the R and A.

Going into the final round Lee Trevino, who shot a third-round 71, was leader on 208 with Jacklin, Nicklaus and another fine American golfer, Doug Sanders, two shots back.

11 JULY

St Andrews, Sunday – Relief and exultation, probably in equal measure, were combined in the excited gesture of triumph made by Jack Nicklaus on the last green of the Old Course this afternoon. Having holed with impassive finality from eight feet he flung his putter high in the air, Open champion again, four years after his first victory at Muirfield. That putt was the only one of any length Nicklaus made during four grinding hours of play, but it came when he wanted it most – to halt at last the brave counter-attack launched by Doug Sanders over the closing stretch of their 18-hole play-off for the title and the prizes of £5250 and £3750 respectively.

Nicklaus's lead of four strokes with five holes to play had been whittled down to one when they came to the seventeenth. There Sanders hit a No.5 iron shot which skirted the Road Bunker and ran to within 15 feet; Nicklaus, with a No.7 iron, struck an even better to follow and was well inside, only to miss the putt. At the last, 358 yards long, Nicklaus unleashed a colossal drive which ran through the fast sweep of the Tom Morris green into the bank behind. Sanders, just short, chipped to four feet, and Nicklaus, fortunate to find the ball lying well, pitched down the slope. Afterwards he said he hit the putt almost before he was ready, but it was firmly struck and fell in.

Sanders, whose tragic mistake yesterday made the play-off necessary, completed the formality of holing out, round in 73 in the strong wind, but beaten by a shot by the 72 of his opponent, par for the 6951-yard course. It was a dramatic ending to a contest whose inevitable result someone compared to the spread of dry rot.

Nicklaus said later that if a player wished to be remembered he must win at St Andrews. The remark confirmed the seriousness of his pre-championship statement of intent that he wanted to win here more than anything else. He had not captured a championship for three years, and he prepared himself with care.

He was the first to admit that he backed into a tie with Sanders on a 72-hole total of 283 and the chance to win where six years before he was runner-up to Tony Lema. That place belonged on this occasion to Sanders, who was joint runner-up to Nicklaus in 1966 and had to accept second best again.

Nicklaus played 15 holes in strict par, having made only one mistake, when he drove into a bunker at the long fifth and putted his third below the green. But he matched Sanders's par with a perfectly judged pitch to three feet and retained the two-stroke lead he had gained when Sanders took three putts at the third and was not up in two at the fourth.

Out in 36 to 38, Nicklaus drew further ahead when Sanders took two shots in the Strath Bunker at the eleventh and half-socketed his approach to the thirteenth, where Nicklaus drove into a good lie in the rough across the sixth fairway.

When Nicklaus missed from three feet at the fourteenth and Sanders holed from five feet the first stirrings of life in what had become a corpse of a contest were evident. They became more so when Sanders made a birdie 3 from 18 feet at the fifteenth and retrieved yet another stroke at the sixteenth, where Nicklaus pitched through the green and took three more. But then came that fine second shot at the Road Hole, which halted the slide.

None of these dramatic events would, of course, have happened if Sanders had not missed that putt of three feet on the home green yesterday. Seldom can a shot of such little length have caused proportionately greater relief to Nicklaus, more inconvenience to hundreds of people, or deeper anguish to Sanders. Except presumably for Nicklaus, the congregate sensation was of having had a handful of cold mud slapped across the heart.

The arguments will last forever about the choice of shot to the green which Sanders might have made. He was quite far back off his drive and a pitch-and-run was a possibility, but at such critical moments a player instinctively goes with the shot he knows best and a ball in the air is not hostage to unpredictable bounces.

When Sanders's shot stopped as far as 30 feet behind the flagstick three putts became alarmingly possible. He had not been past that hole in the three earlier rounds, and the pace of the slope down is notoriously difficult to judge. In the event he left the ball short and did not touch the hole with the second putt. Until the depressing finish Sanders, with his strait-jacket swing, had played one of the best tournaments of his life. In the rough weather he drove well and hit two superb shots out of the Strath and Road bunkers for pars at the eleventh and seventeenth. The latter enabled him to hold his lead over Nicklaus with the least dangerous closing hole on any British championship course to come.

Nicklaus's main problems in the past three years have overtaken him on the greens. He felt he had not struck his putts that badly, but he had 39 of them in his 73, four more than in the play-off round, in which Sanders took 32. His round was a strange mixture of shots struck with great authority and no great conviction at all.

With the hard westerly wind boxing the players' ears, concentration was not easy nor was maintaining the rhythm of a swing. The only player to break the par of 72 was John Panton, who came home in 33 for a magnificent score of 71, lower by two shots than the next best. This effort brought him into twelfth place, worth £1200, the largest single cheque of a long and illustrious career.

Lee Trevino, the leader after the second and third rounds, did not have it on the day to hold on, though his birdie at the last made him joint third with Harold Henning on 285, one stroke ahead of Tony Jacklin. No praise can be too high for the courageous defence Jacklin made of his title. Sooner or later he had to return from the clouds to the world the rest of us live in, and his progressively higher scores, even allowing for the increasingly difficult weather, were all the indication needed to show that he was at last wilting beneath an accumulation of wearing pressures.

Jack Nicklaus allows Doug Sanders a touch of the cup he so nearly won

1971

ROYAL BIRKDALE

The Open was celebrating a second centenary this week. Eleven years ago the championship was 100 years old, having been inaugurated in 1860 but, with the intervention of two world wars and a one-year gap in 1871, it was only now that the oldest and greatest golf tournament in the world would be played for the 100th time.

In 1860 there was no prize-money. In 1960 at the Centenary Open the total prize fund was £5625. This year it is eight times as much at £45,000, with the winner receiving £5500.

Four prominent Americans, including Arnold Palmer, failed to turn up and the draw was done without them. Tony Jacklin and Lee Trevino, the 1968 US Open winner, shared the lead after the first round with two lesser known golfers, American H Johnson and Vicente Fernandez from Argentina, all on 69. The holder, Jack Nicklaus, finished with two 6s for 71.

In the second round Jacklin and Trevino had matching 70s to take the lead on 139, one ahead of an unexpected challenger from Formosa, Liang Huan Lu. Roberto de Vicenzo who said he played the last hole "like my grandmother" was on 141 alongside Gary Player.

Despite unfortunate heckling from the gallery Trevino returned a 69, as did Lu and with Jacklin taking 70, Trevino went into the final round with an aggregate of 208, one ahead of both.

In the final round, Brian Barnes and his South African playing partner, Tienie Britz, set a new record. Out first they covered the 18 holes in 116 minutes.

10 JULY

Lee Trevino won the Open Championship at Royal Birkdale on Saturday because when he came to grips with it his game was in sound order, his thinking consequently more positive than just about every other player who before the start could be taken seriously as a contender. It was Trevino's twelfth event in succession. In the preceding 11 he had been out of the first 10 only twice and in the space of three weeks had gained both the US and Canadian titles, bringing his victories for the season to four and his official prize-money to $196,000.

Trevino still plays like the hungry man he was a little over four years ago, when only his friends and relatives had ever heard of him. His immediate ambition, he frankly admitted, is to win the Western Open which starts on Thursday in Chicago. Such a completely commercial confession sounded strange coming from one who had just carved himself a niche in golfing history by winning the one hundredth Open and in so doing joining three of the most distinguished names in the game – Jones, Sarazen and Hogan – as the only players to have taken both the British and American titles in the same summer.

But the remarkable assumption can be made that part of Trevino's success is due to the fact that he simply loves to play golf. And how he can play. With his muscular thrust from a wide and open stance to the ball set far outside his left foot, Trevino can make all the shots he needs. Moreover when his stroke is right, Trevino can putt the eyes out of a course, as he did on Saturday afternoon. Seven single putts and 11 all told took him out in 31 and increased his lead over Lu and Jacklin from one shot to five and eight respectively.

Liang Huan Lu, or "Mr Lu," as he was known to one and all, became the most unforgettable figure of the championship, even though he did not win. Showing no trace of nervousness and splendidly preserving the rhythm of his rather flat but neat swing, he made hardly an error, and by staying so close to Trevino as he did, he prevented his American partner from turning the championship into a rout,

Trevino dropped shots at the tenth, where he showed he was human by taking three putts, and the fourteenth, where he was bunkered, and so one of his key strokes came at the twelfth, where his recovery from sand hit the flagstick and fell dead into the hole. With five holes to play Lu was three behind and Tony Jacklin, playing just ahead, had cut his own margin to five.

Meanwhile Craig DeFoy had completed the outstanding performance of his career by pitching out of a bunker to within four feet at the last and with a score of 69, set the first genuine target of 281, 11 under par. But Trevino, joking and chattering as he always does to relieve the tension, strode on through the warm, overcast afternoon, apparently in full command.

Then abruptly, just as Jacklin made a last effort, chipping in for a 3 at the sixteenth and following with two more birdies, Trevino's confident step was broken. His drive from the seventeenth tee between the two menacing mounds did not fade back as his shots usually do. The ball plunged into a sandy depression, his attempt to remove it took him into rough on the other side of the fairway, and a 7 was the jolting result.

Had Jacklin holed for an eagle 3 from 10 feet at the last and had Lu been able to make a birdie at the seventeenth instead of under-hitting his second shot, they would relatively have been level with Trevino. Their inability to exploit Trevino's lapse gave the American some breathing space, but not that much as he faced the final ribbon of fairway between the bunkers and the rough and the vast throng of spectators.

Trevino hit two fine shots to the back of the home green, nestling beneath the packed arena of grandstands. Lu's drive left him with a stance on the edge of a bunker below the ball, which he duck-hooked, striking a spectator on the head. Lu pitched his third to nine feet and Trevino putted firmly some 20 inches past. Lu, as he thoroughly deserved to do, holed out for a certain second place, but Trevino, in the classic situation of having "this for the Open" decisively despatched the putt.

The new champion's final round of 70 gave him a total of 278, two shots higher than the championship record established by Arnold Palmer in 1962 at Troon. It earned Trevino £5500, of which he immediately gave £2000 to a Southport orphanage.

Jack Nicklaus was one of seven Americans in the first 16 but duly said farewell to his title, as a final gesture, holing a long putt for an eagle for his great audience to acclaim.

1971, 1972
LEE TREVINO

Lee Buck Trevino was born in Dallas, Texas, near the Mexican border in 1939 and the Merry Mex is credited with having put a lot of the fun back into golf. He was brought up in squalid conditions by his mother and his grandfather. His home was a wooden shack with neither electricity nor plumbing. He never knew his father. His shack was in a field near the Glen Lakes Country Club and when he dropped out of school at 14 he started to caddie and to teach himself how to swing a golf club.

The result was a unique style which at first sight did not seem likely to win anything, never mind six majors. He had an open stance, an out-to-in-swing and took an ungainly lunge at the ball. Beautiful it wasn't, but it worked, especially in money matches which toughened him up. "You don't know what pressure is," he said, "until you play for five bucks with only two in your pocket."

He joined the Marines when he was 17 and this gave him the opportunity to play in the Far East where he was based. He made little impression on the US Tour when he returned and played in his first US Open in 1966, finishing well down the field. The following year he finished fifth and then in 1968, at Oak Hill, he played four rounds under 70, the first man to do so in the US Open, and won by four shots from Jack Nicklaus. He won his second US Open in 1971, again relegating Nicklaus to second place. That year he added the Canadian Open and the Open to his tally, all three within a four-week period. In addition to his two US Open wins he also won the US PGA twice and the Open twice. He was 44 when he won the US PGA for the second time.

Not only was Trevino's swing unorthodox, his whole demeanour on the golf course and his approach to the game at the highest level was alien to most players, in particular his constant wisecracking and his banter with the galleries. At least one English professional specifically requested at one tournament that he be drawn with somebody other than Trevino.

Trevino played in six Ryder Cup matches and was non-playing captain in 1985. He joined the US Seniors Tour in 1990, winning seven events in his first season and has gone on winning. He was elected to the World Golf Hall of Fame in 1981.

1972

MUIRFIELD

A little-known 22-year-old Yorkshire professional stole the first-round thunder of the world's leading golfers. Peter Tupling, a former British boys' champion and leading amateur in the 1969 Open, returned a 68 to lead by one from Tony Jacklin and by two from five others, including Jack Nicklaus.

Brian Barnes, the Anglo-Scot son-in-law of former Open champion, Max Faulkner, had the most rollercoaster round of the day. His par 71 included a 6 at the first, a hole-in-one at the 181-yard fourth, which he promptly followed with a 7 after a 25-minute wait on the tee. He then missed a 10-inch putt at the tenth before having an eagle at the seventeenth.

Brilliant sunshine brought record crowds for the second day. American Doug Sanders looked like taking the second round lead with only one hole to play but closed with a triple-bogey 7 to open the door for Jacklin and holder Trevino who both finished on 141, one ahead of Sanders and Tupling.

Trevino closed his third round with five consecutive birdies, chipping in at the last for a 66 and 207, one ahead of Jacklin who had a 68.

15 JULY

Two Muirfield members were discussing with a marked degree of incredulity the bunker shot and chip Lee Trevino had holed in the third round of the Open. "But don't you know," an American professional remarked as he passed their table in the clubhouse, "that God is a Mexican?"

That exchange on Saturday morning was prophetic as well as wry, for several hours later Trevino, all hope of retaining his title draining away, listlessly chipped at the ball from a lie against the grain of the grass behind the seventeenth green. It ran 15 feet into the hole, the fourth time in the championship Trevino has perpetrated such a recovery, and broke the back of this three-cornered duel with Jack Nicklaus and Tony Jacklin. Whatever outrageous elements it contained, Trevino's victory by one shot with a total of 278, six under par and a record for an Open at Muirfield, established him more firmly than ever in the front rank of world golf.

Trevino will next month complete only his fifth year as a tournament player, yet in that time he has captured four major titles, the British and US opens twice each – as many as Nicklaus, who alone over the same period has won more money.

Trevino's first ambition when he joined the professional circuit was to earn $1m, and at his present rate he expects to reach that target in two years. He is a player of such skill and outstanding golfing intelligence that he will no doubt achieve his aim but, at the age of 32, he also seems certain to add more important championships to those he already has. It will never be dull watching him do so.

As he did last year and as the late Tony Lema did eight years ago, Trevino gave himself only 48 hours to prepare his campaign. This compares with the full week Nicklaus gave himself, but in temperament they are very different men and one suspects that such lengthy preliminaries would not be compatible with Trevino's restless nature. He admitted that the absence for most of last week of a really strong wind was a tremendous help.

In becoming the first player since Arnold Palmer 10 years ago to defend the title successfully, Trevino never went above the par of 71 in any round, a tribute to his ability to avoid the disasters which overtook almost everyone else as well as to the fortune which smiled on him from time to time. Another important factor is Trevino's belief that he can always do well on a British links course because they suit his game.

Of course, Trevino's triumph was Nicklaus's

197

disappointment. His failure was certainly glorious, but it ended his hopes of taking the four major titles in the same season and left him still tied with Bobby Jones's total of 13 championships. Nicklaus, six shots behind Trevino when the fourth round began, knew he had no choice but to charge the course. When he did he changed the character of the championship and lifted the last afternoon towards its concluding dramatic moments.

"I felt I needed 65 to win and I had a 65, but it got away," he said after making his 66, equal to the course record. "It was the first time all week that I was in control of my iron play. I made an adjustment towards the end of the third round which worked, squaring up the face of the club instead of laying it slightly open at the address as I usually do."

Nicklaus in full cry is an awesome sight. He did much of his catching up out of sight of the television cameras, and had the third birdie of his round with two imperial strokes into the easterly breeze on to the green at the long fifth. Inhibitions were lost all over the place and there were 11 scores under 70, one more than in the three previous rounds added together.

Out in 36, Nicklaus became six under par with seven to play and the feeling was strong that a historic round was in the making. But at no comparable stage was Nicklaus able to take a clear lead over his two closest challengers. Behind him the scoreboards told Trevino and Jacklin the story of his dazzling challenge; as if on cue both had eagle 3s at the ninth and birdies respectively at the eleventh and twelfth. Soon they were relatively all level with three holes to play. Then, at the sixteenth, Nicklaus missed the green and shed a stroke. Probably annoyed,

Nicklaus on the next tee swung a little too quickly and hooked into deep rough from where he was never in sight of the birdie he needed so much.

His challengers also missed the short hole green, but Trevino came out of a bunker dead and Jacklin having recovered from another, kept abreast by holing serviceably from eight feet. Jacklin split the next fairway and then Trevino, who had to come away twice from his drive as first one man then another scuttled across the course, bunkered the shot badly. Dispirited, Trevino was through the green in four, Jacklin handily placed on it in three – whereupon Trevino holed out yet again.

Little wonder that Jacklin shook his head in disbelief. After the assault by birdie he had withstood so courageously on Friday evening that further blow was too much and he took three putts.

The spectators in the vast amphitheatre of packed stands round the home green watched in dismay as Jacklin bunkered his second shot, but rose to acclaim Trevino's winning strokes. A long straight drive, and then Trevino with his characteristic thrusting action hit a superb No.8-iron shot to eight feet. He had two for the title and used them both, and so a championship which only half an hour before had teetered in the balance, was suddenly over in an atmosphere of acute anti-climax.

Having now seen the organisation and presentation of the British and US Opens inside a month and the facilities offered to the paying public at both, I can safely say that the Royal and Ancient Golf Club's championship committee have nothing to learn from their opposite numbers.

1973

TROON

Gene Sarazen, aged 71 and playing in his last major, had a hole-in-one at the Postage Stamp eighth in the first round. Ironically 50 years ago when he first played in the Open, also at Troon, he failed to qualify. His ace earned him a magnum of champagne and a bottle of whisky, the latter donated by Arthur Havers who won at Troon all those years ago in 1923. Asked if the ball had bounced, Sarazen said: "I don't know. I couldn't see that far."

On more mundane matters, American Tom Weiskopf, runner-up in the Masters in 1972, led after the first round with a record 68, one ahead of fellow Americans Bert Yancey and Jack Nicklaus and two ahead of Johnny Miller, also from America.

In the second round Tony Jacklin was penalised two shots after being seen on TV unwittingly infringing the rules. Meanwhile Weiskopf broke his own day-old record with a 67 for a 135 total, and a three-shot lead over Miller and Yancey and one more over Nicklaus.

In heavy rain on the third day, Weiskopf's lead was cut to one when he scored 71 to Miller's 69 for 206 and 207 respectively. Yancey had a 73 for 211 while British pair Neil Coles and Brian Barnes had 70s for 213. Nicklaus fell back to 215 with a 76.

14 JULY

The significance of what may be only a coincidence has still to be determined. But the victory of Tom Weiskopf in the Open Championship at Troon a month after Johnny Miller's triumph in the US Open may have ushered in a new phase in golf. Having between them won the last three British titles and four of the previous six American championships, Jack Nicklaus and Lee Trevino have had their grip loosened. This could be a temporary condition but while it lasts a new and not unwelcome dimension is added to the game.

No less an authority than Nicklaus himself said of Weiskopf that he had the best natural talent extant, and of Miller, joint runner-up with Neil Coles to him on Saturday, that he possesses the soundest swing technically of the latest crop of professionals. "You will see at lot more of both of them," he added – and that takes little believing.

The first major is always the hardest to win. In retrospect, and looked at from every possible angle, Weiskopf's breakthrough into a circle to which many are called but few are chosen was fashioned in a truly remarkable manner.

To begin with Weiskopf had never gone into a tournament after a full week of practice so confused as to how to play the course. Yet at the end he had played strongly enough to equal, in totally different conditions, the record aggregate of 276 set by Arnold Palmer 11 years before to win by three shots. Moreover, on Britain's most rugged championship course, its fairways sodden and slow instead of baked and fast, Weiskopf was the first player since Henry Cotton in 1934 to stand alone at the head of affairs after each round. Troon's tradition of establishing precedents was splendidly upheld.

Naturally Weiskopf was able to declare that it was the best tournament shot for shot he had ever played. For one thing he did not once take three putts; for another, despite all his misgivings, he drove the ball consistently well on a course where there is virtually no choice of line from the tee.

Only on the inward half of the third round was the power and grace of Weiskopf's swing not properly synchronised. Like all successful American professionals Weiskopf's holing out was relentless and it is possible to say that he won the championship at the fourth attempt, first by keeping Miller at bay, by getting up and down in two from four bunkers and then gaining a shot, and perhaps a psychological advantage on him, with a par at the fifty-fourth hole.

An hour's practice on Friday night enabled Weiskopf to realign his stance correctly. He did not sleep well – a condition which has, however, preceded all his tournament successes – and had some difficulty in swallowing his breakfast. But having learned to accept adversity he felt reasonably confident.

Weiskopf's single word of advice – "tempo" – to Tony Jacklin on the eve of his 1970 US Open victory was expanded by Nicklaus to "don't play Miller, play your game". Determined not to rush his play, Weiskopf had instant and lasting control of his swing through another dismal rain-drenched afternoon. When he holed from 25 feet for a 4 at the long sixth, Weiskopf was 12 under par and had a lead of three shots for the first time since the end of the second round. There was one uneasy moment when he missed the twelfth and thirteenth greens and dropped his only shot of the round at the latter.

When Weiskopf had rolled a No.3 iron shot down the flagstick at the seventeenth he knew the title was his and his safely played par at the last, before a large, patient, and appreciative audience, simply confirmed his belief.

At 24 years of age to Weiskopf's 30, Miller has slightly the less tournament experience. He will surely be around for a long time yet and although Weiskopf's superior armoury of shots makes him potentially a more dominant figure in world golf, Miller is at least continuing to destroy a reputation for lack of staying power. Miller's holing out was vulnerable towards the end but he was down in two from a bunker at the last to tie with Coles for second place. Coles shortly before had hit a No.6 iron to six feet and holed for a birdie to stay in front of Nicklaus, whom he had seen just ahead of him establish a record of 65 with two almost identical shots.

Coles, by far the most accomplished shot-maker to emerge in British professional golf during the last decade, did himself justice at last in an Open by putting together four solid rounds.

Nicklaus beat his third-round score by no fewer than 11 shots, but as he said after having compiled a score which could easily have been two shots better: "I always think I have a chance as long as there are holes left."

1973

TOM WEISKOPF

Born in Ohio in 1942 Tom Weiskopf started playing golf at 15 and turned pro seven years later. His swing was described as majestic, he was one of the longest hitters in the game and he had a delicate touch around the greens. He should have gone on to become one of golf's "greats" but displayed a lack of ambition. He gained the nickname "Towering Inferno" because of his suspect temperament. He played in two Ryder Cup matches and was chosen for another but turned it down in favour of a hunting trip.

In 1972 he won the World Matchplay Championship and early the following year his father died. In 1973 when he won the Open he also won four other tournaments in America in the space of two months. He was runner-up in the US Open in 1976 and finished in that spot in four US Masters.

He later became involved in course design, his most notable work being the Loch Lomond course, which now hosts its invitational tournament the week before the Open, and is rated one of the finest inland courses in the world.

1974

ROYAL LYTHAM AND ST ANNE'S

Gary Player and little-known John Morgan (Southampton) shared the first-round lead on 69. One stroke back was Bobby Cole of South Africa and Danny Edwards of America. In the second round Player returned a 68 to take the halfway lead on 137, five shots ahead of his nearest rivals, Brian Cole and Peter Oosterhuis with Edwards one shot further back.

Player faded to a 75 in the third round for a total of 212 but his rivals failed to take advantage although Oosterhuis reduced the gap to three with a 73 and Nicklaus returned a third-round 70 to be only four behind on 216.

13 JULY

Before the Open Championship at Royal Lytham and St Anne's last week, Gary Player remarked that finding form was like putting together the pieces of a jigsaw puzzle. In preparation the idea was to fit the bits in gradually and hope that the last ones would fall into place at the right time.

On Saturday afternoon in glorious sunshine, Player completed a picture he had begun to assemble in the first round. Except for some brief moments of hesitation on Friday and in the final round, he never seemed likely to lose his way altogether and, with a final score of 70 for an aggregate of 282, two under par, he won by four shots from Peter Oosterhuis with Jack Nicklaus one further behind.

The ninety-ninth victory of his career was Player's third in the championship and the first to be achieved using the big ball. He has now won eight major world titles. The extent of his achievement, however, goes far beyond adding lines to a record book.

At 37, Player may well have travelled more miles than any other athlete in pursuit of ambitions that have been unquenchable since he turned professional in 1953. It is

19 years since he first entered the Open, 15 years since he first captured the title at Muirfield for the first time, and six since his second victory at Carnoustie. One has to go as far back as the more spacious days of Harry Vardon and J H Taylor to find a winner of the championship in three successive decades.

The span of Player's successes is not confined to the Open. In April he won the Masters 13 years after his first victory at Augusta. As an example of dedication, fitness and a dependable method acquired painstakingly while others were endowed with more natural swings and stronger physiques, Player's is hard to match in any sport. Winning from in front may be the best way – and Player was at the head of affairs after every round, as Tom Weiskopf was at Troon – but it is by no means the easiest. Only a month ago, Player led for more than two rounds in the US Open and was eventually overtaken. "I don't like to lose from a lead," he said, "and this week was agony. Playing last in the two final rounds, there was so much time to kill that I felt as though I had been here for ever." However, from the moment when, in a freshening westerly breeze, Player made birdies at the first two holes and increased his overnight advantage of three shots over Oosterhuis to four, he was not in serious danger. Even dropping shots at the fourth and fifth made no difference for when Oosterhuis, his partner, and Nicklaus, who was immediately ahead, had birdies at the long sixth and seventh holes, Player responded with an eagle and a birdie.

Player had difficulty finding the ball in dense rough a few feet from the seventeenth green but by then was six shots in front of Oosterhuis. He could easily afford to concede one and he let another slip at the last. Player overshot the green and was close to the clubhouse wall but played back on, standing left-handed and using the back of his putter. Another 5 might not have been much of a finish for the packed grandstands, but there was no sense of anti-climax in the spontaneous reception Player received.

Oosterhuis had his best Open. He stuck manfully to an unyielding partner and opponent and upheld what remained of the reputation of Britain's tournament players – a thing of shreds and patches in an international context. One explanation, apart from the obvious one that the great majority are not good enough for this company, was the lack of 72-hole competition in the weeks before the championship.

Nicklaus left yesterday for an enviable change of activity and scene – salmon fishing in Iceland. On Saturday, Nicklaus had two putts on every green going out and was finally deflated by missing from six feet for a birdie at the thirteenth. After that, all he wanted to do was get off the course.

Fears that playing the big ball would lead to an exceptional number of embarrassingly high scores proved groundless. Player's winning total is only two more than Tony Jacklin's in 1969. Player, who thinks the professionals should adopt the 1.68in ball worldwide and leave the 1.62 to the amateurs, contended that he would not have scored better in the first two rounds using the small ball.

The total attendance broke all records. On Saturday there were 17,455 spectators, giving a final count for the week of 90,625. The final touch came at the presentation on Saturday evening when Player received the trophy with his name already inscribed on it. The engraver, who had to work swiftly to make this pleasant gesture possible, was the father of Garry Harvey, the former British boys' champion from Perth.

1975

CARNOUSTIE

Often a controversial course, particularly with Americans, it was a change to hear Johnny Miller, rated second favourite to Jack Nicklaus, describe Carnoustie as "very fair", even if he did qualify this by suggesting that the first fairway looked like it had a hundred elephants buried under it. There was no such thing as a straight bounce, he said.

After the first round the competition was wide open with Peter Oosterhuis, the 1974 runner-up, leading on 68, a group of six on 69, including Jack Nicklaus and David Huish (North Berwick) with four more on 70 and eight on 71, including Tom Watson, Raymond Floyd, Roberto de Vicenzo and Johnny Miller.

In the second round Huish added a 67 to lead by two on 136 from South African Bobby Cole, who scored a record 66, and Oosterhuis and Watson, all three on 138.

Huish had a third-round 76 to fall out of contention while Cole, with another 66, took the third round lead on 204, one ahead of Jack Newton who posted a record 65. Miller was lying third on 206 with Watson one shot further back.

12 JULY

Tom Watson, of the United States, rebuffed in three previous heavy flirtations with a major title in the last 13 months, finally had his suit accepted at Carnoustie yesterday when he won the Open Championship in an 18-hole play-off against Jack Newton, of Australia. On what was only the eleventh such occasion in 104 championships, Watson, an engagingly boyish figure, had a round of 71, one under par, to beat Newton, a chain smoker and stern-faced by comparison, by one shot. As the more finished golfer Watson deserved the victory but both 25-year-olds played creditably.

Watson had begun to build an unfortunate reputation for declining important opportunities after leading by one

shot with a round of the US Open to play last year and by three after the second round of that championship three weeks ago. There was nothing uncertain, however, in the way he hit a No.2 iron shot through the wind and drizzle at the last hole which they had reached, in matchplay terms, all square. The shot was a little heavy but it avoided the many hazards round the green.

Newton, who had played first, dragged his shot with the same club into a bunker and his recovery skidded on the damp green 15 feet past the hole. Watson, as he had done almost throughout, laid his approach putt close and after holing out became champion when Newton's last effort slid past.

It can never be easy for two players, even as strong and ambitious as these contestants, to return with enthusiasm to the starting block after the strains and pressures already experienced in the previous 72 holes. Both were a little jumpy at the start and a crowd, unexpectedly large for a contest involving players less renowned than several whom they finished ahead of in the championship itself, also took time to settle down.

A small boy pocketed Newton's ball at the second and Watson, with justifiable impatience, rounded on a camera man who set his machine into whirring action, causing Watson, who was starting his backswing on the third tee, to pull the shot into rough. That was the last of such irritating incidents.

Newton, generally, did not have as firm control as Watson over his swing and had the rough not been so flimsy the contest might have been resolved sooner. After only three holes, Newton was two shots down. Watson's bunkered drive and third shot at the fifth and a chip at the next less accurate than his opponent's bunker recovery gave Newton openings to square. Watson made an important save at the short eighth by holing from 15 feet for his 3 and both turned in 36.

Newton was fortunate that his stance in a rabbit scrape gave him relief from behind a trap at the eleventh and the chance to halve the hole. Watson played the twelfth poorly and Newton's birdie gave him the lead for the first and only time. The Australian did well to hole from five feet after hitting a bunker recovery through the thirteenth green. But after he had chipped close at the next he could do nothing but watch as Watson chipped in for an eagle 3 from 30 feet and again took the lead.

Watson's tee shot slid off the sixteenth green and so they were again level, but the American kept his composure and holed a nasty left-to-right breaking putt of five feet for the half at the seventeenth, the only hole in the last six not playing into the revived easterly wind. So they came to the last where Watson's four perfect shots avoided extra holes and what would have been the first sudden-death play-off for any major title decided by strokeplay.

Whatever the result and however it is achieved a play-off inevitably is an anti-climax. It tastes of something twice cooked and were it not for the importance of the championship, sudden death immediately after the original 72 holes would seem preferable. That would be the end of the affair, the paying customer would have had his money's worth, and there would be no fall in the crescendo of the championship.

Saturday's play was fascinating, not only for the outcome, but the fashioning of it. For three days the players had had their way with a course in a state of easy virtue; then the bill was presented, written on the westerly wind. Before the final round there had been 79 scores below par, 34 of them lower than 70; during it there were only four players under par and only one, Bob Charles, better than 70. In the end six players beat Ben Hogan's record aggregate for Carnoustie of 282.

All the same the total of 289 on which Bernard Gallacher and Sam Torrance tied for nineteenth place was the same as Gary Player's winning aggregate seven years ago. But still the most treacherous finish of any of Britain's great courses had the last word – on the sixteenth tee Jack Nicklaus, Bobby Cole, and Johnny Miller, as well as Watson and Newton, were all in a position to win.

Nicklaus almost holed a chip at the last and was home in 34, the best by any of the principal contenders. Cole and Miller failed to island hop to complete safety among the twists of the Barry Burn. But Watson holed from over 20 feet at the last for the birdie which made Newton sweat out a par 4 and realise a play-off.

After a bad drive and bunkered second at the fourteenth where a birdie was to be expected, Cole fatally missed the next green with a No.8 iron and dropped shots at the next two holes as well. Miller attempted too much with his recovery from a bunker at the last and left the ball in. So many were so near to joining yesterday's contest.

1975, 1977, 1980, 1982, 1983

TOM WATSON

Tom Watson was born in Kansas City, Missouri, in 1949 into an affluent middle class family and young Tom was introduced to golf early at the local Prairie Dunes Golf Club. He won the state amateur championship and at Stamford University, where he graduated in psychology, he played on the golf team. He turned professional in 1971.

It took him three years to achieve his first tournament win, the 1974 Western Open, and some believed he did not have the temperament to win at the highest level, a notion which is hard to understand today but which at the time had justification following a disastrous final round in the 1974 US Open and poor performances the following year in both the Masters and the US Open again.

The Open at Carnoustie changed all that when he emerged from a group which included Jack Nicklaus and Johnny Miller to tie with Jack Newton and won the 18-hole play-off by one stroke. He went on to win four more Opens, four US Masters and one US Open. He was leading money winner on the US tour five times, including four consecutive years from 1977 to 1980.

Unlike many fellow American professionals, past and future, Watson grew to love links golf and the great golfing traditions which he found at places like St Andrews and Carnoustie and at some of the courses he visited in Ireland. One of his favourites was Ballybunion Old Course on the west coast of Ireland. He would take every opportunity when visiting Europe to play friendly matches on some of the better known links courses not on the Open circuit.

He played in four Ryder Cup Matches and was non-playing captain in 1993.

Tom Watson (right) and Jack Newton dispute the silver claret jug in 1975. Watson won the play off

1 9 7 6

ROYAL BIRKDALE

The Open was marked by a record first-day attendance in excess of 17,500, the previous best being in 1974 when almost 15,500 attended on the first day.

Three players emerged as first-round leaders, Irishman Christy O'Connor, Japan's N Suzuki and the emerging young Spaniard, Severiano Ballesteros, all on 69, closely followed by the American, Tom Kite, Jack Newton of Australia and Anglo-Scot Brian Barnes, all on 70.

The 19-year-old Ballesteros added a second 69 to lead by two from Johnny Miller who carded a 68 for a halfway total of 140. In the third round, playing in rain and a testing south-west wind, Ballesteros played swashbuckling golf to record a 73 and a three-round aggregate of 211 to retain his two-stroke lead on Miller who also returned a 73.

10 JULY

Twelve years ago a promising young California amateur saw the Open Championship cup brought back to his club in San Francisco by Tony Lema and hoped that one day he would repeat that achievement. On Saturday the hope became fact and yesterday the trophy started on its journey back to America under new ownership.

Johnny Miller, aged 29, won the title at the sixth attempt, five years after his first, by coincidence also at Royal Birkdale. His total of 279, nine under par, was completed in bright sunshine and a dwindling breeze with a final round of 66, equalling the course record, and his victory by six shots was the biggest since Arnold Palmer won by the same margin in 1962 at Troon.

Miller, tall and slender and with a mop of blond hair, is a typical product of the American golf system. As an amateur he finished joint eighth in the 1966 US Open for which he qualified although he had expected to be acting as a caddie instead. Since he turned professional he has made the progress expected from one with his talent. For Miller his win was important to his mental attitude and his pride. "A lot of players have won a major title once," Miller said afterwards "but not many have won twice and if I do nothing else this year this victory will have made it a great one for me."

Only three other players were actively concerned in the championship's destiny. The resourceful young Spaniard, Severiano Ballesteros, who was in the lead for three rounds at last gave ground but with no dishonour and distinguished himself by tieing for second place with the inevitable Jack Nicklaus.

Always before an Open one looks for a pointer to an eventual winner. Miller filled the requirements. After his usual flying start to the year on the desert courses, he had lain comparatively fallow. Taking tenth place in the US Open last month rekindled his enthusiasm. Time for only two practice rounds was a close replica of the Lema strategy.

On Friday, Ballesteros was able time and time again to save reckless driving with the recovery play of a sorcerer's apprentice. But at last Miller asserted himself over his presumptuous young partner, whose last act of defiance was to hole for par from 25 feet at the first where Miller took three putts and fell three shots behind.

At three separate holes before the turn there was a swing of two shots in Miller's favour, but the decisive spell came after that. At the eleventh Ballesteros, still swinging flat out, hooked from the tee, was unplayable in three, and took 7 to the 4 of Miller, who promptly struck a No.4 iron shot to 12 feet for a 2 at the next and chipped in from 15 yards for an eagle 3 at the thirteenth.

No-one wanted to see Ballesteros, who had contributed so much colour and life to the championship, disintegrate in a welter of lost shots. The exact opposite happened for Ballesteros, some of his luck and magical short game restored, and unpatronisingly encouraged in his efforts by Miller himself, made three birdies and an eagle in the last six holes.

And so the improbable dream was duly proved impossible. Miller summed up Ballesteros's performance by saying that it was better for someone so young to finish second. "He is not ready yet for the pressures."

This was Nicklaus's fifth second placing in the championship. He set expectations of a lasting challenge alight with birdies at the third and fourth, but hardly had he closed the gap than he let it widen again beyond

recovery by taking 6 at the sixth, where the ball slid off the face of his No.1 iron and vanished forever in the scrub.

Miller is a noted front-runner, liking nothing more than to pile up greater and greater gains and rub the noses of his challengers in his superiority. Somehow, at the moment Nicklaus was experiencing his disaster, one knew that Miller was certain to win. There was never any hint that he might stumble. Miller used his driver from the tee only six times and on 10 occasions drove or played second shots with his No.1 iron, along with an old driver restored to favour, his putter, and pitching sand wedges the only clubs in his bag without graphite shafts.

1976
JOHNNY MILLER

For about three years Johnny Miller was one of the best golfers in the world. The problem was he didn't really want to be or perhaps it would be more accurate to say that it wasn't all that important to him. He had other priorities, in particular his family of six children and his religious beliefs.

Born John Lawrence Miller in San Francisco, California, in 1947 he won the US Junior championship in 1964. He played golf for his university team in 1966 and that same year went to caddie at the US Open at the Olympic Club in California. He was drafted in to play as a reserve and finished eighth while still only 18. Three years later he became a professional and won his first tournament in 1971. In 1973 he went into the final round of the US Open six shots adrift of the lead and fired a stunning 63 to win,

the lowest ever single round in that championship. In 1974 he won the first three tournaments on the US Tour, the first time this had been done, and went on to win a total of eight that year, a feat previously bettered only twice and equalled once. Hardly surprisingly he was leading money winner on the US Tour that year.

In 1975 he was second to Jack Nicklaus in the US Masters and his win in the Open in 1976 elevated him to the elite group of only a handful of players who have won the Open and the US Open. In addition he had been runner-up in the Open at Troon in 1973, the year he won the US Open, and on two other occasions he was runner-up in the US Masters.

He continued to play and to win from time to time into the eighties and nineties with a win as late as 1994, but he is better known now as an outspoken commentator on the game, defending its traditions and high standards of behaviour, which he always maintained as a player.

1977

TURNBERRY

The first round of the Open has produced some unlikely leaders, none more so than this week which marks Turnberry's debut on the Open rota. The early leader was Yorkshireman Martin Foster with a 67. Then, as the sun set over the isle of Arran, an American, John Schroeder, making his first appearance in the competition, finished with two birdies for the outright lead on 66. Jack Nicklaus, Lee Trevino and Tom Watson, all former winners, returned 68s.

In the second round both Schroeder and Foster had 74s while Nicklaus, Watson and Trevino returned 70s for aggregates of 138. Roger Maltbie of Australia carded a 66 to lead on 137 and Hubert Green had a 65 to join his three fellow Americans on 138. The round of the day was reserved for Mark Hayes of Edmond, Oklahoma, who had a 63 to beat Henry Cotton's 1934 record for the lowest single round in the tournament by two strokes.

Ben Crenshaw, who had quietly reached the halfway stage in 140 shots, produced a third-round 66 to lead on 206 only to see Nicklaus and Watson produce 65s to move three ahead going into the final round. Three shots further back were Tommy Horton who also had a third round 65, American Gaylord Burrows and Maltbie.

9 JULY

Before the Open Championship began I suggested that the world of professional golf might be in a period of gestation and not far from giving birth to a new leader in the person of Tom Watson. On the evidence of the outcome of that gripping contest with Jack Nicklaus at Turnberry on Saturday when Watson won the title for the second time in three years there seems to be no reason to change that opinion. Nicklaus has described Watson as being amongst the most positive thinkers and exponents he has known. Defending champion Johnny Miller said

that Watson is one of those few who have that look in their eyes and that indefinable aura that sets the champions apart from their fellows.

Twice now this year Watson has fought unremitting struggles with Nicklaus for a major title and has prevailed twice. In the final round of the Masters they were paired apart: in the Open they played the last two rounds in each other's company, seven-and-a-half hours of confrontation to make lesser mortals steel silently and respectfully away – which in this instance they did in droves.

A not too fanciful interpretation, is that Nicklaus, not only the most prolific winner of major titles there has ever been, but so many times more in the first five, is at 37 ready to give way to a man 10 years his junior and less worn by competition, just as Arnold Palmer did in his due season to Nicklaus.

Watson's boyish appearance conceals a tough, clear-thinking mind. It would need to be to withstand the pressure Nicklaus has inflicted on him. Nicklaus is renowned for the way in which he manages a round; Watson has now shown to be Nicklaus's equal in poise and composure and in their two contests has played the better golf – fractionally but still better.

After all, Watson played the last 36 holes over the Ailsa course in 130 shots, a championship record, Nicklaus in 131 to finish second for the sixth time. Nicklaus broke the old record aggregate by seven strokes yet lost by one to Watson's 268, 12 under par. Watson really outlasted Nicklaus. Throughout the thunderstorm on Friday and the brilliant burning sunshine the next day Watson was once again three shots down, four times two down and four times one down.

Watson in the final analysis drove more accurately over

the two rounds and for all that the rough was sparse that advantage lent Watson an edge in confidence. Just as at the Masters, Nicklaus played well but Watson played better and just as three months ago with Nicklaus in hot pursuit, Watson made the fewer mistakes.

The contest was as exciting and reminiscent of that epic struggle two years ago at Augusta when Nicklaus held off the double challenge of Miller and Tom Weiskopf to win his sixteenth major. There was a further parallel in that two long putts holed near the end in both events determined the issue. In 1975, Nicklaus's huge putt across the sixteenth green gave him the lead. On Saturday Watson's bolted into the hole from off the fifteenth green, also a birdie 2, which squared what to all

intents and purposes was a head-to-head match. That shot had a large element of luck, but no champion can afford to be without that.

Experience prevented Nicklaus disclosing emotion. Yet the fact is that he missed the seventeenth green with a straightforward No.4 iron shot and then a putt of five feet down a quick and teasing borrow to go one shot behind for the first time. Watson's No.7 iron to two feet at the last was the shot of a player in complete command of his swing and nerve; Nicklaus's cut tee shot, remarkably executed recovery from near whins and putt of 30 feet were the shots of a player who knew the game was up but was determined to keep it afoot to the end.

1978

ST ANDREWS

Despite claiming that St Andrews gave him headaches because he had to use his brain too much, Isao Aoki of Japan took the first-round lead with a 68, one ahead of Severiano Ballesteros, Raymond Floyd, Jack Newton and Tom Weiskopf. Jack Nicklaus was handily placed on 71.

Ballesteros should have taken the halfway lead but for dropping two shots by going out of bounds at the seventeenth in a round of 70. He was still tied with Aoki and Ben Crenshaw on 139 with Tom Watson and Tom Kite among several on 141. Nicklaus had a 72 to go into the final 36 holes four shots behind the leaders.

After three rounds Watson moved into the lead with a 70 for a total of 211 where he was joined by Peter Oosterhuis. Nicklaus closed the gap to one shot with a 69, while Aoki, Crenshaw, Nick Faldo, Kite and Weiskopf were all in contention on 213.

15 JULY

The years have been rolled back by Jack Nicklaus's third victory in the Open Championship, his second at St Andrews. His first over the Old Course in 1970 ended a three-year drought for him in the major events: his second on Saturday came after three more lean years, induced, it has been suggested, by the erosions of age.

Skill, ambition, dedication, and pride are the fuels which propelled the careers of the great sports champions. Nicklaus, aged 38, seemed to have lost the art of bringing these ingredients together at the one time: after he had succeeded in winning his fifteenth major title as a professional, pride, it emerged, was principally satisfied – as follows:

"I played my best golf from tee to green this year. I won this tournament without a putter, I can't remember any championship in which I've done so many things right. I played the shots and made the scores to finish the way I had to. I'm a better player in more ways because I'm not as strong as I was and I can't over-power a course as I used to."

Nicklaus's pride is not false, however. He believes that his achievement in winning the British and US Opens, the Masters, and US PGA championship three times or more will be beaten (an arguable view) and he was so affected by his victory that instead of his usual machine-gun recitation of the clubs and shots Nicklaus had some difficulty, in the emotional state of his mind, recalling the details of his final round.

Although a declining ability to concentrate appeared to cause his lack of success in the US and Canadian opens recently, Nicklaus decided his method was at fault. On the advice of his only teacher, Jack Grout, he changed his grip, strengthening the left hand, but another change, on the eve of the last round, had its own significance. Believing he would play well, Nicklaus postponed his departure for the United States on Saturday until early yesterday morning, an arrangement that still left time for his private jet to make the journey to Ohio so that his son, Jack II, could compete in a local event today.

How correct Nicklaus's decision was became clear during an afternoon dappled by sunshine and shadow and complicated by rapid shifts of fortune. If this championship, the 107th of the line, had been slower than many to gather momentum, it more than made up for the deficiency now. Two factors particularly nourished the roots of Nicklaus's victory. Overnight the wind had changed direction from east to west for the first time since Sunday, which many of the players had not therefore experienced during practice. Nicklaus licked his lips at the prospect and remembered how fast the seventeenth green became for putting downwind.

Raymond Floyd's 31 home for 283 set the first serious target, but a challenger emerged on whom no-one, not even Nicklaus, his partner, could have reckoned before the start. Simon Owen, who had been left for dead before the turn, served up five birdies in seven holes from the ninth, completing this sequence by chipping into the fifteenth hole to lead by a shot. The ghastly thought then crossed Nicklaus's mind that he might again be the victim of an outrageous stroke of a kind similar to Tom Watson's putt against him at the same stage last year at Turnberry.

Such moments try a man, but Nicklaus responded and by his resource, shot management, and sheer strength of mind turned the championship irrevocably his way. After Nicklaus's approach to the sixteenth had allowed Owen to have a good look at the ball an ingratiating eight feet from the hole, the New Zealander pitched strong and his bogey to Nicklaus's birdie reversed, at two strokes, the lead.

At the seventeenth Nicklaus tried merely to bounce a No.6 iron shot up on to the plateau. He narrowly failed, but Owen, from rough, went on the road and Nicklaus's recollection of the quickening pace of this green helped him judge his putt up to the holeside from below the bank. The rest, as the saying goes, is history.

On reflection, that one stroke, as a product of nerve and experience, justified the exceptional demands the eccentricities of the Old Course's design make on a player. It must be encouraging for the future of the championship as a powerful international event that Ben Crenshaw and Tom Kite, like Watson, professionals of a younger generation, intend to keep testing their mettle here.

Peter Oosterhuis, who lives in America, is almost in the same category and his fifth-place finish in this company reflects the value of competing in that hard school. Nick Faldo's high placing, a stroke behind Oosterhuis, deservedly rewarded him for steady rounds and the continuing progress of a necessary apprenticeship.

But of course the day belonged to Nicklaus. It seemed, as he approached 40, that his championship days were numbered, but as he walked briskly up the broad expanse of the last fairway, accepting the acclaim of the Scottish spectators with whom he seems to have established a special relationship, it looked as if Nicklaus's championship career had been reborn.

1979

ROYAL LYTHAM AND ST ANNE'S

Fuzzy Zoeller, the Masters champion, was playing this year in his first Open but the bookies' favourites were Tom Watson and last year's winner, Jack Nicklaus.

The now customary surprise leader was this time the Scot, Bill Longmuir, who went to the turn in 29 and came back in 36 for a record 65. Nicklaus, who had a 72, including a hole-in-one, suggested Longmuir was "a fictitious player you put at the top of the leaderboard". Behind the unranked Scot the top players were well spread out with US Open champion Hale Irwin on 68, Steve Pate one stroke more and World Matchplay champion Isao Aoki on 70. Severiano Ballesteros was one of several on 73. Longmuir hung on grimly on the second day, making two birdies in the last three holes for 74 and a halfway total of 139, to lie third behind Irwin who had another 68 for 136 and Ballesteros who equalled the day-old record of 65 for 138. In a cavalier final flourish he played the last five holes in one over 3s. Watson and Nicklaus stayed in touch with aggregates of 140 and 141 on a day when most Britons "needed a ladder to get to the leaderboard". Only two finished in the first 16.

The third day was a wretched summer afternoon of cloud, rain and wind, making scoring difficult. Irwin and Ballesteros both had 75s to occupy the two top spots on 211 and 213 respectively, with Nicklaus and Mark James one shot further back.

21 JULY

The purists may say that the way Severiano Ballesteros won at Royal Lytham and St Anne's on Saturday was no way to win a major title. The reality is that there was no other way Ballesteros could have won the Open Championship. To have done so would have been out of character. It is true that apart from the mistakes others were making he was escaping with ones twice as bad. No-one is supposed to win the Open having hit the fairway only twice with his drives in the final 36 holes.

But Ballesteros said he would like the championship to be played without fairways – and that was how he won this one.

Ballesteros hit nine tee shots into the rough during the final round and that fairly typical ratio could be attributed to the mixture of courage and foolhardiness, aggression, and wilfulness that have made his game so appealing. Kindly lies in trampled rough sometimes saved him, but he also failed only once in 15 attempts to recover in two shots from greenside bunkers.

It was Ballesteros's play over the last six holes that demanded suspension of belief. At the thirteenth he drove into a bunker, at the fourteenth and fifteenth he was in rough, first right then left, at the sixteenth he was in a car park and at the end of the seventeenth in rough again and then bunkered in two. It was, no doubt, thoroughly improper to win the championship in such a way. Indeed, the contention was that he could not have won on an American course where there are trees, water, and uniformly thick rough. But that was not the examination paper last week and links courses are well known for their accommodation of wayward hitting.

It was worth noting that Ballesteros, whether or not he was playing in some kind of state of grace, had one of only four scores below the par of 71 all day. The others, Nick Faldo, Sandy Lyle and Simon Owen, were far removed from the pressures of contention on another day of rough heavy wind.

Thus Ballesteros frustrated not only the United States champion, Hale Irwin, his bemused partner for the final two rounds. He also thwarted the holder, Jack Nicklaus, into second place for the seventh time and left Ben Crenshaw to be joint runner-up for the second successive year. Mark James, equal fifth in 1976 when Ballesteros was equal second, moved up one place. And now, still only 22, Ballesteros becomes the youngest player to win the title since Tom Morris Jr in 1872 and the only winner from the Continent since Arnaud Massy of France in 1907.

1979, 1984, 1988

SEVE BALLESTEROS

Judged on majors alone, Severiano Ballesteros would emerge as a very fine golfer indeed but hardly the remarkable individual that he was and still is. His contribution to and his influence on the development of European golf over the last 30 years is without parallel. The youngest Open winner this century, he was only the second European to take the title since Max Faulkner in 1951, the other being Tony Jacklin, While Americans took the next four Opens, Seve's intervention in 1979 was the beginning of the end of American domination.

Ballesteros, born in Pedrena, Spain, in 1957 was the youngest of four brothers, all of whom became professional golfers and he had an uncle who had competed at international level in Spain. The game was in the family and it wasn't long before Seve began to play. All he had was an old No.3 iron with which he would practise for hours on the Santander Golf Course after the members had left, playing long shots, short shots and little delicate chips, possibly even putting with the same club. There is little doubt that this basic training explains his uncanny ability to manufacture the miraculous recovery shots which he so often required as a result of wayward driving.

Apart from his three Opens and two Masters his winning record is impressive with over 50 tournament wins on the European circuit and at least 20 more worldwide. In 1980, he was the youngest winner of the Masters and he was inspirational in the European victories in the Ryder Cup, culminating in a fine performance as non-playing captain in 1997.

His five majors tell only half the Seve story. He also had that indefinable charisma that Palmer had, the ability to appear almost human while producing golf shots which were verging on alien to mere mortals.

CHAPTER SEVEN

THE MAKING OF MILLIONAIRES

BALLESTEROS LEADS EUROPEAN CHARGE

The shooting star that was Severiano Ballesteros had come of age with his first Open win in 1979. Never mind that the US Open eluded him. He rocked the foundations of American golf the following year by becoming the first European to win the jewel in their crown at Augusta National and repeated that Masters success three years later to begin a European procession. Sandy Lyle, Nick Faldo, Ian Woosnam, Bernhard Langer and Jose-Maria Olazabal all followed suit.

By that time victory in the US Open was no longer absolutely necessary to convince Americans of the strength of golf on this side of the Big Pond. They knew all about it thanks to the revival of that long-time no-contest called the Ryder Cup. The Great Britain team that biennially took on America and usually lost was extended to Europe in 1979. Europe won the cup at The Belfry in 1985 and then beat the Americans in their own back yard at Muirfield Village two years later. This was under the captaincy of Tony Jacklin and included the inspirational figure of Ballesteros, the men who had spearheaded the Open's revival in the preceding two decades. The Americans knew then they had a match.

Against this background, the status of the Open, the only one of the four now well-established majors held outside America, needed no further hype, just consolidation. Spiralling prize-money would count for US Tour purposes as well as world rankings and exemptions into the big tournaments.

More and more top players, moreover, were becoming millionaires in official prize-money and on the back of that were lucrative endorsements. No expense was spared in the pursuit of excellence. Players had managers, coaches, psychologists and physiologists, some even had private jets. Equipment would move into those contradictions in terms, metal woods, with titanium heads, carbon shafts and designs using rocket technology.

Tom Watson would earn his place in Open history with his fifth win in 1983, but such was the worldwide depth of talent that dominations like the Great Triumvirate and Big Three were never likely to happen again, though Nick Faldo emerged with three wins and Greg Norman two. In a surprise link with the old days, Paul Lawrie in 1999 became the first home-based Scot to win the Open for 106 years.

At the forefront of it all was the Open, now a passport to untold riches. It was all such a far cry from the dire poverty of the Open pioneers, those eight men who stood outside the Red Lion Hotel in Prestwick to have the rules read out to them. One thing has never wavered throughout those enormous changes. It remains exactly the same as it was on that cold October day at Prestwick in 1860. It is the dream – to be champion golfer of the world, no more, no less.

1980

MUIRFIELD

For the first time the Open was played from Thursday to Sunday. Lee Trevino and Tom Watson, first and second on the US money list, each returned 68s in the first round in miserable weather to lead by one from Nick Faldo, Mark James, Jack Newton, Vicente Fernandez and G Ralph of Bognor Regis. Holder Severiano Ballesteros, the pre-tournament favourite, was on 72, one ahead of Jack Nicklaus.

Horacio Carbonetti, a former Argentinian lawyer, who had a 78 in the first round, improved on the second day by no fewer than 14 shots to return a Muirfield record of 64. The 32-year-old who had previously twice failed to qualify, said: "I am a good player, I think."

A total of 87 players qualified for the last two rounds with Trevino leading on 135, three ahead of Ken Brown, Steve Pate and Tom Watson. Nicklaus and Ballesteros were in a group of six on 140.

Ken Brown, the only Briton to start the third round in the first 10, had another 68 to share the lead with Trevino on 206, and carry the flag alone into the final round, while Ben Crenshaw, who also had a 68, was in third place on 208.

20 JULY

Tom Watson's position as the world's leading professional golfer, arguable only because of the very human failing of having allowed major titles he perhaps ought to have won to slip away from his grasp, was put beyond any reasonable doubt by his convincing victory in the Open Championship yesterday at Muirfield.

Not this time the gruelling struggles for the other two opens Watson has won – in the play-off against Jack Newton at Carnoustie in 1975 and in that deathless contest at Turnberry two years later with Jack Nicklaus. Now, after an uncertain start, all was certainty.

So it was at the end of another bleak but dry afternoon

that Watson completed a final round of 69 for an aggregate of 271, 13 under par. His reputation, based on a relative handful of examples, for playing erratically and losing last rounds was at least on this occasion unjustified. The margin, once seven strokes, finished at four.

The vain challenge was best carried out by Lee Trevino, whose 69 for 275 gave him his best finish in this championship since he won the title at Muirfield eight years ago, and by Ben Crenshaw, now third after being runner-up in the two previous Opens, having also had a 69 for a total of 277.

Sadly, Ken Brown, who had so gallantly carried the British standard single-handed for two days, fell back with a 76 to 282, to be overtaken by two strokes by Nicklaus and Carl Mason, who, for three days, though withdrawn from the heat of battle, had bobbed on and off the leaderboard with scores below par.

The basis of Watson's victory was established over the last nine holes of the third round. Trevino dropped a stroke at the closing three holes and when Watson made the statutory birdie at the long seventeenth and splashed out of a greenside bunker for his par at the last, he had an inward half of 30 and a score of 64. Deadlock was transformed into a four-shot swing in Watson's favour.

Every seaside course needs its defences strengthened by a wind and some swiftness in its greens. Neither was forthcoming on Saturday when, among them, 89 players produced 38 scores of par or better. Of these 17 were below 70, Isao Aoki leading the procession with his astonishing 63 which equalled the championship record and broke that for the course by a stroke.

Yesterday some dignity was restored by a brisk and chilling north-easter to a links which had yielded four of the five lowest rounds ever recorded in the Open. The wind had the effect of giving holes back their true value but it followed another night of torrential rain which eliminated any last hopes there might have been of any appreciable pace being added to the greens.

Brown's waif-like appearance and unswervingly reserved attitude seemed to be a fragile bulwark against the strength, experience, and achievement of the five Americans ranged against him at the start of the fourth round – Watson, Trevino, Crenshaw and, if only briefly, Hubert Green and Andy Bean.

A major contribution to Watson's success was the failure of any of those closest to him to put on pressure at a time when he himself was not in full confidence. At three of the first four driving holes Watson was in the rough but he dropped only one shot and significant advances were made by no-one.

Crenshaw did hole from 20 feet for a 3 at the first, where Brown took three putts and Trevino went through to record his fourth successive bogey. But the pace of Watson's game picked up as, almost for the last time, he turned his face away from the wind and he made birdies at five out of six holes from the seventh. Gained by putts of no great length, they broke the back of the contest.

Watson dropped a shot at the short thirteenth, his favourite hole on the course, where he was bunkered. Trevino had been bunkered there before him and saved par from 10 feet but his birdies from 12 and 15 feet at the next two holes, taking him relatively to within four shots of Watson, were his last efforts.

Crenshaw's accurate bunker shots to save par at the sixth and seventh could have been the basis for a significant attack. He followed Trevino's putt for a birdie at the eighth with one of his own and at that stage, just before Watson began his vital thrust, the two partners were within three strokes of the leader. But although Crenshaw drove well throughout the championship his iron play, particularly in his judgment of distance, was too frequently at fault.

The reluctance of Brown to come, so to speak, to the starting post – fidgeting interminably around the first tee as he did – was surely nothing more than a reflection of tension. Having stood up manfully to his partnership with Trevino on Saturday, here he was, last out again, in the equally formidable presence of Watson.

Brown's pace of play is as stimulating sometimes as watching glue run down a wall, but his application has to be admired. After his initial slip, Brown gave further ground by missing a very short putt at the fourth and, having matched Watson's 2 at the seventh, he ran out of steam as the last holes took their toll of his limited resources.

1981

ROYAL ST GEORGE'S

The Open returned to Royal St George's at Sandwich for the first time in 32 years. The turnout of Americans was well down, so much so that Arnold Palmer criticised his fellow countrymen for not coming to an event which he considered a must for any serious professional. Had he not won the Open, he said, his career would not have been fulfilled. One of the reasons given for the poor attendance was the continually escalating prices for hotels and other accommodation – up to £2500 being charged to rent a house for a week.

In an afternoon of wind and heavy rain Jack Nicklaus had his worst Open experience, carding an 83, three shots more than his first attempt at Troon in 1962. Nick Job (unattached) shared the lead on 70 with Vicente Fernandez. There were six on 71, including Tony Jacklin, and nine on 72, including Americans, Palmer and Bill Rogers, Scot Sam Torrance and Australian Greg Norman.

Nicklaus improved by an incredible 17 shots on Friday, equalling the course record of 66, while Gordon Brand, the Yorkshire professional, went one better with a record 65. The American, Rogers, who also had a 66, led at the halfway stage on 138, one ahead of Ben Crenshaw and Nick Job and two ahead of the German, Bernhard Langer. Sam Torrance was fifth on 141.

By the end of the third day Rogers had increased his lead to four shots, scoring a 67 for an aggregate of 205. Crenshaw with a 70 was in second place on 209, while Mark James and Langer were one shot further back.

19 JULY

"There is not," said Bill Rogers, after he had taken the lead in the second round, "too much to be gained by letting the expense of the journey get in the way of playing in the Open Championship." At Royal St George's yesterday the 26-year-old American's clear-headedness in establishing his priorities was deservedly rewarded when he won the title by four shots and with it £25,000.

That margin may sound comfortable enough and, indeed, Rogers began the final round with a lead of five strokes. But he had to recover resolutely from a stumble of alarming proportions towards the turn which reduced his advantage over the German, Bernard Langer, to one shot. That Rogers succeeded so quickly and so decisively further endorsed the worth of his victory.

Rogers, who tied for second place in the US Open last month and is rare among professionals in not wearing a glove on his left hand, had a final round of 71 for a total of 276, four under par. For the fifth time this season, Langer had to be content with being runner-up on 280, three strokes ahead of Mark James, for the third time in six years the leading British professional in the Open, and the redoubtable Raymond Floyd. Sam Torrance did himself proud in achieving highest finish by a home-based Scot since Eric Brown in the 1950s. Had he not taken 6 at the last he would have shared third place, not fifth on his own; the financial, loss was heavy, £5000, but Torrance's closing 70 earned him £8500 and handsomely advanced his attempt to get a Ryder Cup place.

By tradition, the third round is the one in which to make a move, the fourth to avoid fatal mistakes. That was perhaps more applicable when the final 36 holes were played in one day, but on Saturday Rogers mastered the course so impeccably that from 13 players being covered by only five strokes only five players were now covered by eight strokes, by five of which Rogers led.

The shake-up was such that Ben Crenshaw, only one shot behind after two rounds, finished the third 10 adrift, and holder Tom Watson went from four shots behind to 12.

Whereas Rogers was accurate, Crenshaw and Watson were wayward and the consistency of Langer and James enabled them to chisel out scores and take up the challenge. The interest now lay in discovering if Rogers, having conquered the course, could also be master of himself.

Rogers, if only by way of the leaderboard, must first have glimpsed the ghostly shadow of pursuers when a poor chip shot cost him one stroke at the fifth and a sequence of glaring errors a dismal 7 at the long seventh. The process of steadying the rocking boat began when Rogers laid a long approach putt dead at the next, just the stroke to give him the breathing space he so urgently required.

Rogers' position could not have become more perilous. After eight holes he was only one shot ahead of Langer, two in front of Floyd, whose four birdies in seven holes from the second constituted the afternoon's most ambitious counter attack, and four ahead of James.

But Rogers held on to win then and he showed singular composure and presence of mind to regain the initiative after only two more holes. Approach shots close to the

ninth and tenth made birdie 3s and he thereby gained two strokes on Langer, one on James and no fewer than four on Floyd who blunted his thrust with two bogeys. When Rogers pitched to four feet at the twelfth for another birdie he was as good as home free. Only at the last did Rogers find the rough and, as if in acknowledgement in the proper manner of the resounding applause from the grandstands around the green, Rogers holed out manfully to save his par.

When he broke 70 in the two final rounds at Muirfield last year Rogers announced he could play seaside courses. The omen was there; it simply was not recognised as such.

Watson, Jack Nicklaus, Arnold Palmer, Hubert Green and Tony Jacklin all finished on 290 – inside the first 25 who will be exempt from qualifying next year.

The amateur medal went to US champion Hal Sutton, who beat the only other survivor of the breed, Geoff Goodwin, after the Englishmen had gone 5, 7 at the last two holes to drop four shots, the very margin by which Sutton finished ahead of him.

1981
BILL ROGERS

Bill Rogers was born in Waco, Texas, in 1951 and played in the 1973 Walker Cup before turning professional. He had five victories on the US Tour and in Britain won the World Matchplay championship two years before his Open win in 1981 at St George's, which proved to be his best year with five wins worldwide.

Rogers, willowy in build, was not a long hitter but the strength of his game matched the very premium of St George's demands, accuracy from the tee. Until then, Rogers was best known for having won the World Matchplay championship and for the more dubious distinction of having earned the most money in a season without actually winning a tournament.

He quickly lost his sparkling form, though he did finish third in the US Open in 1982 and had a US Tour victory in 1983, and made fewer tournament appearances before withdrawing altogether from the tournament scene.

1982

ROYAL TROON

With the absence of many Americans the previous year and one of their reasons being the expense of taking part, the R and A took steps to protect the Open as the world's premier golf tournament. The steadily rising prize fund was increased again with the winner standing to benefit with a first prize of £32,000, up £7000 on 1981.

A 22-year-old American, Bobby Clampett, who finished equal third in this year's US Open alongside Bill Rogers, took the first-round lead with a 67, which included 11 single putts and only 25 in total, two ahead of Tom Watson and Nick Price of Zimbabwe. Ken Brown was one shot back on 70 along with Bernhard Langer and Irishman Des Smyth. Seven players were on 71, including Arnold Palmer and Seve Ballesteros.

With his putter still red hot, Clampett led by five shots after two rounds, carding a record 66 with 10 single putts this time and only 26 in the round. His nearest rival was Price who had another 69 for 138, one ahead of Smyth and Langer with Watson and Sandy Lyle on 140. The holder, Rogers, was 10 strokes behind Clampett.

After five holes of the third round Clampett had increased his lead to seven shots but it was downhill after that and he carded a 78 for an aggregate of 211, one ahead of Price, two ahead of Lyle and Smyth and three ahead of Watson.

18 JULY

The 111th Open Championship will, like it or not, be remembered as much for being lost by Nick Price as won by Tom Watson. At Royal Troon yesterday the South African was three strokes ahead with six holes to play, but over that exacting run, by wont and usage the graveyard of hopes great and humble, he dropped five strokes and was denied even the consolation of second place on his own.

Pedigree and experience were, as they usually are, the factors which determined the outcome. Watson's single error in a score of 70 was to overclub with a No.6 iron to the fifteenth green and drop his only stroke of the final round. At the same hole, by coincidence, Price's final downfall began when, still relatively two strokes ahead, he took 6 and became level with three to play.

The pressure was, not surprisingly, too stifling for Price, whose powerful swing lost its hitherto admirable timing and whose nerve, untutored at the highest level of competition, was so suddenly and brutally broken. Watson, having finished 40 minutes ahead, was powerless to do other than watch as Price's challenge ebbed on a tide of wayward tee shots.

And so Watson captured this ancient title for the fourth time. Watson triumphed in the US Open last month and thus becomes the fifth player, after Bobby Jones, Gene Sarazen, Ben Hogan and Lee Trevino, to win both championships in the same summer.

On an afternoon calculated to gladden the heart of the local tourist authority – warm sunshine with a light breeze shifting off the shimmering waters of the Firth of Clyde – Watson played the waiting game which, at 32, brought him the £32,000 first prize and his seventh major title in eight seasons, by one stroke with his total of 284, four under par, which was two more than his own preliminary estimate.

Price had to be content to divide £38,600 with Peter Oosterhuis, who finished like the hardened professional he is with a birdie to be runner-up for the second time. But for a long period it seemed as if a player eighty-sixth in the money list with £1860, and who missed three cuts in his last seven outings, would prevail. Until his game crumbled, giving Watson the gift of a championship, Price had been doing what few others were able to accomplish – making birdies. It must be rare for a genuine challenger like Price to have six birdies in his final round and not win. Watson had one and one eagle. When Price took his imposing lead with three successive birdies from the tenth, none of which owed anything to his putter, one of the least probable outcomes seemed in the making. But Watson, his brisk swing under the control which the hazardous nature of these links insists upon, had already made his impact at that same crucial stage.

A putt of seven feet saved par for him at the tenth, and at the next Watson struck a No.3 iron shot 203 yards to within three feet of the hole for an eagle 3. Then the drives at the thirteenth and fifteenth to their ill-defined targets undermined Price, and the deep bunker short of the latter's sunken green swallowed waning confidence along with ball. The slide was on.

But it was even more destructive in the case of Bobby Clampett. During an afternoon of struggle and confusion, when the wind was no stronger than on Thursday but the pressures evidently were, the rot set in. Clampett's last two rounds of 78, 77 suggested that when he tried to wind his mechanical game up again to apply it to conditions which require some adaptability, the spring simply broke. But in fairness to the 22-year-old, making his first appearance in this championship, others with more experience of it fared little better or not at all. For instance, Sandy Lyle and Des Smyth took nine shots between them in rough or bunkers over the first four holes.

1983

ROYAL BIRKDALE

The prize fund was substantially raised again with the winner due to collect £40,000, an increase of 25% on 1982. Craig Stadler opened the American challenge with a record first-round score of 64. Bill Rogers, the winner in 1981, holder Tom Watson and Bernhard Langer were three shots back, with five more on 68, including Nick Faldo and Sam Torrance. Amateur Philip Parkin was one of a group of seven on 69.

After two rounds there were six Americans in the first eight, the exceptions being Faldo and Australian Terry Gale. Stadler was leading on 134, one ahead of Lee Trevino and Watson with Faldo on 136 and Hale Irwin on 137. The round of the day was compiled by Denis Durnian, a 33-year-old professional from Northenden, Manchester. He set a first-nine Open record of 28. He came back in 38 for a 66 and a halfway total of 139. Coincidentally he had played with Longmuir when he had a record outward 29 in 1979.

After three rounds Watson had moved into the lead on a total of 205, one ahead of Stadler and Raymond Floyd. Faldo and David Graham were one shot further adrift on 207 with Trevino on 208.

17 JULY

Tom Watson and the Open Championship are becoming inseparable. At Royal Birkdale yesterday the American again belied the engaging boyishness of his appearance with a final round of professional maturity to defend his title successfully. But whereas at Royal Troon Watson rather backed into victory, this time he took it on his own initiative.

Three holes from home Watson was eight under par and knew that his fellow Americans, Andy Bean and Hale Irwin, had finished on that mark. His last best opportunities for birdies were at either of the next two holes, the 415-yard sixteenth, which calls for a firm approach to a plateau green, and the seventeenth, 526 yards long, but in the scoring statistics the second least difficult hole.

Watson stole past them both at the former with a No.8-iron shot through a slackening breeze to 25 feet and that birdie was timely, for a characteristically wayward drive at the next stifled his hopes of the birdie which had become commonplace. And so, Watson came to the last great test to his skill and nerve.

At the 473-yard eighteenth, he struck a superb drive and made absolutely certain with an equally emphatic No.2 iron of 213 yards – "as good as I have ever struck," he said afterwards – to within 18 feet of the flagstick. He sensibly used the two putts he had and the packed stands which make a spectacular arena of the home green did not hold back their acclaim.

There is something appealing to the average golfer about the vulnerability of Watson's game. He made his share of mistakes when sultry heat gave way to a freshening wind and even spots of rain fell, but he can play a patient game and was content to wait until the eleventh for his first birdie.

Watson's No.4-iron shot to 12 feet there launched his challenge, a bunker-shot to two feet for another birdie at the thirteenth strengthened it, and a second putt of six feet at the short fourteenth to save par crucially preserved it. His 34 home made up, as he remarked later, for the disappointing inward half which cost him the US open title at Oakmont last month.

Bean's championship was unusual for not including a double bogey, and the avoidance of such errors often tells as much about a player as any spectacular shots. Thus Bean, having tangled twice with the rough at the tenth, holed from 15 feet to avoid a 6, and he can seldom have contrived as deft a chip as he did to save par at the last. This was Bean's third Open and his first since he was sixth at Muirfield three years ago. Irwin had not entered since 1979, when his conservative sense of proprieties was affronted by the buccaneering style of Severiano Ballesteros's victory. Although he played his grinding sort of golf to the hilt to match Bean's 67, his one extraordinary lapse will surely be remembered longer.

It would be as sensible to maintain that Irwin lost his chance of adding to his two US championships by his careless airshot on a tap-in putt at the short fourteenth on Saturday as that Roger Wethered lost the 1921 Open because he stood on the ball. But a point of speculation will doubtless remain.

The United States game's domination of the championship for the last two decades and more was reflected in American occupation of four of the first five places. All the same, the retreat of such powers as Craig Stadler, Raymond Floyd, and David Graham put into sharper

relief the performances of Lee Trevino, the winner here 12 years ago, and Graham Marsh of Australia.

Trevino, at 43, ageing but still crafty in the best sense of the word, was in the hunt until his second to the seventeenth slid away into an unplayable lie and he drove into rough at the last. But even that achievement paled before the 64 with which Marsh equalled Stadler's course record and took fourth place, having begun the round eight strokes behind Watson.

Nick Faldo played with wonderful pluck, having started the championship with two 6s, showing no little skill once he had recovered from the setbacks and considerable resilience as the sole British golfer on whose shoulders lay the hopes and fears of so many spectators. But when Faldo missed the twelfth green and took three putts at the next two holes, that gallant challenge was over. The Open was watched by a record crowd of 142,894, over 8000 more than the previous best, set at Lytham in 1979. Yesterday's fourth-round attendance was 26,666.

1984

ST ANDREWS

Six amateurs survived final qualifying – US Amateur champion Jay Sigel and British Amateur champion Jose Maria Olazabal from Spain, as well as four English amateurs, Andrew Sherborne, John Hawksworth, Simon Wood and Peter McEvoy.

Severiano Ballesteros was the bookies' favourite even though Americans had won on 16 occasions out of the last 23 and for the second time in five years Bill Longmuir was the "fictitious" player at the top of the first-day leaderboard with a 67, a score he shared on this occasion with Greg Norman and Peter Jacobson. Ian Baker-Finch, playing the Old Course for the first time, was fourth on 68. The 1981 winner, Bill Rogers, ran up a 12 at the fourteenth.

At the end of the second day Baker-Finch led with a 66 for a total of 134, three ahead of Nick Faldo and Ballesteros, who both returned 68s. Longmuir with a 71 was only one shot further back with four players on 139, including holder Tom Watson, and Bernhard Langer. In the third round Watson moved up with a 66 and a total of 205 alongside Baker-Finch who returned a 71. Two shots further back were Ballesteros and Langer.

22 JULY

Severiano Ballesteros yesterday transformed what had been a forlorn, and by his standards fruitless, season in a gripping climax to the Open Championship at St Andrews which had the spectators in the grandstands on the edge of their seats and those on foot on the tips of their toes. Not until the last two holes was the issue decided in his battle for the title with the holder, Tom Watson. They were then level and it almost goes without saying that the seventeenth, the Road Hole of fact and fable, played the crucial part. Yet the last, not so obviously demanding but scarcely less dramatic, raised the drawbridge against Watson's vain attack.

Ballesteros pulled his penultimate drive into a lie in the rough he disarmingly described as "not too good, but not bad". Needing all his skill, strength and composure he executed a perfect No.6-iron shot 200 yards through the light, left-hand breeze and held the ball on that polished shelf. After having had three 5s at this insidious hole, a par was most timely. The seventy-second hole, part of that incomparable arena created by weathered stone buildings and crowded stands, provided a fitting stage for the final, authoritative act. Having seen Watson, playing behind him, securely on the seventeenth fairway and quite capable of making his 4, Ballesteros decided that a birdie was needed to secure victory.

Ballesteros was not, of course, to know that Watson, from 190 yards, had overclubbed the green with a No.2 iron and now had, literally and metaphorically, his back almost to the wall. There is nothing like making sure and to a tumultuous roar that must have sounded in Watson's ears like that of a vengeful mob awaiting his tumbril, the Spaniard holed from some 15 feet, in by the side door with the last roll.

Watson's inevitable 5 was followed by a pitch too far to make even a birdie possible and so Ballesteros could celebrate this second triumph. His final round of 69 for a 12-under-par total of 276 was two strokes lower than the record aggregate for the Old Course, set 24 years ago by Kel Nagle.

Ballesteros's finish earned him £55,000 but Watson, in relinquishing the crown he had worn with distinction and enthusiasm for two years, was denied even the consolation of second place on his own. He was joined by Bernhard Langer, whose own 3 at the last enabled him to be runner-up for the second time in four championships.

The warm, dry weather continued, but the easterly breeze, an element to contend with over the last six holes, was not quite as strong as on Saturday. By the turn Ballesteros, out in 34, had putted well enough to overtake Watson, who had begun two strokes ahead but whose approach shots lacked the authority with which they had burned the paint from the flagsticks in the third round.

Over the last nine holes of championships the shadow boxing ceases and powerful and invisible forces begin to grip body and soul. Neither Ballesteros nor Watson was impervious. Ballesteros took three putts at the tenth, was bunkered at the short eleventh, and missed from five feet to regain a shot at the twelfth. Watson drove the tenth and made his 3 at the next, but having pulled his drive into whins at the twelfth suffered a bogey. Now they were level with the demanding closing stretch confronting them, and Ballesteros's superior golf deservedly prevailed.

The outcome was intensely disappointing for Watson. Had he won he would have gained six of the last 10 championships and thus equalled Harry Vardon's record. He also would have been only the second professional in modern times, since Peter Thomson in 1954-55-56, to have won the title for three successive years.

Langer, the very model of Teutonic thoroughness and determination, had his moments, but not quite enough of them were invested with the inspiration he needed to overhaul the two others.

The Old Course demands some flair and imagination as well as sturdy shot-making, a quality that was not enough to prevent Ian Baker-Finch from subsiding out of the contest. Sheer inexperience at this rarefied elevation finally undermined a game and compromised a level-headedness that had been impressive.

1985

ROYAL ST GEORGE'S

There was optimism in the European camp with Nick Faldo, Bernhard Langer and Severiano Ballesteros all playing well. It was another European, though, who set the pace in the first round. Christy O'Connor, nephew of another famous Irish golfer of the same name, shot a 64, which broke Henry Cotton's record 65 for St George's, set in 1934, and equalled the lowest first round in an Open set in 1983 by Craig Stadler at Royal Birkdale. His seven birdies in a row from the fourth to the tenth was also a first.

Four shots back, tied for second place, were former Amateur champion Philip Parkin, Sandy Lyle, David Graham, Tony Johnstone, and Robert Lee. Five others were on 69, including Fuzzy Zoeller. Peter Jacobson had a 71 that included a 9 at the fourteenth. The main European hopes, Langer, Faldo and Ballesteros, had 72, 73 and 74 respectively.

O'Connor slipped in the second round with a 76 that put him in joint third position on 140, one behind Lyle and Graham who both scored 71 for 139. Also on 140 was Tony Johnstone and the American, D Weibring, with Langer one shot further back after a 69. Jack Nicklaus and Tony Jacklin failed to make the cut.

At the end of the third day Langer had made up even more ground with a 68 and was now joint leader on 209 with Graham. Sandy Lyle dropped back with a 73 for a share of third place on 212 with O'Connor and the American, Mark O'Meara.

21 JULY

The promise which Sandy Lyle had long shown of an ability to capture a major golf title, but which had revealed a marked reluctance to come to terms with the immediate pressures and the wider implications, was at last fulfilled yesterday when he won the 114th Open Championship at Royal St George's.

In becoming the first player with Scottish connections to triumph since 1931, Tommy Armour's year at Carnoustie, and the first British professional since Tony Jacklin at Royal Lytham and St Anne's in 1969, Lyle, aged 27, did not exactly finish the job with authority, but at the climax he played the demanding last five holes more convincingly.

On a warm day and in a wind from the Channel less strong than before, Payne Stewart had a final round of 68 to set the target with his total of 283 and the unruly character of this course being what it is there was no guarantee that his principal pursuers could avoid costly mistakes.

On reaching the fourteenth tee Lyle was three over par, as was behind him the US Masters champion, Bernhard Langer, when he reached the same stage partnering David Graham, with whom he had shared an overnight lead of two strokes and who himself was one over. The stage thus was set to enliven what had been a decidedly subdued afternoon. Lyle made, as it turned out, the crucial thrusts then. To him the telling shots were the No.2 iron and No.6 iron which he hit at the fourteenth and fifteenth, enabling him to hole from the fringe and then from 12 feet for birdies.

Firmly he holed for par at the sixteenth and seventeenth from around a yard and so came to the last, its fairways lined with spectators up to the amphitheatre of the packed stands. Lyle's drive fell into rough that was light but sufficient to muffle clean contact. His No.6-iron shot fell into the fringe below "Duncan's Hollow", so called because the Scot who in 1920 won the Open at the neighbouring club of Deal failed to get down in two from it two years later to tie with Walter Hagen. For a moment it seemed as if fate might deal Lyle a comparable bad card.

Lyle's first chip returned down the slope to almost where he stood and he sank to his knees in anguish. But the two victories he gained last autumn in Hawaii and Japan and the two weeks he spent on the US Tour early this year had clearly helped immeasurably to harden Lyle's resolve.

Lyle got down in two more for a score of 70 and a total of 282, two over par, to assume the lead from Stewart. That final bogey marginally opened the door to Graham and Langer as they pursued their laborious and painstaking contest in tandem around the links.

Graham, a sort of golfing molar in the way he grinds out a score, needed more of the edge of an incisor at the climax. But St George's deep bunkers caught him three times in the last four holes and the dour Australian's hopes of adding this championship to his US Open and PGA titles were dashed.

Langer floundered with startling frequency from the beginning of his round and having limped out in 39, four over par, kept ambition alive only when he saved par from bunkers at the tenth and eleventh. But a putt of 12 feet for a 3 at the fifteenth resembles a solitary ember in the ashes of his score. Yet his chip from the side of the last green to tie actually grazed the flagstick.

The £65,000 first prize will merely be the first of the many hefty rewards to come Lyle's way. Until now the judgment on Lyle was that whatever emotions might seethe within him he was, on the surface anyway, too placid and almost Micawber-like, content to wait for something to turn up and not greatly depressed if it did not. That attitude may harden now.

1985
SANDY LYLE

"The greatest bunker shot in the history of the game." Thus did the golf historian, Herb Warren Wind, describe Sandy Lyle's second shot to the eighteenth green in the final round of the US Masters at Augusta National in 1988. The 10-foot putt went in for birdie and Lyle had become the first Briton ever to don the coveted green jacket.

Alexander (Sandy) Lyle was born in Shrewsbury, England, in 1958. His father, a Scot, was a teaching professional at the nearby Hawkstone Park Club and Sandy was swinging a golf club by the time he was three. When he turned professional he adopted the Scottish nationality of his father.

He had played for England, won the English Amateur Strokeplay championship twice and played in the Walker Cup before turning professional in 1977. His Open win was the first by a Briton for 16 years and the first by a UK-based Scot for 65 years.

Notable among his achievements were the European Open in 1979 and the World Matchplay championship in 1988, one of his best years. He played in five Ryder Cup matches, including 1985 and 1987 when the Europeans won in the UK and in America for the first time ever.

Very much a natural swinger of the golf club, the amiable and approachable Lyle, famed for his regular use of a No.1 iron from the tee, had always had a slightly imperfect backswing but until 1989 it had given him little trouble. After a reasonable start to that year his game went into decline and all of a sudden he was missing cuts, including at the defence of his Masters title, which Nick Faldo won. The more advice he sought and the more he worked on his swing the worse it seemed to get, although he won a few more tournaments. He was awarded the MBE after his successes in the majors.

1986

TURNBERRY

Severe and unpredictable wind conditions, coupled with the difficult Ailsa course at Turnberry, led to high scoring in the first round. More than a third of the field failed to break 80. Leading on 70 was Ian Woosnam, followed on 71 by Nick Faldo, Gordon Brand, Robert Lee and Anders Forsbrand. There were six on 72, including Bernhard Langer, while Greg Norman, runner-up in this year's Masters, was on 74.

In the second round two putts on the last would have given Norman an Open record of 62 but he took three for a mere 63, a two-round total of 137 and a two-shot lead over Brand and two more over Faldo and T Nakajima of Japan. Langer was one shot further back. Last year's winner, Sandy Lyle, and two previous winners, Trevino and Ballesteros, only just made the cut.

Although slipping to a 74 in the third round there were few low scores that day and Norman, with an aggregate of 211, stayed in the lead, one shot ahead of Nakajima and three ahead of Brand and Woosnam.

20 JULY

When after one of his most important victories Gene Sarazen could declare: "All men are created free and equal but I am one shot better than the rest of us" he could not have had in mind an achievement of the magnitude of Greg Norman, winner of the 115th Open Championship and £70,000 at Turnberry yesterday by five strokes.

Norman's final round of 69 gave him a total of 280, the only one to match par over the Ailsa course after three days of turbulent weather and a fourth in which the elements at last relented to allow competitors to play shots for spectators to enjoy in warm and bright sunshine.

The margin of Norman's success, the greatest since Johnny Miller won by six strokes at Royal Birkdale a

decade ago, also laid to rest a spectre that was beginning to haunt the Australian, the third of his countrymen after Peter Thomson and Kel Nagle to capture the world's oldest and most internationally valued of titles.

Both in the US Masters and US Open championship this season Norman led by a stroke entering the last round and did not win. Even at 31, with many productive years ahead and as the current leading money winner on the US Tour with two victories to his name, a bat squeak of alarm may have begun to sound in Norman's ears.

After all, Norman had seen a five-stroke lead by the turn in the third round dwindle to one at the end, just as he had in the US Open last month. This time, however, the tall, ivory-haired golfer with the big, high swing was not to be denied when his composure and technique were again put to the test.

Norman's most direct confrontation was with Tsuneyuki Nakajima, one stroke behind and attempting to become both the first Japanese and the first bespectacled player to win the Open, with Gordon J Brand and Ian Woosnam another stroke in arrears. Unexpectedly the issue was, in retrospect, settled over the first few holes.

Norman, having holed a bunker shot of 25 yards for a birdie 3 at the third then found himself with a five-stroke advantage, for Nakajima took three putts from five feet at the first for a 6 and dropped another when he drove into rough two holes later.

Woosnam had bogeys at the second and third and the distinctive pause in Brand's swing quickly developed into a hiccup. A hooked drive at the long seventh escaped serious punishment and Norman, as he saw it later, closed the door at the next, hitting a No.4-iron shot to nine feet for a birdie.

When he saved par from six feet at the next two holes,

where his momentum began to falter on Saturday, victory became more assured still. To confirm it, Norman struck a succession of iron shots through the south-westerly breeze that "impressed even me" – notably a No.7 iron from rough at the fourteenth which was turned by the flagstick to three feet. After his No.4-iron shot to the eighteenth green found safe sanctuary, the conquering hero was engulfed by enthusiastic spectators.

Brand to his great credit, recovered his rhythm and came home in 32 for his 71 and second place, culminating in a metal wood shot to 18 feet for an eagle 3 at the seventeenth. Brand's reward of £50,000 was the largest in a career so far not distinguished by any victory in Europe but by four in Africa, two of them earlier this year.

Woosnam also finished strongly to share third place with Bernhard Langer who began the inward half with four consecutive 3s, three of them birdies, and completed it in 32 for a £35,000 cheque which will surely help to wet the head of the daughter born to his wife on Saturday. Would an earlier arrival have enhanced Langer's fortunes? Nick Faldo's 70 brought him his best finish since he was equal fourth at Royal Troon four years ago and allowed him to steal in front of Gary Koch and Severiano Ballesteros, whose 64 was the day's lowest score. Koch and Fuzzy Zoeller were the only American players to finish in the first 10 compared with 1977 when they held 11 of the first 12 places.

Ballesteros, with victories behind him in his last four tournaments, was 13 strokes behind Norman going into the final round after scores of 76, 75, 73 – a modest downward progression that picked up a faster pace in the more inviting conditions to come within a stroke of Norman's record for the course. Yesterday in halves of 33, 31 the putts fairly flowed into the hole – one of 40 feet, one of 35 feet, two of 15 feet and three of around four feet – for Ballesteros's seven birdies. His cheque for £22,000 carried him to within £18,000 of becoming the first player to earn £1m in prize-money in Europe.

1986, 1993
GREG NORMAN

Greg Norman is one of the best golfers of the eighties and the nineties and one of the unluckiest. In 1986 he led in all four majors going into the final round and won only one. The Masters he lost by a shot to Jack Nicklaus when he bogeyed the last hole and in the US PGA Bob Tway holed a bunker shot at the last to deny him that title. The following year at the US Masters he tied with Larry Mize after 72 holes only to see that one slip away too when Mize chipped in at the second extra hole. By 1989 he had finished second in the majors five times and won only one. In the 1989 Open at Troon he scored a magnificent 64 to force a three way tie only to see Mark Calcavecchia birdie the fourth extra hole to take the trophy. He is the only golfer to lose play-offs in all four majors. Despite all this he was leading money winner on the US Tour from 1986 to 1990.

Born at Mount Isa, Queensland, Australia in 1955 Greg Norman did not start playing golf seriously until he was nearly 17. Within two years he was playing to scratch and two years after that he turned professional. In his first season he won The West Lakes Classic in Australia and was chosen to play for Australia in the World Cup, an early indication of his talent and potential. In 1980 he won the first of three World Matchplay titles and in 1981 and 1982 he won the Dunlop Masters. He has won the Australian Masters six times.

He has won Open tournaments in at least seven countries, and he was the first golfer to break 70 in all four rounds of the Open when he won at Royal St George's in 1993.

Of all his disappointments, the worst was at the 1996 US Masters when he led Nick Faldo by six shots going into the final round. Playing together with the television cameras of the world on them Norman shot a dismal 78 to Faldo's 67 and Nick Faldo won his second Masters by five shots. On this occasion there was no question of bad luck. To his credit Greg Norman bore that humiliating defeat with the dignity and good grace that he has shown throughout his career, and he has continued to compete at the highest level.

1987

MUIRFIELD

It was now four years since an American won the Open, the longest gap since Arnold Palmer launched the transatlantic invasion in 1961. European favourites were Bernhard Langer and Ian Woosnam.

Rodger Davis, the latest in a long line of Australian players to make their mark in far-off lands, opened with a 64, a record over the new Muirfield layout. He was followed on 67 by three Americans, Lee Trevino, Bob Tway and Ken Green with two more, Paul Azinger and Larry Mize, one shot back alongside the two Nicks, Faldo and Price. Langer was one of a group of 10 on 69.

Azinger moved into the lead with a second-round 68 and a halfway total of 136, one ahead of Davis, another Australian, G Taylor, Faldo and American Payne Stewart. On 138 were Tom Watson, Craig Stadler, Langer and South African, David Frost.

Faldo celebrated his thirtieth birthday on day three with a 71 for an aggregate of 208, tied for second place with Frost, one shot behind Azinger.

19 JULY

In one of the most tense, dramatic and unexpected finishes there has been in the long history of the event, Nick Faldo outlasted Paul Azinger at Muirfield yesterday to win the 116th Open Championship. It was the second time in two years, after Sandy Lyle, and the third in 18, after Tony Jacklin, that the title had been welcomed back into British hands. Azinger, the leading money-winner of the US tour this season so far, and competing here for the first time, was one stroke ahead of Faldo with only two of the 72 holes to play. But whereas Faldo was able to complete a possibly unique final round comprising 18 par figures, the slender American faltered and finished 6, 5 – both bogeys.

First Azinger, who has an exceptionally strong left-hand grip and noticeably open stance, pulled his drive at the seventeenth into a bunker. Meanwhile, Faldo, playing the last hole immediately ahead, safely reached the green with a solid No.5-iron shot. Azinger's only hope of preserving his slender advantage was to get down in two from 100 yards for par, but he could not achieve that and now all eyes were on Faldo.

One of the best putters on the PGA European tour, Faldo's first putt from 25 feet, misread and overhit, ran some four feet past, but the holing out which had sustained his cause several times during the afternoon did not desert him in his moment of greatest need.

Now Azinger was faced with the daunting prospect of making 4 at the 448-yard eighteenth to tie. His tee shot left him some 200 yards to the green, and, perhaps pressing for distance, he pulled his No.5-iron shot into a greenside bunker. His position left him with an awkward stance from which there was little prospect that he would turn three shots into the two he so urgently needed.

Faldo's round gave him a total of 279, five under par, the first prize of £75,000 and, as is the way in sports nowadays, no doubt will bestow substantial fringe benefits. He should take particular pride and satisfaction from his victory – his first in a major championship – as entirely justifying the decision he took three years ago to make fundamental changes in his swing.

It was Faldo's timing that was so surprising, for he had just won his first tournament in the United States and his tenth in Europe, but he believed he required greater consistency in his swing. His mentor in America, David Leadbetter, helped him to develop that.

After two days of mixed weather and a thoroughly vile morning on Saturday, Faldo's thirtieth birthday, a sea

haar obliterated Gullane Hill and the Firth of Forth and spread eerily over the links. That did not make shot judgment any easier, yet Faldo missed only four greens, all of them in a critical run from the seventh, and saved par each time. Had he not, the chances were that Azinger, who had holed four substantial single putts, three of them for birdies, to lead by three strokes with 10 holes remaining, would have run away with the title.

Faldo's much-publicised broken first marriage and a decided difficulty in projecting a withdrawn personality and unbending attitudes to the game have not made him readily approachable. This triumph must surely alter that state.

Azinger, aged 27, has won three times on the US Tour this year, but confessed he had some difficulty in eating his breakfast yesterday. He said that he welcomed the chance of experiencing the pressure of competing for a major title. In that he did acquit himself well. In the alien conditions of foul weather on a course with no water hazards and no trees, he managed his way round this admittedly most uncomplicated and fairest of all the British links with considerable poise. "Don't feel sorry for me," he said. "I proved I can play in any company. It just wasn't to be. I'll be better off next time for this experience."

Azinger admitted to two crucial mistakes in club selection – taking a No.2 iron instead of a No.1 at the tenth, which he bunkered, and his driver at the seventeenth instead of, once again, his No.1 iron for safety. Just when he had most need of a hitherto trustworthy putter, "the club failed me four times and I also slightly misread the breaks on these putts".

Azinger tied for second place with the Australian, Rodger Davis, on 280, a stroke ahead of two other Americans, Ben Crenshaw and Payne Stewart.

1987, 1990, 1992
NICK FALDO

For dedication to the game and to the aim of becoming the best in the world there can be no contender to match Nick Faldo.

Born Nicholas Alexander Faldo in Welwyn Garden City in 1957 he took up golf after watching Jack Nicklaus on television at the Masters in 1971 and four years later became the youngest ever winner of the English Amateur championship. He turned professional in 1976 and the following year won his first tournament and became the youngest player to represent Britain in the Ryder Cup.

He was the new star on the British golf scene but for Faldo it wasn't enough. Despite winning five tournaments in Europe in 1983 he decided his golf swing wasn't good enough to compete at the highest level and he embarked on the task of rebuilding it with the help of David Leadbetter.

In the Open at Muirfield in 1987 his dedication paid off. He went into the final round one shot behind Paul Azinger and shot 18 straight pars while Azinger could manage only 16 and bogeyed the last two to give Faldo his first major.

In 1988 he tied with Curtis Strange in the US Open but lost in the play-off. He did better in the Masters however. In 1989 and 1990 he tied with Scott Hoch and Raymond Floyd respectively and won both play-offs to become, after Sandy Lyle, only the second Briton to take that title and only the second player to take the title two years in a row, the other being Jack Nicklaus. Faldo won the Masters again in 1996, going into the final round six shots behind Greg Norman and carding a 67 while Norman collapsed with a 78.

1988

ROYAL LYTHAM AND ST ANNE'S

To the consternation of some Americans, Tony Jacklin predicted that Royal Lytham would produce another European winner, but with the exception of Severiano Ballesteros at the top of the leaderboard with a 67 the first-round scores did not augur well for this prediction. Brad Faxon (USA) and Wayne Grady (Australia) were second equal one behind Seve with two more Australians on 70 alongside Nick Price of Zimbabwe and another American, Don Pooley. There were 11 on 71 including Nick Faldo and Bob Charles.

Despite a boisterous wind on the second day, the scoring was quite good and the European fortunes improved a little with Ballesteros on 138, one behind the leader, Price, and Faldo sharing third place with Craig Stadler on 140. Andy Bean of America was on 141, with Sandy Lyle, Fred Couples and Bob Tway one shot further back.

On Saturday, torrential rain flooded the course, causing the third round to be postponed until Sunday. Hubert Green was five under after seven holes when play was stopped.

On Sunday conditions were much better and despite a fairly strong breeze the scoring was good. Nick Price took the lead with a 69 for an aggregate of 206, two ahead of Ballesteros who had a 70 and Faldo who had a 68. Sandy Lyle, this year's winner of the Masters, had a 67 to be in fourth place on 209. Price will no doubt not wish to dwell on the fact that at Troon in 1982 he had a lead of three with six holes to play and lost to Tom Watson.

18 JULY

The prodigal was welcomed home yesterday when Severiano Ballesteros won the Open Championship for the third time. He thus became the first player to do so twice at Royal Lytham and St Anne's, and in killing the fatted calf represented by £80,000 in prize-money, Ballesteros ended the four lean years that stretched

behind him to his second victory, at St Andrews. His once undisciplined talent now under strict control, Ballesteros achieved his latest triumph in masterly fashion. The Spaniard had won his two previous Opens having started the final round two strokes behind the leader and he did so again. But there, resemblances, particularly with the manner of his first victory at Royal Lytham in 1979, ended. This was the reformed Ballesteros, at 31 his game nine years older and wiser, more restrained, more thoughtful, and even more accomplished.

Perhaps the most striking confirmation of the transformation came at the 357-yard sixteenth where nine years ago he made an improbable birdie, having cut his drive among parked cars. This time he pitched dead a No.9-iron shot of 135 yards from the centre of the fairway. Finally, although Ballesteros's last drive was slightly pushed into rough and his No.6-iron second ran beyond the green into fringe grass, his chip back with a sand wedge was so finely executed that the ball touched the hole and lay dead.

When his partners, Nick Faldo, who put up a resolute defence of the title, and Nick Price, who hunted Ballesteros to the end, had holed out, Ballesteros was by tradition allowed to complete this smallest of formalities. His score of 65 equalled the best finishing round by a champion, set in 1977 by Tom Watson at Turnberry Hotel, and his aggregate of 273, 11 under par, beat his earlier winning total over the 6857-yard course by 10 strokes.

It also overcame the challenge posed by Price, the overnight leader, whose stubborn 69 left him two strokes adrift. Price, who in 1982 failed to win the championship at Royal Troon after he had led by three strokes with only six holes to play, had nothing to reproach himself for this time. He was simply the helpless victim of inexorable fate

– in other words one of the greatest players in the history of the game.

Afterwards, Ballesteros acknowledged that he had become a little worried at his continuing failure in the major championships. His confidence had been shaken in 1986, when, leading the Masters tournament he had already won twice, he mishit his second shot at the fifteenth into water, and when, the following year, he lost again at Augusta, this time in a play-off. He had clearly brooded on these setbacks.

"It was important for me to win again," he said. "I can remember how I played today. It was one of those rounds that only happens very rarely, and this is the best golf I've played over four days since the Open at St Andrews."

Might that, one wondered, although not in the hearing of Ballesteros, be at least partly because for the first time since then a professional caddie, Ian Wright, and not one of his brothers was working with him?

Ballesteros said afterwards that he had in his bag the same driver, spoon, sand wedge and putter that he used in 1979, and that he was wearing the same colours of clothing. In those more headstrong days he won despite having hit only two fairways from the tee over the last 36 holes and had been in the rough nine times in the final round alone. Apart from his game having matured, the competition is far too strong nowadays to permit such unbuttoned hitting.

Ballesteros turned in 31 to Price's 33 and Faldo's 34, and it was an indication of the intensity of the struggle that Ballesteros could gain six strokes on par over as many holes from the sixth yet pick up only two strokes on Price. Faldo and the Masters champion, Sandy Lyle, the only other player who could be described as a genuine contender, gradually retreated from the forefront of affairs.

When Ballesteros struck a No.5-iron shot to 10 feet at the 590-yard seventh, Price, although he mishit his reply, managed to deliver the ball four feet from the hole for a matching eagle. But three of the four holes after the turn decided the issue.

Having replied to Ballesteros's putt of 20 feet for a 3 at the tenth with one of seven feet and seen Ballesteros hole from 20 feet at the next for another birdie to lead for the first time, Price pitched dead at the thirteenth only to see Ballesteros remain ahead with a putt of 18 feet. Ballesteros was not punished when he took 5 at the fourteenth, for Price did not hit a solid putt from five feet for his 4 and, as it turned out, his last chance to draw level again had gone.

Faldo thought his challenge began to ebb at the seventh which he duly reached in two downwind, but from a difficult place he took three putts. After that he was never quite the same player again and although a 2 at the twelfth with a No. 2-iron shot through the left-hand cross-wind to 20 feet was a rarity, his bunkered second at the tenth and two shots in the rough at the fifteenth were penalised.

Lyle made the ritual birdies at the long sixth and seventh holes, but although he saved par at the next after a weak pitch had left the ball 60 feet from the hole, inspiration left him and he had bogeys at three of the next four holes. It was symptomatic of his dwindling fortunes that he should finish 5, 6, taking two shots in a fairway bunker at the last.

1989

ROYAL TROON

There was strong competition from several sources. Severiano Ballesteros, going for two in a row and a total of four, Tom Watson bidding for his sixth win, Jack Nicklaus at 49 bidding to become the oldest winner, and favourite Nick Faldo.

Again, however, a non-ranked player took the lead after the first round over Old Troon. Jersey-born Wayne Stephens, playing in his first Open, scored a record 66 for a two-stroke lead over seven players, consisting of three Americans, two Spaniards, one Argentinian and an Australian. There were eight others on 69, including Watson and Greg Norman. Faldo was in a group of 17, including the American, Mark Calcavecchia, on 71. More than a quarter of the field was below the par of 72. Holder Ballesteros was on level par.

After the second round Wayne Grady, the 31-year-old Australian, led on 135, following his first round 68 with a 67, two ahead of Payne Stewart who carded a new record of 65, and Watson who was the last player to win here, in 1982. Three shared fourth place on 138, including Stephens. There were eight more on 139, including Norman and Calcavecchia.

At the end of day three Grady had retained the lead with a 69 for a three-round aggregate of 204, but only by one shot from Watson who had closed the gap with a 68, with Stewart one shot further back on 206. David Feherty, Fred Couples and Calcavecchia were another shot back on 207. Norman had slipped back with a 72 to 211.

23 JULY

Mark Calcavecchia, at 29 years of age representing the latest generation of young and upwardly mobile American professionals, yesterday won the Open Championship at Royal Troon in the most dramatic, and even poignant, of circumstances, beating Greg Norman and Wayne Grady, both of Australia, after the first four-hole play-off in the history of the event.

On another day of uncharacteristic Ayrshire weather – hot, sunny, and with only the lightest of breezes from the sea – these three professionals tied on 275, 13 under par and a record aggregate for the championship over these links where it was being played for the sixth time.

Norman, whose closing 64 established a record for the 7079-yard course by a stroke, began, as he had done in the final round, with two birdie 3s, from nine feet at the first and 15 feet at the second after Calcavecchia had holed ahead of him from 18 feet. Grady, who was to become a witness to history rather than an influence on it, left the stage when he bogeyed the short seventeenth. But so also did Norman begin to falter, over-hitting his chip shot from behind the green at the seventeenth (the third play-off hole), as Calcavecchia, from further away, made par to draw level. The last was a tragedy for Norman. He drove too far and right and, unluckily, under the face of a bunker. From there he landed in another bunker, and when his recovery from that went out of bounds he conceded the title.

Calcavecchia, who had struck his ball to 10 feet, then had three putts for the championship, the first to be won by an American since Tom Watson six years ago at Royal Birkdale. With his typically positive approach Calcavecchia holed it. The prize of £80,000 was his, and the victory must have come as considerable consolation for his defeat by one stroke in the Masters tournament by Sandy Lyle last year.

Calcavecchia began to make the championship aware of him in the final round when he pitched out of rough directly into the twelfth hole for a 3 to become 11 under par, a position he preserved by recovering close from a bunker at the short fourteenth. He then caught Norman, long since in the clubhouse, by playing the last three holes in 10 strokes, three fewer than Grady. Following Norman's example Calcavecchia reached the green at the 542-yard sixteenth in two and almost had an eagle. Having safely negotiated the seventeenth, at 223 yards the most difficult hole on the course, he struck a superb approach to the last for a birdie 3 to put his first victory of international importance within his grasp.

On Saturday evening Norman had received, as it were, final instructions from three players of distinction. Jack Nicklaus said: "Play with your brain, not just your game." Raymond Floyd encouraged him: "Now let your reins go." Finally, Tom Weiskopf advised: "Play more finesse shots." Somehow Norman survived, as well as he applied, their good intentions.

Norman uncompromisingly acted on the knowledge that he would have to make his move on the outward half and, starting one hour 40 minutes ahead of the last pair, Watson and Grady, he could set a worryingly formidable aggregate target. To that end Norman, as they habitually say in Wagga Wagga, did not "stand upon the order of his going".

Pitches to within reasonable range of the first three holes, all less than 400 yards long, launched Norman's initiative. And he completed a run of six successive birdies at the 577-yard sixth with "the best pitch I have hit since the one at St Andrews which beat Sam Torrance and Scotland in the Dunhill Cup".

Norman was not rewarded with an eagle at the sixteenth, where he struck a driver from the fairway 277 yards to 18 feet. But he had to work hard for his last two par figures, at the seventeenth holing out by using as a putter the leading edge of his sand iron and getting down in two

from perilously close to the out of bounds at the last which ultimately destroyed his hopes.

To his enormous credit Grady, unaccustomed to the pressures of competing at this rarefied level, kept the rhythm of his three-quarter swing, with its distinctive pause at the top, going as he defended the lead he had taken at the end of the second round.

Having started with a birdie 3, Grady chipped close for par, as he had frequently done during the championship, at the next two holes. That solidity was sustained and when he holed from 12 feet for a 3 at the twelfth he led by two strokes at the point where in 1982 Nick Price had established a three-stroke advantage, which he subsequently lost.

That advantage evaporated on the two remaining short holes, at the fourteenth with three putts and at the seventeenth where he was bunkered short and right. Last year Grady beat Norman for the Australian PGA title after four holes of a play-off, recognised as being the turning point in his career. But yesterday he had be content with second place for the twenty-seventh time.

For the rest, Watson's putting stroke, whose fragility has been partly responsible for denying to him a tournament victory for almost two years, betrayed his ambition to repeat his victory here of 1982 and equal the record of six successes in the championship set in 1914 by Harry Vardon. Three putts at the seventh and a miss for par from eight feet at the ninth were followed by a drive into rough at the next. These three bogeys did irreparable damage and in the end Watson fell from second to fourth place.

1989
MARK CALCAVECCHIA

Mark Calcavecchia was born in Laurel, Nebraska, in 1960, the son of a tenpin bowling centre owner. Mark was a prodigious bowler at the age of 13 and concentrated on golf only after the family moved to Florida. He turned professional in 1981.

He has an unattractive but powerful swing with a fade that turned into a slice at times in his famous battle against

Colin Montgomerie at Kiawah Island in the 1991 Ryder Cup. From four up with four to play, Calcavecchia ended up with a halved match.

His best years were in the late eighties after he won the Southwest Classic in 1986. For four years thereafter he was never out of the top 10 in the US money list. Calcavecchia was the only American to win the Open between Tom Watson's win in 1983 and John Daly's victory in 1995.

1990

ST ANDREWS

Greg Norman began with a 66, tied for first place with American, Michael Allen, one ahead of Faldo and two better than a group of eight, including Ian Baker-Finch and the current US PGA champion, Payne Stewart.

The second round produced even more exceptional scoring with Faldo, the pre-tournament favourite, joining Norman in the lead on 132 after a 65 to the Australian's second 66, equalling the halfway record set by Henry Cotton 56 years before. Two players shared third place on 136, yet another Australian, Craig Parry and Stewart, with another four one shot further back, including Englishman Jamie Spence, who had equalled Faldo's 65 and the exceptional scoring had its downside. On a fine sunny day, Arnold Palmer made an emotional exit. Despite shooting level-par 144, the cut fell at a record low of 143.

By the end of the third day Faldo had established a five-shot lead on 199, a record for the first 54 holes. Sharing second place on 204 were Stewart and Baker-Finch who had a third round 64. Craig Parry was in fourth place one ahead of Ian Woosnam, while Norman, the world No.1, had fallen into a share of sixth after a 76, nine strokes worse than playing partner Faldo.

22 JULY

Nick Faldo yesterday confirmed his position as the leading player in the world when he gained the prize most coveted in the game – an Open Championship victory over the Old Course at St Andrews, golf's spiritual and historical home. The old claret jug and the prize of £85,000 were taken commandingly, convincingly, and deservedly. Faldo, the winner at Muirfield three years ago, set several records at the end of four days which had already served up a rich diet of them. Having led with a total for three rounds of 199, three strokes lower than Tom Watson's at Muirfield in 1980, Faldo won with a total of 270, 18 under par. Watson was a mere 13

under in that championship of 10 years ago.

With his final round of 71 the strappingly built Englishman, 33 last Wednesday, beat Payne Stewart, and Mark McNulty, by five strokes – the widest margin since Johnny Miller's six at Royal Birkdale in 1976 – to become the first home professional since Dick Burton in 1939 to win at headquarters and the first since Henry Cotton in 1937 to win more than once. He is also the first since Watson in 1977 to win this championship and the Masters title in the same season.

In improving by six strokes on the winning total Severiano Ballesteros set at St Andrews six years ago, Faldo put himself on course to deprive Stewart of his title in three weeks' time in Birmingham, Alabama, and become the first player since Ben Hogan in 1953 to take three of the four major championships in the same year. Faldo, who dismissed the flamboyant presence of Greg Norman by nine strokes with his 67 on Saturday, saw off Stewart with the same sort of game he had deployed from the start – intense concentration, exemplary execution, and the complete avoidance of serious error – the same combination which in April helped him to retain his Masters title.

With four major championships now to his credit Faldo has joined Byron Nelson and Raymond Floyd on that number, two behind Lee Trevino, Bobby Jones and Gene Sarazen. He has, of course, some way to go before he catches up with Arnold Palmer on seven, Watson on eight, Gary Player and Hogan on nine, Walter Hagen's 11, let alone the 18 of Jack Nicklaus.

But so successful has Faldo been with his attritional game – he was, after all, only a moderate putt away from tying for the US Open last month – that other championships must come his way. And all this because of his brave, some then said foolhardy, decision to restructure his swing in the interests of greater consistency.

Thus in 72 holes Faldo was in only one bunker – beside the fourth green yesterday which cost him the only other bogey he had in the championship apart from the three he conceded to the seventeenth, by any standards a par 5 on degree of difficulty alone. His iron play was wonderfully accurate and he never took three putts on greens whose vast acreage, great sweeps, and subtle borrows make that error difficult to escape.

Once more great crowds gathered in the sunshine for the final act. There was again a breeze from the north east, but rather lighter now, and on greens, harder and faster than before, holes were cut in more difficult places, entirely justified by the absence of any vigorous defence from the weather. It was Stewart, resplendent in a stars-and-stripes shirt which represented the American National Football League but which looked more appropriate for a burial at sea than a golf championship, who applied the only pressure. Very real that became over the three holes immediately after the turn when Stewart reduced Faldo's advantage to two strokes.

Having turned in 34 to Faldo's 35, Stewart holed from six feet at the tenth, and having saved par from 12 feet after having overhit the short eleventh green, made a 3 from six feet at the twelfth despite having driven into rough. Faldo was well aware of the danger but it receded when he made his par at the twelfth just as Stewart, playing immediately in front, dropped a stroke after having bunkered his drive at the thirteenth.

Faldo was now a more comfortable three strokes clear again and, decisively, his No.6-iron shot to 10 feet for a 3 at the fifteenth plumped the cushion further. Stewart's pitch from between the Principal's Nose bunkers and the old railway line screwed back, denying him the chance of a birdie, and when his second to the seventeenth scampered over the road that was that.

Faldo, playing a No.3-iron shot to below the front bank of the green, cautiously negotiated a 5, but by now Stewart's challenge had subsided in the Valley of Sin. The bogey which resulted meant that Faldo could take his ease playing the last in par and to tumultuous acclamation he was champion again.

Stewart, second in 1985 to Sandy Lyle, was joined by McNulty, whose closing 65, the lowest score of the round, promoted him by almost 20 places. Jodie Mudd, fifth last year at Royal Troon, improved on that placing by one with a 66.

1991

ROYAL BIRKDALE

Severiano Ballesteros, having won two of his last five competitions, opened with a 66 to lead by one from the American, Chip Beck, Santiago Luna of Spain and Martin Gates, with the holder, Nick Faldo, and six others chasing on 68.

Three players shared the lead on 138 after the second round, Mike Harwood (Australia), Gary Hallberg (USA) and Andrew Oldcorn, one shot ahead of Ballesteros, Americans Mike Reid and Mark O'Meara, Australians Wayne Grady and Steve Elkington and David Gilford. Sandy Lyle had a no return after failing to finish the eighteenth. Only four shots separated the first 38 players.

Ian Baker-Finch who had a steady first two rounds of 71, burst into prominence in the third round with a 64 to share the lead on 206 with O'Meara, one ahead of Irishman, Eamonn Darcy, two ahead of Ballesteros and three ahead of Reid.

21 JULY

The Australian connection between Royal Birkdale and the Open Championship, which Peter Thomson established by winning the first and last of his five titles over the Lancashire course, in 1954 and 1965, was triumphantly maintained yesterday when a protege, Ian Baker-Finch, won the title by two strokes – and from a compatriot, no less, Mike Harwood.

In the most benign weather of a decidedly mixed week, Baker-Finch won his first major and the accompanying prize of £90,000 with his final round of 66 for a total of 272, eight under par. Of the 16 players who were on par or better four Americans were in the first seven and five were Australians. Once again in seven championships over this course victory to a European, let alone a British professional, was not to be.

At St Andrews, in 1984, sheer rawness overwhelmed

Baker-Finch when he shared the lead with Tom Watson. He put his first approach into the Swilcan Burn and bled to a 79, and when the championship returned to the Old Course last year he, along with the rest of the field, was overwhelmed by Nick Faldo.

At the third time of asking Baker-Finch was not found wanting. He set out sharing the lead with Mark O'Meara on four under par, but the American, and Harwood and Eamonn Darcy, his next closest rivals, were made, by Baker-Finch's driving start, to resemble nothing so much as cars with stalled engines.

In warm sunshine and a breeze which steadily dwindled to a whisper the 30-year-old Australian built a five-stroke lead with as many birdies in the first seven holes. No defensiveness here from the 6ft 4in graduate of the European Tour, who in 1988 elected to cast his bread in the choppier waters of the American counterpart.

When Darcy, whose flying right elbow cheerfully rejects the orthodoxies of the most sought-after teachers of the game, gave ground towards the end, the biggest threat to Baker-Finch had emerged in the charging shape of Fred Couples as Harwood continued to sustain his challenge. Couples, with five birdies in six holes from the eighth, including four in succession from the turn, proved, with fearless holing out from both medium and long range, that although the greens were now drier and faster, his recent form in finishing third equal in the US Open and first and third in subsequent tournaments had not deserted him in very different surroundings.

But as celebrated as he is for his "catch-up" final rounds, Couples also has a history of failing to drive home challenges. The seventeenth, 525 yards long but all week anyone's birdie and frequently an eagle chance, thwarted him. Bunkered in two, Couples came out to four feet and missed the putt and a chance to become six under and intensify the pressure on Baker-Finch.

Similarly Harwood, who deserted his dogged style to make three birdies in four holes from the eighth and another at the sixteenth with a fine iron shot to 10 feet, came to within two strokes of the tall Australian. But when, at the seventeenth, Harwood failed to hold the fairway from the tee he could score no lower than par and Baker-Finch's task was to some extent eased.

The Australian, whose only concession to par had been at the tenth, where he was bunkered from the tee, made efficiently certain of what had become a commonplace birdie and, as he later admitted, it was only because a three-stroke lead made him over exuberant that he hit his last drive into the rough. Eventually he had three putts to win the championship and he prudently used two of them.

Unlike Thomson, who hit his winning shot 37 years ago with the back of his putter, Baker-Finch did so the conventional way. The suspicion was that his American caddie, Pete Bender, who worked successfully with Greg Norman at Turnberry in 1986, would have somewhat strenuously advised against it.

Before play began a writer from the United States remarked with sour distaste: "If you want a comment on the sorry state of our golf, of the 11 players on par or better at the start of the third round America had one more than Fiji," – referring to the slim majority held by O'Meara and Mike Reid over Vijay Singh.

Ultimately he could salvage some consolation from the final placings and the record score of 63 by Mudd for the total of 277 which set the first serious target. Mudd's performance need have come as no surprise for in his first Open, in 1989, he was fifth and last year equal fourth. "I just seem to take to links courses," he observed. As a further salve to the writer's patriotism, Lee Trevino proved that at 51 there is life yet in his golfing seniority with a score of 67 for 281, only three strokes above the total with which he won the title on this course 20 years ago.

1991
IAN BAKER-FINCH

Ian Baker-Finch was born in Nambour, Queensland, Australia, in 1960. He turned professional in 1979 and won regularly in Australia, Japan and Europe. Among his successes were the New Zealand Open in 1983 and the Scandinavian Open in 1985. He also had a successful spell on the US Tour.

He said of sports phsychologist Bob Rotella: "The biggest thing he did for me – the key to my success – was to get me to try to hole every shot, to try to focus wholly on knocking every shot into the cup from the fairway."

No psychology could help him after his 1991 Open success. Inexplicably, he suddenly lost form and over the next few years it was difficult to believe that this was the same man who had won at Birkdale. He struggled to make cuts to the extent it began to become almost embarrassing before he conceded his golfing career was over.

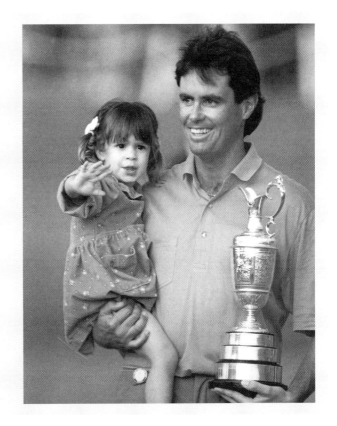

1 9 9 2

MUIRFIELD

In benign weather, the first-round scores were exceptional. No fewer than 56 players broke the par of 71, almost half of them Americans or players owing allegiance to the US Tour. Steve Pate and veteran Raymond Floyd shared the lead on 64, one ahead of Gordon Brand Jr and Ian Woosnam and two ahead of Lee Janzen, Nick Faldo, Ernie Els and John Cook. Floyd was motivated by his desire to become only the fifth player to win all four majors.

Faldo, playing in a brisk westerly breeze, had a second round of 64 with 3s at seven of eight holes from the ninth, comprising an eagle, four birdies and two pars. His halfway total of 130 was a record and gave him a lead of three over Cook and Gordon Brand Jr with Pate one shot further back, and on 135, Floyd, Els and another American, Donnie Hammond.

At the end of the third day Faldo equalled his 54-hole record of 199, established two years before at St Andrews, and had a four-stroke lead. His nearest rivals on 203 were Pate and Cook, with Brand, Hammond and Els two shots further back. The holder, Ian Baker-Finch, was 15 shots behind Faldo.

19 JULY

Where Nick Faldo won his first Open Championship, in 1987 at Muirfield, yesterday he won his third – neither, however, as convincingly as five years ago nor as commandingly as in 1990 at St Andrews. But having appeared to be about to snatch defeat from the grasp of victory Faldo, a day after his thirty-fifth birthday, re-found his game and his composure just in time.

Faldo was three strokes ahead of John Cook with eight holes to play but only six holes later Cook was one stroke in front as Faldo bogeyed three of the next four holes and the blond-haired American had three birdies in five holes from the twelfth. This transformation was eerily reminiscent of another such in 1982 at Royal Troon. Then

Nick Price, three ahead with six to play, eventually lost to Tom Watson, and when Cook, making only his second appearance in the event, narrowly missed for an eagle at the seventeenth he still had a putt of less than a yard to increase his advantage to two strokes. But rather as Tony Jacklin did 20 years ago on that same green, Cook missed by misreading the line and the championship was truly open again.

Behind, Faldo was wondering why he had to make life so difficult for himself and realised he would have to play the best last four holes of his life if he was to retrieve an apparently lost cause. He played their 1603 yards in 14 strokes, two under par, to Cook's 15, one under, the most iron-willed performance and technically efficient shot-making possible in the circumstances.

Having birdied the fifteenth with "a half No.5 iron" to three feet, and saved par from behind the sixteenth green, Faldo struck two magnificent shots on to the penultimate green, the second with a No.4 iron for the birdie with which he again drew level.

Ahead, Cook, winner of two tournaments on the US Tour early this season, was facing up to the most intense moment of pressure of his career. But he pushed his No.2-iron second shot into the gallery and despite a brave pitch over the greenside bunker he could not save par.

Incredibly, Faldo now faced a similar situation to that he had overcome five years before when, playing ahead of Paul Azinger, he hit a No.5-iron shot 190 yards to the heart of the green. Then, Faldo succeeded in turning the screw on Azinger. Now the full stress of the occasion was on him. The green, surrounded by packed grandstands, must have looked like a pocket handkerchief to him but a great roar went up to the leaden, windswept skies as, from 196 yards out, Faldo's No.3-iron shot cut against the wind and covered the flagstick. The ball finished at the back edge of the green from where Faldo trundled it down the quick slope. His knees, he said later, were shaking, but the putt was steady and sure as he urged it closer to the hole. The few inches that remained he completed after his partner, Steve Pate, had holed out.

Faldo's final round of 73 meant that he would not become the first champion to break 70 in every round but, more important to him, his total of 272, 12 under par, enabled him to become the only professional since James Braid in 1901 and 1906 to win the title twice at the home of the Honourable Company of Edinburgh Golfers.

Victory brought Faldo the first prize of £95,000, a return to the top of the world rankings, and a place in the Johnnie Walker World Championship in Jamaica in December. Faldo also gained his fifth major title, after twice having the US Masters, and his defeat of Cook and Pate prevented Americans from holding all four majors for the first time in eight years.

Faldo also equalled the third victory at Muirfield in 1948 of Henry Cotton, with whom he shares the further distinction of being the only British professional to have won the Open Championship more than once since the First World War – in his case, as it happens, all of them in Scotland.

Faldo began the round with a four-stroke lead, but the almost magnetic pull of the first fairway bunker cost him a stroke and it was an indication of the playing difficulties that he could reach the turn in 37, one over par, without a birdie on his card, yet had his lead reduced by only one over Pate with Cook still four strokes in arrears at that point.

If, despite the westerly wind, punctuated by an occasional rain burst, birdies were not impossible to come by, bogeys and worse were all too easy to make. A low-scoring challenge from the anonymity of the pack was highly improbable. Faldo would have to come back if his closest pursuers hoped to offer a serious challenge and even overtake him.

And come back Faldo did. His lead, three strokes after 10 holes, shrank to two after 11 and one after 13. Faldo bunkered a wedge shot at the eleventh, took three putts at the short thirteenth, and bunkered his tee shot at the next. He thought to himself: "This is absolutely stupid. What are you doing?"

At this point, none too soon, Faldo reasserted himself. Cook hit a No.7 iron to six feet at the fifteenth to draw level and Faldo matched the birdie. Cook hit a No.5 iron to 20 feet for a 2 at the sixteenth to lead, but then Faldo, with much more experience of competition at this level, made the 4 which caused Cook to overclub his 200 yard second shot at the last from an uphill lie.

It was ironic that Cook, having until then played the three long holes cumulatively in 13 under par, should hook out of bounds at the ninth and take a 7 before his fatal miss at the seventeenth. He lasted the course longer, however, than Pate, who dropped a stroke at the fourteenth and two at the fifteenth not only to fall out of the race but to be overtaken by Jose Maria Olazabal.

At the turn there was no sign of a challenge developing from Olazabal, who was playing in his first event in Europe since the PGA championship in May. This was because he had missed three putts of around a yard before the turn, but an inward half of 32 gave him a 68, equalling the scores of the holder, Ian Baker-Finch, and his fellow Australian, Greg Norman, as the lowest of the day.

1993

ROYAL ST GEORGE'S

In 11 Opens played at Royal St George's in the last 100 years eight winners had never previously won the title, the exceptions being Harry Vardon and Walter Hagen. Nick Faldo and Greg Norman were no doubt hoping to emulate them and not just for the prize-money which had risen from a first prize of £25,000 in 1981 to £100,000.

Four players shared the first-round lead on 66 – Peter Senior, Greg Norman, Mark Calcavecchia and Fuzzy Zoeller. There were 10 players on 67 and no fewer than 69 players separated by only four shots. The European challenge was still alive with Severiano Ballesteros on 68, Faldo on 69, and Sandy Lyle on 70.

In a blustery wind and with testing pin positions Faldo played the second round in a record of 63 and a halfway total of 132, the same score as Henry Cotton had in 1934. Whereas on that occasion Cotton had led by nine, Faldo had an advantage of only one over Bernhard Langer and two over Norman, Fred Couples and Corey Pavin with Peter Senior only one shot further adrift. There were two more players on 136.

In the third round, Pavin drew level with Faldo in first place with a 68 to the holder's 70, with Langer and Norman only one shot behind them on 203. Paul Lawrie had a three-round total of 209.

18 JULY

All the doubts over Greg Norman's psychological resilience and technical mastery to win a major title again were swept away yesterday at Royal St George's by the Australian's second victory in the Open Championship. The shots which finally laid to rest the ghosts raised by previous titles lost when 38-year-old Norman was in a position to win them were those he struck to the home green. Having just taken three putts at the seventeenth for his only bogey, Norman's lead over the holder, Nick Faldo, shrank from three to two strokes and the spectre of another setback loomed.

But Norman, one of the greatest straight, as well as long, hitters the game has known, executed two of the finest shots of his life when they were needed most. His last drive split the fairway and his second, a nerveless No.4-iron shot, bisected with equal accuracy the air between the crowded grandstands and safely held the green.

Two careful putts later the title and first prize of £100,000 were his. That par 4 for a two-stroke victory not only re-established the Queensland-born professional's return to the heights of the game, it confirmed all sorts of Open records.

Norman's aggregate of 267, 13 under par, beat Tom Watson's by a stroke, and his closing round of 64 was the best by a winner, lower by a stroke than the score previously made by Watson and Seve Ballesteros. Moreover, Norman, with his rounds of 66, 68, 69, and 64, became the first winner to better 70 in all four rounds of an Open, indicative of the welter of low scoring which more docile conditions than this corner of Kent is accustomed to invite. In all there were 116 scores below 70, 14 more than the record set in 1991 at Royal Birkdale. Norman, before and after his victory in Ayrshire, endured many disappointments, usually a combination of his own failings and the opportunism or steadiness of other players, and sometimes the result of poor thinking and club selection. Somehow the sight of those long, blond locks inspired rivals and turned fortune against him. Not this time. Norman's margin over Faldo spoiled what would have been an even more eventful thirty-sixth birthday celebration for the Englishman, who had won the championship three times in the previous six years. But Faldo had nothing to reproach himself for as his 67 gave him second place over Bernhard Langer, the US Masters champion, by a stroke. Langer also shot a 67.

Understandably elated with his success Norman, who seven years ago became the third of his countrymen, after Thomson and Kel Nagle, to win "the world's Open," said: "In my entire career I've never had a round like that. I never mishit a shot and I was almost in awe at the way I struck the ball. Faldo was tenacious and Langer was gracious, for as we came down the last fairway Bernard said to me: 'That's the greatest golf I've ever seen in my life. You deserve to win.'

"I've been playing well for the last 12 months, a tremendous relief after my down period of the two years before that. But with a lot of work I got my swing back to where I could trust it."

In fact, Norman, when the final round began in mild weather freshened by a westerly breeze, immediately made his intentions clear of closing the one-stroke gap he and Langer shared behind Faldo and Corey Pavin. He hit his first approach to four feet, and with three more birdies in seven holes from the third, he succeeded in completely altering the balance of power.

At the turn Norman, out in 31, was 11 under par, and Faldo and Langer, each having bogeyed the fourth, were now two strokes behind. Norman went from strength to strength, picking up three more birdies, including the long fourteenth after two imperious shots through the left-hand wind almost on to the green. The blip caused by that missed short putt at the seventeenth proved a blessing in disguise. "It gave me a kick up the backside," said Norman. He had looked at the leaderboard for the first time in the round just before he made the error which reconcentrated his mind, with results that were to

be resoundingly achieved and acclaimed. Faldo it was who, on the way to winning the 1990 championship at St Andrews, had swept aside Norman, then in the lead by a stroke, with 67 to 76 in the third round. They were not paired together on this occasion, Norman being with Langer and Faldo with Pavin, but they were of course sensitive to each other's presence even at a distance. Pavin, short of length by comparison with the others but renowned as a tactician and fierce competitor, never recovered from having made three bogeys in the first six holes.

Nothing in Faldo's nature allows him to give up without a fight. He almost holed his tee-shot at the short eleventh and saved par from 10 feet after being bunkered from the thirteenth tee. But when he left his birdie putt at the seventeenth short, in the jaws of the hole, his last chance had gone.

Langer's fatal error of striking as well as of club selection at the fourteenth set him back for good. In the first three rounds he had conservatively taken a No.1 iron from the tee; now he risked the driver and cut the ball over the fence on to the adjoining Prince's course. His two birdies on either side of the double bogey 7 were in turn resolute and unavailing.

It was left to Peter Senior, Norman's compatriot, to wield his broom-handle putter effectively again on an inward half of 32 to join Pavin on 272, two strokes behind Langer and two in front of Aberdeen's Paul Lawrie, the second British player behind Faldo, and the two Southern Africans, Ernie Els and Nick Price, the US PGA champion, who never quite came to terms with this championship.

1994

TURNBERRY

The last 15 majors had produced 15 different champions and the Open title had not been taken by the same player two years in a row since Tom Watson's victory in 1983. Statistics therefore did not favour Greg Norman but the Australian was playing well.

Conditions on the first morning were bright and breezy but deteriorated in the afternoon when New Zealander Greg Turner set the pace with a 65 containing two eagles, the second at the par-4 sixteenth where he holed his second with a No.2 iron. He had a one shot lead over the young Shropshire professional, Jonathan Lomas who had led for five hours. The American, Andrew Magee, was third on 67 with 11 more chasing on 68, including Jean Van de Velde, Tom Watson, John Daly and Jesper Parnevik.

Old-timer Watson shot a 65 in the second round for the halfway lead on 133. He was one ahead of Brad Faxon, who also had a 65, and Parnevik, with Nick Price on 135 and four others on 136, including Lomas. The holder, Norman, was two shots further back.

On Saturday the top honour went to Fuzzy Zoeller who carded a 64 for an aggregate of 201 and a share of the lead with his compatriot, Faxon, just one ahead of Watson, Parnevik and Price, with David Feherty one shot more and Mark James on 205. Norman was six shots off the lead.

17 JULY

Nick Price, deprived of the title once by his own hand and once by a rival's brilliant golf, put these frustrations firmly behind him at Turnberry yesterday by the manner in which he won the 123rd Open Championship by a stroke. This time Price was the architect of his own triumph and the instrument of the destruction of another's hopes, although Jesper Parnevik also contributed to his own downfall.

When, towards the end of a glorious summer's afternoon, Parnevik holed from 15 feet at the sixteenth and chipped out of rough dead at the long seventeenth for another birdie, he stood 12 under par and, relatively, was three strokes ahead of Price, in the match immediately behind. But there then followed one of the championship's quickest and most dramatic reversals of fortune.

Parnevik's putter had operated to magical effect five times after the turn but the club could not save him when he needed its powers most. He missed the home green into the thick rough that more than compensates for the absence of any bunkers and his chip was not close enough for par to be saved.

Price, who seemed as if he needed to play the last three holes in three under to tie, now had been given an opening to win. He made a nine-foot putt at the sixteenth, but when his second at the next ran to the back of the green some 65 feet from the hole, a birdie appeared the limit of his ambition. Instead, Price holed it and leapt in the air in jubilation as the putt died in on the low side. There never was any doubt that Price would make the par he needed at the last after a long and accurate drive and an approach to the heart of the green.

The "long and hard road since 1982," as Price himself later described it, had, at last, found its happy abode. But as vital as that lethal advance was, Price probably will recall as crucial to his cause the pars he saved at the tenth, eleventh, and fourteenth. The last was particularly adept, for having comprehensively overshot the green in two, Price played a bump-and-run back so close to the hole that the putt was a formality.

Thus, a final round of 66 gave Price a total of 268, 12 under par, and equal to the record for the Ailsa course set in 1977 by Tom Watson, and the £110,000 first prize. Although Price did not play well in this season's first two majors – thirty-fifth in the Masters and a missed cut in the US Open – his victory, by no means, was unexpected. Price had experience of winning a major, the 1992 US PGA Championship, and has won three times on the US Tour this season, remarkably the only player to have done so more than once.

With four victories in 1993, Price emerged as America's Player of the Year, but he still had to lay the ghost of those two Open defeats. At Royal Troon 12 years ago, Price led by three strokes with six to play but his inexperience cost him the title, which went to Watson. In 1988, he led by two strokes at Royal Lytham, but was overtaken by Severiano Ballesteros' brilliant 65 in the final round. Now aged 37, the Zimbabwean clearly is in the prime of his golfing life.

Parnevik, at 29, has time on his side to overcome his disappointment. Sweden, in sport better known for its tennis players and footballers than its golfers, very nearly had its first major championship winner to justify and advance the great strides taken by the game in that country over the last decade and more.

The 1993 Scottish Open champion, who finished third last week defending the title, made a tremendous thrust for victory when, after having played the first 10 holes each in par, he made birdies at five of the next seven. One suspects, however, that recollection of that damaging bogey will linger longer in Parnevik's thoughts. Nevertheless, Parnevik brought to life a championship which, at the end of a week generally conducted on a low key, seemed to be proceeding peacefully to a close.

Such was the potential for victory in so many candidates that none firmly recommended himself as favourite. No doubt Fuzzy Zoeller would, at 42, have been the sentimental choice, but the former US Open and Masters champion, whose equal of the late Julius Boros he must be for the nonchalant approach to the game, could not respond to the occasion, although he led by two strokes after he had birdied the second. His final round of 70 gave him third place.

Similarly, David Feherty, with one bogey and one birdie, also had a par round of 70, but that was still adequate enough to share fourth place with Mark James, who covered the last four holes in four under, and Parnevik's compatriot, Anders Forsbrand, who came home in 31 for 64 to share the score as the day's lowest with Nick Faldo. The light breeze which tempered the warm sunshine perhaps ruffled the sparkling waters of the Firth of Clyde more than the flags or the composure of the competitors. All the same, it almost boxed the compass as the day progressed, from east for the early starters to north-east for the leading groups. By the end of the day 29 of the 81 players had bettered the 6957-yard links' par of 70.

Watson's hopes vanished with quite startling rapidity. When he pitched to two feet to birdie the seventh, he held a share of the lead at nine under. Two holes late Watson, having missed both greens, first took three putts and then stubbed his first chip shot, put two 6s on his card, and retreated to a woebegone distance.

Colin Montgomerie, not unexpectedly, was the leading Scottish player of the eight who survived the cut. But 15 par figures surrounding the only lively action – birdies at the eleventh and thirteenth and a bogey at the twelfth – was not inspirational enough to advance him significantly from his starting point of four under.

1994
NICK PRICE

Nick Price was born in Durban, South Africa, in 1957 but moved to Rhodesia as a child and would later serve in the Rhodesian Air Force before the country became Zimbabwe. His parents being British, it would be safe to say he was international even before his golfing talents came to the fore.

He started golf as a child and played as a serious amateur before he did his military service, after which he turned professional.

His Open win came after two near misses, in 1982 when he threw away a three-shot lead with six holes to play, and in 1988 as the result of brilliant play by Severiano Ballesteros. Having "paid his dues" no-one grudged this popular player his success which came, aged 37, at the height of his career. He topped the US money lists in 1993 and 1994. He also won the US PGA title in 1994 making him one of only three players in the 1990s to win two majors in one season (the others being Nick Faldo in 1990 and Mark O'Meara in 1998). His book, *The Swing*, was published in 1997, the same year that he lost his good friend and caddie Jeff 'Squeeky' Medlen to leukaemia.

Price is a fully paid-up member of the airways, owning a private jet which he bought from Greg Norman. Yes, he would buy a second-hand jet from that man.

Nick Price admires the Claret Jug, as a disconsolate Parnevik looks on.

1995

ST ANDREWS

Arnold Palmer, who played in his first Open at St Andrews 35 years ago, was back for a nostalgic last crack at the Old Course and the championship to which he contributed so much, while at the other end of the scale the Amateur champion, Gordon Sherry, was having his first crack. The young Scot, enjoying a great season, had a hole in one in practice.

Tom Watson, together with Ben Crenshaw, John Daly and Mark McNulty of Zimbabwe, led with 67s after the first round. Sherry had a 70.

Three players were in the joint lead after two rounds, Brad Faxon, Daly and K Tomori of Japan, all on 138, with six more one shot back, including Crenshaw, John Cook and the Italian, Costantino Rocca. Sherry, playing in the exalted company of Tom Watson and Greg Norman, added a 71 for 141, just three behind the leaders. A total of 100 players made the cut.

Sadly Palmer, at the age of 65, didn't qualify for the last two rounds, but his two younger buddies, Gary Player and Jack Nicklaus, survived.

On the third day, Michael Campbell of New Zealand with a 65 jumped into the lead on 207, two clear of Rocca who had returned one of the better scores of 70. Steve Elkington of Australia had a 69 for 210 and third place, with Tomori, Daly, Corey Pavin (USA) and the South African, Ernie Els, sharing fourth place on one shot more. Sherry had a third round of 74.

23 JULY

John Daly, very much the enfant terrible of the US Tour, shook the world of golf when in 1991 he emerged from total obscurity to win the US PGA title. At St Andrews yesterday he stirred it by capturing the 124th Open Championship, soundly beating the Italian Costantino Rocca, after a four-hole play-off.

The two players had tied with 72-hole totals of 282, six under par, over an Old Course ravaged by wind, with respective final rounds of 71 and 73, Rocca's shot to tie having been achieved in as melodramatic a way as can ever have been witnessed in the long and ancient history of the headquarters of the game.

But the play-off itself, conducted over the first, second, seventeenth, and eighteenth holes as the gale which had gusted to 35mph subsided in the evening sunshine, was a severe anti-climax for the many spectators who hoped that Rocca would ensure that America's recent victory drought in this championship lasted for another year.

Instead Daly, aged 29, became the seventh player from the United States to win the Open at St Andrews in 14 attempts since the First World War when he took the venerable claret jug and the first prize of £125,000 by no fewer than four strokes, 15-19 on aggregate.

Rocca, aged 37, who came to professional golf comparatively late in life, was halted in his tracks when he took three putts at the first, having overrun the hole by six feet, to go 4-5, one behind, and when Daly ran in an unlikely 40-footer for a birdie at the next to win 3-4, the margin had increased to two.

The end came for the amply-built Rocca at the third extra hole. The Road Bunker, the nemesis of so many ambitions over the years, gathered another victim in its embrace when Rocca's second shot finished under the face and he needed three more to extricate himself. Daly's carefully crafted approach from the rough on to the green won him the seventeenth by 4-7. The last thus became routine, although Rocca put a slightly better complexion on his defeat with a birdie 3 to Daly's 4.

Daly said: "I was disappointed when Rocca's putt went in, but Corey Pavin, Brad Faxon and Bob Estes told me I could do it. Muirfield in 1992, when I finished last, was a tough initiation for me, but I proved the next year at

Royal St George's [where he was equal fourteenth] that I was improving at this style of golf. There was more pressure on me than in 1991, when I didn't think I could win the US PGA – and neither did anyone else."

Rocca consoled himself with the knowledge that his second prize of £100,000 ensured he had retained his European Ryder Cup team place. "It wasn't easy to marshall my thoughts after that putt and I knew I was up against it in the play-off because Daly hits the ball so far. Those three putts on the first green gave me the feeling it wasn't going to be my day and Daly's birdie at the next confirmed it. When my second at the next went into the bunker, I really did have that sinking feeling."

That this outcome, only the second since the reduced and immediate play-off system was introduced in 1985, was necessary and came at the end of a tumultuous afternoon, during which the ferocity of the westerly wind, buffeting the competitors on the exposed and firm greens and hard and running fairways, had really too much influence to allow skill to outplay endurance.

It seemed as if Daly had the title for the taking when, with only three holes to play, he led by three strokes from Michael Campbell and Rocca, two games behind, and from Steve Elkington who was in the penultimate pair, and Steven Bottomley who, in the by now well-tried phrase, had risen without trace eventually to share third place.

But the tail of the course wagged in the most dramatic manner. Daly dropped one stroke by three-putting the sixteenth. From his next drive pulled into the rough, the ball fell under the vertical face of the Road Bunker and having had to play well away from the flagstick, two putts from 30 feet gathered in a commonplace bogey.

When Daly's last approach was not close enough to give him a plausible chance of a birdie to soften the cushion to a two-stroke lead and the bogeys of Campbell and Elkington at the sixteenth and seventeenth respectively eliminated them from the championship's climax, Rocca became the last remaining threat. But even he must have thought his last hope had gone when his second, also from rough, ran over the seventeenth green on to the tarmac of the road beyond. Instead, he improvised such a remarkable shot with his putter that the ball, lofted as in a chip, finished only four feet from the hole.

That par saved, Rocca had to birdie the last, 354-yards long but, downwind, within driving distance all week. Rocca's tee shot came up short of the Valley of Sin and then disaster seemed about to prevail over that other great impostor, triumph. After a lengthy reconnaissance Rocca hit the ground behind the ball which rolled ignominiously into that famous depression.

The collective intake of breath was similar to that taken when Doug Sanders had that awful four-foot miss which ultimately cost him the 1970 Open. But the roar, echoed even by those hardened and sceptical inhabitants of the media centre, which greeted the next shot was as resoundingly rendered. Rocca, probably with the hopes and fears of every Italian in or out of captivity riding on the shot, holed out from some 35 feet for the 3.

Astonishingly the leading British player was Bottomley, a 30-year-old Yorkshireman who in 20 tournaments this season has missed 11 cuts and withdrawn twice.

1995
JOHN DALY

"Wild Thing" John Daly was born in Sacramento, California, in 1966. One of the longest hitters the game has ever seen – his catchphrase is "grip it and rip it" – his touch around the greens is also on a par with the best. He unexpectedly won the 1991 US PGA Championship after being allowed to play due to a late withdrawal and despite having no time for a practice round.

Daly has packed into a troubled life divorce, drink, and drug problems, and suspension from the US Tour after having been involved in a brawl. Much of his considerable winnings have been used to settle gambling debts.

After his 1995 Open win, Daly paid tribute to the part played in his rehabilitation by wife Paulette, whom he married earlier that year. He said: "She's very special and she's been through a lot with me. I love her more than golf and we have a wonderful little baby girl. She'd better get ready as we'll definitely have a lot more."

Typically, preparation for the greatest round of his life was a gastric nightmare. "This morning I had about 10 croissants with chocolate in them, and some eggs, to help while away the time before I teed off."

1996

ROYAL LYTHAM AND ST ANNE'S

Just three years after the first prize reached the seemingly staggering figure of £100,000 the winner will receive exactly double that amount. Small wonder that Nick Faldo celebrated his thirty-ninth birthday on the first day by arriving at the practice area at 6.30am, where to his surprise some of his fans also turned up to wish him a happy birthday. He continued his celebration with a 68 but still found himself three shots off the lead.

With the sun blazing down from a cloudless sky Paul Broadhurst set the first round pace with a 65, equalling the course record set by Severiano Ballesteros in his winning final round in 1988. H Tanaka of Japan shared second place on 67 with seven Americans, including Tom Lehman and Loren Roberts, respectively runners-up in the 1994 US Masters and US Open. Former winners Bob Charles and Gary Player, both aged 60, scored 70.

Irishman Paul McGinley returned a second-round 65 for a 134 total and a share of the lead with Lehman, playing in only his third Open, one ahead of Jack Nicklaus, Peter Hedblom of Sweden, who also had a 65, and Ernie Els.

In the third round Lehman returned a 64 to establish an Open record of 198 for the first 54 holes, beating Faldo's mark by one. This gave Lehman a six-stroke advantage over Faldo going into the last round. In joint third place on 205 were Fijian Vijay Singh and the American Marc Brooks, with Fred Couples and Els, one stroke further back.

21 JULY

So, in the end, Tom Lehman wasn't Greg Norman, Royal Lytham wasn't Augusta National, and this morning Nick Faldo isn't Open champion. In a fourth round that began with an eerily familiar script – the six-stroke lead, the cold-eyed Faldo marking his card, the potential for disaster almost tangible in the sweltering heat – Lehman, a 37-year-old Minnesotan, now resident in Arizona,

finally put paid to one of golf's more tedious statistics. Now an American pro has won an Open at Lytham.

Lehman singled out one ill-mannered spectator for the part he played in his victory. As Lehman lined up a putt on the seventh green, the 'fan' shouted out: "Knock it in, Greg."

Lehman took it as a reference to Norman's last-day collapse against Faldo at the US Masters in April and said after collecting the trophy: "He was basically calling me a choker and I really wanted to bury the ball right in the middle of the hole and say 'take that'. Nobody likes to be called a choker or be ridiculed. I didn't hole the putt, but it made me more determined. You don't want to have on your gravestone that you couldn't win the big one."

The history books will tell us that the endearingly blue-collar Lehman shot a final two-over-par round of 73 and won by two strokes from former US Open champion Ernie Els and Mark McCumber. And that Faldo was fourth, a stroke further away. Lehman's aggregate of 271 moreover is the lowest winning score ever recorded over these famous links.

But this was no procession. Lehman never looked completely comfortable until his No.8-iron second shot to the final green found its target. That nervous neck twitch of his was up to about one every three seconds by the time he reached the last tee needing a 5 for victory. "I saw then that I had a two-shot lead," he said. "I knew that if I could stay out of the bunkers off the tee I'd win." He was right. Coming up the last he didn't cry, but it was a close run thing. "I had tears in my eyes walking up there," he admitted. "When the ovation you have watched and listened to on television so many times is for you, it's a great feeling."

He then talked of the contrast between his early – and

long – struggles on almost every tour imaginable and the feelings engendered by lifting the claret jug. Only five years ago he was on the Nike Tour. "I'd get almost as nervous on the mini-tours," he said later. "It's just that the Open is so huge. But when you have a chance to win anywhere the feeling is the same. Now I just want to sit down and think about it."

Such sentiments were understandable. It had been a long day. Almost immediately the field made inroads into that six-shot cushion of his. At no time before the last was he allowed the luxury of relaxation. "I didn't feel comfortable with my swing or the putter," he claimed. "It felt like a lead mallet. When I feel like that the rest of my game always suffers."

Five holes into his final round Lehman's lead had been halved, Couples the man in second place, four birdies in the first six holes, dragging the American Players' champion past Faldo. Then came two holes, both par-5s, at which Lehman needed birdies but didn't get them.

"I was concerned for Tom at that point," said the sporting and fast-finishing McCumber after completing his round of 66. But, luckily for Lehman, none of his nearest challengers managed two birdie 4s either.

The sixth hole, the easiest on the course, produced Lehman's first moment of crisis. A snap-hooked drive – always his bad shot when that rather agricultural action ("It isn't pretty, but it's good enough") gets a little quick – into bushes was found and playable. Two hacks later he was just short of the green, from where he saved par. Five pars followed. Then Lehman had to face the treacherous 198-yard twelfth. Later he would call the No.4-iron shot he struck to 12 feet the "best shot of the week." He identified the resulting birdie as "the turning point and a huge lift. I felt as if I was in charge."

Faldo was reduced to the level of Lehman's "subordinate." He did birdie the fourth from about six yards, but when he spilled short putts on the next three greens three men were in front of him. Thereafter he was never closer to Lehman than three shots. It was left to Els and Couples to get closest. A birdie at the ninth took the American to 12 under. But it was a false dawn. As so often with this talented, yet lackadaisical, figure, three careless bogeys in the space of four holes followed. He eventually meandered home in 41 strokes. Bye-bye Freddie.

Els, although displaying a similarly phlegmatic exterior, was made of sterner stuff, at least for a while. Six times in 15 holes he dipped below par, only a bogey at the third slowing his methodical progress towards the leader.

Until, that is, his tee-shots at the sixteenth and eighteenth found sand. "I had it going," he said at the end. "I was right in there, but hit two bad shots. I tried to cut a No.2 iron at 16 and it went straight. And at the last I played the wrong club. I just couldn't finish it."

Els's bogeys gave the new champion the breathing space he so desperately needed. Showing signs of strain, Lehman three-putted the fourteenth from long range and pulled his No.6-iron approach into sand at the ever dangerous fifteenth. "My uncertainty returned about then," he said.

The up-and-down he made there was perhaps the most important of his life. "That was a key putt," he claimed. Three holes later it was over and Lehman had lost forever his "nearly man" tag. This was his fourth visit to major championship contention.

The course, long since transformed from its usual slog to a test of distance control rather than pure distance, came away from all of this looking almost as good as the winner. It still isn't pretty, even when the sun shines and shines, but Lytham established itself as the best Open venue in England this week.

Three men, the new champion, Faldo and Vijay Singh, began the last day with the chance to shoot four rounds in the 60s. None of them managed it. The only pity is the wind didn't blow.

1996
TOM LEHMAN

Tom Lehman was a late developer, and his Open victory at the age of 37 was testimony to his never-say-die spirit. From 1983 to 1987, the young Lehman played in 77 US Tour events and won a mere $39,027. "We got down to a thousand bucks one time," said the father-of-three. "That's pretty close to zero, and I had just lost my sponsors."

He came close to giving up, but never did, even when offered the security of the position of golf coach at his alma mater, the University of Minnesota. He played instead on mini-tours where the players compete for their own money and also on the tours in Asia, South Africa and South America.

"Confidence is everything," Lehman said. "But the competition is great. If you have a swing that will repeat and hold up, you start to believe in it."

His salvation was the Hogan, now Nike Tour, in the States. The Hogan was started in 1990 to give those like Lehman, who did not have their tour cards, a place to compete. The top 10 players on the money list would win their US Tour cards.

Lehman, noted for being unfailingly polite, was seventeenth in his first year. In 1991 he won four events and more than $100,000. At the end of the year he was "player of the year" and ready for the US Tour. "I started to believe in myself then," Lehman said. "You get to the point where you believe no-one can beat you".

That first year, aged 32, he finished in the top 10 nine times and won $440,000. The first win came at the Memorial Tournament in 1994. The next step was major championship play. That same year he finished second to Jose Maria Olazabal at the US Masters. At the final hole, needing a birdie, Lehman took an iron from the tee and hit into the left-hand bunker. Nine months later he was third in the 1995 US Open, playing with Greg Norman in the final round. A month before his Open win only a last-hole bogey prevented him playing off with Steve Jones in the US Open.

1 9 9 7

ROYAL TROON

The by now customary strong international field was illustrated by David Leadbetter, Nick Faldo's guru, predicting his five most likely winners – an American, a South African, an Australian, an Englishman and a Scotsman.

An interesting qualifier was amateur Barclay Howard, a self-confessed former alcoholic, having a fine season at the age of 44. A Walker Cup player and holder of the Scottish Amateur Strokeplay championship, this was his first attempt at the Open.

First-round leaders on 67 were the American Jim Furyk and Irishman, Darren Clarke, two ahead of Greg Norman, Fred Couples and a new American talent, Justin Leonard. Howard was one of a group on 70, which also included Jesper Parnevik. Colin Montgomerie, who despite his enormous success has a poor Open record, started with a 76. American prodigy Tiger Woods had a 72. Holder Tom Lehman had a 74 which included two penalty strokes for a breach of the rules relative to replacing a marked ball on the green. Sadly Ian Baker-Finch continued his decline and returned a 92.

In the second round Clarke followed up his 67 with a 66 for a two-round total of 133 and a lead of two over Leonard. Parnevik also had a 66 to be one stroke further back. Howard qualified on 144, the only amateur to do so, thus assuring himself of the amateur medal.

Meanwhile Steven Bottomley was quietly writing himself into the history books with two visits to the par-3 Postage Stamp eighth hole, where in 1973 the 71 year old Gene Sarazen scored a hole in one in the first round and followed it with a 2 in the second. Steven managed a 7 on the first day, a mere quadruple bogey, and, determined to do better in the second round, put together a 10 (would this be a septuple bogey?), a total of 11 over par.

At the end of the third day things were looking good for Clarke, who had increased his lead over Leonard to three, with a 71 for

a 54-hole total of 204. Sharing second place with Leonard was Fred Couples. Barclay Howard had a 54-hole total of 220.

20 JULY

One is so square he is divisible by four. The other one wears flashing, bleeping sunglasses on aeroplanes to unite the left and right sides of his brain. One is seemingly as sweet as mom's apple pie. The other one subsisted for three months on fruit and volcanic sand.

The first thing one of them does upon entering a new hotel room is unpack. The other checks to see that he is not only in the right hotel but the correct city. One would like to play golf in a collar and tie. The other wears trousers so tight they restrict his hip turn.

One, according to his family, "makes lists of lists." The other listens to faith healers who tell him he has "scars in his stomach". One was recently named one of the world's most eligible bachelors by *Cosmopolitan* magazine. *Sports Illustrated* called the other an eccentric.

Never mind, they can both play golf. What started as a fairly pedestrian day's play evolved into a feast of birdies, and the destination of the 126th Open Championship at Royal Troon came down to a straight fight between Texan Justin Leonard (the boring one) and Sweden's Jesper Parnevik (the weird one).

One of them shot an eight-birdie, two-bogey round of 65 yesterday. The other plodded to a 73, dipping under par only three times in the process. So, as sometimes happens, boring won in the most exciting way imaginable. Let's start with the numbers. He would, after all.

Leonard, 25, from Dallas, is the Open Champion of 1997. His four-round total of 272, 12 under par, for the 72 holes he played, was three shots better than both Parnevik, courtesy of a Swedish bogey at the last and his own birdie, and halfway leader Darren Clarke of Ireland. Leonard becomes the third 20-something – after Tiger Woods and Ernie Els – to win a major this year. Do I hear new era? Truly, majors are weird things. Who would have imagined that Justin Leonard would win one before the likes of Davis Love, Phil Mickelson and our own Colin Montgomerie?

He did it in style, though. In contrast with the third round, where he hit the ball well and holed nothing, Leonard made every putt he looked at over the closing holes. A 15-footer for par at the fifteenth was followed by another on the sixteenth for a birdie. The 20-footer he holed at the short seventeenth after a perfectly-struck tee-shot gave him his eighth birdie of the day and he safely two-putted from long range for par at the last. "Those putts were the tournament," he said. "I didn't allow Jesper any breathing room."

That analysis was confirmed by Parnevik, who struggled all day to find his rhythm. "My game didn't feel good all week," he claimed. "For three days I was riding a wave of forward momentum, but today the pressure was too much. The shots were not there. I felt like I had to hole from six feet on every hole for par."

Still, this isn't the first time Parnevik has folded on a Sunday. Last year on the US Tour he averaged 69.92 before the cut and 69.50 in his third rounds. Pretty good. However, his final-round average is 71.63, more than two shots more. Not good. There is better news in the fact that, unlike three years ago at Turnberry, where he went for the flag at the last when a par would have put him in a play-off with Nick Price, Parnevik did look at every scoreboard.

Leonard goes back to Dallas and the friends and family who caused him to break down in the middle of his victory speech. He will also now be at Valderrama for the Ryder Cup. American captain Tom Kite, a close pal, even made the effort to return from Prestwick Airport to see the youngster's victory first hand. "Welcome to the team," he said as the pair embraced beside the eighteenth green.

According to the new champion, the key to victory, apart from all those putts, was, not surprisingly, "playing conservatively off the tees. I went with the long irons a lot," he said. "Those bunkers are in play for me, so I had to play short of them. I had good distance control today, too. I hit a lot of good shots to eight or 10 feet and made them."

It is not as easy as that, of course. Leonard is one of the more diligent practicers on the US Tour. "I enjoy being last off the range," he said. No kidding. Late on Saturday evening he was the only man left on the practice putting green.

Clarke's high hopes of the morning all but evaporated when he hit his first shank in seven years as a professional on to the beach at the second and took 6. "I don't know where it came from," he claimed. "But I struggled from then on." Still, the 28-year-old will have learned much from his first exposure to the unique pressures induced by being in contention in a major championship. "I'm disappointed," he said. "Finishing second in the Open is pretty good, but first is better."

He was not alone in his misery. For Tiger Woods, the talk before the off had been of 61 or 62. When the young Master birdied the fourth and fifth, that sort of score looked as if it might be on. But a short putt for a third consecutive birdie was spilled at the next, then another at the seventh. He looked a little annoyed. Ten minutes later that had changed to a lot. After pushing his tee-shot into the right hand bunker, Tiger took two to escape and compounded his error by three-putting. The thought that 24 years ago a 71-year-old man had played the same hole in five strokes fewer was irresistible. The shot is obviously a wee No.5 iron, Tiger.

In the end he shot 74 for a level par total of 284, a number which put him in the company of such as defending champion Tom Lehman, Montgomerie, Phil Mickelson and Ian Woosnam.

1997

JUSTIN LEONARD

Justin Leonard, from Dallas, Texas, had a long track record as a winner before his Open victory. In 1992, while a second-year student at the University of Texas in Austin, Leonard won the US Amateur championship. A year later he was the best player in the US Walker Cup side. In 1994 he won the NCAA title, college golf's most prestigious, before turning professional that autumn by which time he had graduated with a degree in business.

Immediately, he did well in the paid ranks. A third-place finish in only his third tournament won him $74,000. He finished No.126 on the money list, good enough to avoid a trip to the qualifying school. In 1995 Leonard was No.22, and in 1996 he was eleventh and won his first tournament, the Buick Open. Before his win at Troon, aged 25 – the youngest Open winner since Severiano Ballesteros in 1979 – he had won his second US Tour event, the Kemper Open. His record in the other major championships revealed a similar upward trend. In two Masters he was twenty-seventh and seventh; in three US Opens, sixty-eighth, fiftieth and thirty-sixth; in two US PGAs, eighth and fifth.

Leonard, regarded as mentally tough, worked with sports psychologist Fran Pirazzola from the age of 18. Every week he would fax Pirazzola his goals for the next seven days. Leonard is also regarded as having much more of a body than a hands and arms swing, which is why he doesn't hit it too far. He has a highly individual low-and-around follow through, though by that time the ball is well on its way.

Off the course, Leonard is known for his organisation. When his sister moved into his flat, Justin made it a condition that she would have to make her bed every morning before leaving, without fail. She was more amused than irked. "Justin makes lists of his lists," she says.

Leonard hails from an upper-middle class background. His father is an administrator at a medical lab. Leonard has remained faithful to the one teacher throughout his career. Randy Smith, head pro at the Royal Oaks Country Club has taught the Open champion for 15 years.

"The reason I think Justin won the Open is because he has the ability to adapt to the elements and control the height of his ball," he said. "Whatever the shot requires, he has the ability to do it. Ever since he was 19, the more people he has played in front of, the better he has responded. He draws energy from the crowd."

Leonard's family is involved in his career. His mother handles travel, father does his finances and sister handles public relations.

He holed the putt that ultimately won the Ryder Cup for USA at Brookline in 1999 and sparked the controversial green invasion when Jose Maria Olazabal still had a long putt to keep the contest alive.

1998

ROYAL BIRKDALE

Royal Birkdale, the venue for eight Opens, is the course where the fastest round of golf in the history of the Open was played in 1971 when Brian Barnes and South African Tienie Britz out first in the final round, covered the 18 holes in 116 minutes; where Irishman Denis Durnian in 1983 covered the first nine holes in a record 28 strokes; and where, also in 1983, Hale Irwin had an air shot on the fourteenth green, missing a tap-in putt, and went on to lose the Open to Tom Watson by one stroke.

In the first round, John Huston and Tiger Woods took the lead on 65 with two more Americans, Fred Couples and Loren Roberts, and Nick Price of Zimbabwe one shot further back. There were five on 67 and nine on 68, including three Scots, Raymond Russell, Andrew Coltart and Sam Torrance. Holder Justin Leonard had a 73, as did Colin Montgomerie.

Outright leader after two rounds was Brian Watts (USA) on 137, one ahead of Woods, Price and the young English amateur, Justin Rose, who had a second round of 66. Mark O'Meara was on 140 and Montgomerie missed the cut.

Scoring in the third round was high and Watts, despite returning a 73, retained the lead on 210, two ahead of O'Meara, Parnevik and Jim Furyk. Rose was on 213, three shots off the lead.

19 JULY

America's domination of the Open Championship continued last night when course specialist Mark O'Meara beat countryman Brian Watts by two shots in a four-hole play-off to take his second major of the year. The 41-year-old O'Meara, who captured the US Masters in dramatic style, was always in control in extra time against the unknown Watts at Royal Birkdale. The winner's cheque was £300,000, but it will mean much more to O'Meara that his career has flourished in mid-life.

He is the first player since Zimbabwean Nick Price in 1994 to win two majors in the same year. He is also the oldest to win two majors in the same year, surpassing Jack Nicklaus and Ben Hogan, who each won multiple majors in their fortieth years.

O'Meara is a man who lives up to golf's highest traditions. That was evidenced when applauding the spectacular greenside bunker shot to 18 inches by Watts that took him into the play-off. The defining moment came on the very first hole of a play-off that had already ensured that the claret jug was heading back to America for the fourth year in succession.

On the 544-yard fifteenth, Watts hit his third to three feet, O'Meara was two feet further away, but it was he who showed the composure necessary to hole for a birdie, whereas his younger and vastly more inexperienced rival missed. Watts may have won 10 events on the Japanese Tour, but these achievements do not stack up against those of O'Meara.

On the 416-yard sixteenth, O'Meara made a solid par, two-putting from 18 feet, but Watts, who was some five feet closer on the same line, could not take advantage. Again O'Meara was solid and assured in making par on the 547-yard seventeenth, whereas Watts made an improbable 5. Showing signs of the pressure of the greatest minutes of his career, Watts sent his drive into heavy rough and could only hack out. Then his third shot was again blocked wide and he required a pitch and putt from seven feet to stay in the hunt. His chances ended when he bunkered his approach on the eighteenth while his rival flew the flag to land 18 feet away. Watts could not get up and down in two and O'Meara two-putted effortlessly.

O'Meara, who won the Lawrence Batley event over the

Lancashire links and finished tied for third in the Open of 1991, admitted: "I was amazed at how relaxed I felt in the play-off with so much riding on this event. I'm pretty impressed with myself. I think I took something from my Masters win and played real solid. This course has been very, very special to the O'Meara family, but I thought when I was third here that this would be the closest I'd get to winning. It is an incredible feeling to have won a championship which I love so dearly. This championship is the most special there is. It is a worldwide event with great players and changing conditions every day. That is its challenge."

O'Meara carded a two-under-par 68 to eliminate the two-shot advantage Watts enjoyed going into the final round. Having finished no better than tied fortieth place in six previous attempts, it was a magnificent effort by Watts when confronted by the greatest challenge of his career. He reflected ruefully: "I knew I just had to hole that bunker shot on the last play-off hole to have any chance. But Mark is a great guy, a class act." Tiger Woods, who closed with a 66 to miss out on the play-off by a single stroke, had predicted that O'Meara, who he regards as his big brother, would win. "You know the guy is capable of gutting it out and winning championships," he said.

Raymond Russell, who equalled Woods' 66 with a bogey-free round, finished in a four-way tie for fourth place – the highest a Scot has been placed since Sandy Lyle won in 1985 at Sandwich. The performance of the Prestonpans player was all the more creditable as he has just recently been given the all-clear after a six-month bout of hepatitis.

English amateur international, Justin Rose, aged 17, holed his pitch at the last for a birdie 3 and a round of 69 to finish on the same mark as Russell and the teenager immediately afterwards declared his intention to turn professional.

1998
MARK O'MEARA

Mark O'Meara said modestly of his two majors in one season at the age of 41: "What I have done does not give me a place in the history of the game. I am a good player, but I do not classify myself as a great player. The greats are Nicklaus, Hogan, and Byron Nelson. You can go on down the list to Sam Snead and Arnold Palmer who have won lots of majors and have been incredible golf ambassadors."

O'Meara, of course, does have his place in history and he, too, has been a great ambassador by projecting the proper image of golf in his 18-year career until he became Open champion and beyond.

His emergence as a force in the majors in his mid-life was due in part to his relationship and rivalry with Tiger Woods, a near neighbour at Isleworth Golf Club in Orlando.

Serious money was wagered on their games and O'Meara more than held his own because of his relaxed and extremely effective putting stroke. Woods, who regards his mentor as the greatest putter in the world, borrowed a putter from him before competing in the Open where he came within a shot of making it a three-way play-off. O'Meara joked: "That was my back-up putter Tiger used. I finished first, he finished one shot behind so you know why it is my second choice putter."

O'Meara is a world player, having won events in the USA, Japan, Europe and Australia plus the US Amateur in 1979. The father-of-two is a laid-back character as witness an incident at the 1991 Open at Royal Birkdale. On the practice area he opened his bag and a large amount of money went fluttering away in the wind. As spectators ran about trying to collect it, he told them not to bother, with the words: "Easy come, easy go." As if to prove it, he went on to finish third, collecting a cheque for £55,000.

1 9 9 9

CARNOUSTIE

This century the Open has been won by players of 11 different nationalities. Leaders are America (22, including two Scots-born immigrants), England (12), Scotland (5), Australia (4), South Africa (2), and one apiece for Argentina, France, Spain, Ireland, Zimbabwe and New Zealand. None of the Scots were home-based at the time of winning.

The championship was back at Carnoustie after 24 years and even before the first round was under way many talented players were expressing serious misgivings about the narrow fairways and the thick rough. The Americans were looking for a fifth consecutive victory, something they hadn't achieved since the 1920s, and were looking to their new star, Tiger Woods, to do the needful.

There was a brisk westerly wind on the first day but hardly enough to account for the level of the scoring which was even worse than the gloomy predictions. Sergio Garcia, the new Spanish prodigy with the Irish Open under his belt after only 12 weeks as a professional, scored 89, Sandy Lyle had 85, Mark O'Meara 83, Tom Watson 82 and Severiano Ballesteros 80.

Rodney Pampling, a little-known Australian, led with a 71, one ahead of Bernhard Langer and the American, Scott Dunlap, with seven players on 73, including Justin Leonard and Aberdeen's Paul Lawrie, who has three times finished in the top 25. Garcia failed to qualify and so did first-round leader Pampling who hit the eighties having had his moment of fame. At the end of the second round, Frenchman Jean van de Velde, leading player in the qualifying rounds, shot 68 for 143 and was one ahead of Angel Cabrera of Argentina. Jesper Parnevik was one behind Cabrera on 145, with Greg Norman, Tiger Woods and another Swede, Patrick Sjoland, on one more. There were five players on 147, including Leonard and Lawrie. Nine former Open winners missed the cut.

After three rounds van de Velde had increased his lead to five shots with a 70 for a 54-hole total of 213, level par. Joint second

on 218 were Leonard and Australian Craig Parry who had a third round of 67. David Frost of South Africa and Tiger Woods shared fourth place, two shots further back. Lawrie had fallen well back with a 76 and was 10 shots behind the leader.

23 JULY

Amid ecstatic scenes, Paul Lawrie last night became the first home-bred Scot to win the Open Championship since the "Silver Scot", Tommy Armour, at Carnoustie all of 68 years ago. (Armour had become an American citizen at the time of his success.) The 30-year-old Aberdonian also made history by becoming the first player to survive the qualifying process and lift the old claret jug since Arnold Palmer at Royal Birkdale in 1962. Lawrie, 10 shots behind overnight leader Jean van de Velde when the day began, outplayed the Frenchman and former Open champion Justin Leonard for a momentous three-stroke victory over the American in a four-hole play-off. Apart from the wealth that will accrue in addition to his £350,000 first prize, Lawrie, who is attached to the Newmachar club, will now achieve his dream of playing in his first Ryder Cup match at Brookline in September and will gain entry to all the majors.

Yet even he did not give himself any chance of achieving his greatest triumph, despite a closing 67 that left him at six-over par for the tournament. However, he was handed his chance as they all self-destructed in their different ways down the stretch and how he seized it, holding his nerve and game when the 128th Open Championship moved into over-time.

Neither of his rivals could match his magnificent birdies on the seventeenth and eighteenth holes, which brought rapturous applause and raised the Saltire among the galleries that savoured this long-awaited triumph on home soil.

"I can't really believe it – it's amazing," admitted Lawrie, who developed his game on the links courses around Aberdeen. "There was no way I thought I could make the play-off at six-over-par, but when it happened I tried to stay focused and take every shot at a time. Pretty damn good it feels. It cannot get any better than this.

"Before starting, I knew Andy Coltart was ahead of me and I was thinking about the Dunhill and World Cup. Then I put all that nonsense out my head and got on with the job. And I did play beautifully. Making the Ryder Cup team is another bonus. Just great – terrific. I didn't moan or bitch about the course. I just did my thing and it worked out. It was very tough and you just had to pass the exam. Every kid dreams about this. I'm delighted that I have done it. But Jean had the tournament in his pocket. All he needed was a 6 at the last to win."

Much credit must go to his coach and fellow Scot, Adam Hunter, the former European Tour player, who took him aboard earlier this year. Their partnership assisted Lawrie to the Qatar Masters and, since then, his swing has continued to improve. Hunter said: "Paul is a very

dedicated and single-minded player, very much in the Nick Faldo mould, and deserves this win because no-one works harder. He will win more, just wait and see."

Yet even Lawrie, whose 67 had elevated him only to fifth place on the leaderboard when he completed his round over an hour before, conceded that he was presented with the most prestigious and oldest of the majors by van de Velde, who held a three-stroke advantage playing the eighteenth and struggled into the play-off with a 7 that contained all the elements of a French farce.

Each player was affected by the enormous pressure in the play-off, but it was the Scot who proved the most resolute. Each pulled their tee shots on the fifteenth, but the Frenchman was forced to drop out under penalty from a gorse bush, could not find the green in three shots and took 6, whereas his two rivals managed bogeys from poor lies in the deep rough. All three missed the short sixteenth, Leonard in the left rough and the two others bunkered. All again made bogeys.

Lawrie's telling thrust came on the danger-fraught seventeenth hole. With all three on the green, the American two-putted from the front edge, the Frenchman holed from 16 feet to birdie, and the Scot

followed him in from around a foot less to forge a stroke ahead. With the title riding on the last, van de Velde ended his hopes by pulling his drive into the left rough. His two rivals split the fairway, but when Leonard dumped his approach in the Barry Burn, Lawrie smote a superb No.4 iron to three feet and the trophy was his.

He now joins an illustrious cast of Armour, Henry Cotton, Ben Hogan, Gary Player, and Tom Watson who have prevailed on this formidable Angus links.

In regulation play, van de Velde, the pro from Disneyland Paris, produced a finale that not even old Walt could have dreamed of. His white-knuckle ride through 71 holes reached a crescendo on the last. Despite holding a three-stroke lead over Leonard and Lawrie, he went for glory with a driver instead of trying to find the fairway with an iron. His caddie should have insisted on a safety-first approach but sadly did not. The tee shot was blocked

and came to rest on a bank of the Barry Burn. He should have hit out on to the short grass but instead went for a grandstand finish. He did, too, but not the way he wanted with his errant ball rattling off the stanchions into deep rough. His recovery found the water and, when he climbed in to try and play his ball out, the huge gallery could not believe their eyes. "If you wait a bit longer the tide will go out," quipped Parry, in an attempt to lessen the tension. However, van de Velde dropped under a one-stroke penalty, sent his fifth shot into a greenside bunker and got up and down for a 7.

Leonard's three victories have been achieved by coming from five shots behind on the final day. When the Texan, who started five strokes adrift, birdied the par 5 Spectacles to earn a share of the lead there was a sense of deja vu. However, he found the Barry Burn at the last to drop a shot and that cost him a second Open title.

1999
PAUL LAWRIE

At the age of 17, some 13 years before his Open victory, Paul Lawrie was more interested in football than golf, at which he was a four-handicapper. A chance meeting, however, with Doug Smart, the late professional at Banchory, gave him his start as an assistant professional, learning his trade through the PGA training scheme.

Through a great deal of hard work his game quickly developed to the point where he won the Scottish Assistants championship in 1990 and then the Scottish PGA championship two years later. The following year he showed his potential on the international stage by finishing sixth in the Open at Royal St George's, closing with a five-under-par 65, holing a No.3-iron shot at the seventeenth with a "soft draw" he had been practising. He has always taken the view that if you can't raise your game for the Open then there's something wrong. Asked then if he was aware that no home-based Scot had won the Open since Willie Auchterlonie in 1893 he said: "Really! It would be nice to change that." It took him another six years to do so.

Life has not always been easy for Lawrie, who was born

on January 1, 1969. By 1995 he was languishing at No.107 on the European Tour order of merit and considering quitting the tour to take up a club job. "I was struggling badly and my wife, Marian, looked at the bankbook. There wasn't much left. It was a case of quit and get a club job or work harder," he said.

Lawrie, who was world No.159 at the time of his Open success, chose the latter course, linking up with sports psychologist Dr Richard Cox, of Moray House in Edinburgh. His coach, Adam Hunter, who gave up the European Tour in favour of a teaching career, concentrated on shortening his swing and changing his leg action. He also improved Lawrie's attitude and motivation. Victory in the European Tour's Qatar Masters in 1999 preceded his Open win.

Hunter is not averse to playing mind games as well, for he told Lawrie that his six-over-par total was good enough to win at Carnoustie, certainly enough to earn a play-off, when, in fact, Hunter believed that his man had taken one stroke too many.

Lawrie went on to make a successful debut in the Ryder Cup at Brookline and now divides his time between the European and US tours.

LEADING SCORES
1860 – 1999

1860   PRESTWICK
Willie Park Sr, Musselburgh 55, 59, 60 – 174;
Tom Morris Sr, Prestwick 58, 59, 59 – 176;
Andrew Strath, St Andrews 180
   (no further record of individual round scores);
Robert Andrew, Perth – 191;
George Brown, Blackheath – 192;
Charles Hunter, Prestwick St Nicholas – 195.

1861   PRESTWICK
Tom Morris Sr, Prestwick 54, 56, 53 – 163;
Willie Park Sr, Musselburgh 54, 54, 59 – 167;
William Dow, Musselburgh 59, 58, 54 – 171;
David Park, Musselburgh 58, 57, 57 – 172;
Robert Andrew, Perth 58, 61, 56 – 175;
Peter McEwan, Bruntsfield 56, 60, 62 – 178.

1862   PRESTWICK
Tom Morris Sr, Prestwick 52, 55, 56 – 163;
Willie Park Sr, Musselburgh 59, 59, 58 – 176;
Charles Hunter, Prestwick 60, 60, 58 – 178;
William Dow, Musselburgh 60, 58, 63 – 181;
Mr James Knight, Prestwick 62, 61, 63 – 186;
Mr J F Johnston, Prestwick 64, 69, 75 – 208.

1863   PRESTWICK
Willie Park Sr, Musselburgh 56, 54, 58 – 168;
Tom Morris Sr, Prestwick 56, 58, 56 – 170;
David Park, Musselburgh 55, 63, 54 – 172;
Andrew Strath, St Andrews 61, 55, 58 – 174;
George Brown, St Andrews 58, 61, 57 – 176;
Robert Andrew, Perth 62, 57, 59 – 178.

1864   PRESTWICK
Tom Morris Sr, Prestwick 54, 58, 55 – 167;
Andrew Strath, St Andrews 56, 57, 56 – 169;
Robert Andrew, Perth 57, 58, 60 – 175;
Willie Park Sr, Musselburgh 55, 67, 55 – 177;
William Dow, Musselburgh 56, 58, 67 – 181;
William Strath, St Andrews 60, 62, 60 – 182.

1865   PRESTWICK
Andrew Strath, St Andrews 55, 54, 53 – 162;
Willie Park Sr, Musselburgh 56, 52, 56 164;
William Dow, Musselburgh 171
   (no record of individual round scores);
Robert Kirk, St Andrews 64, 54, 55 – 173;
Tom Morris Sr, St Andrews 57, 61, 56 – 174;
Mr William Doleman, Glasgow 62, 57, 59 – 178.

1866   PRESTWICK
Willie Park Sr, Musselburgh 54, 56, 59 – 169;
David Park, Musselburgh 58, 57, 56 – 171;
Robert Andrew, Perth 58, 59, 59 – 176;
Tom Morris Sr, St Andrews 61, 58, 59 – 178;
Robert Kirk, St Andrews 60, 62, 58 – 180;
Andrew Strath, Prestwick 61, 61, 60 – 182;
Mr William Doleman, Glasgow 60, 60, 62 – 182.

1867   PRESTWICK
Tom Morris Sr, St Andrews 58, 54, 58 – 170;
Willie Park Sr, Musselburgh 58, 56, 58 – 172;
Andrew Strath, St Andrews 61, 57, 56 – 174;
Tom Morris Jr, St Andrews 58, 59, 58 – 175;
Robert Kirk, St Andrews 57, 60, 60 – 177;
Mr William Doleman, Glasgow 55, 66, 57 – 178.

1868   PRESTWICK
Tom Morris Jr, St Andrews 51, 54, 49 – 154;
Tom Morris Sr, St Andrews 54, 50, 53 – 157;
Robert Andrew, Perth 53, 54, 52 – 159;
Willie Park Sr, Musselburgh 58, 50, 54 – 162;
Robert Kirk, St Andrews 56, 59, 56 – 171;
Charles Hunter, Prestwick 60, 54, 58 – 172;
John Allan, Westward Ho! 54, 55, 63 – 172.
   (published R and A records for 1868 and 1869 have been corrected
   by Prestwick Golf Club, whose versions are used here).

1869   PRESTWICK
Tom Morris Jr , St Andrews 50, 55, 52 – 157;
Robert Kirk, St Andrews 53, 58, 57 – 168;
David Strath, St Andrews, 53, 56, 60 – 169;
Jamie Anderson, St Andrews 60, 56, 57 – 173;
Mr William Doleman, Musselburgh 60, 56, 59 – 175;
Tom Morris Sr, St Andrews 56, 62, 58 – 176.

1870   PRESTWICK
Tom Morris Jr, St Andrews 47, 51, 51 – 149;
Bob Kirk, Royal Blackheath, 52, 52, 57 – 161;
David Strath, St Andrews 54, 49, 58 – 161;
Tom Morris Sr, St Andrews 56, 52, 54 – 162;
Mr William Doleman, Musselburgh 57, 56, 58 – 171;
Willie Park Sr, Musselburgh 60, 55, 58 – 173;
Jamie Anderson, St Andrews 59, 57, 58 – 174.

1872   PRESTWICK
Tom Morris Jr, St Andrews 57, 56, 53 – 166;
David Strath, St Andrews 56, 52, 61 – 169;
Mr William Doleman, Musselburgh 63, 60, 54 – 177;
Tom Morris Sr, St Andrews 62, 60, 57 – 179;
David Park, Musselburgh 61, 57, 61 – 179;
Charles Hunter, Prestwick 60, 60, 69 – 189.

1873   ST ANDREWS
Tom Kidd, St Andrews 91, 88 – 179;
Jamie Anderson, St Andrews 91, 89 – 180;
Tom Morris Jr, St Andrews 94, 89 – 183;
Bob Kirk, Blackheath 91, 92 – 183;
Davie Strath, St Andrews 97, 90 – 187;
Walter Gourlay, St Andrews 92, 96 – 188;
Tom Morris Sr, St Andrews 93, 96 – 189;

1874   MUSSELBURGH
Mungo Park, Musselburgh 75, 84 – 159;
Tom Morris Jr, St Andrews 83, 78 – 161;
George Paxton, Musselburgh 80, 82 – 162;
Bob Martin, St Andrews 85, 79 – 164;
Jamie Anderson, St Andrews 82, 83 – 165;
David Park, Musselburgh 83, 83 – 166;
W Thomson, Edinburgh 84, 82 – 166.
(Scores for the nine-hole course are recorded in 18-hole aggregates).

1875   PRESTWICK
Willie Park Sr, Musselburgh 56, 59, 51 – 166;
Bob Martin, St Andrews 56, 58, 54 – 168;
Mungo Park, Musselburgh 59, 57, 55 – 171;
Robert Ferguson, Musselburgh 58, 56, 58 – 172;
James Rennie, St Andrews 61, 59, 57 – 177;
David Strath, St Andrews 59, 61, 58 – 178;

1876   ST ANDREWS
Bob Martin, St Andrews 86, 90 – 176;
Davie Strath, North Berwick 86, 90 – 176
   (Martin won after Strath refused to play off);
Willie Park Sr, Musselburgh 94, 89 – 183;
Tom Morris Sr, St Andrews 90, 95 – 185;
W Thompson, Elie 90, 95 – 185;
Mungo Park, Musselburgh 95, 90 – 185.

1877   MUSSELBURGH
Jamie Anderson, St Andrews 82, 78 – 160;
Bob Pringle, Musselburgh 82, 80 – 162;
Bob Ferguson, Musselburgh 80, 84 – 164;
William Cosgrove, Musselburgh 80, 84 – 164;
David Strath, North Berwick 85, 81 – 166;
William Brown, Musselburgh 80, 86 – 166.

1878   PRESTWICK
Jamie Anderson, St Andrews 53, 53, 51 – 157;
Bob Kirk, St Andrews 53, 55, 51 – 159;
Jamie Morris, St Andrews 50, 56, 55 – 161;
Bob Martin, St Andrews 57, 53, 55 – 165;
Mr John Ball, Hoylake 53, 57, 55 – 165;
Willie Park Sr, Musselburgh 53, 56, 57 – 166;
W Cosgrove, Musselburgh 55, 56, 55 – 166.

1879   ST ANDREWS
Jamie Anderson, St Andrews 84, 85 – 169;
James Allan, Westward Ho! 88, 84 – 172;
Andrew Kirkaldy, St Andrews 86, 86 – 172;
George Paxton, Musselburgh – 174
   (no further individual round scores recorded);
Tom Kidd, St Andrews – 175;
Bob Ferguson, Musselburgh – 176.

1880   MUSSELBURGH
Bob Ferguson, Musselburgh 81, 81 – 162;
Peter Paxton, Musselburgh 81, 86 – 167;
Ned Cosgrove, Musselburgh 82, 86 – 168;
George Paxton, Musselburgh 85, 84 – 169;
Bob Pringle, Musselburgh 90, 79 – 169;
David Brown, Musselburgh 86, 83 – 169.

1881   PRESTWICK
Bob Ferguson, Musselburgh 53, 60, 57 – 170;
Jamie Anderson, St Andrews 57, 60, 56 – 173;
Ned Cosgrove, Musselburgh 61, 59, 57 – 177;
Bob Martin, St Andrews 57, 62, 59 – 178;
Tom Morris Sr, St Andrews 58, 65, 58 – 181;
Willie Campbell, Musselburgh 60, 56, 65 – 181;
Willie Park Jr, Musselburgh 66, 57, 58 – 181.

1882   ST ANDREWS
Bob Ferguson, Musselburgh 83, 88 – 171;
Willie Fernie, Dumfries 88, 86 – 174;
Jamie Anderson, St Andrews 87, 88 – 175;
John Kirkaldy, St Andrews 86, 89 – 175;
Bob Martin, St Andrews 89, 86 – 175;
Mr Fitz Boothby, St Andrews 86, 89 – 175.

1883   MUSSELBURGH
Willie Fernie, Dumfries 75, 84 – 159;
Bob Ferguson, Musselburgh 78, 81 – 159;
   (Fernie won play-off 81, 77 – 158;
   Ferguson 82, 77 – 159);
W Brown, Musselburgh 83, 77 – 160;
R Pringle, Musselburgh 79, 82 – 161;
W Campbell, Musselburgh 80, 83 – 163;
G Paxton, Musselburgh 80, 83 – 163.

1884   PRESTWICK
Jack Simpson, Carnoustie 78, 82 – 160;
Douglas Rolland, Elie 81, 83 – 164;
Willie Fernie, Felixstowe 80, 84 – 164;
Willie Campbell, Musselburgh 84, 85 – 169;
Willie Park Jr, Musselburgh 86, 83 – 169;
Ben Sayers, North Berwick 83, 87 – 170.

1885   ST ANDREWS
Bob Martin, St Andrews 84, 87 – 171;
Archie Simpson, Carnoustie 83, 89 – 172;
David Ayton, St Andrews 89, 84 – 173;
Willie Fernie, Felixstowe 89, 85 – 174;
Willie Park Jr, Musselburgh 86, 88 – 174;
Bob Simpson, Carnoustie 85, 89 – 174.

1886   MUSSELBURGH
David Brown, Musselburgh 79, 78 – 157;
Willie Campbell, Musselburgh 78, 81 – 159;
Ben Campbell, Musselburgh 79, 81 – 160;
Archie Simpson, Carnoustie 82, 79 – 161;
Willie Park Jr, Musselburgh 84, 77 – 161;
Thomas Gossett, Musselburgh 80, 81 – 161;
Bob Ferguson, Musselburgh 82, 79 – 161.

1887   PRESTWICK
Willie Park Jr, Musselburgh 82, 79 – 161;
Bob Martin, St Andrews 81, 81 – 162;
Willie Campbell, Prestwick 77, 87 – 164;
Mr J E Laidlay, Honourable Company 86, 80 – 166;
Ben Sayers, North Berwick 83, 85 – 168;
Archie Simpson, Carnoustie 81, 87 – 168.

1888   ST ANDREWS
Jack Burns, Warwick 86, 85 – 171;
D Anderson Jr, St Andrews 86, 86 – 172;
Ben Sayers, North Berwick 85, 87 – 172;
Willie Campbell, Prestwick 84, 90 – 174;
Mr Leslie Balfour, Edinburgh 86, 89 – 175;
Andrew Kirkaldy, St Andrews 87, 89 – 176;
Davie Grant, North Berwick 88, 88 – 176.

1889   MUSSELBURGH
Willie Park Jr, Musselburgh 78, 77 – 155;
Andrew Kirkaldy, St Andrews 77, 78 -155
   (Park won play-off 82, 76 – 158; Kirkaldy 85, 78 – 163);
Ben Sayers, North Berwick 79, 80 – 159;
Mr J E Laidlay, Honourable Company 81, 81 – 162;
David Brown, Musselburgh 82, 80 – 162;
Willie Fernie, Troon 84, 80 – 164.

1890   PRESTWICK
Mr John Ball Jr, Royal Liverpool 82, 82 – 164;
Willie Fernie, Troon 85, 82 – 167;
Archie Simpson, Carnoustie 85, 82 – 167;
Willie Park Jr, Musselburgh 90, 80 – 170;
Andrew Kirkaldy, St Andrews 81, 89 – 170;
Mr Horace Hutchinson, Royal North Devon 87, 85 – 172.

1891   ST ANDREWS
Hugh Kirkaldy, St Andrews 83, 83 – 166;
Andrew Kirkaldy, St Andrews 84, 84 – 168;
Willie Fernie, Troon 84, 84 – 168;
Mr R Mure Fergusson, Royal and Ancient 86, 84 – 170;
W D More, Chester 84, 87 – 171;
Willie Park Jr, Musselburgh 88, 85 – 173.

1892   MUIRFIELD
Mr Harold Hilton, Royal Liverpool 78, 81, 72, 74 – 305;
Mr John Ball Jr, Royal Liverpool 75, 80, 74, 79 – 308;
Hugh Kirkaldy, St Andrews 77, 83, 73, 75 – 308;
Sandy Herd, Huddersfield 77, 78, 77, 76 – 308;
J Kay, Seaton Carew 82, 78, 74, 78 – 312;
Ben Sayers, North Berwick 80, 76, 81, 75 – 312.

1893   PRESTWICK
Willie Auchterlonie, St Andrews 78, 81, 81, 82 – 322;
Mr J E Laidlay, Honourable Company 80, 83, 80, 81 – 324;
Sandy Herd, Huddersfield 82, 81, 78, 84 – 325;
Andrew Kirkaldy, St Andrews 85, 82, 82, 77 – 326;
Hugh Kirkaldy, St Andrews 83, 79, 82, 82 – 326;
J Kay, Seaton Carew 81, 81, 80, 85 – 327;
Bob Simpson, Carnoustie 81, 81, 80, 85 – 327.

1894   ROYAL ST GEORGE'S
J H Taylor, Winchester 84, 80, 81, 81 – 326;
Douglas Rolland, Limpsfield 86, 79, 84, 82 – 331;
Andrew Kirkaldy, St Andrews 86, 79, 83, 84 – 332;
A Toogood, Eltham 84, 85, 82, 82 – 333;
Willie Fernie, Troon 84, 84, 86, 80 – 334;
Ben Sayers, North Berwick 85, 81, 84, 84 – 334;
Harry Vardon, Bury 86, 86, 82, 80 – 334.

1895   ST ANDREWS
J H Taylor, Winchester 86, 78, 80, 78 – 322;
Sandy Herd, Huddersfield 82, 77, 82, 85 – 326;
Andrew Kirkaldy, St Andrews 81, 83, 84, 84 – 332;
G Pulford, Hoylake 84, 81, 83, 86 – 334;
Archie Simpson, Aberdeen 88, 85, 78, 85 – 336;
Willie Fernie, Troon 86, 79, 86, 86 – 337;
David Brown, Malvern 81, 89, 83, 84 – 337;
D Anderson Jr, St Andrews 86, 83, 84, 84 – 337.

1896   MUIRFIELD
Harry Vardon, Ganton 83, 78, 78, 77 – 316;
J H Taylor, Winchester 77, 78, 81, 80 – 316
   (play-off Vardon 157; Taylor 161);
Mr F G Tait, Black Watch 83, 75, 84, 77 – 319;
Willie Fernie, Troon 78, 79, 82, 80 – 319;
Sandy Herd, Huddersfield 72, 84, 79, 85 – 320;
James Braid, Romford 83, 81, 79, 80 – 323.

1897   HOYLAKE
Mr Harold Hilton, Royal Liverpool 80, 75, 84, 75 – 314;
James Braid, Romford 80, 74, 82, 79 – 315;
Mr F G Tait, Black Watch 79, 79, 80, 79 – 317;
G Pulford, Hoylake 80, 79, 79, 79 – 317;
Sandy Herd, Huddersfield 78, 81, 79, 80 – 318;
Harry Vardon, Ganton 84, 80, 80, 76 – 320.

1898   PRESTWICK
Harry Vardon, Ganton 79, 75, 77, 76 – 307;
Willie Park Jr, Musselburgh 76, 75, 78, 79 – 308;
Mr Harold Hilton, Royal Liverpool 76, 81, 77, 75 – 309;
J H Taylor, Winchester 78, 78, 77, 79 – 312;
Mr F G Tait, Black Watch 81, 77, 75, 82 – 315;
D Kinnell, Leven 80, 77, 79, 80 – 316.

1899   ROYAL ST GEORGE'S
Harry Vardon, Ganton 76, 76, 81, 77 – 310;
Jack White, Seaford 79, 79, 82, 75 – 315;
Andrew Kirkaldy, St Andrews 81, 79, 82, 77 – 319;
J H Taylor, Richmond 77, 76, 83, 84 – 320;
James Braid, Romford 78, 78, 85, 81 – 322;
Willie Fernie, Troon 79, 83, 82, 78 – 322.

1900   ST ANDREWS
J H Taylor, Richmond 79, 77, 78, 75 – 309;
Harry Vardon, Ganton 79, 81, 80, 77 – 317;
James Braid, Romford 82, 81, 80, 79 – 322;
Jack White, Seaford 80, 81, 82, 80 – 323;
Willie Auchterlonie, St Andrews 81, 85, 80, 80 – 326;
Willie Park Jr, Royal Musselburgh 80, 83, 81, 84 – 328.

1901   MUIRFIELD
James Braid, Romford 79, 76, 74, 80 – 309;
Harry Vardon, Ganton 77, 78, 79, 78 – 312;
J H Taylor, Richmond 79, 83, 74, 77 – 313;
Mr Harold Hilton, Royal Liverpool 89, 80, 75, 76 – 320;
Sandy Herd, Huddersfield 87, 81, 81, 76 – 325;
Jack White, Seaford 82, 82, 80, 82 – 326;
J Kinnell, Royal Norwich 79, 85, 86, 78 – 328;
Mr J E Laidlay, Honourable Company 84, 82, 82, 80 – 328.

1902   HOYLAKE
Sandy Herd, Huddersfield 77, 76, 73, 81 – 307;
Harry Vardon, Ganton 72, 77, 80, 79 – 308;
James Braid, Romford 78, 76, 80, 74 – 308
Mr R Maxwell, Tantallon 79, 77, 79, 74 – 309;
Tom Vardon, St George's 80, 76, 78, 79 – 313;
J H Taylor, Mid Surrey 81, 76, 77, 80 – 314;
J Kinnell, Royal Norwich 78, 80, 79, 77 – 314;
Mr Harold Hilton, Royal Liverpool 79, 76, 81, 78 – 314.

1903   PRESTWICK
Harry Vardon, Totteridge 73, 77, 72, 78 – 300;
Tom Vardon, St George's 76, 81, 75, 74 – 306;
Jack White, Sunningdale 77, 78, 74, 79 – 308;
Sandy Herd, Huddersfield 73, 83, 76, 77 – 309;
James Braid, Romford 77, 79, 79, 75 – 310;
A H Scott, Elie 77, 77, 83, 77 – 314;
R Thomson, North Berwick 83, 78, 77, 76 – 314.

1904   ROYAL ST GEORGE'S
Jack White, Sunningdale 80, 75, 72, 69 – 296;
J H Taylor, Mid-Surrey 77, 78, 74, 68 – 297;
James Braid, Walton Heath 77, 80, 69, 71 – 297;
Tom Vardon, Royal St George's 77, 77, 75, 72 – 301;
Harry Vardon, South Herts 76, 73, 79, 74 – 302;
J Sherlock, Oxford 83, 71, 78, 77 – 309.

1905   ST ANDREWS
James Braid, Walton Heath 81, 78, 78, 81 – 318;
Rowland Jones, Wimbledon Park 81, 77, 87, 78 – 323;
J H Taylor, Mid-Surrey 80, 85, 78, 80 – 323;
James Kinnell, Purley Downs 82, 79, 82, 81 – 324;
Ernest Gray, Littlehampton 82, 81, 84, 78 – 325;
Arnaud Massy, North Berwick 81, 80, 82, 82 – 325;
R Thomson, Romford 81, 81, 82, 83 – 327.

1906   MUIRFIELD
James Braid, Walton Heath 77, 76, 74, 73 – 300;
J H Taylor, Mid-Surrey 77, 72, 75, 80 – 304;
Harry Vardon, South Herts 77, 73, 77, 78 – 305;
Mr John Graham Jr, Royal Liverpool 71, 79, 78, 78 – 306;
Rowland Jones, Wimbledon Park 74, 78, 73, 83 – 308;
Arnaud Massy, La Boulie 76, 80, 76, 78 – 310.

1907   HOYLAKE
Arnaud Massy, La Boulie 76, 81, 78, 77 – 312;
J H Taylor, Mid-Surrey 79, 79, 76, 80 – 314;
Tom Vardon, Royal St George's 81, 81, 80, 75 – 317;
G Pulford, Hoylake 81, 78, 80, 78 – 317;
James Braid, Walton Heath 82, 85, 75, 76 – 318;
Ted Ray, Ganton 83, 80, 79, 76 – 318;
George Duncan, Timperley 83, 78, 81, 77 – 319;
T Williamson, Notts 82, 77, 82, 78 – 319;
Harry Vardon, South Herts 84, 81, 74, 80 – 319.

1908   PRESTWICK
James Braid, Walton Heath 70, 72, 77, 72 – 291;
Tom Ball, West Lancashire 76, 73, 76, 74 – 299;
Ted Ray, Ganton 79, 71, 75, 76 – 301;
Sandy Herd, Huddersfield 74, 74, 79, 75 – 302;
Harry Vardon, South Herts 79, 78, 74, 75 – 306;
D Kinnell, Prestwick 75, 73, 80, 78 – 306.

1909   ROYAL CINQUE PORTS
J H Taylor, Mid-Surrey 74, 73, 74, 74 – 295;
James Braid, Walton Heath 79, 75, 73, 74 – 301;
Tom Ball, West Lancashire 74, 75, 76, 76 – 301;
C Johns, Southdown 72, 76, 79, 75 – 302;
T G Renouf, Manchester 76, 78, 76, 73 – 303;
Ted Ray, Ganton 77, 76, 76, 75 – 304.

1910   ST ANDREWS
James Braid, Walton Heath 76, 73, 74, 76 – 299;
Sandy Herd, Huddersfield 78, 74, 75, 76 – 303;
George Duncan, Hanger Hill 73, 77, 71, 83 – 304;
L Ayton, Bishop's Stortford 78, 76, 75, 77 – 306;
J Robson, West Surrey 75, 80, 77, 76 – 308;
W Smith, Mexico 77, 71, 80, 80 – 308;
Ted Ray, Ganton 76, 77, 74, 81 – 308.

1911   ROYAL ST GEORGE'S
Harry Vardon, South Herts 74, 74, 75, 80 – 303;
Arnaud Massy, La Boulie 75, 78, 74, 76 – 303
   (Play-off, Massy conceded at 35th hole, Vardon 143 after 35,
   Massy 148 after 34);
Mr Harold Hilton, Royal Liverpool 76, 74, 78, 76 – 304;
Sandy Herd, Coombe Hill 77, 73, 76, 78 – 304;
James Braid, Walton Heath 78, 75, 74, 78 – 305;
Ted Ray, Ganton 76, 72, 79, 78 – 305;
J H Taylor, Mid-Surrey 72, 76, 78, 79 – 305.

1912   MUIRFIELD
Ted Ray, Oxhey 71, 73, 76, 75 – 295;
Harry Vardon, South Herts 75, 72, 81, 71 – 299;
James Braid, Walton Heath 77, 71, 77, 78 – 303;
George Duncan, Hanger Hill 72, 77, 78, 78 – 305;
Sandy Herd, Coombe Hill 76, 81, 76, 76 – 309;
L Ayton, Bishop's Stortford 74, 80, 75, 80 – 309.

1913   HOYLAKE
J H Taylor, Mid-Surrey 73, 75, 77, 79 – 304;
Ted Ray, Ganton 73, 74, 81, 84 – 312;
Michael Moran, Royal Dublin 76, 74, 89, 74 – 313;
Harry Vardon, South Herts 79, 75, 79, 80 – 313;
T G Renouf, Manchester 75, 78, 84, 78 – 315;
Johnny McDermott, Atlantic City, USA 75, 80, 77, 83 – 315.

1914   PRESTWICK
Harry Vardon, South Herts 73, 77, 78, 78 – 306;
J H Taylor, Mid-Surrey 74, 78, 74, 83 – 309;
H B Simpson, St Anne's Old Links 77, 80, 78, 75 – 310;
Abe Mitchell, Sonning 76, 78, 79, 79 – 312;
T Williamson, Notts 75, 79, 79, 79 – 312;
R G Wilson, Croham Hurst 76, 77, 80, 80 – 313.

1920   ROYAL CINQUE PORTS
George Duncan, Hanger Hill 80, 80, 71, 72 – 303;
Sandy Herd, Coombe Hill 72, 81, 77, 75 – 305;
Ted Ray, Oxhey 72, 83, 78, 73 – 306;
Abe Mitchell, North Foreland 74, 73, 84, 76 – 307;
L Holland, Northamptonshire 80, 78, 71, 79 – 308;
Jim Barnes, Sunset Hill, USA 79, 74, 77, 79 – 309.

1921   ST ANDREWS
Jock Hutchison, Glenview, USA 72, 75, 79, 70 – 296;
Mr Roger Wethered, R and A 78, 75, 72, 71 – 296
      (play-off, Hutchison 74, 76 – 150; Wethered 77, 82 – 159);
Tom Kerrigan, USA 74, 80, 72, 72 – 298;
Arthur Havers, West Lancashire 76, 74, 77, 72 – 299;
George Duncan, Hanger Hill 74, 75, 78, 74 – 301;
F Leach, Northwood 78, 75, 76, 73 – 302;
Walter Hagen, USA 74, 79, 72, 77 – 302;
J H Kirkwood, Australia 76, 74, 73, 79 – 302;
Arnaud Massy, La Nivelle 74, 75, 74, 79 – 302;
Sandy Herd, Coombe Hill 75, 74, 73, 80 – 302;
Jim Barnes, USA 74, 74, 74, 80 – 302;
T Williamson, Notts 79, 71, 74, 78 – 302.

1922   ROYAL ST GEORGE'S
Walter Hagen, Detroit, USA 76, 73, 79, 72 – 300;
George Duncan, Hanger Hill 76, 75, 81, 69 – 301;
Jim Barnes, USA 75, 76, 77, 73 – 301;
Jock Hutchison, USA 79, 74, 73, 76 – 302;
Charles Whitcombe, Dorchester 77, 79, 72, 75 – 303;
J H Taylor, Mid-Surrey 73, 78, 76, 77 – 304.

1923   TROON
Arthur Havers, Coombe Hill 73, 73, 73, 76 – 295;
Walter Hagen, USA 76, 71, 74, 75 – 296;
Macdonald Smith, USA 80, 73, 69, 75 – 297;
J Kirkwood, Australia 72, 79, 69, 78 – 298;
T R Fernie, Turnberry 73, 78, 74, 75 – 300;
George Duncan, Hanger Hill 79, 75, 74, 74 – 302;
Charles Whitcombe, Lansdown 70, 76, 74, 82 – 302.

1924   HOYLAKE
Walter Hagen, USA 77, 73, 74, 77 – 301;
E R Whitcombe, Came Down 77, 70, 77, 78 – 302;
Frank Ball, Langley Park 78, 75, 74, 77 – 304;
Macdonald Smith, USA 76, 74, 77, 77 – 304;
J H Taylor, Mid-Surrey 75, 74, 79, 79 – 307;
Len Holland, Northampton 74, 78, 78, 78 – 308;
Aubrey Boomer, St Cloud, Paris 75, 78, 76, 79 – 308;
George Duncan, Hanger Hill 74, 79, 74, 81 – 308.

1925   PRESTWICK
Jim Barnes, USA 70, 77, 79, 74 – 300;
Ted Ray, Oxhey 77, 76, 75, 73 – 301;
Archie Compston, North Manchester 76, 75, 75, 75 – 301;
Macdonald Smith, USA 76, 69, 76, 82 – 303;
Abe Mitchell, unattached 77, 76, 75, 77 – 305;
J W Gaudin, Alwoodley 78, 81, 77, 74 – 310;
Percy Alliss, Wanstead 77, 80, 77, 76 – 310;
J H Taylor, Mid-Surrey 74, 79, 80, 77 – 310;
W H Davies, Prenton 76, 76, 80, 78 – 310;
S Wingate, Templenewsam 74, 78, 80, 78 – 310.

1926   ROYAL LYTHAM AND ST ANNE'S
Mr Bobby Jones, USA 72, 72, 73, 74 – 291;
Al Watrous, USA 71, 75, 69, 78 – 293;
Mr G Von Elm, USA 75, 72, 76, 72 – 295;
Walter Hagen, USA 68, 77, 74, 76 – 295;
Abe Mitchell, unattached 78, 78, 72, 71 – 299;
T Barber, Cavendish 77, 73, 78, 71 – 299;
F McLeod, USA 71, 75, 76, 79 – 301.

1927   ST ANDREWS
Mr Bobby Jones, Atlanta, USA 68, 72, 73, 72 – 285;
Aubrey Boomer, St Cloud, France 76, 70, 73, 72 – 291;
Fred Robson, Cooden Beach 76, 72, 69, 74 – 291;
Ernest Whitcombe, Bournemouth 74, 73, 73, 73 – 293;
Joe Kirkwood, USA 72, 72, 75, 74 – 293;
Charles Whitcombe, Crews Hill 74, 76, 71, 75 – 296.

1928   ROYAL ST GEORGE'S
Walter Hagen, USA 75, 73, 72, 72 – 292;
Gene Sarazen, USA 72, 76, 73, 73 – 294;
Archie Compston, unattached 75, 74, 73, 73 – 295;
Percy Alliss, Germany 75, 76, 75, 72 – 298;
Fred Robson, Cooden Beach 79, 73, 73, 73 – 298;
Jim Barnes, USA 81, 73, 76, 71 – 301;
Aubrey Boomer, St Cloud, France 79, 73, 77, 72 – 301;
Jose Jurado, Argentina 74, 71, 76, 80 – 301.

1929   MUIRFIELD
Walter Hagen, USA 75, 67, 75, 75 – 292;
Johnny Farrell, USA 72, 75, 76, 75 – 298;
Leo Diegel, USA 71, 69, 82, 77 – 299;
Abe Mitchell, unattached 72, 72, 78, 78 – 300;
Percy Alliss, Germany 69, 76, 76, 79 – 300;
R Cruikshank, USA 73, 74, 78, 76 – 301.

1930   HOYLAKE
Mr Bobby Jones, USA 70, 72, 74, 75 – 291;
Macdonald Smith, USA 70, 77. 75, 71 – 293;
Leo Diegel, Agua Caliente, Mexico 74, 73, 71, 75 – 293;
Horton Smith, USA, 72, 73, 78, 73 – 296;
Fred Robson, Cooden Beach 71, 72, 78, 75 – 296;
Jim Barnes, USA 71, 77, 72, 77 – 297;
Archie Compston, Coombe Hill 74, 73, 68, 82 – 297.

1931   CARNOUSTIE
Tommy Armour, USA 73, 75, 77, 71 – 296;
Jose Jurado, Argentina 76, 71, 73, 77 – 297;
Percy Alliss, Germany 74, 78, 73, 73 – 298;
Gene Sarazen, USA 74, 76, 75, 73 – 298;
Johnny Farrell, USA 72, 77, 75, 75 – 299;
Macdonald Smith, USA 75, 77, 71, 76 – 299.

1932   PRINCE'S, SANDWICH
Gene Sarazen, USA 70, 69, 70, 74- 283;
Macdonald Smith, USA 71, 76, 71, 70 – 288;
Arthur Havers, Sandy Lodge 74, 71, 68, 76 – 289;
Alf Padgham, Royal Ashdown Forest 76, 72, 74, 70 – 292;
Percy Alliss, Beaconsfield 71, 71, 78, 72 – 292;
Charles Whitcombe, Crews Hill 71, 73, 73, 75 – 292.

1933   ST ANDREWS
Densmore Shute, USA 73, 73, 73, 73 – 292;
Craig Wood, USA 77, 72, 68, 75 – 292
      (play-off, Shute 75, 74 – 149; Wood 78, 76 – 154);
Gene Sarazen, USA 72, 73, 73, 75 – 293;
Leo Diegel, USA 75, 70, 71, 77 – 293;
Syd Easterbrook, Knowle 73, 72, 71, 77 – 293;
Olin Dutra, USA 76, 76, 70, 72 – 294.

1934   ROYAL ST GEORGE'S
Henry Cotton, Waterloo, Belgium 67, 65, 72, 79 – 283;
Syd Brews, Durban 76, 71, 70, 71 – 288;
Alf Padgham, Sundridge Park 71, 70, 75, 74 – 290;
Macdonald Smith, USA 77, 71, 72, 72 – 292;
Marcel Dallemagne, St Germain, France 71, 73, 71, 77 – 292;
Joe Kirkwood, USA 74, 69, 71, 78 – 292.

1935   MUIRFIELD
Alf Perry, Leatherhead 69, 75, 67, 72 – 283;
Alf Padgham, Sundridge Park 70, 72, 74, 71 – 287;
Charles Whitcombe, Crews Hill 71, 68, 73, 76 – 288;
Mr W Lawson Little, Presido, USA 75, 71, 74, 69 – 289;
Bert Gadd, Brand Hall 72, 75, 71, 71 – 289;
Henry Picard, Hershey, USA 72, 73, 72, 75 – 292.

1936   HOYLAKE
Alf Padgham, Sundridge Park 73, 72, 71, 71 – 287;
James Adams, Romford 71, 73, 71, 73 – 288;
Marcel Dallemagne, St Germain, France 73, 72, 75, 69 – 289;
Henry Cotton, Waterloo, Belgium 73, 72, 70, 74 – 289;
Percy Alliss, Templenewsam 74, 72, 74, 71 – 291;
Gene Sarazen, USA 73, 75, 70, 73 – 291;
Tom Green, Burnham Beeches 74, 72, 70, 75 – 291.
Mr Bobby Locke, State Mines, South Africa 75, 73, 72, 74 – 294;

1937   CARNOUSTIE
Henry Cotton, Ashridge 74, 73, 72, 71 – 290;
Reg Whitcombe, Parkstone 72, 70, 74, 76 – 292;
C Lacey, USA 76, 75, 70, 72 – 293;
Charles Whitcombe, Crews Hill 73, 71, 74, 76 – 294;
Byron Nelson, USA 75, 76, 71, 74 – 296;
Ed Dudley, USA 70, 74, 78, 75 – 297.

1938   ROYAL ST GEORGE'S
Reg Whitcombe, Parkstone 71, 71, 75, 78 – 295;
James Adams, Royal Liverpool 70, 71, 78, 78 – 297;
Henry Cotton, Ashridge 74, 73, 77, 74 – 298;
A Dailey, Wanstead 73, 72, 80, 78 – 303;
J J Busson, Pannal 71, 69, 83, 80 – 303;
Alf Padgham, Sundridge Park 74, 72, 75, 82 – 303;
Richard Burton, Sale 71, 69, 78, 85 – 303.

1939   ST ANDREWS
Richard Burton, Sale 70, 72, 77, 71 – 290;
Johnny Bulla, Chicago, USA 77, 71, 71, 73 – 292;
S L King, Knole Park 74, 72, 75, 73 – 294;
Reg Whitcombe, Parkstone 71, 75, 74, 74 – 294;
Alf Perry, Leatherhead 71, 74, 73, 76 – 294;
W Shankland, Templenewsam 72, 73, 72, 77 – 294;
J Fallon, Huddersfield 71, 73, 71, 79 – 294.

1946   ST ANDREWS
Sam Snead, USA 71, 70, 74, 75 – 290;
Bobby Locke, South Africa 69, 74, 75, 76 – 294;
Johnny Bulla, USA 71, 72, 72, 79 – 294;
Norman von Nida, Australia 70, 76, 74, 75 – 295;
C H Ward, Little Aston 73, 73, 73, 76 – 295;
Henry Cotton, Royal Mid-Surrey 70, 70, 76, 79 – 295;
Dai Rees, Hindhead 75, 67, 73, 80 – 295.

1947   HOYLAKE
Fred Daly, Balmoral, Belfast 73, 70, 78, 72 – 293;
R W Horne, Hendon 77, 74, 72, 71 – 294;
Mr Frank Stranahan, USA 71, 79, 72, 72 – 294;
W Shankland, Templenewsam 76, 74, 75, 70 – 295;
Richard Burton, Coombe Hill 77, 71, 77, 71 – 296;
Johnny Bulla, USA 80, 72, 74, 71 – 297;
C H Ward, Little Aston 76, 73, 76, 72 – 297;
S L King, Wildernesse 75, 72, 77, 73 – 297;
Arthur Lees, Dore and Totley 75, 74, 72, 76 – 297;
Norman von Nida, Australia 74, 76, 71, 76 – 297;
Henry Cotton, Royal Mid-Surrey 69, 78, 74, 76 – 297,

1948   MUIRFIELD
Henry Cotton, Royal Mid-Surrey 71, 66, 75, 72 – 284;
Fred Daly, Balmoral 72, 71, 73, 73 – 289;
Norman von Nida, Australia 71, 72, 76, 71 – 290;
J Hargreaves, Sutton Coldfield 76, 68, 73, 73 – 290;
C H Ward, Little Aston 69, 72, 75, 74 – 290;
Roberto de Vicenzo, Argentina 70, 73, 72, 75 – 290.

1949   ROYAL ST GEORGE'S
Bobby Locke, South Africa 69, 76, 68, 70 – 283;
Harry Bradshaw, Kilcroney, Eire 68, 77, 68, 70 – 283
      (play-off, Locke 67, 68 – 135; Bradshaw 74, 73 – 147);
Roberto de Vicenzo, Argentina 68, 75, 73, 69 – 285;
C H Ward, Little Aston 73, 71, 70, 72 – 286;
S L King, Knole Park 71, 69, 74, 72 – 286;
Arthur Lees, Dore and Totley 74, 70, 72, 71 – 287;
Max Faulkner, Royal Mid-Surrey 71, 71, 71, 74 – 287.

1950   TROON
Bobby Locke, South Africa 69, 72, 70, 68 – 279;
Roberto de Vicenzo, Argentina 72, 71, 68, 70 – 281;
Fred Daly, Balmoral 75, 72, 69, 66 – 282;
Dai Rees, South Herts 71, 68, 72, 71 – 282;
E Moore, South Africa 74, 68, 73, 68 – 283;
Max Faulkner, Royal Mid-Surrey 72, 70, 70, 71 – 283.

1951   ROYAL PORTRUSH
Max Faulkner, unattached 71, 70, 70, 74 – 285;
A Cerda, Argentina 74, 72, 71, 70 – 287;
C H Ward, Little Aston 75, 73, 74, 68 – 290;
James Adams, Wentworth 68, 77, 75, 72 – 292;
Fred Daly, Balmoral 74, 70, 75, 73 – 292;
W Shankland, Templenewsam 73, 76, 72, 72 – 293;
Bobby Locke, South Africa 71, 74, 74, 74 – 293;
Harry Weetman, Croham Hurst 73, 71, 75, 74 – 293;
Peter Thomson, Australia 70, 75, 73, 75 – 293;
N Sutton, Leigh 73, 70, 74, 76 – 293;

1952   ROYAL LYTHAM AND ST ANNES
Bobby Locke, South Africa 69, 71, 74, 73 – 287;
Peter Thomson, Australia 68, 73, 77, 70 – 288;
Fred Daly, Balmoral 67, 69, 77, 76 – 289;
Henry Cotton, Royal Mid-Surrey 75, 74, 74, 71 – 294;
A Cerda, Argentina, 73, 73, 76, 73 – 295;
S L King, Knole Park 71, 74, 74, 76 – 295.

1953   CARNOUSTIE
Ben Hogan, USA 73, 71, 70, 68 – 282;
Mr Frank Stranahan, USA 70, 74, 73, 69 – 286;
A Cerda, Argentina 75, 71, 69, 71 – 286;
Peter Thomson, Australia 72, 72, 71, 71 – 286;
Dai Rees, South Herts 72, 70, 73, 71 – 286;
Roberto de Vicenzo, Argentina 72, 71, 71, 73 – 287.

1954   BIRKDALE
Peter Thomson, Australia 72, 71, 69, 71 – 283;
Bobby Locke, South Africa 74, 71, 69, 70 – 284;
S S Scott, Carlisle City 76, 67, 69, 72 – 284;
Dai Rees, South Herts 72, 71, 69, 72 – 284;
James Adams, Royal Mid-Surrey 73, 75, 69, 69 – 286;
J Turnesa, USA 72, 72, 71, 71 – 286;
A Cerda, Argentina 71, 71, 73, 71 – 286.

1955   ST ANDREWS
Peter Thomson, Australia 71, 68, 70, 72 – 281;
J Fallon, Huddersfield 73, 67, 73, 70 – 283;
F Jowle, Edgbaston 70, 71, 69, 74 – 284;
Bobby Locke, South Africa 74, 69, 70, 72 – 285;
Ken Bousfield, Coombe Hill 71, 75, 70, 70 – 286;
A Cerda, Argentina 73, 71, 71, 71 – 286;
Bernard Hunt, Hartsbourne 70, 71, 74, 71 – 286;
Flory van Donck, Belgium 71, 72, 71, 72 – 286;
Harry Weetman, Croham Hurst 71, 71, 70, 74 – 286.

1956   HOYLAKE
Peter Thomson, Australia 70, 70, 72, 74 – 286;
Flory van Donck, Belgium 71, 74, 70, 74 – 289;
Roberto de Vicenzo, Argentina 71, 70, 79, 70 – 290;
Gary Player, South Africa 71, 76, 73, 71 – 291;
John Panton, Glenbervie 74, 76, 72, 70 – 292;
Henry Cotton, Temple 72, 76, 71, 74 – 293;
E Bertolino, Argentina 69, 72, 76, 76 – 293.

1957   ST ANDREWS
Bobby Locke, South Africa 69, 72, 68, 70 – 279;
Peter Thomson, Australia 73, 69, 70, 70 – 282;
Eric Brown, Buchanan Castle 67, 72, 73, 71 – 283;
A Miguel, Spain 72, 72, 69, 72 – 285;
Dave Thomas, Sudbury 72, 74, 70, 70 – 286;
Mr W D Smith, Prestwick 71, 72, 72, 71 – 286;
Flory van Donck, Belgium 72, 68, 74, 72 – 286;
Tom Haliburton, Wentworth 72, 73, 68, 73 – 286.

1958   ROYAL LYTHAM AND ST ANNE'S
Peter Thomson, Australia 66, 72, 67, 73 – 278;
Dave Thomas, Sudbury 70, 68, 69, 71 – 278
   (play-off, Thomson 68, 71 – 139; Thomas 69, 74 – 143);
Eric Brown, Buchanan Castle 73, 70, 65, 71 – 279;
Christy O'Connor, Killarney 67, 68, 73, 71 – 279;
L Ruiz, Argentina 71, 65, 72, 73 – 281;
Flory van Donck, Belgium 70, 70, 67, 74 – 281.

1959   MUIRFIELD
Gary Player, South Africa 75, 71, 70, 68 – 284;
Flory van Donck, Belgium 70, 70, 73, 73 – 286;
Fred Bullock, Prestwick St Nicholas 68, 70, 74, 74 – 286;
S S Scott, Roehampton 73, 70, 73, 71 – 287;
Christy O'Connor, Royal Dublin 73, 74, 72, 69 – 288;
John Panton, Glenbervie 72, 72, 71, 73 – 288;
Mr Reid Jack, Dullatur 71, 75, 68, 74 – 288;
S L King, Knole Park 70, 74, 68, 76 – 288.

1960   ST ANDREWS
Kel Nagle, Australia 69, 67, 71, 71 – 278;
Arnold Palmer, USA 70, 71, 70, 68 – 279;
Bernard Hunt, Hartsbourne 72, 73, 71, 66 – 282;
Harold Henning, South Africa 72, 72, 69, 69 – 282;
Roberto de Vicenzo, Argentina 67, 67, 75, 73 – 282;
Mr Guy Wolstenholme, Sunningdale 74, 70, 71, 68 – 283.

1961   ROYAL BIRKDALE
Arnold Palmer, USA 70, 73, 69, 72 – 284;
Dai Rees, South Herts 68, 74, 71, 72 – 285;
Neil Coles, Coombe Hill 70, 77, 69, 72 – 288;
Christy O'Connor, Royal Dublin 71, 77, 67, 73 – 288;
Eric Brown, unattached 73, 76, 70, 70 – 289;
Kel Nagle, Australia 68, 75, 75, 71 – 289.

1962   TROON
Arnold Palmer, USA 71, 69, 67, 69 – 276;
Kel Nagle, Australia 71, 71, 70, 70 – 282;
Brian Huggett, Romford 75, 71, 74, 69 – 289;
Phil Rodgers, USA 75, 70, 72, 72 – 289;
Bob Charles – New Zealand 75, 70, 70, 75 – 290;
Peter Thomson, Australia 70, 77, 75, 70 – 292;
Sam Snead, USA 76, 73, 72, 71 – 292.

1963   ROYAL LYTHAM
Bob Charles, New Zealand 68, 72, 66, 71 – 277;
Phil Rodgers, USA 67, 68, 73, 69 – 277
   (play-off, Charles 69, 71 – 140; Rodgers 72, 76 – 148);
Jack Nicklaus, USA 71, 67, 70, 70 – 278;
Kel Nagle, Australia 69, 70, 73, 71 – 283;
Peter Thomson, Australia 67, 69, 71, 78 – 285;
Christy O'Connor, Royal Dublin 74, 68, 76, 68 – 286.

1964 ST ANDREWS
Tony Lema, USA 73, 68, 68, 70 – 279;
Jack Nicklaus, USA 76, 74, 66, 68 – 284;
Roberto de Vicenzo, Argentina 76, 72, 70, 67 – 285;
Bernard Hunt, Hartsbourne 73, 74, 70, 70 – 287;
Bruce Devlin, Australia 72, 72, 73, 73 – 290;
Christy O'Connor, Royal Dublin 71, 73, 74, 73 – 291;
Harry Weetman, Selsdon Park 72, 71, 75, 73 – 291.

1965 ROYAL BIRKDALE
Peter Thomson, Australia 74, 68, 72, 71 – 285;
Brian Huggett, Romford 73, 68, 76, 70 – 287;
Christy O'Connor, Royal Dublin 69, 73, 74, 71 – 287;
Roberto de Vicenzo, Argentina 74, 69, 73, 72 – 288;
Bernard Hunt, Hartsbourne 74, 74, 70, 71 – 289;
Kel Nagle, Australia 74, 70, 73, 72 – 289;
Tony Lema, USA 68, 72, 75, 74 – 289.

1966 MUIRFIELD
Jack Nicklaus, USA 70, 67, 75, 70 – 282;
Dave Thomas, Dunham Forest 72, 73, 69, 69 – 283;
Doug Sanders, USA 71, 70, 72, 70 – 283;
Gary Player, South Africa 72, 74, 71, 69 – 286;
Bruce Devlin, Australia 73, 69, 74, 70 – 286;
Kel Nagle, Australia 72, 68, 76, 70 – 286;
Phil Rodgers, USA 74, 66, 70, 76 – 286.

1967 HOYLAKE
Roberto de Vicenzo, Argentina 70, 71, 67, 70 – 278;
Jack Nicklaus, USA 71, 69, 71, 69 – 280;
Clive Clark, Sunningdale 70, 73, 69, 72 – 284;
Gary Player, South Africa 72, 71, 67, 74 – 284;
Tony Jacklin, Potters Bar 73, 69, 73, 70 – 285;
Harold Henning, South Africa 74, 70, 71, 71 – 286;
S Miguel, Spain 72, 74, 68, 72 – 286.

1968 CARNOUSTIE
Gary Player, South Africa 74, 71, 71, 73 – 289;
Jack Nicklaus, USA 76, 69, 73, 73 – 291;
Bob Charles, New Zealand 72, 72, 71, 76 – 291;
Billy Casper, USA 72, 68, 74, 78 – 292;
Maurice Bembridge, Little Aston 71, 75, 73, 74 – 293;
Brian Barnes, Burnham and Berrow 70, 74, 80, 71 – 295;
Neil Coles, Coombe Hill 75, 76, 71, 73 – 295;
Gay Brewer, USA 74, 73, 72, 76 – 295.

1969 ROYAL LYTHAM AND ST ANNES
Tony Jacklin, Potters Bar 68, 70, 70, 72 – 280;
Bob Charles, New Zealand 66, 69, 75, 72 – 282;
Roberto de Vicenzo, Argentina 72, 73, 66, 72 – 283;
Peter Thomson, Australia 71, 70, 70, 72 – 283;
Christy O'Connor, Royal Dublin 71, 65, 74, 74 – 284;
D M Love Jr, USA 70, 73, 71, 71 – 285;
Jack Nicklaus, USA 75, 70, 68, 72 – 285.

1970 ST ANDREWS
Jack Nicklaus, USA 68, 69, 73, 73 – 283;
Doug Sanders, USA 68, 71, 71, 73 – 283
  (play-off, Nicklaus 72, Sanders 73);
Harold Henning, South Africa 67, 72, 73, 73 – 285;
Lee Trevino, USA 68, 68, 72, 77 – 285;
Tony Jacklin, Potters Bar 67, 70, 73, 76 – 286;
Peter Oosterhuis, Dulwich and Sydenham Hill 73, 69, 69, 76 – 287;
Neil Coles, Coombe Hill 65, 74, 72, 76 – 287.

1971 ROYAL BIRKDALE
Lee Trevino, USA 69, 70, 69, 70 – 278;
Liang Huan Lu, Formosa 70, 70, 69, 70 – 279;
Tony Jacklin, Potters Bar 69, 70, 70, 71 – 280;
Craig DeFoy, Coombe Hill 72, 72, 68, 69 – 281;
Charles Coody, USA 74, 71, 70, 68 – 283;
Jack Nicklaus, USA 71, 71, 72, 69 – 283.

1972 MUIRFIELD
Lee Trevino, USA 71, 70, 66, 71 – 278;
Jack Nicklaus, USA 70, 72, 71, 66 – 279;
Tony Jacklin, Potters Bar 69, 72, 67, 72 – 280;
Doug Sanders, USA 71, 71, 69, 70 – 281;
Brian Barnes, Fairway Driving Range 71, 72, 69, 71 – 283;
Gary Player, South Africa 71, 71, 76, 67 – 285.

1973 TROON
Tom Weiskopf, USA 68, 67, 71, 70 – 276;
Neil Coles, Holiday Inns 71, 72, 70, 66 – 279;
Johnny Miller, USA 70, 68, 69, 72 – 279;
Jack Nicklaus, USA 69, 70, 76, 65 – 280;
Bert Yancey, USA 69, 69, 73, 70 – 281;
Peter Butler, Golf Domes 71, 72, 74, 69 – 286.

1974 ROYAL LYTHAM AND ST ANNE'S
Gary Player, South Africa 69, 68, 75, 70 – 282;
Peter Oosterhuis, Fiji 71, 71, 73, 71 – 286;
Jack Nicklaus, USA 74, 72, 70, 71 – 287;
Hubert Green, USA 71, 74, 72, 71 – 288;
Danny Edwards, USA 70, 73, 76, 73 – 292;
Liang Huan Lu, Taiwan 72, 72, 75, 73 – 292.

1975 CARNOUSTIE
Tom Watson, USA 71, 67, 69, 72 – 279;
Jack Newton, Australia 69, 71, 65, 74 – 279
  (play-off, Watson 71, Newton 72);
Jack Nicklaus, USA 69, 71, 68, 72 – 280;
Johnny Miller, USA 71, 69, 66, 74 – 280;
Bobby Cole, South Africa 72, 66, 66, 76 – 280;
Graham Marsh, Australia 72, 67, 71, 71 – 281.

1976 ROYAL BIRKDALE
Johnny Miller, USA 72, 68, 73, 66 – 279;
Jack Nicklaus, USA 74, 70, 72, 69 – 285;
Severiano Ballesteros, Spain 69, 69, 73, 74 – 285;
Raymond Floyd, USA 76, 67, 73, 70 – 286;
Mark James, Burghley Park 76, 72, 74, 66 – 288;
Hubert Green, USA 72, 70, 78, 68 – 288;
Tom Kite, USA 70, 74, 73, 71 – 288;
Christy O'Connor Jr, Shannon, 69, 73, 75, 71 – 288;
Tommy Horton, Royal Jersey 74, 69, 72, 73 – 288.

1977 TURNBERRY
Tom Watson, USA 68, 70, 65, 65 – 268;
Jack Nicklaus, USA 68, 70, 65, 66 – 269;
Hubert Green, USA 72, 66, 74, 67 – 279;
Lee Trevino, USA 68, 70, 72, 70 – 280;
G Burns, USA 70, 70, 72, 69 – 281;
Ben Crenshaw, USA 71, 69, 66, 75 – 281.

1978 ST ANDREWS
Jack Nicklaus, USA 71, 72, 69, 69 – 281;
Simon Owen, New Zealand 70, 75, 67, 71 – 283;
Raymond Floyd, USA 69, 75, 71, 68 – 283;
Ben Crenshaw, USA 70, 69, 73, 71 – 283;
Tom Kite, USA 72, 69, 72, 70 – 283;
Peter Oosterhuis, England 72, 70, 69, 73 – 284.

1979 ROYAL LYTHAM AND ST ANNE'S
Severiano Ballesteros, Spain 73, 65, 75, 70 – 283;
Ben Crenshaw, USA 72, 71, 72, 71 – 286;
Jack Nicklaus, USA 72, 69, 73, 72 – 286;
Mark James, Burghley Park 76, 69, 69, 73 – 287;
Rodger Davies, Australia 75, 70, 70, 73 – 288;
Hale Irwin, USA 68, 68, 75, 78 – 289.

1980 MUIRFIELD
Tom Watson, USA 68, 70, 64, 69 – 271;
Lee Trevino, USA 68, 67, 71, 69 – 275;
Ben Crenshaw, USA 70, 70, 68, 69 – 277;
Jack Nicklaus, USA 73, 67, 71, 69 – 280;
Carl Mason, unattached 72, 69, 70, 69 – 280;
Craig Stadler, USA 72, 70, 69, 71 – 282;
Andy Bean, USA 71, 69, 70, 72 – 282;
Hubert Green, USA 77, 69, 64, 72 – 282;
Ken Brown, Ridge Engineering 70, 68, 68, 76 – 282.

1981 ROYAL ST GEORGE'S
Bill Rogers, USA 72, 66, 67, 71 – 276;
Bernhard Langer, West Germany 73, 67, 70, 70 – 280;
Raymond Floyd, USA 74, 70, 69, 70 – 283;
Mark James, England 72, 70, 68, 73 – 283;
Sam Torrance, Scotland 72, 69, 73, 70 – 284;
Bruce Lietzke, USA 76, 69, 71, 69 – 285;
Manuel Pinero, Spain 73, 74, 68, 70 – 285.

1982 ROYAL TROON
Tom Watson, USA 69, 71, 74, 70 – 284;
Peter Oosterhuis, England 74, 67, 74, 70 – 285;
Nick Price, Zimbabwe 69, 69, 74, 73 – 285;
Tom Purtzer, USA 76, 66, 75, 69 – 286;
Nick Faldo, England 73, 73, 71, 69 – 286;
M Kuramoto, Japan 71, 73, 71, 71 – 286;
Des Smyth, Ireland 70, 69, 74, 73 – 286.

1983 ROYAL BIRKDALE
Tom Watson, USA 67, 68, 70, 70 – 275;
Hale Irwin, USA 69, 68, 72, 67 – 276;
Andy Bean, USA 70, 69, 70, 67 – 276;
Graham Marsh, Australia 69, 70, 74, 64 – 277;
Lee Trevino, USA 69, 66, 73, 70 – 278;
Severiano Ballesteros, Spain 71, 71, 69, 68 – 279;
Harold Henning, South Africa 71, 69, 70, 69 – 279.

1984 ST ANDREWS
Severiano Ballesteros, Spain 69, 68, 70, 69 – 276;
Bernhard Langer, West Germany 71, 68, 68, 71 – 278;
Tom Watson, USA 71, 68, 66, 73 – 278;
Fred Couples, USA 70, 69, 74, 68 – 281;
Lanny Wadkins, USA 70, 69, 73, 69 – 281;
Nick Faldo, England 69, 68, 76, 69 – 282;
Greg Norman, Australia 67, 74, 74, 67 – 282.

1985 ROYAL ST GEORGE'S
Sandy Lyle, Scotland 68, 71, 73, 70 – 282;
Payne Stewart, USA 70, 75, 70, 68 – 283;
Jose Rivero, Spain 74, 72, 70, 68 – 284;
Christy O'Connor Jr, Ireland 64, 76, 72, 72 – 284;
Mark O'Meara, USA 70, 72, 70, 72 – 284;
David Graham, Australia 68, 71, 70, 75 – 284;
Bernhard Langer, West Germany 72, 69, 68, 75 – 284.

1986 TURNBERRY
Greg Norman, Australia 74, 63, 74, 69 – 280;
Gordon J Brand, England 71, 68, 75, 71 – 285;
Bernhard Langer, West Germany 72, 70, 76, 68 – 286;
Ian Woosnam, Wales 70, 74, 70, 72 – 286;
Nick Faldo, England 71, 70, 76, 70 – 287;
Severiano Ballesteros, Spain 76, 75, 73, 64 – 288;
Gary Koch, USA 73, 72, 72, 71- 288.

1987 MUIRFIELD
Nick Faldo, England 68, 69, 71, 71 – 279;
Rodger Davis, Australia 64, 73, 74, 69 – 280;
Paul Azinger, USA 68, 68, 71, 73 – 280;
Ben Crenshaw, USA 73, 68, 72, 68 – 281;
Payne Stewart, USA 71, 66, 72, 72 – 281;
David Frost, South Africa 70, 68, 70, 74 – 282;
Tom Watson, USA 69, 69, 71, 74 – 283.

1988 ROYAL LYTHAM AND ST ANNE'S
Severiano Ballesteros, Spain 67, 71, 70, 65 – 273;
Nick Price, Zimbabwe 70, 67, 69, 69 – 275;
Nick Faldo, England 71, 69, 68, 71 – 279;
Fred Couples, USA 73, 69, 71, 68 – 281;
Gary Koch, USA 71, 72, 70, 68 – 281;
Peter Senior, Australia 70, 73, 70, 69 – 282.

1989 ROYAL TROON
Mark Calcavecchia, USA 71, 68, 68, 68 – 275;
Wayne Grady, Australia 68, 67, 69, 71 – 275;
Greg Norman, Australia 69, 70, 72, 64 – 275
   (Calcavecchia won the four-hole play-off);
Tom Watson, USA 69, 68, 68, 72 – 277;
Jodie Mudd, USA 73, 67, 68, 70 – 278;
Fred Couples, USA 68, 71, 68, 72 – 279;
David Feherty, N Ireland 71, 67, 69, 72 – 279.

1990 ST ANDREWS
Nick Faldo, England 67, 65, 67, 71 – 270;
Mark McNulty, Zimbabwe 74, 68, 68, 65 – 275;
Payne Stewart, USA 68, 68, 68, 71 – 275;
Ian Woosnam, Wales 68, 69, 70, 69 – 276;
Jodie Mudd, USA 72, 66, 72, 66 – 276;
Ian Baker-Finch, Australia 68, 72, 64, 73 – 277;
Greg Norman, Australia 66, 66, 76, 69 – 277.

1991 ROYAL BIRKDALE
Ian Baker-Finch, Australia 71, 71, 64, 66 – 272;
Mike Harwood, Australia 68, 70, 69, 67 – 274;
Mark O'Meara, USA 71, 68, 67, 69 – 275;
Fred Couples, USA 72, 69, 70, 64 – 275;
Jodie Mudd, USA 72, 70, 72, 63 – 277;
Eamonn Darcy, Ireland 73, 68, 66, 70 – 277;
Bob Tway, USA 75, 66, 70, 66 – 277.

1992 MUIRFIELD
Nick Faldo, England 66, 64, 69, 73 – 272;
John Cook, USA 66, 67, 70, 70 – 273;
Jose Maria Olazabal , Spain 70, 67, 69, 68 – 274;
Steve Pate, USA 64, 70, 69, 73 – 276;
Donnie Hammond, USA 70, 65, 70, 74 – 279;
Andrew Magee, USA 67, 72, 70, 70 – 279;
Ernie Els, South Africa 66, 69, 70, 74 – 279;
Ian Woosnam, Wales 65, 73, 70, 71 – 279;
Gordon Brand Jr, Scotland 65, 68, 72, 74 – 279;
Malcolm Mackenzie, Chile 71, 67, 70, 71 – 279;
Robert Karlsson, Sweden 70, 68, 70, 71 – 279.

1993 ROYAL ST GEORGE'S
Greg Norman, Australia 66, 68, 69, 64 – 267;
Nick Faldo, England 69, 63, 70, 67 – 269;
Bernhard Langer, Germany 67, 66, 70, 67 – 270;
Corey Pavin, USA 68, 66, 68, 70 – 272;
Peter Senior, Australia 66, 69, 70, 67 – 272;
Nick Price, Zimbabwe 68, 70, 67, 69 – 274;
Ernie Els, South Africa 68, 69, 69, 68 – 274;
Paul Lawrie, Scotland 72, 68, 69, 65 – 274.

1994 TURNBERRY
Nick Price, Zimbabwe 69, 66, 67, 66 – 268;
Jesper Parnevik, Sweden 68, 66, 68, 67 – 269;
Fuzzy Zoeller, USA 71, 66, 64, 70 – 271;
Anders Forsbrand, Sweden 72, 71, 66, 64 – 273;
Mark James, England 72, 67, 66, 68 – 273;
David Feherty, N Ireland 68, 69, 66, 70 – 273.

1995 ST ANDREWS
John Daly, USA 67, 71, 73, 71 – 282;
Costantino Rocca, Italy 69, 70, 70, 73 – 282
   (four-hole play-off: Daly 15, Rocca 19);
Steven Bottomley, England 70, 72, 72, 69 – 283;
Mark Brooks, USA 70, 69, 73, 71 – 283;
Michael Campbell, New Zealand 71, 71, 65, 76 – 283;
Vijay Singh, Fiji 68, 72, 73, 71 – 284;
Steve Elkington, Australia 72, 69, 69, 74 – 284.

1996 ROYAL LYTHAM AND ST ANNES
Tom Lehman, USA 67, 67, 64, 73 -271;
Mark McCumber, USA 67, 69, 71, 66 – 273;
Ernie Els, South Africa 68, 67, 71, 67 – 273;
Nick Faldo, England 68, 68, 68, 70 – 274;
Jeff Maggert, USA 69, 70, 72, 65 – 276;
Mark Brooks, USA 67, 70, 68, 71 – 276.

1997 ROYAL TROON
Justin Leonard, USA 69, 66, 72, 65 – 272;
Darren Clarke, N Ireland 67, 66, 71, 71 – 275;
Jesper Parnevik, Sweden 70, 66, 66, 73 -275;
Jim Furyk, USA 67, 72, 70, 70 – 279;
Stephen Ames, Trinidad and Tobago 74, 69, 66, 71 – 280;
Padraig Harrington, Ireland 75, 69, 69, 67 – 280.

1998 ROYAL BIRKDALE
Mark O'Meara, USA 72, 68, 72, 68 – 280;
Brian Watts, USA 68, 69, 73, 70 – 280
   (four-hole play-off: O'Meara 17, Watts 19);
Tiger Woods, USA 65, 73, 77, 66 – 281;
Raymond Russell, Scotland 68, 73, 75, 66 – 282;
Justin Rose, amateur, England 72, 66, 75, 69 – 282;
Jim Furyk, USA 70, 70, 72, 70 – 282;
Jesper Parnevik, Sweden 68, 72, 72, 70 – 282.

1999 CARNOUSTIE
Paul Lawrie, Scotland 73, 74, 76, 67 – 290;
Justin Leonard, USA 73, 74, 71, 72 – 290;
Jean van de Velde, France 75, 68, 70, 77 – 290
   (four-hole play-off: Lawrie 15, Leonard 18, van de Velde 18);
Angel Cabrera, Argentina 75, 69, 77, 70 – 291;
Craig Parry, Australia 76, 75, 67, 73 – 291;
Greg Norman, Australia 76, 70, 75, 72 – 293.

REFERENCES

Barret, Ted, and Hobbs, Michael: *The Ultimate Encyclopedia of Golf*, 1995.

Burnett, Bobby: *The St Andrews Opens*, 1990.

Campbell, Malcolm: *The Encyclopedia of Golf*, 1991.

Chapman, Kenneth: *The Rules of the Green*, 1997.

Colville, George: *Five Open Champions* and *The Musselburgh Golf Story*.

Ferrier, Bob, and Hart, Graham: *The Johnnie Walker Encyclopedia of Golf*, 1994.

Green, Robert: *The Illustrated Encyclopedia of Golf, 1987*.

Hamer, Malcolm: *The Ryder Cup: The Players*, 1992.

Hobbs, Michael: *Great Opens*, 1976.

McDonnell, Michael: *The Complete Book of Golf*, 1985.

Phillips, Alastair: *Glasgow's Herald: Two Hundred Years of a Newspaper*, 1982.

Price, Charles: *The World of Golf*, 1963.

Robertson, James: *St Andrews: Home of Golf*, 1967.

Ryde, Peter: *Royal and Ancient Championship Records 1860–1980*.

Scott, Tom, and Cousins, Geoffrey: *The Ind Coope Book of Golf*, 1965.

Smail, David Cameron: *Prestwick Golf Club: Birthplace of the Open*, 1989.